The Ringlemere Cup

Precious Cups and the Beginning of the Channel Bronze Age

Editors
Stuart Needham, Keith Parfitt and Gillian Varndell

Contributors
Aaron Birchenough, Chris Butler, Caroline Cartwright, Stuart Needham, Susan La Niece, Keith Parfitt, Gillian Varndell

Illustrations by
Barry Corke and Stephen Crummy

Publishers

The British Museum
Great Russell Street
London WC1B 3DG

Series Editor

Dr Josephine Turquet

Distributors

The British Museum Press
38 Russell Square
London WC1B 3QQ

The Ringlemere Cup: Precious Cups and the Beginning of the Channel Bronze Age

Editors: Stuart Needham, Keith Parfitt and Gillian Varndell
Contributors: Aaron Birchenough, Chris Butler, Caroline Cartwright,
Stuart Needham, Sue La Niece, Keith Parfitt, Gillian Varndell
Illustrations by Barry Corke and Stephen Crummy

ISBN-13   978-086159-163-3
ISBN-10   086159-163-1
ISSN   0142 4815

Front cover: Cups (from left to right) from Saint-Adrien (no. 8),
Ringlemere (no. 1), Farway (no. 14) and Hove (no. 11);
design Stephen Crummy

Note: the British Museum Occasional Papers series is now entitled
British Museum Research Publications. The OP series runs from
1 to 150, and the RP series, keeping the same ISSN and ISBN preliminary
numbers, begins at number 151.

For a complete catalogue of the full range of OPs and RPs see the series
website: www/the britishmuseum.ac.uk/researchpublications
or write to:
Oxbow Books, Park End Place
Oxford OX1 1HN, UK
Tel: (+44) (0) 1865 241249
e mail oxbow@oxbowbooks.com
website www.oxbowbooks.com
or
The David Brown Book Co
PO Box 511, Oakville
CT 06779, USA
Tel: (+1) 860 945 9329; Toll free 1 800 791 9354
e mail david.brown.bk.co@snet.net

Printed and bound in the UK by 4-Print

Contents

List of Figures

List of Tables

List of Plates

List of Colour Plates

Foreword

The pursuit of a context for such a rare thing as an Early Bronze Age gold cup was a must. Little did we realise how rich a site at Ringlemerethe cup was signposting, moreover one previously unknown. Indeed, not just an unknown site, but an unknown prehistoric monument complex with the first secure henge to be recognized in Kent and the additional reward of an overlying Anglo-Saxon cemetery, itself of considerable significance.

Initial thoughts of a modest exploratory cutting to see whether an immediate context for the artefact could be found were overtaken by greater ambition even before a spade went in as it emerged from geophysical survey that the cup lay within a large ditched monument. Trench 1 in the spring of 2002 revealed not only the basal structure of a mound, but also the richest assemblage of Grooved Ware, associated lithics and features yet known from Kent. With the threat of the plough biting ever deeper into the surviving intact deposits, the scope of the campaign was scaled up again. Total excavation of the upstanding part of the monument became the only sensible option.

However, scaling up a fieldwork campaign always means lengthening the delay before final reporting on the results. So, rather than allow the detailed study of the cup and its parallels to languish for longer than necessary, we have decided on a bipartite report structure for the prehistoric evidence. Even so, a hard line has not been drawn between star find and excavated evidence; this project was above all about seizing a rare opportunity to place an iconic object in multi-level context. Five years on from its discovery, we can already point to a specific context on the site that we think the cup came from and we can begin to relate this to a longer site history involving a henge monument and a barrow. So we make no apology for outlining that history even though some aspects of it are necessarily provisional. In addition to a future companion volume on the full array of prehistoric evidence, it is already apparent that the Anglo-Saxon cemetery merits its own detailed publication.

But the focus of this volume is the find that started it all off – the Gold Cup... .

Summaries

In 2001 an Early Bronze Age gold cup was discovered by Cliff Bradshaw, a metal-detectorist, at Ringlemere Farm, Woodnesborough, in east Kent. It belongs to a well known series of 'precious' cups made of gold, silver, amber and shale, and has much in common with the celebrated gold example from Rillaton, Cornwall. The find set in motion a campaign of survey work and excavation on the site; preliminary results are given here.

The cup was found to have come from a circular ditched monument (M1), originally over 50m in diameter. The monument is interpreted, in its original form, as a Late Neolithic henge with an external bank, a single entrance and a central rectilinear timber structure; a mound was later added to the interior. Henges with comparable diameters, orientations, central structures or added mounds are discussed. No evidence for prehistoric burials has been found at Ringlemere M1, but a precise context for the cup has been deduced, placing its deposition with a contemporary amber pendant, one of two amber objects from the site, at an advanced phase of the site's life.

Fieldwork has also demonstrated the presence of other monuments clustered around M1 and occupying gently sloping ground near the headwaters of the Durlock Stream. This volume gives a synthesis of current knowledge of the elusive Neolithic and Early Bronze Age monuments of east Kent. It also contains a summary of the long sequence of activity revealed by excavation, including intensive Grooved Ware occupation preceding and/or contemporary with the henge, and much later use of the denuded mound as a focus for an early Anglo-Saxon cemetery.

The 15 other precious cups from north-west Europe are reviewed afresh in terms of form and contexts largely on the basis of new study. Their stylistic and technological backgrounds are elicited and their function argued to be highly specialized. Despite the presence of common features, most of the cups are seen to be individual creations, probably the products of their respective regions of discovery. This has significant implications for what the cups represent and how they relate to growing waterborne exchange along an axis from the English Channel to the lower Rhine and the Frisian coast. The cups are interpreted as key elements in a ritual package that helped 'service' a specific maritime contact network operating in this zone.

One of the key materials being exchanged westwards within this network was amber, highly prized for cosmological reasons in southern Britain and Brittany. While amber was clearly much sought in Wessex for the manufacture of spacer-plate necklaces and other ornaments, it is argued that southern coastal communities were those responsible for supply of the precious raw material. A range of distinctions is brought out between the two regions – Wessex proper and the southern English littoral – to demonstrate that, although articulating with one another,

they had rather different identities, craft skills and ritual preoccupations. Ringlemere adds further evidence to help undermine the joint fallacies that all Early Bronze Age valuables stem from a Wessex-led ideology and that a 'Wessex culture' or 'Wessex series' is a meaningful term for the varied ritual and material expressions in Early Bronze Age southern Britain.

Resumée

En 2001, une coupe en or du Bronze Ancien a été découverte par Cliff Bradshaw, au détecteur à métaux, à Ringlemere Farm, Woodnesbourgh, dans l'est du Kent. Elle appartient à une série bien connue de coupes 'précieuses' en or, argent, ambre et schiste bitumineux et présente de nombreux points communs avec le célèbre exemplaire en or de Rillaton, Cornouailles. La découverte a été à l'origine d'une campagne de prospection et fouille du site dont les résultats préliminaires sont présentés ici.

Il s'est avéré que la coupe provenait d'un monument circulaire ceint d'un fossé (M1) d'un diamètre de plus de 50m à l'origine. Le monument a été interprété comme un 'henge' (cercle) du Néolithique final, doté d'un talus externe, d'une entrée unique et d'une structure centrale rectiligne, en bois; un tertre a été ajouté postérieurement, à l'intérieur. La discussion porte ici sur les 'henges' de diamètres et orientations comparables, à aménagements internes ou tertres ajoutés. À Ringlemere M1, aucune sépulture préhistorique n'a été mise en évidence, mais le contexte précis de la coupe a pu être déduit, associant son dépôt à celui d'un pendentif contemporain en ambre, un des deux objets en ambre du site, à une phase avancée de l'occupation du site.

Les fouilles ont aussi révélé la présence d'autres structures groupées autour de M1, occupant un terrain légèrement en pente proche des sources de la Durlock. La publication présente une synthèse des connaissances actuelles sur les monuments assez insaisissables du Néolithique et du Bronze Ancien, dans l'est du Kent. Elle résume également la longue séquence d'activités révélée par les fouilles, avec une forte occupation pendant de la culture des 'Grooved Ware', antérieure et/ou contemporaine du 'henge', puis, beaucoup plus tard, une utilisation du tertre erodé comme centre d'un cimetière anglo-saxon précoce.

La typologie et les contextes des quinze autres coupes précieuses du nord-ouest de l'Europe font l'objet d'une actualisation fondée principalement sur de nouvelles études. Styles et techniques sont clarifiés et la fonction de ces coupes s'avère hautement spécialisée. Bien qu'elles présentent des caractéristiques communes, la plupart d'entre elles sont des créations uniques, probablement produites dans leurs zones de découverte. Les implications sont considérables pour le statut de ces coupes et leur lien avec l'expansion des échanges maritimes le long d'un axe reliant la Manche, l'embouchure du Rhin et les côtes frisonnes. Les coupes sont considérées comme des éléments clefs d'un mobilier rituel qui aide à l'instauration d'un réseau spécifique d'échanges maritimes dans cette région.

Au sein de ce réseau, un des principaux matériaux acheminés vers l'ouest était l'ambre, hautement prisé pour des raisons cosmologiques dans le sud de la Grande-Bretagne et en Bretagne. Bien que l'ambre ait été clairement recherché dans le Wessex surtout pour la fabrication d'espaceurs pour colliers et d'autres ornements, il est proposé que ce soient les communautés installées sur la côte sud qui soient responsables de la fourniture de la précieuse matière brute. Un ensemble de différences est mis en évidence entre les deux régions – le Wessex proprement dit et le littoral sud de l'Angleterre – qui montre que, bien que liées l'une à l'autre, ces deux régions ont des identités, des savoir-faire et des préoccupations rituelles assez différents. Ringlemere apporte des arguments supplémentaires pour dénoncer les liens erronés qui associent tous les objets de valeur du Bronze Ancien à une idéologie orchestrée par le Wessex et qui font de la 'culture du Wessex' ou des 'séries du Wessex' un terme qui englobe la variété des expressions rituelles et matérielles du Bronze Ancien du sud de la Grande-Bretagne.

Catherine Louboutin

Zusammenfassung

Im Jahr 2001 entdeckte Cliff Bradshaw, ein Sondengeher, in der Nähe der Ringlemere Farm bei Woodnesborough in Ost Kent eine frühbronzezeitliche Goldtasse. Sie gehört zu einer bekannten Serie solcher 'kostbarer' Tassen aus Gold, Silber, Bernstein oder Schieferton und hat viel gemeinsam mit dem berühmten Goldexemplar aus Rillaton, Cornwall. Der Ringlemere Fund führte zu einer Kampagne von Geländesurveys und Ausgrabungen; vorläufige Ergebnisse werden hier präsentiert.

Es stellte sich heraus, daß die Tasse aus einem runden, von einem Graben umgebenden Monument (M1) stammte, das ursrpünglich einen Durchmesser von über 50m gehabt hatte. In seiner originalen Form wird dieses Monument als spätneolithisches Kreismonument ('henge') mit vorgelagertem Graben, einem einzigen Eingang und einer zentralen, rechteckigen Holzstruktur interpretiert; zu einem späteren Zeitpunkt wurde im Inneren ein Hügel hinzugefügt. Kreismonumente mit vergleichbaren Durchmessern, Ausrichtungen, Zentralstrukturen und hinzugefügten Hügeln werden hier diskutiert. Es konnte keinerlei Nachweis für prähistorische Bestattungen bei Ringlemere M1 erbracht werden, aber es war möglich einen präzisen Kontext für die Tasse zu folgern. Dieser plazierte ihre Deponierung, die zusammen mit einem gleichdatierenden Bernsteinanhänger – einem von zwei Bernsteinobjekten vom Grabungsgelände – erfolgte, in eine fortgeschrittene Phase des Fundplatzes.

Weitere Untersuchungen zeigten, daß andere Monumente, um M1 herumgruppiert und auch auf dem leicht abfallenden Terrain in der Nähe des Oberlaufs des Durlock Baches, vorhanden waren. Der vorliegende Band enthält eine Synthese des gegenwärtigen Wissenstandes der schwer fassbaren neolithischen und frühbronzezeitlichen Monumente in Ost Kent. Die Publikation beinhaltet außerdem eine Zusammenfassung der langen Aktivitätssequenz, die die Ausgrabung offenlegte, einschließlich der intensiven 'Grooved Ware' Besiedlung, die dem Kreismonument voranging und/oder gleichzeitig mit ihm stattfand, sowie der viel späteren Nutzung des inzwischen stark verflachten Hügels als Fokus eines frühangelsächsischen Friedhofes.

Die 15 anderen 'kostbaren' Tassen aus Nordwesteuropa werden im Hinblick auf ihre Form und Fundzusammenhänge besprochen, auf der Basis einer weitgehenden, neuen Studie. Ihr stilistischer und technologischer Hintergrund wird eruiert und es wird argumentiert, daß ihre Funktion hochspezifisch war. Trotz des Vorhandenseins gemeinsamer Züge werden die meisten Tassen als individuelle Kreationen angesehen, vermutlich als Produkte der jeweiligen Region, in der sie entdeckt wurden. Dies hat signifikante Implikationen für den Bedeutungsgehalt der Tassen und für die Frage wie sie mit dem wachsenden Austausch auf dem Wasserweg entlang einer Axe vom Ärmelkanal zum Niederrhein und der friesischen Küste im Zusammenhang stehen. Die Tassen werden interpretiert als Schlüsselelemente in einem Ritualpaket, das half ein spezifisches maritimes Kontaktnetz, das in dieser Zone bestand, zu 'erhalten'.

Eines der Schlüsselmaterialien, die innerhalb dieses Netzwerkes nach Westen ausgetauscht wurden, war Bernstein, der aus kosmologischen Gründen im Süden Englands und in der Bretagne hochgeschätzt war. Während Bernstein offensichtlich in Wessex hochgefragt war für die Herstellung von Schiebern für Halsketten und von anderen Schmuckstücken, wird hier argumentiert, daß Gemeinschaften an der Südküste für die Versorgung mit dem wertvollen Rohmaterial zuständig waren. Eine Reihe von Unterschieden zwischen den beiden Regionen – Wessex im eigentlichen Sinne und der südenglischen Küstenzone – wird herausgearbeitet, um darzulegen, daß sie trotz aller Interaktion eher verschiedene Identitäten, Handwerkstraditionen und rituelle Glaubens- und Ausdrucksformen besaßen. Ringlemere hilft weither dabei die Trugschlüsse, daß alle frühbronzezeitlichen Wertobjekte aus einer Wessex-orientierten Ideologie stammten und dass 'Wessexkultur' und 'Wessexserie' aussagefähige Begriffe für die vielfältigen rituellen und materiellen Ausdrucksformen der Frühbronzezeit im Süden Englands und in Wales seien, zu unterminieren.

Sonja Marzinzik

Acknowledgements

Thanks are due first and foremost to the landowners – Andrew, Robert, Christopher, Jeremy and other members of the Smith family at Ringlemere Farm – who readily allowed access to their ground and have taken a keen interest in the progress of the work from the first. The excavations have been funded by substantial grants from the British Museum, the British Museum Friends (Townley Group), the British Academy, English Heritage, the BBC and the Kent Archaeological Society, together with a donation from Cliff Bradshaw, the finder of the site. At English Heritage, David Miles, Peter Kendall and Sarah Jennings have provided assistance and support throughout the early stages of the project up to completion of Trench 1 and the production of an assessment report on its results. Louise Martin and A. Payne undertook the initial geophysical survey work with some valuable results and demonstrated the potential for further work. Thanks are also due to the staff at Kent County Council's Heritage Conservation Group: Simon Mason monitored the earlier stages of the project, examined the available air photograph cover and conducted a preliminary contour survey of the site, whilst Stuart Cakebread provided details of local sites recorded in the county.

Roger Bland, Michael Lewis and Andrew Richardson of the Portable Antiquities Scheme attended to the reporting requirements of the gold cup under the terms of the Treasure Act and have given much support and encouragement to the subsequent fieldwork undertaken on the site.

Unpaid volunteers have conducted the bulk of the excavation work, led by a small number of full-time, salaried staff from the Canterbury Archaeological Trust (C.A.T). Of the full-time team, Grant Shand, together with Enid Allison and Richard Helm have made substantial contributions to the project, whilst Barry Corke has acted as site records officer, surveyor and draughtsman. C.A.T.'s Director, Paul Bennett has given much support, guidance and practical help throughout.

Volunteers from various local archaeological societies, including those of Lenham, Maidstone, Otford and Thanet, and most particularly the Dover Archaeological Group, have made a valuable contribution to the work, together with a number of other local helpers. Of the individual volunteers, Don and Tassa McGregor, Tina Parfitt, Geoff Halliwell, David Holman, Richard Hoskins, Leslie Smith and John Smythe deserve a special mention for their long-term commitment to the project, whilst Cliff Bradshaw tirelessly worked on his barrow between 2002 and 2004, undertaking both metal-detecting and excavation as required. Geoff Halliwell kindly funded some initial radio-carbon dates from the site. Help in kind has also been provided by Ovenden's plant hire.

The excavation campaign would not have been possible without the wholehearted support of Leslie Webster, Keeper of Prehistory & Europe at the British Museum, the British Museum's Research Board and the Townley Group. Similarly, Richard Bradley and Alison Sheridan have given magnificent support for grant applications. Valuable specialist assistance and advice has also come from Sonja Marzinzik (Anglo-Saxon curator), Saul Peckham (photographer), Tony Simpson (scientific technician) while several members of the Conservation Department are involved in the painstaking removal of fragile Anglo-Saxon artefacts from soil, notably Denise Ling, Fleur Shearman, Clare Ward and Duygu Cleere.

In the context of this volume, one really vital contribution has been the willingness and enthusiasm of museum curators and private owners to allow new study of precious cups in their respective collections: Jost Bürgi and Urs Leuzinger (Museum des Kantons Thurgau), Richard Le Saux (Brighton & Hove Museums), Julien Parsons (Exeter Museum), Alison Roberts (Ashmolean Museum, Oxford), Peter Saunders (Salisbury & South Wiltshire Museum), Peter Woodward (Dorset County Museum) and the private owner of the Gölenkamp cup. Sir Hugh Roberts of the Royal Collection Trust kindly gave permission for a fresh thorough inspection of the Rillaton cup, and we also thank Elizabeth Stuart, Duchy of Cornwall, for her continued support. Tobias Springer was of immense help in providing study facilities at the Germanisches Nationalmuseum, Nürnberg, when two of the continental cups were on loan for an exhibition there. We also thank Alison Sheridan and the National Museums of Scotland for allowing reproduction of their images of some cups, and Jane Marchand of Dartmoor National Park and Jacky Nowakowski of Cornwall Archaeological Unit for bringing the contemporary watercoloured sketch of the Rillaton cup to our attention. Mr Jim Woollcombe kindly gave permission to reproduce the sketch. It is thanks to Mary Cahill, National Museum of Ireland, that we are aware of the Liscahane amber pommel.

We are extremely grateful to Catherine Louboutin and Sonja Marzinzik for their translations of the summary into French and German respectively. Finally, Richard Bradley and Ann Woodward cannot go unmentioned in their roles as peer-reviewers of the text; they provided valuable pointers which resulted in significant improvements to the text.

Chapter 1: Background and Survey Work
Keith Parfitt

In early November 2001 Cliff Bradshaw of Broadstairs was metal-detecting in a recently harvested potato field at Ringlemere Farm, near Sandwich in Kent (**Fig. 1**), when he discovered a gold vessel buried at a depth of about 0.40m below the surface (**Front cover**). Suspecting it to be an important object, he was able to find a parallel in the celebrated Rillaton gold cup, recovered from an Early Bronze Age cairn on Bodmin Moor in Cornwall during the 19th century (Smirke 1867; Needham 2000a). Having informed the farmers and all the relevant authorities, Mr Bradshaw invited Keith Parfitt, Field Officer with the Canterbury Archaeological Trust, to visit the find-spot soon after the discovery (Parfitt 2001). The vessel had been found on a low, but quite distinct, rise in the middle of the field. Mr Bradshaw suspected that this might be the remains of an otherwise unrecorded round barrow, an opinion supported by preliminary inspection.

The site lies in the parish of Woodnesborough, about 1.5km west of the parish church (NGR TR 2938 5698; **Fig. 2**). The neighbouring parish church of Ash is 1.55km to the north, with Ringlemere Farm some 400m to the south-east and Black Pond Farm on Fleming Road 150m to the south-west (**Fig. 3**). The mound is situated at an elevation of between 10 and 13m above O.D. and in subsequent fieldwork has been designated Monument (M)1.

At the British Museum, a more detailed examination of the gold vessel confirmed its Bronze Age identification. With only the Rillaton vessel in Britain and four or five more parallels in gold on the Continent, it was clear that the Ringlemere cup would be of both national and international importance. Versions of these cups are also known in other materials, including amber and shale in southern England and silver in Brittany. The distribution of such cups thus ranges from southern England to the Alps and the new find from Kent represents a pivotal addition to this select corpus.

Given the importance of the find and its apparent association with the remains of a previously unknown round barrow, it was agreed through a Steering Group,[1] consisting of a partnership of local and national archaeological organisations, that the find-spot should be investigated on three grounds:

- it provided an unparalleled opportunity to identify the immediate context of one of these rare cups in unusual materials;
- it was crucial to prospect the site further because of the risk of damage and looting when the find became public knowledge;
- there was an on-going threat of damage to the context of the find and the remains of the monument from annual ploughing.

A programme of field-walking, geophysical survey and

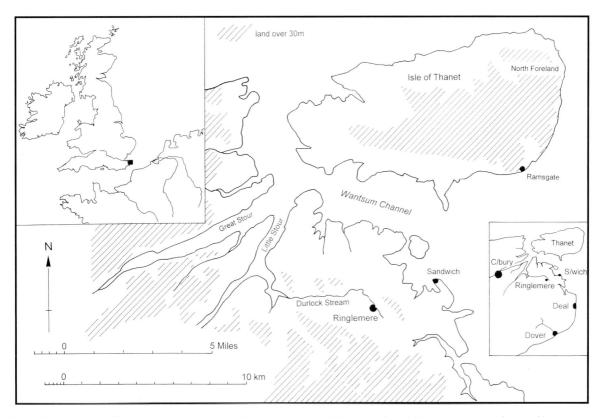

Figure 1 Location map for Ringlemere. Coastline around north-east Kent showing the Wantsum channel at its maximum extent during prehistory.

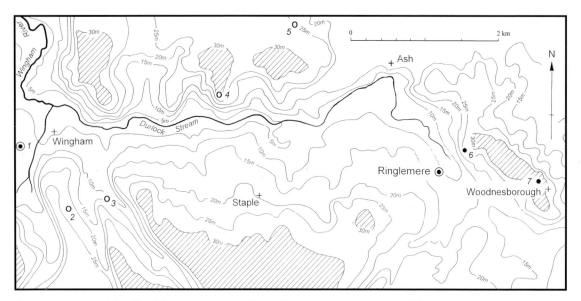

Figure 2 Ringlemere and the valley of the Durlock Stream. Other possible Bronze Age monuments around the valley are shown. Key to sites: 1, Wingham Bridge, monument complex (see **Figure 17c**); 2, Neavy Downs, ring-ditch with beaker; 3 & 4, ring-ditches on air photographs; 5, double ring-ditch on air photograph; 6, RAF Ash, destroyed mound; 7, Woodnesborough Church, destroyed mound

excavation was agreed, and from this has evolved the Ringlemere Ancient Landscape Project, led by the Canterbury Archaeological Trust. The full excavation of monument M1 is a collaborative project between the Trust and the British Museum. At the time of writing six separate excavations have taken place over four years, 2002–2005.

Finds have been acquired by the British Museum, the gold cup through the Treasure process and the bulk of the assemblage through generous donation by the Smith family.

Geology and topography of the region

Ringlemere lies some 3.75km west of the ancient Cinque Port town of Sandwich in Kent (**Fig. 1**), towards the bottom of a long north-east facing slope. This slope constitutes the southern side of the broad, shallow valley of the Durlock Stream (**Fig. 2**). The underlying geology around the site is Thanet Beds, partially sealed by deposits of gravel and head brickearth. Rolling chalkland of the North Downs dip-slope rises gently to the south, its heights lying 21km away.

Today, the Durlock Stream begins at a spring which rises in the immediate environs of the site (**Fig. 3**) and flows for about 8km westwards to join the Wingham River, which in turn empties into the Little Stour near Ickham (**Fig. 2**). A ridge of Eocene sands separates the Durlock valley from the south-western edge of an extensive tract of drained marshland which represents the now silted remains of the former Wantsum Channel (**Figs 1 & 2**). Throughout the prehistoric and Roman periods the Wantsum appears to have been open water (Champion 1980). Archaeological evidence for settlement around its shores suggests it was a much-used waterway, providing a more sheltered alternative to rounding the North Foreland for vessels traveling between the Thames estuary, the southern North Sea and the English Channel.

The Wantsum Channel divided the Isle of Thanet from the Kentish mainland until medieval times. It seems to have been formed by rising sea-levels at the start of the Neolithic period, if not a little before, and by the Bronze Age the silting-up process must have been underway (**Fig. 1**). On the evidence of prehistoric finds recovered from the surrounding area, however, it would seem that the shores of the Wantsum were well

populated, and received a disproportionate share of metalwork deposits during the Middle and Late Bronze Age (Champion 1980, 229; Perkins *et al.* 1994, 310).

Ringlemere lies just over 4km from the Wantsum shore which seems significant in terms of the continental connections of the Early Bronze Age items from the site – the gold cup and two pieces of worked amber. The Wingham River may once have formed a fairly broad inlet opening off the main Wantsum Channel and its lower reaches might have been usable by ancient vessels with shallow draught. A rare example of such a craft, of Bronze Age date and sewn-plank construction, has been discovered in the valley of the river Dour, at Dover, just 16km to the south of Ringlemere (Clark, ed. 2004a & 2004b; **Fig. 1**).

The lower reaches of the Wingham River are, however, now infilled with a complex sequence of riverine clays and peats (Dover Archaeological Group archives) and peat samples recovered north-west of Wingham church (**Fig. 27**) provided Harry Godwin with some of the material for his pioneering paper on the 'Vegetational History of the Kentish Chalk Downs as seen at Wingham and Frogholt'. This work produced a series of pollen diagrams suggesting that the region had been extensively deforested, presumably through agriculture, by the earlier Bronze Age (Greenfield 1960; Godwin 1962; see Chapter 5).

Accepting a general absence of woodland, as is suggested by Godwin's research, reasonably long views would have been available from the summit of the mound at Ringlemere inland, in a wide arc extending from north-west, through west and south to south-east. The view across the Durlock valley in the opposite direction, between east and north, however, is limited by the well-defined ridge which lies in that direction. This high ground generally reaches an elevation of between 25 and 35m OD (**Fig. 2**). It effectively obscures any view from Ringlemere to the Wantsum Channel, the Isle of Thanet and the open sea beyond, all of which can be clearly seen from the top of the ridge. If such coastal vistas were of interest to the local prehistoric inhabitants, they were apparently not important in the siting of M1.

The region around Ringlemere is generally rich in archaeological remains, with numerous prehistoric, Roman,

Anglo-Saxon and later sites. However, the bulk of the recorded information has been the result of antiquarian investigation, chance discovery or, in more recent years, development-led intervention. With the notable exception of the extensive research work carried out at Richborough (Cunliffe 1968; Millett and Wilmott 2003), there have been few large-scale excavations or detailed programmes of field survey in the area. There can be no doubt that much awaits discovery and the intensive survey and excavation work conducted at Ringlemere since 2002 is salutary on this point. The following account provides an overview of discoveries made up to the end of 2005 and must be treated as an interim statement on work still incomplete.

Field walking and metal detector surveys 2002–2004

Initial field walking in 2002 involved detailed surface artefact collection over an area centred upon Bradshaw's mound (M1). All material of archaeological significance was collected and bagged by individual 5m squares. Prehistoric calcined flint and worked flint was found to be spread across the entire survey area with noticeable concentrations being plotted around the mound. Other finds included occasional Roman, medieval and post-medieval pottery and some fragments of Roman tile but there were no significant concentrations of these. In 2003 and 2004 the survey area was extended across the valley, using a slightly less intensive search pattern based on 30m squares. By Easter 2004 more than 130 such squares had been surveyed. It is now apparent that an unbroken scatter of prehistoric struck flint and calcined flint is present across the area examined, although its density is generally less than recorded in the area of M1.

Gridded metal-detector surveys have also been undertaken. Typically for the region, these yielded a light scatter of late Roman coins together with other artefacts of Roman, Anglo-Saxon, medieval and post-medieval date. There have also been two important prehistoric finds. At a point about 200m to the north-east of M1, a rare cast bronze brooch of Hallstatt D2/D3 type was discovered (**Fig. 3**; Parfitt 2005). The type is well known on the Continent but there are very few close parallels from Britain; it is almost certainly an import.

The second find comprises fifteen objects found scattered in the ploughsoil around 150m to the south of M1 (**Fig. 3**): a 37mm length of thin gold wire with a diameter of 2.7mm and weighing 3.27g; the mouth fragment of a broken socketed axe with wing decoration; a plate-like fragment of copper alloy, possibly from an artefact; an unidentified tang fragment, and 11 pieces of raw metal. Some of the last are from copper plano-convex ingots, others are more amorphous small lumps, perhaps casting waste. The axe is datable to the Ewart stage, c. 1000–800 BC. Much of this material could derive from a closed hoard deposit, but alternatively the group could indicate a metalworking site. More work in the area is planned.

The suggestion has been made that the gold wire piece may have been residual from the manufacture of the rivets in the gold cup, for it has roughly the correct diameter. There are two obstacles to such a conclusion: firstly, the piece would appear to be associated, albeit loosely, with considerably later material – almost a millennium later. Secondly, the composition of the wire does not correspond, for it has a much higher gold content and correspondingly less silver (approximately 87% and 12 % respectively based on non-destructive surface analysis; compare the cup's composition – Chapter 3).

Geophysical surveys 2002–2003
by Aaron Birchenough

The application of geophysical survey techniques to adjacent areas has suggested that M1 is, in fact, the focal point of a more extensive prehistoric ceremonial landscape, now effectively invisible on the surface due to centuries of plough erosion (**Figs 3 & 4**).

An initial survey, covering some 1.4ha around the cup's findspot, was undertaken by staff from English Heritage's Centre for Archaeology. As well as magnetometry, earth resistivity was applied and this revealed the approximate outline of monument M1, together with two smaller ring-ditches (M2 and M3) situated immediately to the south-west (Martin 2003). Further magnetometry surveys were undertaken by the writer in 2003 in adjoining areas. This fieldwork produced some significant new information and the results were submitted as an undergraduate dissertation to Bournemouth University (Birchenough 2004). The Ringlemere site currently appears to comprise at least 12 major magnetic anomalies of archaeological significance, of which 9 are ring-ditches (**Figs 3 & 4**). These vary considerably in both size and morphology. It has also been possible to recognise at least three on aerial photographs of the area.

The following provides a summary and interpretation of the main results of the geophysical survey work to 2003. None of the major anomalies identified, other than M1, has yet been tested by excavation and it seems certain that other features remain to be located. Indeed, concentrations of minor anomalies, considered likely to be archaeological in nature, are also present in a number of places. The ring-ditches seem to fall into two distinct linear arrangements, one running south-east from M1, the other lying immediately to its west (**Fig. 3**). There is every reason to suppose that an extension of the survey area would reveal more features.

The 2003 survey was conducted using a standard Geoscan FM36 fluxgate gradiometer (vertical probe separation 0.5m) fitted with a Ps1 automatic data logger, employing parallel traverses over a 30m grid system. The resolution was set at 0.1 nT and the digital average was set at 16. Readings were taken every 0.5m. In total, the surveyed area amounted to more than 52,000m^2. The most obvious anomalies represented on the data-plot are recent: two parallel linear responses along the eastern margin of the survey area represent the bed of the now dismantled East Kent Light Railway, built in the early 20th century (Lawson Finch and Garrett 2003; **Fig. 4**). Further exaggerated readings were produced by electricity poles which run across the field (T1, T2, T3). The other main anomalies, however, all appear to relate to more ancient monuments.

The survey evidence indicates the existence of a clear linear arrangement of at least four ring-ditches (M6, M7, M8, and M9) extending in a south-easterly direction from the main monument, M1 (**Fig. 3**). These run along the contour of the valley. Monument M6 lies just under 60m from M1 and despite the weak nature of the magnetic response, the results indicate that its ditch is approximately 24m in external diameter. Worthy of particular note is the strong circular anomaly, perhaps a pit-like feature, which occurs within this ring-ditch. Located upon the northern side of M6, but even more ephemeral in its magnetic response is M7. This appears as a very small ring-ditch, approximately 8m in diameter. Its apparent placement over, or

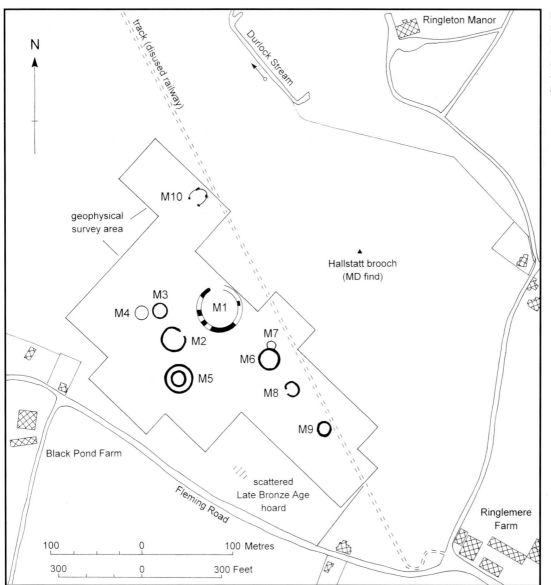

Figure 3 Ringlemere monument complex; M1 is the site of the gold cup (**see Figs 7 & 10**), M2-10 are those revealed by aerial photography and geophysical prospection.

as an appendage to, the north side of the ditch of M6 could suggest that it is the later of the two monuments.

Some 20m from M6 lies M8, another ring-ditch, with a diameter of about 18m. Of interest here is the apparent break in its circuit on the south-western side (**Figs 3 & 4**). Inside the ditch there is an indistinct, arc-like, central anomaly represented by an area of raised magnetic response. There are also a considerable number of magnetic anomalies outside the presumed break in the ditch circuit. These are presently difficult to interpret but may be of archaeological origin.

The last ring-ditch on this alignment is M9, 40m to the south-east of M8 and about 160m from M1. It is approximately 10m in diameter and impinges on (or *vice versa*) the north-western end of an irregular rectilinear feature measuring about 25 x 40m . The exact nature of this structure (M12) remains unclear (not shown on **Fig. 3**).

The other group of ring-ditches (M2, M3, M4 and M5), occurs to the west of the main monument (M1) and occupies a slightly raised outcrop of natural gravel. The most responsive of the anomalies here was M2, previously located in the English Heritage survey, but also known from aerial photographs (Pitts 2002, 452) and visible from the ground in growing crops. Approximately 28m in diameter, it would seem that this slightly irregular feature represents a fairly large, possibly penannular

ring-ditch, the potential entrance facing M1. The ditch terminals are apparently marked by two anomalies, perhaps pits or large post holes. A positive interpretation of the penannular nature of the ring-ditch is, however, hampered by the presence of an angled linear anomaly, presumed to be a later field boundary ditch, running across the ditch circuit. The trench for a modern gas main also runs east-west across the centre of this monument. Less distinct to the east, and intertwined with M2, is a possible rectangular feature and associated enclosure which is seen more clearly on aerial photographs of the site (not shown on **Fig. 3**).

Some 14m to the south of M2 lies monument M5. Whilst the magnetic response given was weak, it is apparent that it is a circular, double-ditched monument. Also recorded on an aerial photograph, the outer ditch is of almost equal proportions to M2, at about 28m in diameter, whilst the inner ditch is some 16m across (**Figs 3 & 4**). The two remaining ring-ditch anomalies (M3 and M4) lie to the north of M2 and are of more modest proportions. Monument M3 is approximately 18m in diameter and also seems to have been crossed by a later field boundary ditch. As with M2 and M5, this monument has been identified on aerial photographs (see Pitts 2002, 452) and also by ground observation.

Situated several metres to the west of M3 is the faint trace of

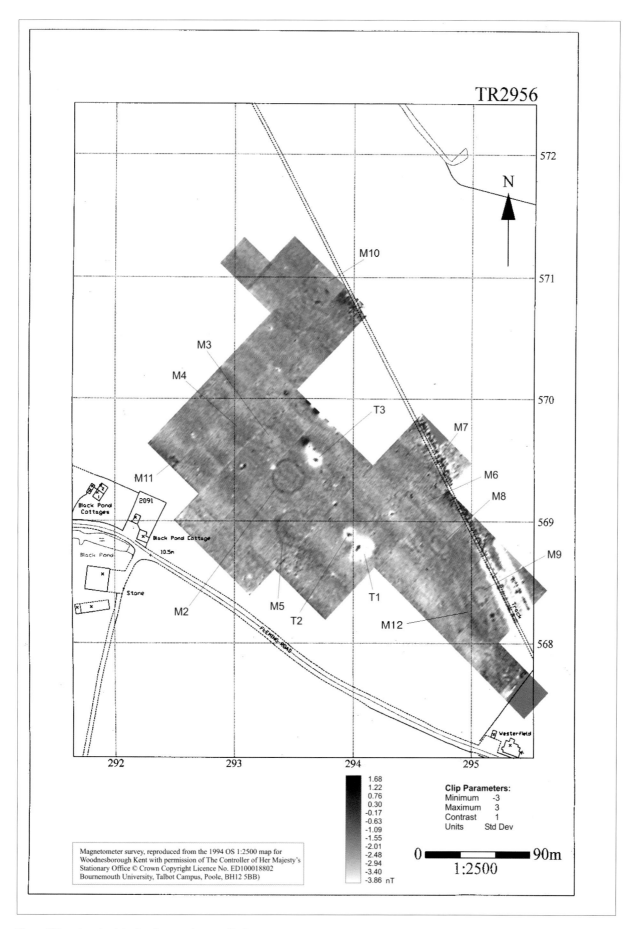

TR2956

Figure 4 Magnetometry data plot of surveyed areas at Ringlemere

another circular ring-ditch, M4, whose diameter is roughly 14m. The narrow width of ditch indicated suggests that it may represent a post trench rather than a barrow quarry ditch.

Monument M10, located 60m to the north of M1, is

altogether a much more difficult feature to interpret. Its most obvious characteristics are the four irregular anomalies that occur close to the cardinal points of the compass, at a distance of around 14m from each other (**Fig. 3**). These could represent large irregular pits or post settings. They appear to be either incorporated into, or superimposed onto, a faint ring-ditch. A subtle, yet discernible, central anomaly recognisable from the data might represent another pit.

Feature complex MII is located some 120m to the west of MI and has again been transected by the gas pipe trench. It may represent a series of circular pits, or is perhaps just one large pit (not shown on **Fig. 3**).

Note

1 Representatives of English Heritage, Kent County Council, The Portable Antiquities Scheme, Canterbury Archaeological Trust, Dover Archaeological Group, Dover Museum and the British Museum.

Plate 1 Aerial photograph of Trench 1 fully excavated

Plate 2 Site under excavation, Trench 5

Chapter 2: Excavations 2002–2005
Keith Parfitt

Following the initial survey work in 2002, it was clear that the only prospect of establishing a useful context for the Ringlemere gold cup would be to excavate a sizable area around the findspot. Accordingly, English Heritage provided funds for the excavation of an area measuring 10 x 30m on the north-western side of mound M1 (**Pl. 1**, **Fig. 5** Trench 1; Parfitt 2003a; 2003b). This work confirmed the presence of surviving mound material, encircled by a substantial ditch. The mound sealed an earlier soil profile and cut-features associated with large quantities of struck flints, calcined flints and Late Neolithic Grooved Ware pottery (Chapter 4).

The immediate context of the cup appeared to be a position at the ploughsoil/subsoil interface which was not very informative (but see further below). Despite this, the wealth of data and artefacts recovered demonstrated that further work on the site would be of considerable value. Indeed, since the plough was continuing to erode the mound, with the tines of the sub-soiler cutting down into the pre-mound land surface, total excavation of the upstanding monument seemed highly desirable. The large area of the monument, the survival of some stratified deposits and the scale of the ditch meant that with limited funding the work would have to be spread over a number seasons. To date, funds to cover the cost of the work have come from the British Museum, the Townley Group (British Museum Friends), the British Academy, English Heritage, the BBC, the Kent Archaeological Society and Cliff Bradshaw.

In the autumn of 2002 Trench 2 was excavated on the lower, downhill, part of the monument, at an angle to Trench 1, with the specific aim of testing the preservation of the monument in this area (**Fig. 5**). Initially, it was hoped that preservation might be better here than in Trench 1, but in the event, the work showed that the edge of the mound and ditch had been severely truncated by a deep terrace or negative lynchet, perhaps connected with cultivation or quarrying. In 2003, Trench 3 was cut south-eastwards from the south-east end of Trench 1 in order to examine further the central area, complete a NW–SE section through the monument and determine an overall diameter for the enclosing ring-ditch. It also established the presence of another terrace or lynchet on the south-east side of the mound more or less perpendicular to that through Trench 2. Later in 2003 Trench 4 was set alongside Trench 1 to extend exploration of the interior (a small part of this trench was finished in 2005). An unexpected result was to find that the enclosing ditch was broken by a causeway on the north side (**Fig. 5**). Trench 5 followed in 2004 on the opposite side, alongside Trench 3; it examined much of the southern quadrant and demonstrated that there was no entrance opposite that on the north. The latest work, Trench 6 in 2005, saw the western quadrant of the mound between Trenches 1 and 5 fully excavated along with two flanking segments of ditch. By the end of the 2005 season about three-quarters of the enclosed area had been examined (**Fig. 5**).

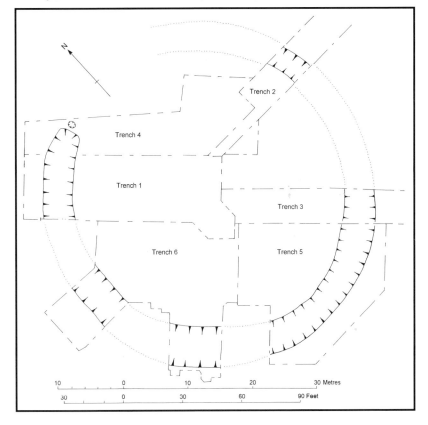

Figure 5 Excavated trenches at Ringlemere M1, 2002–2005.

Trench 2

Trench 4

Trench 1

Trench 3

Trench 6

Trench 5

| 10 | 0 | 10 | 20 | 30 Metres |
| 30 | 0 | 30 | 60 | 90 Feet |

Overall, the site has proved to be a difficult one to investigate, with the similarity in colour and texture of the clayey soils, the frequent lack of clearly defined edges to cut features and the occurrence of extensive animal burrows dug through most of the stratified deposits (**Pl. 2**), combining to hamper progress. Despite these problems, the information recovered from Trenches 1–6, now allows a provisional account of the development of the site of Monument M1 to be set out. It is hoped that detailed analysis of all the data once the excavations are completed will allow this sequence to be further refined.

Early Occupation
Mesolithic activity
A small proportion of the large quantities of prehistoric flintwork recovered from Ringlemere may be dated to the Mesolithic period (see Butler, Chapter 4). In addition, a microlith and a tranchet axe (not yet studied by Butler) were found in 2005, although no associated features or implement concentrations have yet been identified to indicate activity on this very spot. The presence of fresh running water, in the form of the nearby Durlock Stream, would have made the area attractive to Mesolithic people.

Finds of Mesolithic date are not at all common in north-east Kent and are largely confined to isolated surface discoveries of axes and adzes (e.g. Ogilvie 1981; 1983; Hoskins 1995). The only significant local site is that at Lower Farm, Finglesham, located some 5.5km south-east of Ringlemere. Like Ringlemere, the Finglesham site is situated at the foot of the downs, on brickearth. It is an occupation site with an extensive flint assemblage (Parfitt and Halliwell 1983), which is characterised by a large number of heavy axes, sharpening flakes and an absence of microliths. Associated luminescence dates indicate a late Mesolithic date (Parfitt and Halliwell 1988, 80; Butler 2005, 118).

The new Mesolithic finds from Ringlemere thus represent a very useful addition to this comparatively poorly represented period in east Kent. The low yield of microliths within the excavated assemblage, despite careful sieving of the deposits, further reinforces the view previously arrived at by the writer that microliths were seldom used in this region. Overall, the Mesolithic industry at Ringlemere presently appears to be of a broadly similar character to Finglesham. It is tempting to suggest a similarly late date but much more work is required.

Neolithic Settlement
Preserved below the mound of M1 is a buried soil profile. To date about 730m^2 of this artefact-rich soil have been excavated and totally dry-sieved through a 1cm mesh. Sealed under it are more than 150 cut-features, in the form of variously sized hollows, pits, post-holes and three hearths (**Fig. 6**). These features are most numerous on the south-western side of the enclosed area,

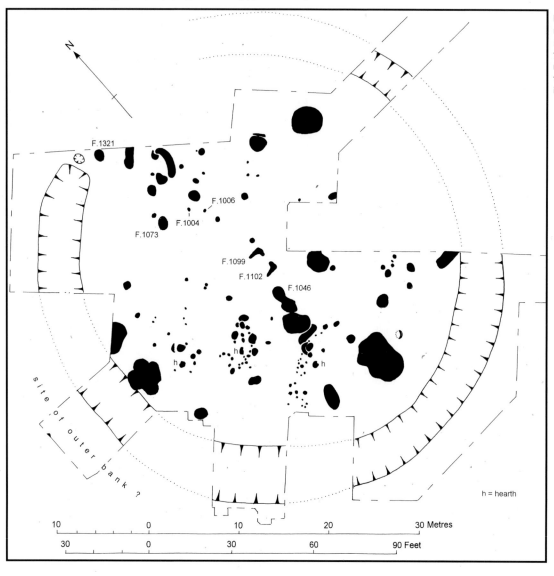

Figure 6 Plan of all pre-mound features within M1. Those discussed in text (including flint report) are numbered; the hearths/ovens are indicated by 'h'.

F.1321

F.1006

F.1004

F.1073

F.1099

F.1102

F.1046

site of outer bank ?

h = hearth

10   0   10   20   30 Metres

30   0   30   60   90 Feet

where the hearths are located. Indeed, pits and post-holes seem to be clustered around the hearths. An arc of 15 post-holes, possibly relating to a large building, occurs in the area of the south-east hearth. Collectively, these remains provide clear evidence for occupation on the site prior to the erection of the barrow mound.

The buried soil, cut-features and turf stack of the mound have together yielded over 5,000 sherds of pottery, large quantities of calcined flint, struck flint including many finely worked scrapers and other tools, together with parts of ground stone axes of non-local rock. The particular contents of several pits suggests that they include special 'placed' deposits of pottery and flintwork. Despite the large quantities of lithic and ceramic material recovered, however, there are no corresponding assemblages of prehistoric faunal remains. Disappointingly, animal bone and marine shell simply have not survived in the brickearth and there is virtually no such material from any of the prehistoric deposits investigated. By analogy with the faunal assemblages recovered from other Neolithic and Bronze Age sites it may be reasonably surmised that considerable quantities of bone and shell were once present at Ringlemere but that these have all decayed without trace.

The pottery recovered from the pre-mound deposits and features consists almost exclusively of Late Neolithic Grooved Ware. The same is true of the material in the turf mound and it is likely that this material was taken directly from the same occupied land surface nearby. A small number of Beaker sherds have been recognized in both the pre-mound topsoil and the mound core. Some of the pits have contained large sherds of Grooved Ware, perhaps deliberately placed, and one pit has yielded a radio-carbon date of 2890–2600 cal BC (2 sigma; Beta-183862; **Table 3**) from contained charcoal. Collectively, these finds provide clear evidence for intensive use of the site before the construction of the barrow mound. Their relationship with the enclosing ditch has yet to be established – at present they are thought to belong at least in part to pre-monument occupation, perhaps only fortuitously preserved in this area because of the protecting cover of the mound. Nevertheless, the question is raised as to whether such earlier activity on the site in some way influenced the positioning of the later monument. Interestingly, Cleal has previously highlighted the close correlation between Bronze Age barrow sites and the occurrence of earlier Grooved Ware (Cleal and MacSween 1999, 6).

Analysis suggests that the majority of the flintwork recovered from Ringlemere is of later Neolithic date (Chapter 4) and there can be little doubt that most is contemporary with the Grooved Ware pottery. In addition to the Mesolithic material identified (see above), another small group of flints appears to be of earlier Neolithic date. So far no associated pottery or features of this period have been identified.

Grooved Ware is not well represented in Kent and the present assemblage is by far the largest yet recovered from the county. Locally, small assemblages of Grooved Ware have previously been recovered from the submerged land-surface of the Lydden Valley north of Deal (Halliwell and Parfitt 1985, 40) and in pits at Mill Hill, Deal, where associated radiocarbon-dates suggest a period of use between 2880 and 2450 BC. (Parfitt 1998a, 377; see **Table 3**). Finds of derived Grooved Ware occur in several east Kent round barrows, including Eastling Wood, Sutton (Grinsell 1992, Sutton 2; Parfitt, Allen and Rady 1997),

Haynes Farm, Eythorne (Grinsell 1992, Eythorne 1; Parfitt 2004, fig. 5) and Ringwould Free Down, Ringwould (Grinsell 1992, Ringwould-with-Kingsdown 2; Woodruff 1874, 26, plate II, fig. 7). The quantity of material so far recovered from Ringlemere, however, is far in excess of the combined total from all these earlier explorations.

The Neolithic period, in general, is still poorly understood in east Kent. Major field monuments, well known in other southern counties, appear to be sparse in the landscape (Barber 1997), although the recent excavation of a large causewayed camp near Ramsgate, on the Isle of Thanet (Shand 2001), together with the discovery of a possible second, noted on an aerial photograph between Eastry and Tilmanstone, just south of Ringlemere (Oswald *et al.* 2001, 153 no. 47), suggests that this is likely to be mainly due to intensive later cultivation of the land rather than any genuine Neolithic lacuna (see Chapter 5 for further discussion). Known occupation sites are mostly represented by isolated pits and surface scatters of lithic material. Indeed, such evidence appears to be typical of large areas of southern Britain (Holgate 1988, 32, 67) and clearly much has been lost to the plough over the centuries. The site preserved below Ringlemere M1 thus provides excellent prospects for the recovery of detailed Neolithic occupation evidence which has elsewhere been destroyed.

Monument M1

The geophysical survey and excavation have now confirmed that the low mound initially identified by Bradshaw is a man-made structure of prehistoric date. It is a circular monument comprising a central barrow encircled by a ditch. There is also some evidence for an outer bank. When upstanding, the mound had provided a convenient home for generations of burrowing animals and conceivably it may have served as a medieval rabbit warren belonging to the manor house at Ringleton, on the opposite side of the valley (**Fig. 3**). The animal activity, however, has led to much disturbance of the mound structure and has probably caused some movement of artefacts.

The pre-mound land surface

Survival of part of the mound had preserved an earlier land surface beneath. A distinctive but discontinuous layer of brown to black manganese, about 10–20mm thick, separated the mound from the buried topsoil, and was best preserved under the central part of the turf core. It apparently represents decayed vegetation. Preliminary analysis of the buried soil has revealed no evidence for cultivation of the ground prior to the construction of the mound; instead it suggests long-term pasture following possible woodland clearance (Heathcote 2003). As already described, large quantities of Grooved Ware and flintwork were recovered from the buried profile, some of which may precede the first monumental phase. However, we now believe that some of the features and finds under the mound are likely to relate to a pre-mound enclosure phase (see below).

The mound

Exceptionally for the heavily ploughed landscape of east Kent, the base of the barrow mound survived at Ringlemere, with a maximum thickness of 0.50m at the centre. A core of soft, decayed turf (**Figs 7 & 8**) was enclosed by an outer deposit of

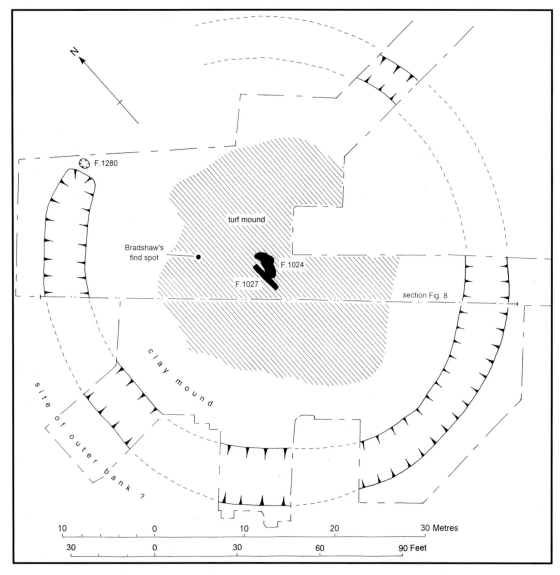

Figure 7 Plan of surviving and interpreted earthworks constituting M1, features cut into the turf mound, and Bradshaw's location for the cup.

orange-brown clay; although they are different in character, the interface between the two elements was diffuse and in many places difficult to closely define. The turf core contained much residual domestic rubbish in the form of struck flint, calcined flint and broken pottery (mostly Grooved Ware with small amounts of Beaker), clearly derived from earlier activity on the site (as described above). Despite the fuzzy definition, it was possible to map the extent of the central turf stack and show that it survived to between 25 and 29m across (**Fig. 7**). It appears to have been somewhat irregular in outline, with a tendency towards a vaguely sub-rectangular, rather than neatly circular, plan. This shape might imply that the turf stack was simply a dump which lay in the centre of a broader mound and not a free-standing structure in its own right.

The outer part of the mound seems to have been composed of fairly clean clay. It sits on a surface that is often a little lower than the old ground surface under the turf stack and which, moreover, does not have as well developed a soil profile. This might suggest that the turf had been stripped in order to contribute to the body of the central core, the clay later being dumped on the resulting lowered surface. The outer mound appears to have originally extended as far as the lip of the enclosing ditch (**Fig. 9**, context 1020) but it had been partially cut away by later terracing in most areas (see below). Within the

make-up of the outer mound, an absence of material derived from the distinctive lower clay and gravel deposits through which the ditch was cut implies that the material of the mound did not include up-cast from the ditch.

The ditch and bank

The enclosing ditch is of substantial size, 41.5m in diameter internally and 50m externally (**Figs 7 & 8**). The ditch itself survives between 4 and 5m across and about 2m deep, with a broad, flat bottom (**Fig. 9**). Analysis of laminar sediments in the base of the ditch has shown that they were water-laid, implying that the ditch had held water, at least in wetter seasons. This is likely to be a reflection of the nature of the clayey subsoil rather than any specific design feature, however. The higher ditch fills in excavated segments from the north-west to the south-west show that more material was slipping in from the outside than the inside (**Fig. 9**), suggesting the former presence of an external bank, of which no trace now survives. The bank was evidently made from the spoil from the ditch, for it had a proportion of gravel derived from the natural gravel bands which are sealed under the brickearth.

None of the deposits filling the ditch were rich in artefacts and many of the layers were sterile. Most of the finds recovered seem to represent residual material derived from earlier activity

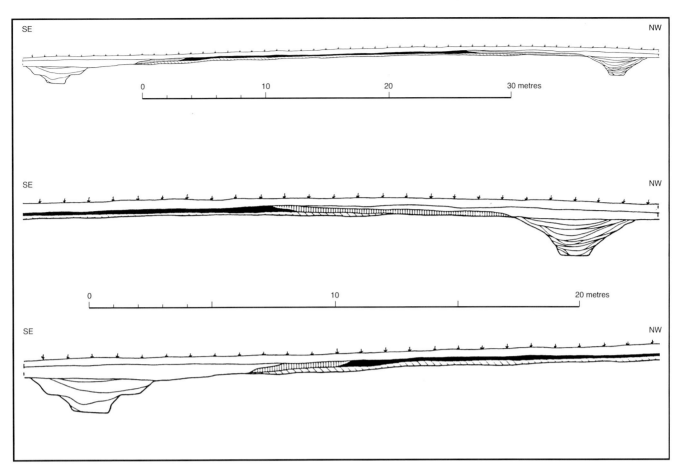

Figure 8 Cross-section of monument M1, south-east to north-west (Trenches 1 and 3). Turf core in solid black; outer mound shaded vertically

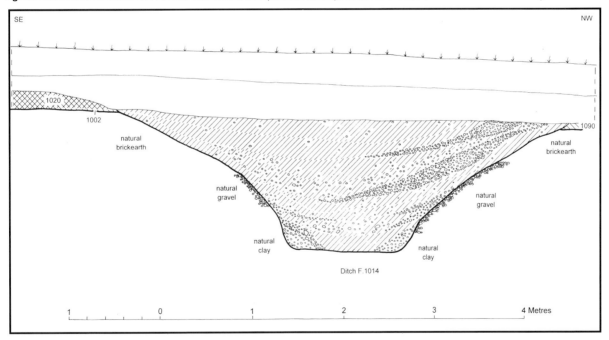

Figure 9 Cross-section of excavated ditch in Trench 1, north-west side of the monument

on the site. On the south side, however, two areas of deliberately laid flint cobbles were found lying on the base of the ditch. These included a small amount of humanly struck flint but, overall, the date of the construction and filling of the ditch remains to be ascertained.

On the northern side, a deliberate break in the circuit of the ditch formed an entrance causeway at least 3m across. What appears to be a large post-pit (F. 1280) is set immediately adjacent to the terminal (**Fig. 6**), but complete excavation of the entrance and phasing of the interior features is required before

its full significance can be determined.

Evidence for human burial

Given the character of the monument, it initially seemed likely that Early Bronze Age burials would be associated. This prospect was encouraged by the gold cup, since some of the parallels are from graves. However, after excavation of almost 80% of the mound no formal prehistoric burials have yet been located and evidence for the presence of human remains on the site is still extremely sparse. Tiny flecks of calcined bone, possibly human, were recovered from a large oval pit, F. 1073, sealed under the mound 12m NNW of the monument's centre (**Fig. 6**). The burnt bone was mostly confined to the upper layers of the north-eastern half of the pit and may represent a scattered, unurned cremation deposit. It is possible it relates to the Grooved Ware phase of activity rather than later and there is currently no evidence that the addition of the mound was connected with interments.

Central structures

Although excavation of the central area of the monument has failed to produce unequivocal evidence for a burial or grave, it has revealed a noteworthy sequence of structures absolutely at the centre of the monument. These merit detailed discussion here because one feature produced one of the Early Bronze Age amber objects from the site and may also have contained the cup.

Immediately beneath the modern ploughsoil, the mound remnant was found to have been cut by an irregular pit (**Figs 10 & 11**; F. 1024), which showed some evidence of disturbance from burrowing animals. This pit was roughly oval in shape and measured 3.30m (N–S) by 1.45m (E–W). It survived to a depth of 0.13m, with steeply sloping sides and a slightly undulating base, which was somewhat banana-shaped in plan. The main filling consisted of a grey-brown silty clay-loam with decayed wood fragments (Context 1026), which contained a few prehistoric sherds, a quantity of struck flints and calcined flints. The pottery is likely to be residual; four sherds are tiny and another is from a thick base, probably Grooved Ware. This main fill was sealed by a 0.02m thick layer of decayed wood (Context 1025) which

occupied the top of the pit (as truncated). It has been possible to identify some of the wood as coming from three species (Cartwright – Chapter 4). The amber object – a pendant fragment – was the only find from this upper layer (Chapter 4).

Below the pit and cut from a lower horizon was a pair of narrow L-shaped slots (**Fig. 11**; Fs 1099 and 1102). These were sealed under the mound material and became visible only after the buried topsoil horizon had been excavated. The main axis linking them roughly aligns on the entrance to the north (**Fig. 10**). The slots seem most suited to holding upright contiguous posts or planks; indeed, highly degraded woody remains were recorded in the base of the southern L-slot, F. 1102. Such a timber structure would form a rectangular 'cove', 2.4m across and open to the west. This was potentially a mortuary structure (cf Ashbee 1960, 52–4) or a focal point for ritual performance at the very centre of the enclosure such as can be paralleled in certain Late Neolithic ritual monuments (discussed later in this Chapter). No internal floor or specific occupation deposits were associated with the cove. A few small pottery sherds were found in the feature fills, together with some struck flints including three scrapers (Butler, Chapter 4) but all this material is probably residual.

Four samples containing wood and charcoal from the southern slot were assessed for their identification potential by Rowena Gale (2003) and later fully analysed (Cartwright – Chapter 4). Some charcoal fragments were subsequently extracted from two of the samples (Samples 2 and 3) and sent for radio-carbon dating in the hope of obtaining at least a broad indication of the age of the feature, which at the time of excavation did not seem at all certain. They gave very different

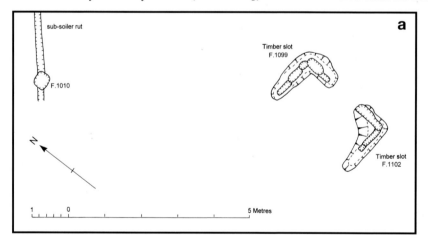

Figure 10 Detail plans of central features: a) pre-mound; b) post-mound

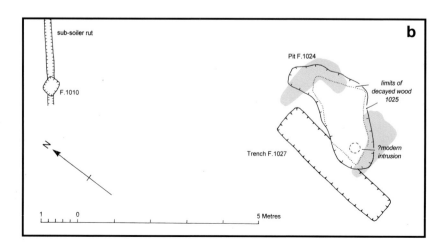

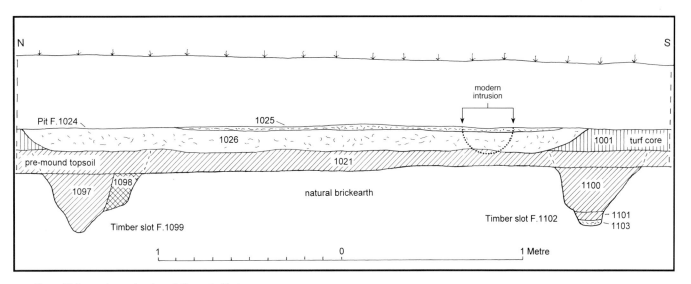

Figure 11 Composite section through the central features

results. Sample 2 produced a determination of 3460 ± 40 BP (Beta- 180487; 1890 – 1680 cal BC; **Table 3**), whilst Sample 3 gave a determination of 1750 ± 40 BP (Beta-180488; AD 130–410). Given that it was well sealed by the main fill of the slot and the mound, presumed contamination is likely to be from percolation of organic matter or adjacent animal disturbance. It is hard to account for a Roman period date otherwise. If contaminant organic matter was responsible, it is possible that it had also affected Sample 2 from the same context, thereby making the radiocarbon measurement fall later than the true age of the sample. On balance, therefore, neither date can presently be rated with much confidence.

Immediately west of the three features so far described was a long rectangular trench (**Figs 7 & 10**; F. 1027). This was parallel to the main axis of the cove, but in contrast was clearly dug through the mound core. As recorded it was 3.68m long and 0.78–0.88m wide, surviving to a depth of 0.23m, the top having been truncated by the plough. The trench penetrated the subsoil much less deeply than the cuts for the cove (**Fig. 11**), which is consistent with the feature being dug in from a higher level (0.35m difference between the deepest parts of the two features). This slot had, however, been clipped on its eastern edge by the later pit (F. 1024). Like the earlier and later intercutting features, F. 1027 too contained some decayed wood, this time small quantities scattered through the fill of fine brown loam (Context 1028); none could be retrieved for identification. Three small sherds of pottery are probably residual.

There are two questions to resolve in relation to this set of central features. Firstly, the presence of unburnt wood remnants in all phases of the sequence initially seemed to suggest they were not particularly ancient (cf Parfitt 2003b, 36). The material present in the L-slot (F. 1102), in fact contains a mixture of unburnt wood, partially burnt wood and charcoal, but no burnt material was discovered in layer 1025. Wood is known to survive, exceptionally, under barrows even when there is no waterlogging. The second problem was the conundrum that the trench F. 1027 on the one hand seemed to relate to the cove structure, closing its western side, yet on the other was cut from a different stratigraphic horizon to the cove slots. This can actually be resolved by interpreting a sequence which encompasses the building of the turf mound and for which the northern alignment remained important. On this basis we offer

the following interpretation of the sequence.

1) A timber cove, c. 2.4 x 1.2m in plan, was erected at the exact centre of the enclosure at the time of its original construction or during later use. The main axis was aligned approximately on the north-facing entrance through the ditch. The cove was apparently originally open to the west, while the gap between the L-slots could have offered a narrow (0.85m) window facing east – in effect a portal. The posts set at right angles at either end were in shallower slots and may have been braces for the main alignment. The surviving depth of the post-emplacements below the old ground surface (up to 0.50m) could have easily supported a structure 2m or so high. Indeed it is possible that the uprights would have been linked by lintels, in which case the structure could have been a little taller.

2) Either while the cove remained standing or later, a turf mound or platform was built around it covering the central area within the ditched enclosure. It was probably not especially high, to judge from the next phase.

3) A trench (F. 1027) was dug through the centre of the turf mound, again respecting the N–S axis. This is now presumed to be a foundation trench for a later façade of timbers set in the top of the mound. It may be coincidence that this new façade largely closed the open side of the original cove for it is offset a little to the south. As an entirely new façade it could still easily have respected the original north-south alignment. The difference in positioning of this new façade could perhaps reflect a slight shift in the apparent centre of the monument following the construction of the turf mound.

4) Finally, an irregular pit (F. 1024) was dug into this central spot from the top of the turf platform, or from a higher level if the mound had been raised in between times. The pit occupies more or less the full area of the underlying cove and this must by now have decayed or been truncated. The western side of the pit clipped the façade bedding trench, potentially when the posts were still standing. Indeed, it is possible that the façade and pit were functionally linked, one dug quickly after the other had been erected. The overall dimensions of the pit, at about 3.30 by 1.45m, are rather large for a grave and, in the absence of any skeletal material, other ritual functions for this pit seem more likely (see below); there is no reason to think the new pit was intended to contain a replacement façade.

5) The woody layer present across virtually the whole pit is

likely to represent a lining, perhaps a 'floor' of branch material; had it been timber subsiding from higher it is less likely to have resulted in such a uniformly horizontal layer. As found, the lining was 0.10m above the base of the pit, but we cannot know the original depth of the pit, nor whether the soil below the decayed wood was early silting while the feature stood open or deliberate backfill. The amber ornament recovered from this woody layer had presumably originally lain on top prior to decay; if not a grave good, it seems highly likely to be another form of ritual offering.

6) Close to the south end of F1024 was a small intrusion, a pit of about 0.30m diameter. It was filled with loose soil and some decayed vegetation and appeared to be of very recent origin. We now believe that this could have been Bradshaw's original excavation to unearth the gold cup. If so, the findspot is placed 1.5m to the south-west of the estimated centre of the monument but some 8m from Bradshaw's stated findspot.

Re-establishing the gold cup findspot

The primary objective of English Heritage-funded Trench 1 had been to establish a context for the burial of the gold cup. Bradshaw had marked the spot, but his marker was removed by ploughing before archaeological inspection of the site thirteen days later. Fortunately, Bradshaw had also at the time of discovery paced out the location from a nearby electricity pole, 38 paces away, and by repeating this exercise he felt confident he could re-establish the findspot to within a metre or so. This exercise was repeated at intervals over the following three years and resulted in locations varying by about 2m. The original stated position is shown in **Fig. 10** (F.1010).

Bradshaw was also able to describe something of the soil around the cup. He particularly remarked on a thin black/brown deposit (*c.* 1cm thick) of organic material like decayed wood below the ploughsoil of about 0.25m depth. The original Treasure Receipt Form (filled out by Michael Lewis, then Finds Liaison Officer for Kent) stated that he had 'noticed narrow black/brown band around hole'. Shortly after, Bradshaw drew a sketch section of the soil profile with his hole dug through it, the cup lying at the bottom. About half way down through the soil his sketch shows the horizontal band; at the hole it is shown belling upwards a little, this presumably being a convention to show it curving round the back wall of his hole as if viewed from a little above the horizontal. When asked later about the relationship, Bradshaw replied that he was unsure whether the organic layer had gone across the soil containing the cup; he evidently did not remember seeing the layer first, before reaching the cup. The cup lay in what he described as a 'light sandy soil' below the level of the organic layer.

The cup lay on its side with the heavily dented face uppermost. It contained a quantity of organic material which Bradshaw carefully tapped out (dry) and placed in sealed bags. These were submitted to the British Museum with the cup and are reported on in Chapter 4.

Careful excavation around the spot first indicated by Bradshaw revealed a shallow depression, cut about 0.22m deep below the base of the ploughsoil and containing some modern vegetation (F. 1010). No ancient sub-soil features were found within a radius of 4m. This might be Bradshaw's original hole, but its re-excavation revealed no traces of gold, no other artefacts and, most importantly, no evidence for the distinctive

dark organic layer previously described by Bradshaw. The location is 8–9m to the north-west of the centre of the monument (**Fig. 10**). The surrounding deposits are riddled with animal burrows and there was also a deep sub-soiler furrow running across the spot which might have accounted for the damage sustained by the vessel.

However, there is now strong evidence that the findspot was really at the centre of the mound – the hole recently dug into pit F. 1024 (see above). There are reasonable grounds for accepting that the thin organic layer Bradshaw noted in the side of his original excavation is the same deposit as the woody layer (Context 1025) subsequently discovered in the top of pit F. 1024. No other comparable organic deposits have been found at the relevant level anywhere else on the site, including the area of Bradshaw's stated findspot for the cup. The sample of organic material which Bradshaw had found within the cup proved to contain decayed wood without any charcoal not unlike that exposed in the top of F. 1024; moreover, one piece was identifiable as possibly *Acer campestre* which matches one of the species from F. 1024 (Cartwright, Chapter 4).

In order to argue that the cup originally lay within the fill of pit F. 1024, we would need to assume that the presumed plough impact had not moved it far. Farmer Andrew Smith and his ploughman Cedric Marsh, from their long experience of working this field, are both of the opinion that a fragile vessel such as the gold cup could not have been pulled any distance through the ground by a plough or sub-soiler tine without being very much more extensively damaged than the present find. Impact by the plough, however, could well have pressed the cup through the woody layer in F. 1024 if the vessel had originally lain upon it. This would have punched a hole through the layer, but the finder's observations were not specific enough to know whether this was the case.

Bradshaw remains adamant that his paced-out location to the north-west of F. 1024 is the true findspot of the gold cup, but given the loss of his definitive marker before scientific investigation of the site, the writers of this report favour the vessel's original place of deposition as being within F. 1024, along with the amber pendant.

Post-monument activity

Later prehistoric to Roman activity

At monument M1 itself, later prehistoric activity may be attested by struck and burnt flints recovered from the plough soil and, particularly in the upper filling of the ditch. Some of this material may be reworked from the artefact-rich underlying deposits. However, Trench 6 also revealed a broad scatter of charcoal with occasional sherds spread across the levelled ditch; the pottery includes a rim and neck of Earliest Iron Age type, *c.* 850–600 BC. This shows that the ditch was already totally full with the implication that the outer bank was also largely or entirely denuded; certainly material from the bank is inferred from the ditch fills. A likely explanation is that agriculture early in the 1st millennium BC was levelling these already eroded features. Broadly contemporary, or only a little earlier would be the scatter of copper and copper alloy material recovered from 150m south of M1 (Chapter 1), with the slightly later Hallstatt brooch to the north-east (**Fig. 3**; Parfitt 2005).

Finds of Roman date are similarly thinly scattered, but coins, pottery, tile and other odd artefacts recovered from both the survey work and excavation imply activity somewhere in the vicinity during the Romano-British period. The nearest site presently known is that at Black Pond, located near the top of the slope, several hundred metres to the south-west (Ogilvie 1982). However, the more immediate source of small Roman finds is likely to be manuring scatters, especially given the evidence for persistent ploughing around the mound at this time. Indeed, as excavations have proceeded on different sides of the mound, it has become clear that a distinct negative lynchet is present on three sides; it cuts laterally into the west, south and east sides leaving a steep erosion scarp through the mound remnant and underlying profile. Only on the northern side does this feature appear to be of slight gradient.

Having bitten into the mound, at some point erosion ceased, and accumulation of soil, presumably gradually transported from up-slope, began to fill the negative lynchet. The resulting profile, accumulated over a lengthy period from before the 5th century AD to some time after the 6th century, is in places 0.70m deep. The soil comprises three layers of different character and ultimately laps up onto the sides of the mound. However, only the modern ploughsoil has been found extending unbroken right across the surface of the remnant mound.

Anglo-Saxon occupation and cemetery

The clearest evidence for Anglo-Saxon settlement in east Kent is generally provided by cemeteries, rather than occupation sites and the region around Ringlemere is well endowed with such remains (see Meaney 1964; Richardson 2005). Collectively, the evidence suggests that this general locality had been extensively occupied by Anglo-Saxon settlers from the start of the 6th century and it seemed that this was an area of early, if not primary, colonisation (Everitt 1986, 116–7). Before excavation work commenced at Ringlemere, the possibility had been considered that the ancient mound might have served as the focus for a subsequent Anglo-Saxon 'flat' cemetery because such post-Roman re-use of prehistoric burial sites is now becoming an increasingly familiar situation in east Kent and beyond (Parfitt and Brugmann 1997, 4). Indeed, Bradshaw had initially speculated that the mound (M1) might be of Anglo-Saxon date. Nor did it seem to be pure chance that the Ringlemere site was overlooked from the north-east by the important 6th century Anglo-Saxon burial site at Coombe, some 750m away(Davidson and Webster 1967).

A number of metalwork items known from around the Ringlemere site had implied some sort of Anglo-Saxon activity in the immediate area from the outset of the fieldwork and the discovery in 2002 of a complete 6th-century pottery vessel set into the outer mound of M1 further raised expectations. Nevertheless, the discovery the following year of a classic Anglo-Saxon sunken hut cut into the north-western side of M1, not far

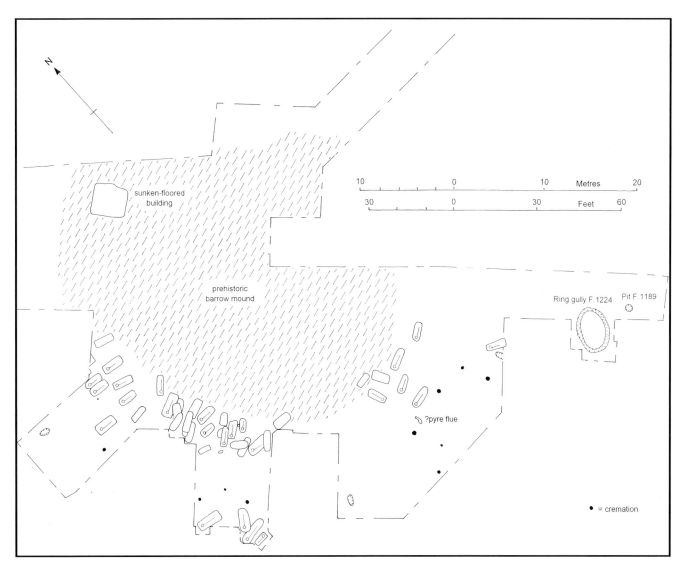

Figure 12 Plan of Anglo-Saxon use of M1

from the findspot of the pot, was completely unexpected (**Fig. 12**). Probably in-filled during the 7th century, the hut-pit is so far an isolated structure but it serves to alert us to the possibility of further buildings. On topographical grounds, any focus of settlement might well be found sheltering low on the valley slopes, close to the Durlock stream – presumably always a reliable source of fresh running water.

Despite the examination of several substantial areas outside the barrow ditch no trace of any Anglo-Saxon burial ground around the mound had been discovered by the end of the 4th season of excavation (Trench 4) and it began to seem unlikely that there had been such a re-use of Ringlemere M1. Then, new excavations on the south side of the mound in 2004 (Trench 5) led to the discovery of no less than 13 burials of Anglo-Saxon date, perhaps part of a larger cemetery extending away from the mound to the south.

The excavation of Trench 6 in 2005 led to the discovery of another much larger group of Anglo-Saxon graves, tightly packed onto the terraced area along the south-west and west side of the mound. These cut through the earliest soils filling the terrace and over 50 graves have now been excavated in all, with every suggestion of more lying beyond the investigated area (**Fig. 12**). Most of the burials are inhumations, but there are also a dozen cremations – a burial rite rarely encountered in east Kent during the early Anglo-Saxon period. On the south side, a small oval pit with heavily burnt sides located adjacent to cremation Grave 2 may represent the base of an associated cremation pyre flue, although no datable evidence was recovered from the feature, which had been partially disturbed by burrowing animals.

Preliminary inspection of the cremation urns and grave goods associated with the inhumations indicates that the bulk of these burials are of 5th-century date. Objects recovered from the inhumations include fine glass vessels, beads, brooches, silver rings and pins, buckles and various iron objects, including knives. No weapon-graves have been discovered as yet.

Some exceptionally important early graves appear to be represented at Ringlemere and these will require detailed study. Their analysis will form the basis of a separate report in due course but already it seems that this new cemetery site is going to be of considerable significance for Kentish Anglo-Saxon studies.

Later history

According to historical records, the Ringlemere monument complex once lay on land belonging to Ringleton Manor. The site of the manor house is situated across the valley 300m to the north-east of the excavated site (**Fig. 3**). The history of this manor has been previously outlined by Hasted (1800) and Davidson and Webster (1967). Here, we may usefully note that it is recorded in the Black Book of St Augustine's Abbey (1070–82) and Domesday Book (1086) and thus was in existence by late Anglo-Saxon times (Davidson and Webster 1967, 6).

Evidence for cultivation of the adjacent lands during the medieval period and early post-medieval periods is provided by a scatter of medieval peg-tile, together with smaller amounts of pottery and metal-finds, presumably brought out to the field with the manure. No doubt this material originated from the farms at Ringleton Manor and Ringlemere.

Recent changes to the landscape seem to have been relatively few. In 1912 the East Kent Light Railway line was laid across the area, just below the barrow site (Lawson Finch and Garrett 2003), although the associated earthmoving seems to have been quite limited and no archaeological discoveries are recorded. A number of old field boundaries have been removed in recent years to create larger fields and a substantial length of the Durlock stream has been confined within an underground pipe (Andrew Smith pers. comm.)

The field containing Monument 1 has been regularly under the plough since at least the 1930s (Andrew Smith pers. comm.) and the Tithe map implies that this was the case 100 years earlier. In all probability, the area had been cultivated for many centuries before this; indeed, we have described above the evidence for prolonged agricultural activity in or around the Roman period. Even if the mound itself remained out of cultivation at this stage and later, the persistent attrition of the edges could have given rise to enhanced erosion off its slopes. Finally, given the extent of animal burrowing encountered during excavation, it may not be unreasonable to speculate that the mound served as a rabbit warren during medieval times. Such burrowing activities can lead to deflation and accelerated erosion of mound structures.

From henge to barrow: Ringlemere M1 and comparable monuments
by Stuart Needham

Once it had been established that a remnant of a mound survived at the site and, moreover, that this was encircled by a ditch, the initial assumption was that the monument was, straight-forwardly, a round barrow. The diameter of the ditch suggested that it would have been an unusually large example, but such are known scattered across the country; Ann Woodward has termed them aggrandised barrows (Woodward 2000, 139–40). However, any initial assumptions that the mound once rose to a considerable height or that it was contemporary with the digging of the ditch now have been reconsidered (Parfitt and Needham 2004).

Certainly by the 7th century AD the outer skirt of the mound would not have been very much higher than it is today to judge from the sunken-floored building cut into the northern side (**Fig. 12**). This might be explained by previous agricultural activity. A little earlier, probably mainly during Iron Age and Roman times, the mound had been subjected to lateral plough erosion, causing the negative lynchets all around. However, we can now also argue that the core mound of turf was never particularly high, for the comparatively narrow second-phase façade trench described above, which survived to a depth of 0.23m, if correctly interpreted as a foundation for prehistoric timber uprights cut through the thickness of the mound, seems unlikely to have ever been more than say 0.75–1.0m deeper. This would suggest a first phase mound little more than 1m high.

It is likely that the mound was enlarged later. This depends on reconstructing the thin surviving layer of orangey clay encircling the core as originally having formed a capping over the turf mound, a bipartite structure familiar in conventional Early Bronze Age barrows. Often such mound additions followed secondary interments in an already established burial monument. Again, it is the erection of the timber façade in the top of the turf core which suggests the outer mound would not have been added immediately.

Monument phase 1

Whatever the original size of the turf mound, we have to take account of the implications of the first central structure, the cove, which preceded it. It seems unlikely that the cove stood before the ditch was constructed and it is possible that it was added secondarily to the centre of an existing enclosure and was part of a sequence of activity leading to construction of the inner mound.

Small rectilinear structures of varied forms can be found under Early Bronze age barrows (Ashbee 1960, 52–4). Two examples very like the Ringlemere cove are worth drawing attention to. A cove structure in a probable burial context has recently been excavated at Llanfair Discoed, Monmouthshire (Chadwick and Pollard 2005). Slot foundations on three sides are very similar in plan and orientation to the Ringlemere cove, but at Llanfair it occupies the base of a pit interpreted as a grave, itself central within a small ring cairn. Barbed and tanged arrowheads and Beaker sherds suggest it is a Beaker period grave with associated mortuary structure.

Another cove-like setting with a maximum width of 2.3m occurred under the burial mound of a barrow at Arreton Down, Isle of Wight (Alexander et al. 1960). Again the cove is formed of two angled slots, each formed of two intersecting pits. In this case association with a burial deposit is not in doubt; a cremation was placed centrally within the structure and was accompanied by a riveted bronze flat dagger and possibly also a

bone belt-hook. Clare (1986) covers other examples of square settings inside small ring ditches which are most likely burial sites. While these are plausible comparisons for the cove at Ringlemere, here there is no evidence for associated burials and, moreover, we can point to a quite different setting for such structures.

The early phase of Ringlemere M1 can be reconstructed as a penannular enclosure with substantial ditch and an external bank enclosing a level interior surface of some 42m diameter (**Fig. 13**). The entrance points a little west of north and, if contemporary, the cove is situated at the very centre of the enclosure. It remains to be determined from full excavation of the interior and post-excavation analysis how many other features are contemporary, rather than belonging to earlier settlement activity. The first-phase monument is clearly a henge, apparently with just one entrance (class 1 – Atkinson et al. 1951; Harding and Lee 1987).

Enclosures accepted as henges or hengi-form have widely varying diameters, orientations, earthwork morphologies and internal structures and, taking account of all these constituent features, they have defied any simple classification (Burl 1969; Clare 1986). One should not therefore necessarily expect to match all features closely between individual sites, for there was clearly an element of 'bricolage' in the designed or accretive plan of henges. Nevertheless, some important comparisons can already be made between Ringlemere and other henges. This

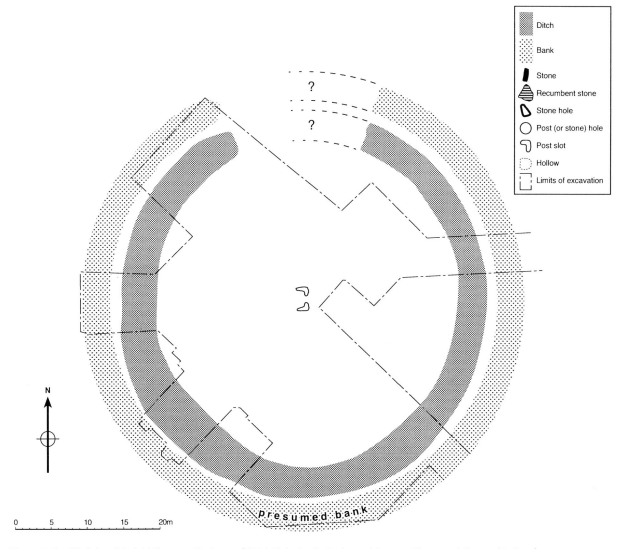

Ditch
Bank
Stone
Recumbent stone
Stone hole
Post (or stone) hole
Post slot
Hollow
Limits of excavation

Figure 13 Simplified plan of the initial henge at Ringlemere. (NB It is likely that further internal features will prove to belong to this phase.)

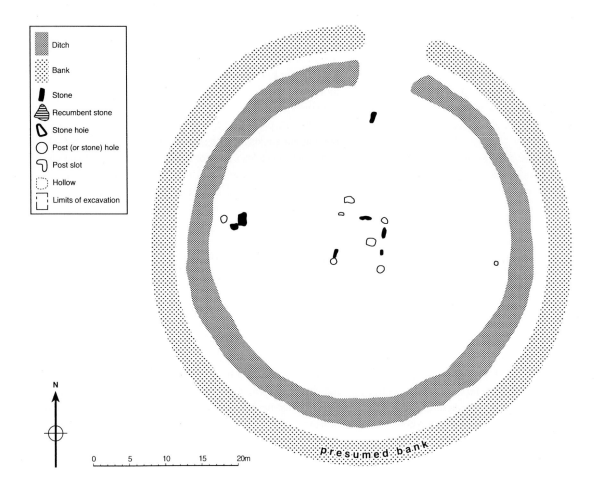

▨	Ditch
⣿	Bank
▌	Stone
◭	Recumbent stone
◖	Stone hoie
○	Post (or stone) hole
⌐	Post slot
⬚	Hollow
⌐	Limits of excavation

N

0 5 10 15 20m

Figure 14 Simplified plan of henge at Site IV, Mount Pleasant, Dorset; Wainwright's phase 2 structures are shown (after Wainwright 1979)

will need more refined consideration later when more is understood of which features belong to the first monumental phase at Ringlemere MI.

The diameter of the Ringlemere example corresponds with the main peak for class 1 monuments, 40–50m internally (Harding and Lee 1987, 39 fig. 28B). Orientations in the north-east quadrant are also the most frequent for single-entrance classic henges, with a smaller number facing in the opposite direction (Harding and Lee 1987, 37, 38 fig. 27a). In these respects, therefore, the Ringlemere monument fits into the modal plan for class 1 henges. More intriguing, however, is the fact that at least two class 1 henges not only match the diameter and approximate orientation of MI, but also have similar rectilinear central structures.

The first is the 'Site IV' henge situated inside the vast 'henge enclosure' of Mount Pleasant, Dorset (Wainwright 1979, 29 fig. 16). The internal layout shown in **Figure 14** is that interpreted as phase 2 by Wainwright in which stone monoliths and pits or post holes are used to define a central rectilinear space 6.5m^2 and, just inside the ditch, three 'cardinal' points. The latter are in fact systematically rotated a few degrees clockwise from west, north

and east thus conforming to the enclosure's alignment, just east of north. Like Ringlemere MI, the ditch describes a good circle; it has an internal diameter of 43m, an external one of 49m.

Dating of the Mount Pleasant IV enclosure relies on pottery and three radiocarbon dates for primary ditch silts. The latter are in good agreement with one another (**Table 1**), but may not date the very first construction phase. The antler and bone objects sampled came from ditch segment VII from the top of a pit, but immediately beneath the basal profile of the main ditch (Wainwright 1979, 17 fig. 10). The pit in question is one of several surviving beneath the ditch cut-line and may well indicate an original circuit formed of pits or shafts, not unlike Maumbury Rings (Bradley 1976). The dates, calibrating to the middle of the 3rd millennium BC, would thus relate to the backfilling of those pits with the main enclosure ditch dug thereafter, perhaps immediately thereafter. Associated pottery from the ditch is principally Grooved Ware, but two Beaker sherds in the lower fills (Longworth 1979, 75, P139, P221), although possibly intrusive from higher(one belongs with a larger number of sherds stratified a little higher), are actually unproblematic at a date shortly after 2500 BC (Needham 2005).

Table 1: Selected radiocarbon dates for Formative and Class 1 henges

Orientation	Site	Context	14C Result (BP)	Calibrated date* (cal BC; 2 sigma)	Lab. Ref.	Reference	Sample Details
?	*Flagstones, Dorset*	Child burial at base of ditch	4490 ± 70	3370–2920	Har-9158	Healy 1997, 38 table 1	Human bone
		Base of ditch	4450 ± 90	3360–2900	OxA-2322		Red deer antler
		Child burial inserted into lower ditch silts	4210 ± 110	3100–2450	OxA-2321		Human right femur
		Base of ditch	4030 ± 100	2900–2300	Har-8579		Red deer antler
WSW	*Llandegai A, Gwynedd*	Internal pit FA 370	4480 ± 50	3360–3010 (2950–2930)	GrN-22954	Lynch & Musson 2004, 118	Cremated bone; adult female
		Internal pit FA 1	4450 ± 40	3340–2920	GrN-27192		Mature oak charcoal
		Ditch middle fill (level 4)	4420 ± 140	3550–2650	NPL-221		Mature oak charcoal
		Cove – feature ACC3	4480 ± 145	3650–2750	NPL-224	Lynch & Musson 2004, 119	Charcoal: mainly oak, some hazel
		Cove – feature ACC2	4420 ± 40	3330–3220 3180–2910	GrN-26818		Charcoal: mainly one oak plank?
		Cove – feature ACC4	4320 ± 30	3020–2880	GrN-26817		Oak charcoal
SW	*Arminghall, Norfolk*	Base post hole 7	4440 ± 150	3650–2650	BM-129	Harding & Lee 1987, 195	Charcoal
N	*Stones of Stenness, Orkney*	Ditch, basal fill	4425 ± 50	3340–2910	OxA-9763	Ashmore 2000; 2001	Cattle hoof core
		Ditch, basal fill	4405 ± 50	3330–2900	OxA-9765	Ashmore 2000; 2001	Cattle mandibular ramus
		Ditch, basal fill	4390 ± 50	(3330–3230) (3180–3150) 3120–2890	OxA-9764	Ashmore 2000; 2001	Cattle left radius
		Ditch, basal fill	4310 ± 70 (110)	3350–2550	SRR-350	Ritchie 1975–6	Animal bone
		Ditch, basal fill	4240 ± 45	2920–2660	OxA-9762	Ashmore 2000; 2001	Wolf bone
		Burnt deposit in central feature	4190 ± 70 (110)	3100–2450	SRR-351	Ritchie 1975–6	Charcoal
		Bedding trench of square structure	3680 ± 270 (380)	–	SRR-592	Ritchie 1975–6	Decomposed wood
NE	*Stonehenge, Wiltshire*	Ditch primary fill	4432 ± 22	(3310–3230) (3180–3150) 3110–2920	UB-3794	Pitts 2000, App. 1; Cleal et al. 1995	Antler
		Ditch primary fill	4430 ± 18	(3279–3230) 3110–2920	UB-3789		Antler
	→	Ditch primary fill	4410 ± 60	3340–2900	BM-1583		Antler
	Excavation of ditch	Ditch primary fill	4393 ± 18	3090–2910	UB-3793		Antler
	3015 – 2935 BC	Ditch primary fill	4390 ± 60	3330–2880	BM-1617		Antler
		Ditch primary fill	4381 ± 18	(3080–3060) 3030–2910	UB-3788		Antler
		Ditch primary fill	4375 ± 19	(3080–3060) 3030–2910	UB-3787		Antler
		Ditch primary fill	4367 ± 18	3030–2910	UB-3790		Antler
		Ditch primary fill	4365 ± 18	3030–2910	UB-3792		Antler
(?NE)	*Balfarg Riding School, Fife*	Ditch middle fill	4425 ± 50	3340–2910	GU-1670	Barclay & Russell-White 1993, 160–2	Charcoal: hazel
		Ditch middle fill	4385 ± 55	(3330–3220) 3180–2880	GU-1904		Charcoal: alder, birch, hazel
		Structure 2, boundary post	4330 ± 85	3350–2650	GU-1907		Charcoal: oak, alder
		Structure 2, internal post	4285 ± 55	3090–2680	GU-1905		Charcoal: alder
		Structure 2, boundary post	4155 ± 70	2900–2560 2520–2490	GU-1906		Charcoal: oak, alder
ENE	*Coneybury, Wiltshire*	Central structure post hole	4370 ± 90	3350–2700	OxA-1409	Richards 1990	Animal bone
		Ditch primary fill	4200 ± 110	3100–2450	OxA-1408		Animal bone
?	*Briar Hill inner circuit, Northamptonshire*	Primary silts in segment 176A(1), west side	4130 ± 150	3100–2200	Har-5216	Bamford 1985, 127	Small-counter sample
		Primary silts in segment 165B(1) [?late pit cutting segment 162]	3900 ± 90	2650–2000	Har-5125		Small-counter sample
		Cove	4010 ± 90	2900–2200	Har-2607		Charcoal: various sp.
N	*Mt. Pleasant IV, Dorset*	Ditch primary fill or prior shaft fill	3988 ± 84	2900–2200	BM-667	Wainwright 1979	Animal bone
		Ditch primary fill or prior shaft fill	3931 ± 72	2620–2190	BM-666		Antler
		Ditch primary fill or prior shaft fill	3911 ± 89	2700–2050	BM-663		Charcoal
		'Hearth' low in ditch middle fill (pale loam)	3630 ± 60	2200–1770	BM-668		Oak charcoal
		'Hearth' high in ditch middle fill	3274 ± 51	1690–1430	BM-669		Oak charcoal

Table 1: Selected radiocarbon dates for Formative and Class 1 henges cont.

Orientation	Site	Context	14C Result (BP)	Calibrated date* (cal BC; 2 sigma)	Lab. Ref.	Reference	Sample Details
N	*Maumbury Rings, Dorset*	Bottom of shaft 1 (pre-henge)	3970 ± 50	2620–2300	BM-2282N	Bowman *et al.* 1990, 65, 71	Red deer antler
		Uppermost fill of shaft 3 (pre-henge)	3940 ± 130	2900–2000	BM-2281R	Bowman *et al.* 1990, 65, 71	Red deer antler
NNE	*Woodhenge, Wiltshire*	Ditch floor	3817 ± 74	2470–2030	BM-677	Pollard 1995a	Antler
		Ditch, primary silts	3755 ± 54	2470–2030	BM-678		Animal bone
NNW	*Gorsey Bigbury, Somerset*	Ditch secondary silts, 'occupation' layer (Beaker-associated; various levels)	3800 ± 74	2470–2030	BM-1088	Harding & Lee 1987, 261–2	
			3782 ± 62	2460–2030	BM-1089		
			3666 ± 117	2500–1650	BM-1090		
			3663 ± 61	2210–1880	BM-1086		
			3606 ± 67	2150–1740	BM-1091		
			3602 ± 71	2140–1740	BM-1087		

* Ranges in brackets have relatively low probability

On Wainwright's phasing, the central square arrangement was introduced later, as indicated by the occurrence of an 'extensive spread of ash and charcoal, fresh sarsen flakes, stone mauls, flint artefacts, animal bones and numerous sherds of Beaker pottery' at the base of the pale loam in the upper ditch fills (Wainwright 1979, 28). An associated radiocarbon date on oak charcoal is 3630 ± 60 BP (BM-668). On this chronology, the stone setting is later than the multiple timber circles, but the spatial coherence between the two structure sets is striking and Pollard suggests instead that they were pene-contemporaneous (1992, 218–9). At the very least the positions of the first structure were still visible when the second was laid out.

The second excellent parallel is the Stones of Stenness on Mainland, Orkney, which again is a good circle (**Fig. 15**). The interior is 43m in diameter, the outer lip of the ditch 54m; excavations have revealed a 6m wide bank outside (Ritchie 1975–6). The central structure is a 3 x 3m square setting of low sill-stones, thus similar in dimension to the Ringlemere cove, but differing in being an apparently closed space which has been interpreted as a hearth by Colin Richards (2005, 218–25); burnt material was recovered from its interior. The stone phase may well be a late 'monumental' version of an earlier structure on the same spot (ibid); Richards finds evidence for earlier demarcation of the same space by an equi-armed L-shaped slot

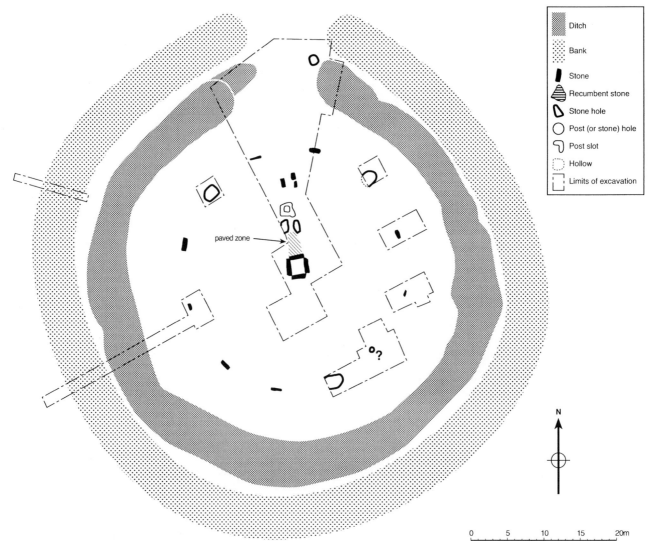

Ditch
Bank
Stone
Recumbent stone
Stone hole
Post (or stone) hole
Post slot
Hollow
Limits of excavation

paved zone

N

0   5   10   15   20m

Figure 15 Simplified plan of Stones of Stenness henge, Orkney (after Ritchie 1975–6)

and this too he sees as a hearth. However, if these were slots for timbers, as seems most likely, they imply an angled wall or facade rising above the ground surface.

The limited areas excavated in the interior of the Stones of Stenness also revealed a range of other features, particularly on the line between the central structure and the entrance (Ritchie 1975–6). Moving outwards, there is first a 3m length of 'paving' leading to the gap between two stone-holes, perhaps forming a portal. Immediately beyond is a small square slot, 1.5m across, the foundation trench for a four-sided structure of timber or upright stones that were later removed. Next on this line is a 'dolmen' of three stones defining a similar ground area, but already by 1974 a restoration set in concrete. Finally, the whole central zone is encircled by a ring of 11 or 12 colossal upright stones about 30m in diameter; 4 remain *in situ*.

Dating of the Stones of Stenness henge has recently been amplified by a new suite of radiocarbon dates (Ashmore 2000; 2001). Most are for material from the primary ditch silts, presumably therefore dating the early life of the enclosure (**Table 1**). They show conclusively that construction must have been around the turn of the 4th to 3rd millennia BC. A single date for burnt material from the central structure seems to relate to continuing use of the site into the earlier half of the 3rd millennium.

Ringlemere, Mount Pleasant IV and Stones of Stenness are only the most closely comparable in plan among a growing body of henges and contemporary ceremonial sites which have small rectilinear structures associated. Several such associations have been noted and discussed by past researchers (Ritchie 1975–6; Wainwright 1979; Clare 1986; Burl 1988; G. Barclay 1999), but it is now possible to add a number of further examples, not all certain on extant evidence; these are introduced below.

The 'rectilinear' structures concerned are by no means all of the same form, nor necessarily function. Graham Ritchie (1975–6, 19ff; followed by Burl 1988, 3–5) felt that the square structures in the centre of some monuments should not be equated with the three-sided 'coves' in others, whereas Clare (1986, 300) loosely grouped all rectilinear structures together and saw their origins to lie in earlier Neolithic mortuary structures (see for example Burl 1979, 116 fig. 5). Both positions are defensible, but at the same time unhelpful for understanding specific functionalities. Clearly the element of a small to medium sized rectilinear structure was well embedded in Neolithic structural principles; that might mean the basic form could be drawn upon for a variety of purposes and this supports Ritchie's case for scrutinizing the evidence available for any differentiation. Precise lay-out in plan may not, however, be as important as evidence as to how the feature was used, as derived from position in the site, size, reconstruction of superstructure and excavated debris (eg Pollard 1992). Such factors might, for example, override formal differences between those seemingly four-sided in plan and those apparently with only three sides.

The Coneybury Hill class 1 henge, Wiltshire, is 'sub-oval' in shape, encloses an area of 32 to 38.5m diameter and faces east-north-east (J. Richards 1990), in these respects differing from the previous class 1 henges discussed. Julian Richards thought that the excavated pits/post-pits at the centre might have formed part of a circle (1990, 134), but this looks unlikely, even allowing for what remained unexcavated. As Pollard has recognised (1995b, 125), three of the most substantial features – 1177, 1601, 1603 – are very similar in character and would make a neat rectangle 4 x 4.5m with the addition of a fourth outside the excavated area (**Fig. 16**). Smaller features adjacent would seem to have supported smaller timbers partially filling three sides, but remaining open away from the entrance, in this way comparable to the Mount Pleasant IV structure. As at Mount

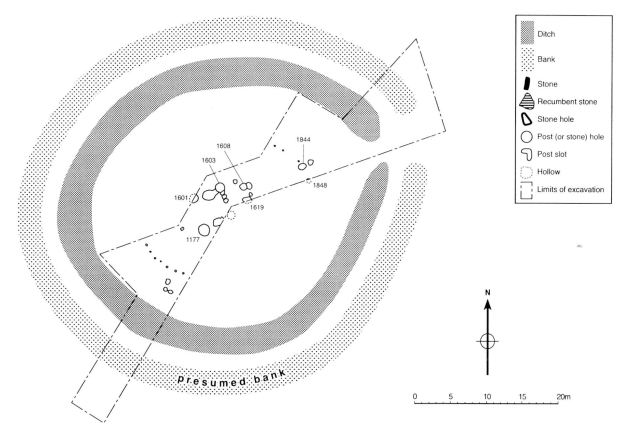

Figure 16 Simplified plan of Coneybury henge, Wiltshire (after Richards 1990)

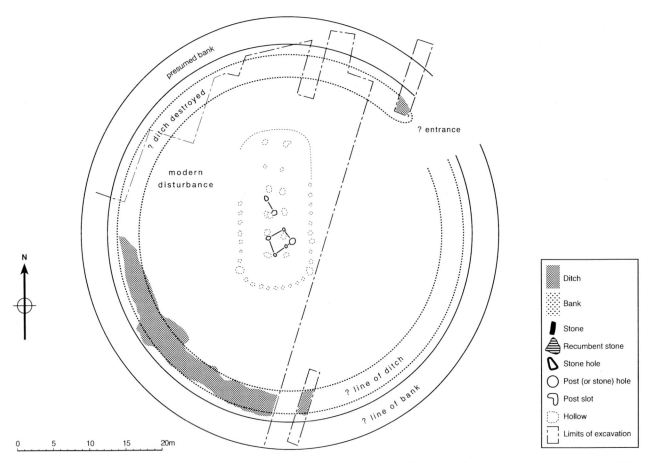

Figure 17 Simplified plan of possible henge at Balfarg Riding School, Fife (adapted from Barclay and Russell-White 1993). The internal features are suggested to belong to two main phases.

Pleasant and Stones of Stenness, the rectangle is aligned with the axis through the entrance and this alignment is enhanced by two intermediate pairs of posts noted by Richards (1990, 134–9; posts 1844 with 1848, and 1608 with 1619), these again recalling the arrangements at Stones of Stenness.

The dating of Coneybury relies on two rather imprecise radiocarbon dates. Bone from one of the larger central structure features, 1601, was dated 4370 ± 90 BP, and that from primary ditch fills, 4200 ± 110 BP (**Table 1**). These dates would relate best to pre-Beaker Grooved Ware phases, but sherds of Beaker pottery suggest continuing activity after the middle of the 3rd millennium BC. In fact most of the Beaker pottery is in layers also yielding still later pottery, down to the Middle Bronze Age, suggesting it was already old when deposited in the higher ditch fills, perhaps in the course of ploughing.

On the evidence of an early depiction, four monoliths once stood in a square arrangement in the middle of the large class 1 henge of Mayburgh, Cumbria (Topping 1992, 250–3); only one now survives. The enclosure has an internal diameter of 88m and is unusual in being ditchless, the massive bank being made up of imported pebbles.

A partly destroyed enclosure which is likely to have been a classic henge monument was excavated at Balfarg Riding School, Fife (Barclay and Russell-White 1993). It was also found to have suffered marked subsoil truncation in its northern half. The original shape of the enclosure is uncertain, as is the position of the ditch and entrance(s). However, the excavated ditch circuit has an internal diameter of about 40m. Grooved Ware and material datable by radiocarbon were associated with both the middle ditch fills and parts of the interior surface. A

most striking structure was revealed in the interior – a large rectangular building with bowed end walls – and was interpreted by the excavators as an unroofed mortuary house. A second, very similar in plan, lay outside, 35m away to the south west.

The post holes at the southern end of the earthwork-enclosed building were more numerous than elsewhere in this or the second house and five superfluous features can be made into a small slightly trapezoid cove, aligned diagonally to the superimposed building and enclosing 3 x 2.5m (**Fig. 17**). One corner post lies at the predicted centre of the ditch, assuming near circularity. The henge can feasibly be constructed with a north-east facing entrance which might thus have aligned with the long axis of the cove.

Class 2 henges can also have related central structures. Arbor Low, Derbyshire (**Fig. 18**), is famous for its central setting of up to seven stones, some of which are recumbent, which is often regarded as a collapsed cove (Gray 1903, pl. XXXVIII; Barnatt 1990, 35–8; Hart 1981, 39 fig. 4.4, 41). Gray's excavations found no evidence for holes in between the two large recumbent stones and if they were ever upright they must cover their respective sockets, as Barnatt has conjectured. They would have been on opposite sides facing the entrances and forming a cove 3m or more across. Standing 3m high, they would have effectively blocked the view of the cove's interior from the direction of the entrances (Barnatt 1990, 38). The henge's interior is about 43 x 54m across.

Another relevant class 2 henge is that of Cairnpapple Hill, West Lothian (**Fig. 19**). The interior was fully excavated by Piggott (1947–8). Again the internal platform is of very

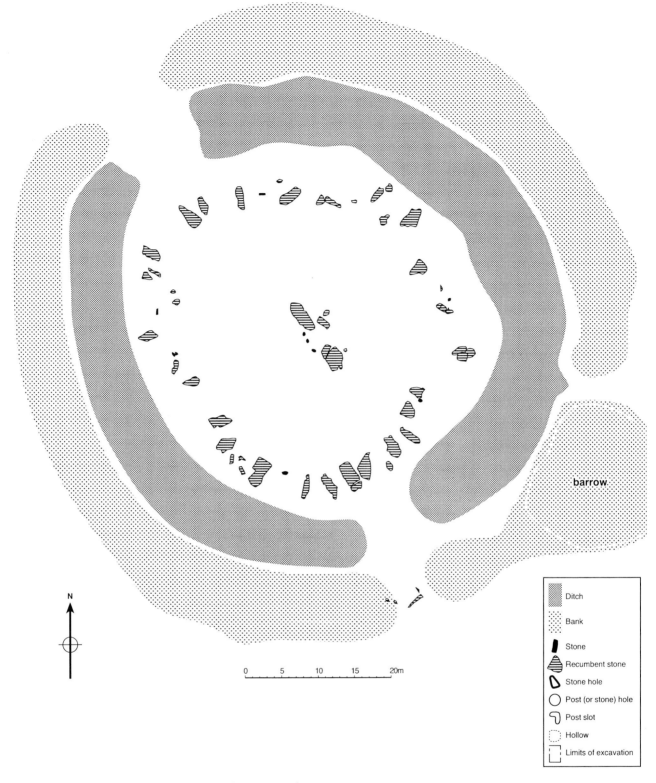

Figure 18 Simplified plan of Arbor Low henge, Derbyshite (after Gray 1903)

comparable size to those discussed so far, 35 x 40m, and it contained two relevant structures. The site sequence has been reconsidered by later writers, most recently by Gordon Barclay (1999), and there is considerable debate about the exact phasing of the early (pre-cairn) structures. The 'structure' nearest the centre is represented by three linear 'pits', or slots, set on the edges of a larger hollowed zone, which might be contemporary or later. The slots are likely to have held upright stones or timbers (Ritchie 1975–6). Piggott had reservations about whether they belonged with the initial henge phase (his period II) because of their eccentricity to the ditch and bank (1947–8,

79). However, the henge itself is one of those that seem to have been deliberately made to be asymmetric around the axis through the entrances. Moreover, it may be that he was expecting the wrong element to be central. Rather than the setting as a whole, it appears that it was the large socket, up to 6m long, that was intended to be central. The feature is aligned on the south entrance and perhaps also on a narrow gap through the terminal to the west of the north entrance (**Fig. 19**). It recalls the phase 2 façade at Ringlemere.

A revised perspective on Cairnpapple can be gained by developing Ritchie's suggestion that this central rectilinear

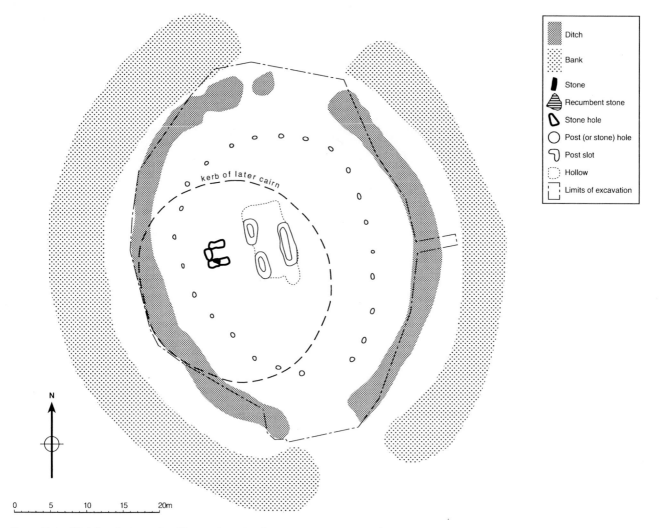

▨	Ditch
⣿	Bank
◣	Stone
◭	Recumbent stone
◖	Stone hole
○	Post (or stone) hole
⌐	Post slot
⸛	Hollow
⌐⌐	Limits of excavation

N

0   5   10   15   20m

Figure 19 Simplified plan of Cairnpapple Hill henge, West Lothian (adapted from Piggott 1947–8)

structure went together with another early structure immediately to the west – the 'cove' (this is followed by Barclay in his phase 2; 1999, 39). The structure has a maximum external width of 3.5m and although most sockets are now empty, they are best seen as for modest sized stones. Indeed one upright is surely still essentially *in situ*; it is incorporated into, but out of character with, an oval stone-slab surround for a subsequent Beaker grave, which will have truncated the eastern end of its socket (Piggott 1947–8, 91 fig. 10, pl. IX.2). The cove faced east with a potential sight line through a portal formed by the westerly two uprights of the 'central' setting and thus onto the flat face of, or through a window in, the central façade. It is also noteworthy that the outer circle of uprights, probably timber posts, is flattened on the east side, opposite the westerly offset position of the focal structures, and this gives a symmetry about an axis perpendicular to the axial passage through the entrances (itself offset from the centre line of the monument) .

There is no stratigraphic evidence against these features at Cairnpapple belonging to a contemporary structural set. They pre-date two graves, one with two Long-Necked Beakers, the other with a Food Vessel, and an encircling two-phase cairn (Piggott's periods III–IV). The structure set should pre-date the 2nd millennium BC and could be significantly earlier (Barclay 1999, 32–4). Beaker sherds (unillustrated) were apparently recovered from the fill of one of the central structure sockets (Piggott 1947–8, fig. 5), but they might relate to demolition as much as construction.

The Devil's Quoits, a class 2 henge in Oxfordshire, yielded a cluster of shallow post holes at its centre (A. Barclay *et al.* 1995, 43 fig. 26). Most survived to no more than 11cm deep, possibly having been truncated by agricultural activity, including medieval ridge-and-furrow. Alistair Barclay was concerned that a structure may have survived incompletely and suggested that the post holes represented an oval setting (ibid 71–3). However, the main arc of post holes forms a semi-circular setting 9m across and open towards the western entrance. The presence of close-set and double post holes suggests the structure went through two-phases or was repaired. Within the cresecent defined are five further post holes, one of which (F90) is equidistant from the crescent's ends. It is just possible that three of the others may have belonged to a rectilinear setting, but if so one had been destroyed or missed. This arrangement of posts as a crescent is reminiscent of what may be reconstructed at the centre of Balfarg henge.

Balfarg is an atypical henge with two entrances set at about 100° from each other, the ditch enclosing an area of around 65m diameter (Mercer 1981; Mercer *et al.* 1988). It lies close to the Balfarg Riding School enclosure already discussed. Despite considerable erosion and a difficult glacial till subsoil, the excavator was able to identify many internal features, some of which could be reconstructed as concentric circles or arcs thereof, mainly for timber uprights. The main circle, A, had a 'portal' structure facing west and this seems to define the main axis of approach to the centre (**Fig. 20**). Inside was a lighter

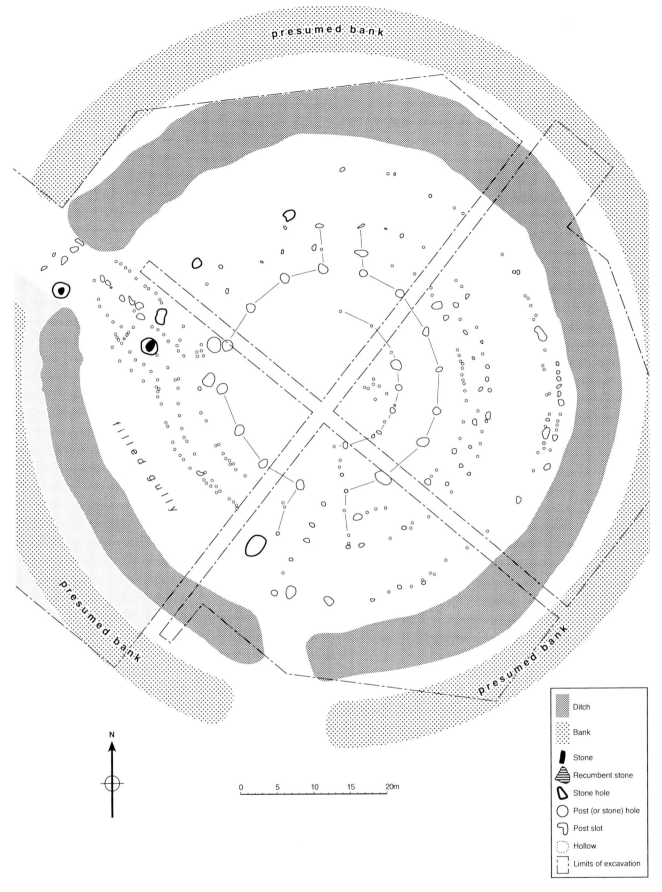

Figure 20 Simplified plan of Balfarg henge, Fife (adapted from Mercer 1981). Only selected internal features are shown here.

semi-circular structure screening the back (east) side of the inner space, away from the main approach. Focally sited towards the back of the semi-circle and a few metres behind the centre of the whole monument was a cluster of small post holes, some having evidence of burning (Z9 – Z15). These are not unambiguously reconstructed and may not all be post holes, but a small rectilinear or trapezoid structure is possible. The very centre of the site is almost bare of features, but a late Beaker grave was inserted, presumably considerably later than the site's foundation.

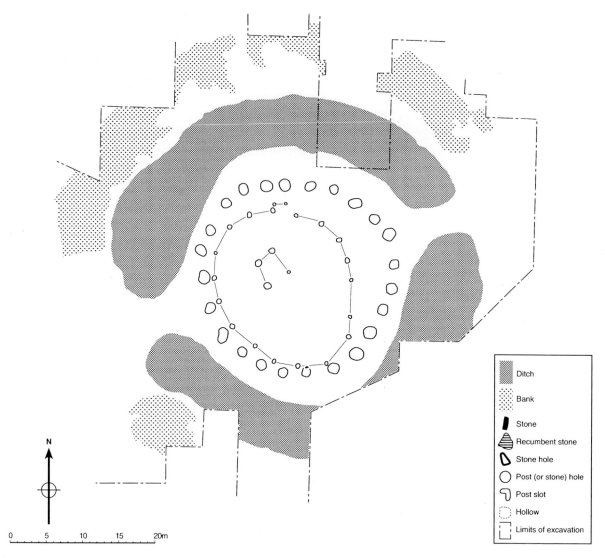

	Ditch
	Bank
	Stone
	Recumbent stone
	Stone hole
	Post (or stone) hole
	Post slot
	Hollow
	Limits of excavation

0   5   10   15   20m

Figure 21 Simplified plan of North Mains henge, Perthshire (adapted from Barclay 1983)

At North Mains, Perthshire, there is again the possibility of a small cove or quadrangular structure near to the centre of a henge of 35 x 32m internal diameter (**Fig. 21**). A sequence was recognised by the excavator in which the ring of substantial posts, circle A, must have been erected before the henge earthwork was constructed because of the consistent orientation of their ramps outwards, towards the ditch; had the ditch already existed, this would have made erection of the big timbers even more difficult a task than it already was (G. Barclay 1983, 180). Inside circle A was an egg-shaped ring of slighter posts, circle B, whose eccentricity relative to circle A and the enclosure has led to the suggestion that it was earlier still (Gibson 1998, 36–7). This need not necessarily be the case since there is no overlap between the two 'circles' and an alternative explanation for their eccentricity could lie in the deliberate creation of a forecourt area between them on the east side, arguably the main approach.

Four pits or post holes – F40, F41, F43, F45 (G. Barclay 1983, 152–4) – form a slightly trapezoid setting, about 3.5m long and contracting from 3.5 to 2.5m in width. Although not central in the monument, it is sited focally within ring B, just north-west of its centre, its wide end facing the centre (south-east). If this was the open side of a cove, it may have faced away from the entrance to ring B, for such is potentially defined by F37 and F38 which were recognized by the excavator to form a pair lying

immediately outside the north of ring B. None of the relationships here prove contemporaneity between the various structural elements and there may have been a sequence of additions. Nonetheless, it is possible to see all these elements as constituting a unitary plan at some point in the site's history.

The single-entrance henge-like enclosure at Llandegai A, Gwynedd, atypical in having an internal bank only really repeated at Stonehenge, may also have a cove structure, but unlike the classic henges discussed so far, the cove lies immediately outside the entrance. A set of pits and postholes containing cremated human bone deposits at that location has hitherto been described as a 'cremation circle' (Lynch and Musson 2004, 48–54). However, this is something of a misnomer; the three main features are elongate slots, each between four and 5m long. Together they form what can readily be reconstructed as a cove enclosing an area of 7 x 4.5m and facing NNE. Other features in the group are modest by comparison although some may have held single posts, two being situated in front of the putative open side of the cove.

Although described as pits, the long oval features could have been slots for upright timbers and/or stones. The westerly one, ACC2, even contained in its centre the base of a broken and partially keeled over monolith, but concentrations of charcoal to either side suggest that it stood between or replaced timbers which had burned *in situ*. The back-wall slot, ACC3, had a central linear bed of charcoal all along its base, and another against its northern edge; they are suggested to have originated in planks (ibid, 51), in which case they could be the base of one or more phases of a timber-framed wall. Deposits of cremated bone are recorded in plan as having formed a neat ring around the central line of the slot and would be consistent with having been buried at the foot of a wall panel, both internally and externally (ibid, 49 fig. 22).

The eastern slot, ACC4, contained less charcoal occurring as five patches fairly regularly distributed along its length and suggestive of burnt post positions. Three radiocarbon dates, one for charcoal from each of the three slots, show broad contemporaneity with the earthwork of the 'formative' henge, ie towards the end of the 4th millennium cal BC (**Table 1**).

A slot foundation for a slightly trapezoid timber cove 5m long, 2.5m wide and facing east was excavated at Briar Hill, Northamptonshire. It stood in the southern part of the innermost circuit of a triple segmented ditch enclosure, the whole of which was initially taken to constitute an earlier Neolithic causewayed enclosure (Bamford 1985, 43 fig. 22). The innermost enclosure was 95 x 85m across, but the cove itself is dated by radiocarbon and Grooved Ware sherds to the Late Neolithic, as are three other internal features. There is also an undated linear façade trench, 6m long, placed immediately behind the cove.

The Late Neolithic features must be much later additions to the original causewayed enclosure; Chris Evans (1988, 85–6) was first to challenge the notion that all three ditch circuits were part of the 'coherent design' originally argued by the excavator. It is now much more likely that most of the inner circuit was appended to a stretch of the middle circuit to form a near-circular enclosure with an external bank, contrasting with the existing internal banks (Mercer 1990, 63–4; Bradley 1998b, 79; Oswald et al. 2001, 55, 56, 77, 133–4, 153). The earthwork in this rejuvenated phase is not well dated; sparse finds are still of earlier Neolithic material, perhaps residual, and two radiocarbon measurements are on small samples. Nevertheless, the latter do suggest contemporaneity with the enclosed cove and associated features at a date around 3000 cal BC and the complex may qualify as a 'formative henge' in Jan Harding's terms (2003, 10–20).

Flagstones in Dorset is another enclosure that may fit into this category and has much in common with Briar Hill's inner circuit – very small ditch segments and an internal diameter of 97m (Healy 1997). Radiocarbon dating again places its construction and early use to either side of 3000 cal BC. Only about half of the interior was available for excavation and it is not certain where the entrance or entrances lay. One strong candidate on the north side was defined by a wider gap than normal and shallower flanking ditch segments of distinct profile than elsewhere, possibly incorporating post sockets (ibid 33, fig. 20 section J). A little south and west of that gap, 20m distant overall, were three contiguous shallow pit features (ibid, 41). Unfortunately these had been partly destroyed by medieval field boundaries, but they define three sides of a space of 4 x 2m open to the south-east. It seems quite possible that this too was the foundation for a timber cove.

In the south-west quadrant of the enclosure, immediately inside the ditch, was a semi-circular ditch about 7m across, three enclosed pits each contained cremated human bone (ibid, 41).

Although semi-circular, this mini-enclosure is highly reminiscent of the Llandegai A cove in its size, position on the south-west perimeter and association with bone.

Another monument created in this 'formative' phase was Stonehenge; there may even be indications of a rectilinear feature here amidst the considerable ground surface losses caused by the subsequent stone settings in the central zone. The timber structures are generally believed to have belonged to pre-stone phases and are ascribed to Stonehenge 2 (Cleal et al. 1995). This may be an over-simplification arising from the fragmentation of the evidence, but a thorough consideration of this problem cannot be tackled here. However, a trench opened by Atkinson close to the centre of the site yielded just two post holes 3.5m apart (Cleal et al. 1995, 149 fig. 69). Moreover, these would be consistent with one side of a square or quadrilateral four-post setting symmetrically disposed around the theoretical centre of the enclosure. It is tempting, on this limited evidence, to hypothesise that an early phase of Stonehenge had a central rectilinear structure.

Similar questions need to be asked of the features that have been revealed by geophysical survey at the centre of the Stanton Drew great stone circle which is now seen to lie immediately inside a ditch enclosing a space of 125m diameter (David et al. 2004, 344–9). At least two major features here are now shown to lie at the centre of as many as nine concentric circles of pits and/or post holes. For the sake of completeness, we should also mention the record of a possible cove inside a now lost earthwork – perhaps a henge – at Tisbury, Wiltshire (Bradley, in Barrett et al. 1991, 106).

Related structures also occur within circular stone and timber monuments that lack an immediately enclosing earthwork; even so, some of these are associated with great-henge enclosures or with large palisade enclosures. The great majority of the 'open' circles have a maximum diameter much smaller than the henges and formative henges discussed. The stone circle at Balbirnie, part of the Balfarg complex in Fife, is only 14m in diameter and central within it is a closed kerb-defined square about 3.5 x 3m which only really finds structural parallel at Stones of Stenness (Ritchie 1975–6). In contrast is the North circle within Avebury great henge, some 97 x 93m across, with its equally grand stone cove facing north-east and enclosing about 8 x 4.5m (Smith 1965, fig. 68; Burl 1976, 307 fig. 50a, 320–33; Gillings and Pollard 2004, 13 fig. 4). The southern circle inside Avebury is of similar size and had instead the tall 'obelisk' stone at its centre. To the west of the obelisk Keiller excavated stone holes forming a three-sided setting of smallish stones, the long side being 32m long, but the short axis (7m) may be incomplete if the setting extended beyond the excavation trench (Smith 1965, 198–201; Gillings and Pollard 2004, 122 fig. 16, 13 fig. 4).

The two timber circles inside the Durrington Walls great henge both feature four-post central settings which are slightly trapezoid and comprise substantial timbers (Wainwright and Longworth 1971). Dimensions are 5 x 5m tapering to 4m within the North circle and a little larger within the South circle. Similar arrangements of comparable dimensions are becoming recurrent in timber 'circles', some having extended entrance features. Examples are now known at Knowth, Co Meath (Eogan and Roche 1997, 101 ff), and Ballynahatty, Co Down (Hartwell 1998, as well as nearby at Durrington 68, sealed under a later barrow mound (Pollard 1995b), and perhaps some more Irish sites (Sheridan 2004, 28–9). An additional structure was set inside the Ballynahatty four-poster (BNH6): 14 posts defining a 3 x 3m square which Hartwell sees as having supported an excarnation platform (1998, 39–40). Ten metres outside the entrance of this structure was excavated a three-sided cove foundation of similar dimensions; a second matching example is deduced from geophysical survey.

A variation on this pattern may be evident at the north-east stone circle at Stanton Drew (David *et al.* 2004, 352). Here, the long-known stone circle of about 33m diameter with a short approach avenue facing east has recently been found to enclose substantial features, presumably once holding big timbers – a four-post setting (*c.* 6m^2) with a narrower appended 'portal' facing east. A similar but larger 'portalled four-poster' has appeared inside the south-south-west circle in the same complex. It is as much as 17m square and the portal instead faces NE. In fact, the addition of an earth resistance survey here suggests that this timber-cum-stone circle is enclosed by a ditch of a little over 40m internal diameter (David *et al.* 2004, 350–3); it may well be a second henge to go alongside that found around the great stone circle.

Yet another variant on the theme appears at West Kennet structure 2. A small rectilinear setting of posts, 3.5 x 3m, lies immediately outside the inner of a double-ring palisade, itself set within the large palisade enclosure 2 (Whittle 1997, 76–85). It appears to have been an annexe to the inner ring of posts which has a gap at this point, thus forming an entrance porch, but its posts would have been much less substantial than the ring itself. This particular structure was not dated by radiocarbon, but did contain Grooved Ware. The palisaded enclosures at West Kennet are mainly datable to the later 3rd millenniun BC.

Two final coves should be mentioned, neither apparently inside an enclosure, but both associated with complexes already discussed. The destroyed stone cove at Beckhampton was again trapezoid, faced south-east and enclosed a relatively large space, about 10 x 8m. It stood at the end of and perpendicular to the Beckhampton stone-lined avenue leading west out of Avebury, but was as much as 1.5km from that great henge (Burl 1988, 4 fig. 3). However, it is also necessary to consider its relationship to a previous unknown enclosure alongside; this was subsequently traversed by the avenue (Gillings and Pollard 2004, 79–81). The outlying stone cove at Stanton Drew is again situated south-west of the complex of three stone circles, but is much smaller in scale, about 3 x 2m. These 'external' locations bring back to mind Llandegai A, where the cove lies outside the henge's south-west entrance.

Three other class 1 henges have yielded dating evidence and offer parallels for Ringlemere in terms of orientation and/or area enclosed. Maumbury Rings, not far from Mount Pleasant, is difficult to reconstruct in detail because of the substantial alterations made to convert it into a Roman amphitheatre (Bradley 1976). This involved significant reduction of the internal ground surface which will have removed any internal prehistoric features, including all but traces of the ditch. Nevertheless, Bradley's careful calculations leave little doubt that a ditch was originally present directly above the ring of deep shafts which penetrate well below the later destruction level. As far as can be estimated the internal diameter of the ditch would have been in the region of 45m and the outer

diameter 55m or more. The probable single entrance was just east of north. Two radiocarbon dates have been obtained from red deer antlers from the early excavations by H. St George Gray: 3970 ± 70 BP (BM-2282N) for the bottom of shaft 1 and 3940 ± 130 BP for the uppermost fill of shaft 3 (BM-2281R).

Other class 1 henges of similar orientation to Ringlemere are less comparable in dimensions and regularity. Woodhenge has a slightly oval plan and its diameter is larger (internally around 50m); the entrance faces about 30° east of north. Two radiocarbon dates are from early contexts within the ditch; antler from the ditch floor produced a result of 3817 ± 74 BP (BM-677) and animal bone from the primary silts gave 3755 ± 54 BP (BM-678). Another somewhat irregular example is that at Gorsey Bigbury, Somerset, it points just west of north and has an internal diameter of between 20 and 24m. A rich deposit of occupation debris in the secondary silts of the ditch yielded many Beaker sherds and six radiocarbon dates on charcoal falling between 3800 and 3600 BP (**Table 1**; Harding and Lee 1987, 261–2).

As a henge in its first manifestation, the Ringlemere M1 enclosure would belong to a tradition of 'Late Neolithic' monument design. In reality, the construction of such monuments spans the very end of the fourth and much of the 3rd millennium BC (J. Harding 2003, fig. 6), the last part of which is contemporary not only with continuing Grooved Ware, but also with early Beaker material and the earliest metallurgy. Nevertheless, there is little evidence that classic henges (*sensu* Harding and Lee 1987) were constructed after 2000 BC; indeed, the latest good dating for an early phase of a class 1 henge is around 2200/2100 BC (**Table 1**).

In this context the current dating of the cove at Ringlemere, 1890–1680 cal BC, might suggest that it was a later addition to the enclosure and related more to those examples known from Early Bronze Age burial contexts. However, there are significant uncertainties relating to its radiocarbon dating (Chapter 4) and there must be a strong presumption, given the emerging pattern of evidence for Late Neolithic ceremonial monuments, that it was a key feature of the original henge. From this non-exhaustive survey it can be seen that up to 15 earthwork enclosures share with Ringlemere the presence of a cove or similar rectilinear structure – a *secretum*; in 11 or 12 cases the secretum lies at the heart of the monument. Furthermore, there are nine 'open' circles of timber or stone uprights that again, with one exception, have central secretums. These open circles tend to be smaller in diameter, but often set within a larger monumental complex involving great henges and large palisade enclosures. The same is true of two known 'outlying' coves, one of which is linked to its associated complex by an avenue.

It should be emphasized that in drawing together this set of broadly comparable sites in terms of their lay-out, it is not to be suggested that all functioned in exactly the same way, either at secretum or whole-site level. This is an aspect that will be explored in greater detail in another context.

Monument phases 2 and 3

In its second phase as a monument a turf mound was added in the interior of Ringlemere M1. Aside from the off-centre pit (F. 1073) with possible flecks of cremated bone, there is no evidence that it was erected to cover a burial deposit. A berm may have been left between it and the lip of the ditch, but the later edge truncation makes this impossible to ascertain with certainty. Given the arguments presented above, that the turf mound was never more than about 1m high, it would seem that the intention was not to impress viewers with sheer monumental scale, but rather to create a raised platform for the enactment of ritual activities. Although not high, such a platform set amidst gently sloping topography would have distinctly enhanced visibility of the performances from the immediate surrounds. It may for example have off-set the partial barrier effect of the encircling bank.

The turf platform was given a new structural focus, the linear façade of timbers (F. 1027), again respecting the previously important northerly orientation. Together, platform and post setting would have provided an excellent dais for performing ceremonies (Fox 1959, 139–43; Barrett 1988, 38; Barrett *et al.* 1991, 128). Attention has also recently been given to the potential role of barrow mounds to enhance inter-visibility between critical parts of the landscape (Woodward 2000, 139–140, 142). Dating of this Ringlemere phase is not yet very precise, but some Beaker sherds occur in the old ground surface sealed by the mound and in the turf of the mound itself. The mound is unlikely to have been erected before the last quarter of the 3rd millennium BC (see Chapter 4, Beaker pottery).

Periodic activity in the centre of the platform around the façade could help explain the curious survival of wood fragments in the central cut features. It is possible that regular trampling there would have compacted and depressed the surface locally, acting to exacerbate puddling whenever rain fell. This might just have tipped the balance towards longer periods of wetness in the underlying deposits, at the same time producing a less permeable capping which prevented rapid drying out. The latter effect might also have been aided by the later capping with a clayey mound.

The third monument phase may, perhaps, have related to a burial, but even this is uncertain. The pit (F. 1024) dug into the centre of the turf mound contained a raft of wood, perhaps a 'floor' lining, the amber pendant fragment and quite probably the gold cup. Had this been a burial by inhumation, the skeletal remains would have decayed badly or totally; furthermore, any fragments surviving above the wood layer could have been dispersed by modern ploughing. If the orange clay deposit encircling the turf core is the basal remains of a secondary capping mound, this would traditionally be seen to be associated with a significant secondary burial. However, the shape and large size of the phase 3 central feature is far from classic for an Early Bronze Age grave, and it must be considered equally possible that the pit had another ritual purpose connected to the activities on the mound. Whatever, it continues the sequence of events that make it clear that the centre of the henge-cum-barrow retained a focal position for some time.

The addition of a mound within or attached to a classic henge (ie discounting small sites which merge into conventional barrows – see Chapter 5 for some discussion of Kentish examples) is not a particularly common phenomenon, but a growing number of examples are known. The most celebrated are the large mounds at Knowlton, Mount Pleasant and Marden (Bradley, in Barrett *et al.* 1991, 105; Woodward 2000, 92) and the smaller one attached to Arbor Low (Gray 1903). The Knowlton mound has not been excavated, but on the aerial photographic evidence it would seem that the large mound stood within its own ditch and then, separated by a wide berm, the earthworks of a substantial henge with a narrow entrance facing north-east (Grinsell 1959, 159 fig. 6, 174 – Woodlands 1; Woodward 2000, colour plate 17). The mound itself is about 38m in diameter and 6.1m high, while the internal diameter of the henge ditch is about 100–102m (Harding and Lee 1987, 127 fig., 129).

At Cairnpapple, West Lothian, much of the interior, including the early structures discussed above, was covered by a cairn erected in two phases (Piggott 1947–8). One difference from Ringlemere is that the cairn was offset to the west rather than being centrally placed; secondly, it was clearly erected to commemorate formal burials, which seems not to have been the case at Ringlemere. At Catterick, North Yorkshire, the reverse sequence has been found; the bank of a henge incorporated a pre-existing cairn (Richard Bradley pers. comm.).

An unexcavated monument – either disc-barrow or henge – at Eggardon Hill (Grinsell 1959, 169 Powerstock 4a), Dorset, has two mounds, one impinging on the south-west side of the bank, the other centrally placed with a maximum diameter of about 14m leaving a wide berm outside (Piggott and Piggott 1939, 151 fig. 8; RCHME 1952, xxxii, 185 no. 29). The internal platform diameter is about 40 x 45m and two possible entrances aligned NW–SE have been noted in the past. On the ground these are unconvincing as original entrances, instead appearing as partly denuded earthworks due to later traffic. It may be no coincidence that these two breaches align on the nearby road junction, suggesting a past footpath crossing the monument. There is also good evidence for a second, outer ditch, grouping this site with Grinsell's 'Dorset' variant of disc barrow (Grinsell 1959, 18).

A similar monument on the South Dorset Ridgeway (Grinsell 1959, 171 Bincombe 60f, pl III; Woodward 2000, 141 ill. 73) is more promising as a henge-with-barrow. There is today a good break in the bank on the north side, although the internal ditch seems to continue uninterrupted. Grinsell noted that the berm around the mound was not of constant width, which might perhaps signify a two phase design with the original site centre not closely re-located in the second phase. The internal diameter of the ditch is about 54m. If nothing else, sites like these emphasise the grey boundary that may exist between classic henges and the succeeding 'fancy' barrows with ditch and external bank.

At Maxey, Cambridgeshire, a circular ditched enclosure of large diameter, some 120m, has an east facing entrance which straddled an oval barrow. At some point in its history a ditch-enclosed turf mound 32 x 36m in internal diameter was added at the centre (Pryor and French 1985; Bradley 1993, 101–2). Francis Pryor regarded the enclosure as a henge (class 1), but the combination of large diameter and yet relatively slight ditch profile is not normal for such monuments and an alternative possibility is that it is akin to the perimeter enclosures seen round Neolithic round barrows at Duggleby Howe and Maes Howe, or it is a 'formative' henge.

Flagstones enclosure is in many ways similar to Maxey and has much more secure dating evidence. Almost centrally in the original enclosure of 97m diameter a burial was inserted much later, in the early 2nd millennium cal BC. The grave was enclosed by a new ring-ditch about 25m internal diameter and covered by a mound (Healy 1997, 39).

A much smaller monument – class 2 henge or hengi-form –

at Ballymeanoch, Argyllshire, may also relate in that it has a low surviving mound (Craw 1930–1, 278–9; RCAHM Scotland 1988, 52). The entrances are aligned ENE–WSW and the internal diameter is a maximum of 20m. The presence of two cists might suggest that this was initially constructed as a burial monument, but neither is central or obviously primary.

A possible mound remnant has been suggested at Balfarg Riding School, the probable henge discussed above. The post holes of the southern end of the internal building were sealed by a stoney layer, doubtless originally more extensive, but surviving here due to a surface hollow (Barclay and Russell-White 1993, 84). The excavators considered it possible that this was the last vestige of a low mound erected over the site of the former building. Although they suggest that the ditch was dug after the building already existed, this is not supported by any stratigraphic or radiocarbon evidence. If a mound was indeed once present, it is clear that it need not be contemporary with initial ditch digging.

A final site to be discussed in this context is Bryn Celli Ddu, Anglesey (Hemp 1930). Frances Lynch has argued that its passage grave set within a circular mound is concentrically placed over an earlier circular monument comprising a ditch and internal circle of stone uprights (Lynch 1969, 110–12 fig. 29). The internal diameter of the enclosure was about 21m. This provides another possible parallel sequence, although no evidence has been found for an external bank or an entrance causeway. This leaves some uncertainty over the relationship of the first Bryn Celli Ddu monument to henges, a difficulty compounded by the fact that the passage grave is best dated to the late 4th millennium BC. Moreover, a number of variant sequences have been proposed for the site, in one of which the ditch initially encircled a mound with a peripheral ring of monoliths. These features were later all covered when the mound was enlarged to the diameter of the now largely silted ditch, in the top of which was set a new mound-edge kerb (Bradley 1998a, 8–9). Intriguingly, just outside the ditch at the entrance to the passage grave Hemp uncovered a small cove-like setting of stones in the centre of which was the burial of an ox. The cove is 3.5 x 2m but not datable relative to the main monument phases.

Chapter 3: The Gold Cup
Stuart Needham

General condition and problems

The image presented by the Ringlemere cup is striking partly because of the obvious quality of the original workmanship, but also because of the severe crumpling it has suffered (**Colour Pls 1 & 2**). The greater part of the damage appears to be due to impacts of similar nature – heavy blows with a hard, pointed object or objects. The most swinging blow was received to the middle of the side opposite the handle at or just below the carination, leaving this side with a deep cleft. Diametrically opposite is a lesser dent just below the handle, presumably arising from resistance to this impact. Because of the rigidity of the corrugated conical lower body the main cleft has caved in as a roughly triangular shape with crisp surrounding arrises. To the right of it the original morphology is little affected, but to the left of the cleft there is another lesser dent, again with a linear central crease running vertically up the body. This is the only significant damage to encroach on the uncorrugated, basal part of the body (**Pl. 12**).

It is probable that the main blow and the opposing resistance, which nearly pinched together part of the middle of the body, also accounts for the flattening of the upper body roughly into a narrow pointed ellipse (**Pl. 3**). At the two ends of this ellipse the rim and neck have been crushed on a near-vertical axis into acute angles. The remainder of the circumference features other more or less severe buckles interspersed with seemingly more intact stretches. The stresses involved have acted unevenly causing the sheet metal to fold at a limited number of points on the circumference. The stretch of wall inside the handle has been partially flattened, the handle itself having been pressed up against it and almost folded double towards the top (**Pl. 4**). A tear runs half way across this fold, and there is a further substantial tear across the lower end where it joins the carination because the handle has been pulled upward in the process of being crushed (**Colour Pl. 2**).

Another substantial blow has caused damage of different character. It has badly gashed the side of the vessel to the right

of the handle base (**Pl. 5**). The metal immediately around the gash shows marked but local crumpling on both faces and part of a rectangular impression has been left on one edge.

As close inspection proceeded, it became apparent that there was a sudden turn in profile at the top of the 11th rib (numbered from the bottom rib upwards) for the greater part of the circumference. The upper body (neck) has partially collapsed, or concertinered, into the lower body, leading to a marked double bend at the carination. This leaves the body immediately above for the most part inaccessible because it is tucked inside the double bend.

Explaining this collapse is not straightforward. One possibility considered was that it derives from an earlier phase of damage, due to strong or sustained pressure on a vertical axis through the cup. Further reflection, however, makes this unlikely. It would have had to be uneven compression which allowed one side to survive unaltered, in which case one would expect evidence of a gradational change between the intact profile on one side and the markedly altered profile opposite. Instead, the change is sudden at two creases – one negative the other positive – associated with the main crushing. This strongly suggests that the partial concertinering was integrally linked to the other major damage and caused by multi-directional stresses acting on a complex three-dimensional geometry.

It would be extremely important to determine how much of the damage was modern and how much ancient, for example, deriving from pre-depositional rituals. Although there are at least four major aspects of damage – two large dents, the gash, the vertical concertinering – these do not necessarily imply separate events. All could actually be reconciled with the

Plate 3 Top view showing crushing of the mouth

Plate 4 Profile view showing crushed handle

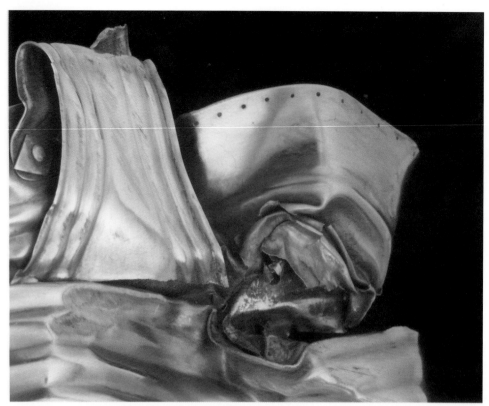

Plate 5 Detail of gash in side of body

incidence of a single massive blow from agricuatural machinery with consequent crumpling effects due to soil resistance and the geometry of the hollow object. Equally, there is no certainty that the damage was all simultaneous.

What may be significant, however, is that there are no occurrences of multiple contiguous or overlapping dents that might be expected had the object been subjected to a sequence of blows from an ancient implement. If, therefore, we are to contemplate the possibility of ancient damage, it has to be seen as 'single-strike' in any given orientation. On balance the character of the damage observed seems much more likely to be the result of one accidental, but substantial encounter with a massive object.

Surface patination
by Susan La Niece

The gold has a distinctive, fine-grained, red patina, preserved in the recesses, particularly in the folds of the damaged area, and inside the rim. On some areas just inside the rim there are unexplained linear marks in the patina. Endoscopic examination shows the patina layer is thinner inside the cup. It is not present on the most accessible areas of the outer surface, where it had been rubbed with a cloth previously used by the finder for polishing coins. Traces of corundum (alpha-alumina, Al_2O_3) were identified by X-ray diffraction analysis in the pointillé decoration and crevices where the handle joins the body of the cup. This is an abrasive, here probably representing modern residues of chrome polish on the cloth.

The red patina was identified by X-ray diffraction analysis as silver gold sulphide (AgAuS) (JCPDS 19-1146). This patina was first published from research into silver-rich gold antiquities from Egypt (Frantz and Schorsch 1990). This is the first recorded instance of the patina from Britain, perhaps because it is rare for gold objects to be examined straight from excavation, before thorough cleaning.

Reconstructing the original form

No restoration of the cup has been attempted because of concern that opening the severe buckles might alter the metal structure. This made even more important the need to create a virtual restoration to allow good visualisation of the object in antiquity. This has proved to be doubly important given that the profile reconstructed was not that initially assumed from casual inspection.

Undistorted segments of the cup show good circularity in plan and we can assume that it was close to circular from top to bottom. Virtual restoration then depends on three types of observation:

partial profiles taken from intact segments;
total surface length of the profile along any radial slice;
circumferences at a range of planes through the full depth of the vessel.

The sheet metal being relatively thick, it is thought that any stretching due to distortion is likely to be insignificant. Taken together these observations act as a constraint on one another and, if sufficient data can be obtained, there is little margin for error in the overall reconstruction. Judging a segment to be intact depends on observing an even radial curvature, a lack of any obvious dents and creases, and internal 'coherence' between the features (mainly ribs) contained. There are three segments of near-intact profile which are large enough to offer valuable information on shape.

Intact segment A: The first is obvious – one side of the lower body running all the way from the base up to rib 11. The profile (**Fig. 22; Pl. 6**) must be very close to the original even though there may be slight distortion of some radii due to the severe damage to either side. As a double-check on radii, circumferences were measured around ribs 1 and 11, a process made difficult by the deep cleft in the front of the body.

Intact segment B: A smaller segment situated within one side of the pronounced cleft is somewhat surprisingly intact. This was not at first appreciated, but is of enormous significance because in addition to the smoothly cusping profile of ribs 6–10 of the lower body, it shows the profile to turn at rib 11 and continue at a new angle for ribs 12 and 13 before any significant distortion intervenes (**Fig. 22; Pls 7 & 8**). What this segment shows beyond any doubt is that the middle of the cup was not the weak or

moderate carination familiar on its parallels. Instead the upper body turns suddenly inward at rib 11 producing a shoulder occupied by ribs 12 and 13. The shoulder is sloped, forming an angle of about 110° with the body below and thus nearer to the horizontal than the vertical. The presence of this strong

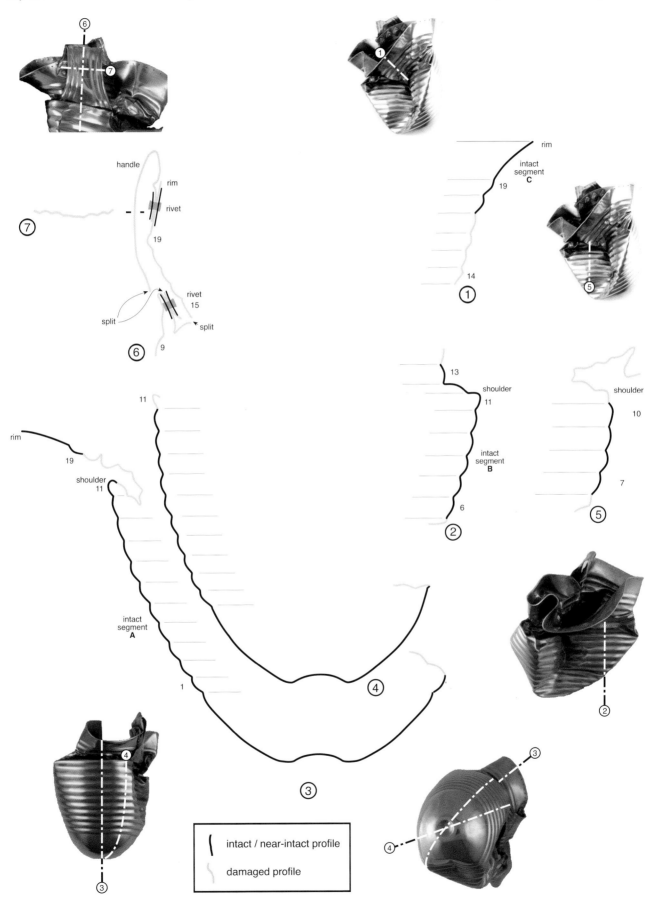

Figure 22 Drawn profiles of the crushed vessel at selected points (scale 100%)

Plate 6 Profile of intact segment A, the lower body

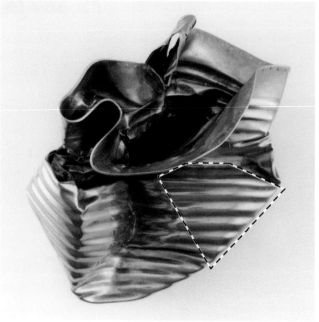

Plate 7 Face view of intact segment B (outlined)

shoulder undoubtedly explains the concertinered damage described above.

Intact segment C: Fortunately the third segment encompasses part of the rim and extends down through the smooth band and then ribs 19 and 18 before some flattening or buckling of ribs 17 onwards (**Fig. 22; Pl. 9**). This segment is not pristine, but undulations are minor and the broad form unlikely to be much altered. It gives a good basis for the angle at which the rim stood and the profile of the upper neck. Although difficult due to the severe contortions, it was possible to obtain circumference measurements at the rim itself and on rib 19 and thus a reliable reconstruction of the mouth of the cup.

The mouth portion is, however, left floating free relative to the lower body and shoulder. Ribs 14–16 are disfigured all round and, moreover, these plus ribs 12–13 are inaccessible for much of their circumferences because of the concertinering. The shape of the neck is therefore the least well documented empirically and has to be interpolated between the other profile stretches. In

practice, the established angles of the latter in conjunction with the measured depth of ribs 14–16 leave little uncertainty in the linkage.

For the virtual restoration (**Colour Pl. 3**), the body was generated through a 'lathed profile' and the handle was based on a 'swept profile', both available in standard computer 3D-graphics packages. The work was undertaken by Stephen Crummy.

Description of the reconstructed form

The Ringlemere cup would have stood around 123mm tall, the greater part, 78mm, being the lower body to the shoulder (**Fig. 23**). The diameter at the shoulder was 96mm, that at the neck a minimum of about 76mm and at the rim 109mm. It currently weighs 183.7g, which should be close to the original weight since very little if any metal has been removed at the gash. Further dimensions, both measured and calculated, are given in the catalogue.

Plate 8 Profile of intact segment B

Plate 9 Face view of intact segment C (outlined) with the rim horizontal

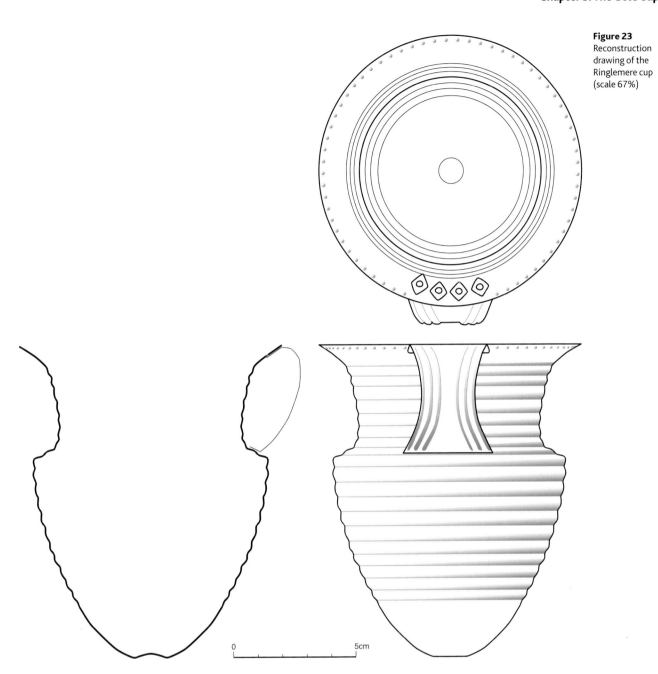

Figure 23
Reconstruction
drawing of the
Ringlemere cup
(scale 67%)

0   5cm

Starting at the base, there is an incredibly neat omphalos just 12mm in diameter and 2.0mm deep. The wall initially rises in a smooth gently convex profile and this sweeping curve is maintained for the ribbed part. The wall is essentially vertical by the time it reaches the shoulder. The ribs both here and higher each present an even curve in profile and meet at sharp creases between. The only rib with a different profile is that on the shoulder, rib 11; a relatively sharp (but not angular) turn divides this broader rib into two, a vertical lower part and a more horizontal upper part.

Above rib 11 the upper body presents a strongly concave and slightly asymmetric profile overall. The minimum diameter would have been below the centre with a strong curve to the shoulder and a more gradual curve sweeping out to the well flared rim. Most of this is ribbed, but the uppermost band of 15mm returns to a smooth metal profile and presents the rim at around 35° to the horizontal. The rim itself is in the same order of thickness as the rest of the walls and is basically flat-topped. Immediately beneath the rim is a row of 62 dots punched from the outside of the vessel and interrupted only at the handle.

While the body of the vessel has all been raised out of a single piece of gold, the handle is a separate piece of sheet metal attached top and bottom by four rivets passing through tab extensions. The handle has a fairly symmetrical hour-glass shape in face view, is about 0.3mm thick at the edges and is decorated and strengthened by ribbing outlining either side (**Pl. 6; Colour Pl. 2**). The ribbing is again cuspate with two ribs between three grooves in each set. The central zone was flat, but is now a little buckled. The handle expands to its broadest at the tabs which are turned inwards to rest flush on the corresponding parts of the body. The upper tab is attached to the smooth wall immediately below the rim and, as reconstructed, would have only needed to be gently angled from the top of the handle. The lower one must instead have turned inwards sharply, approaching a right-angle, and is affixed to rib no 12, that on the shoulder closest to horizontal.

For the top fixing, the nature of the riveting is easily observed inside the vessel (**Pl. 10**), but for the outside the crushing of the handle means that only the outermost rivets are really visible. The lower fixing is much more difficult to view. The collapse of the shoulder on this side of the cup has taken the tab down into the tight double fold. Very little of the outside

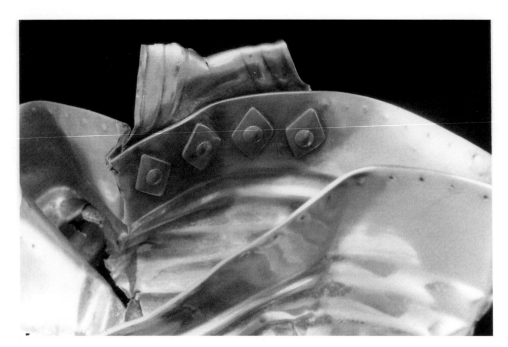

Plate 10 Detail of the inner upper rivet fixings

rivets can be seen by looking into the external fold beside the handle, while the internal ones are tucked up a similar fold not visible from the mouth of the cup. A boroscope, operated by Tony Simpson (the British Museum, Dept. Conservation, Documentation and Science), enabled something to be seen of the latter and about half of one outer rivet can be seen from the inside through a tear in the vessel wall (**Pl. 11**). Radiography confirms that size of rivets and their washers, plus orientation of the latter, are consistent throughout the lower tab.

All rivet ends show the same arrangement with circular, slightly domed and probably only slightly expanded heads barely protruding beyond their diamond-shaped 'washers'. The shallow dome meets the washer almost seamlessly to the naked eye and there are no visible cracks from the clenching process. Slight hammer marks are evident under magnification, but the heads have probably been well polished after closure. Dimensions are typically around 3mm for the diameter of the

heads, 8.5–10mm for the length of (accessible) washers and 7–8mm for their width. In three positions the washers have their long axis horizontal relative to the body; this was advantageous in terms of the ease of fitting the washers on and in a rib (lower fixing) or under the turn (upper fixing). However, inside the vessel at the top they are instead set vertically, presumably for design effect where they would have been most visible.

Metal composition
by Susan La Niece

The gold composition was identified by X-ray fluorescence analysis. It was possible to analyse the main components, the cup and the handle, on both the surface as found, and on small areas of fresh metal, where there was already some damage. The results illustrate the extent of surface enrichment caused by burial corrosion, or perhaps by the manufacturing process. A similar degree of enrichment might also be surmised for the

Plate 11 Detail of inside of cup showing a lower outer rivet head through a tear

rivets and the washers, on which only surface analysis was attempted.

The gold composition, with only trace levels of copper but a significant quantity of silver in the metal, is consistent with the use of alluvial gold with no refining or deliberate alloying. This is typical of Early Bronze Age British goldwork (Hartmann 1982).

		wt %		
		Au	Ag	Cu
Cup	– surface	82	18	0.2
	–- clean metal	76.9	22.9	0.2
Handle	–- surface	74	26	0.4
	–- clean metal	71.6	27.5	0.9
Rivet	–- surface	77	23	0.8
Washer	–- surface	78	21	0.5

The analyses have a precision (a measure of reproducibility) of $c. \pm$ 2% relative for gold, $c. \pm 5\%$ for silver and $c. \pm 20\text{-}50\%$ for copper, the precision deteriorating as the detection limit of 0.1% is approached. The accuracy of the analyses on clean metal should be of a similar order.

Traces of manufacture, wear and damage
Rivet washers
There is an important difference in detailed shape between the upper washers under the handle and those inside the mouth. The former are rather crisp around all their edges including the corners. This is also the state of the one visible outer washer in the lower row. In contrast, all of the exposed corners and edges on the upper internal washers are rounded off to some degree (compare **Pl. 5** with **Pl. 10**). Only the outermost tip of washer 4 under the handle is similar in this respect. These differences are all consistent with the fact that the inner rivets and washers would have been much more exposed to rubbing during finishing and/or use. It seems rather unlikely that differential rubbing would have resulted just from the finishing; surfaces under the handle could easily have been reached by burnishing tools if there had been the desire to bring the whole surface to a consistent level of polish. So while it is possible that some 'wear' occurred during finishing, it is suggested that the strong differential in wear was due to repeated attrition over a period of use. Logically, it could have arisen through regular cleaning of the inside of the vessel which was not so necessary under the handle.

Rim
Evidence from around the rim has similar implications. The one stretch relatively inaccessible to casual contact, that alongside the handle, has a flat top with crisp angles, although the inner, more exposed one is fractionally more rounded under magnification. By contrast, for the rest of its circuit the 'angles' are significantly rounded both internally and externally, leaving just a narrow flat band in between. It may be inferred that the rim started with a crisp square profile when the body was finished and before the handle was attached. Subsequent rubbing, probably mainly during its use-life, progressively reduced this to a sub-square profile.

Base
The omphalos is still very neat in outline and profile (**Pl. 12**). Its surround shows two possible patches of wear in diametrically opposing segments, but these are so slight as to be of uncertain significance. Other subtle dents and creases around the unribbed zone are side effects of the major damage or, in some cases perhaps, original hammer marks not fully planished out.

Striations
There are many very fine striations running circumferentially all over the body which result from finishing, re-polishing in antiquity and the finder's cleaning. Striations of similar grade run instead vertically on the handle, but this is to be expected since the best surface finish would be obtained by polishing in line with its linear mouldings.

A series of coarse parallel striations aligned diagonally on the handle are clearly secondary (**Pl. 5**). They are limited to the flattened central stretch in between the double bend at top and a slight bend towards the bottom, hence formed at the time of the crushing, or subsequently.

There is a third, intermediate grade of striations, in the order of 0.05mm wide, in two locations on the plain band below the rim. In both cases a band of roughly horizontal striations continues round a tight bend in the mouth. Their formation must therefore precede the major damage and, while a phase of slight abrasion due to movement in the ground is possible, the relative fine-ness of these scratches and their alignment favours that they are due to rotational rubbing/scouring of the mouth during use.

There is a multitude of other small marks over the surface, some clearly associated with the major damage episode and others, running parallel to major lines of buckling, almost certainly due to cleaning.

Dot decoration
The punched dots frequently have a slight lip to the left of the impression, suggesting that the tool used was being struck from the right at a slight angle to the perpendicular.

Plate 12 Detail of base showing the omphalos

Technology of production
by Susan La Niece

The body of the cup was made in one piece by hammering. A goldsmith today would take a flat disc of gold and hammer it while holding it firmly against a stake to force the metal progressively into the form of a hollowed vessel of the required proportions (Armbruster 2000, 159 fig. 88). Annealing, that is heating to relieve stresses in the metal, is required at regular intervals in the process. Working from the centre, the metal is beaten while continually rotating the gold against a series of stakes until the required diameter of the cup is obtained. At intervals the craftsman will ensure that the rim is thickened by tapping at right angles to the edge. Once the shaping is completed, the surface can be planished by gently tapping against a support, to smooth out any hammer indentations. The corrugations can be shaped by working the cup from the outside against a former held inside. The former need only be a block of wood into which a number of grooves are cut. The cup is rotated a few degrees and repositioned on the former, to continue the grooves around the circumference. The surface can then be polished with fine abrasives.

The handle was hammered out as a flat strip then cut to the required shape. The longitudinal grooves were worked from one face, leaving rounded ribs between. Once completed, the strip was bent to form the handle, the ends turned to form attachment tabs, perforated and then secured with domed rivets. These were hammered tight from the inside of the cup while the cup was supported.

No advanced tools or materials would have been required for making a vessel of this type; the technology can have changed very little since the Ringlemere cup was made. However, the quality of the workmanship does indicate that the goldsmith had considerable experience in making fine goldwork.

Chapter 4: Other Prehistoric Material

The amber artefacts
by Stuart Needham

Two amber artefacts were recovered during the excavation of Trench 1. Both have been identified as of Early Bronze Age types broadly contemporary with the cup (although one was at first thought to be so fresh as to be more recent!) A pommel fragment was unfortunately not *in situ*, having come from an animal run somewhere in the eastern half of the trench (not precisely located). The second fragment is identified as from a pendant and came from the pit (F. 1024) cut into the turf mound at the centre of the monument (**Figs 10–11**). It was retrieved from spoil immediately after it had been excavated from the upper, woody layer (1025) towards the southern end of the feature. These are the first Early Bronze Age amber artefacts to be recognized from east Kent, although an amber bead necklace has recently been discovered at a barrow site near Longfield in west Kent (Askew 2001).

Pommel fragment
Condition

Approximately half of the object, or a little more, survives (**Fig. 24a; Colour Pl. 4**). All of the original surfaces are crazed and weathered to a matt orangey-brown colour. Fractured surfaces along one side of the mouth and at the main break are the glass-like dark orange of freshly fractured amber. At these breaks the weathered surface is seen to be extremely thin (< 0.1mm). Minor loss by chipping close to the pointed end and along the near-intact side of the mouth appears to be ancient.

Form

The top of the pommel had an elliptical or more probably a lenticular plan; uncertainty is due to removal of a chip to one side of the apex. In side view the top is very gently domed and extends to a pronounced lip, the socket wall beneath contracting sharply. The lip itself is flattened all round with a vertical facet between 1.5 and 2.0mm deep. The undersides of the lip meet in a ridge on the longitudinal axis running out towards the apex. Where the mouth is intact, the socket wall is 1.2mm thick. The socket was lenticular in plan and tapers slightly in profile towards a flat to rounded end.

The intact perforation is an exceedingly neat cylindrical drilling, 1.5mm in diameter; it would have continued through to the other face, where a fragment may survive in the break. If a second peg hole existed towards the other end, reconstruction suggests that the two would not have been symmetrically placed.

Dimensions

Extant length 13.4mm   Estimated original length 20–21mm
Extant width 8.8mm   Estimated original width 9mm
Depth 6.7mm

Depth of socket 3.7mm
Extant length mouth 9mm
Width mouth (one side damaged) 5.5mm

Identification, parallels and dating

The form of this pommel compares well generally with several in Hardaker's group II (1974), most of which are made of bone or similar organic materials. More specifically, it is similar in proportions and size to two of only three previously known amber pommels, those from the Manton barrow, Preshute G1a, Wiltshire (ibid, 10-11 no. 7; Annable and Simpson 1964, 47 no. 208; Cunnington 1907-8, 7 no. 1, pl.) and Winterbourne Stoke G9, Wiltshire (Annable and Simpson 1964, 60 no. 453; Thurnam 1871, 503 fig. 196). The Manton pommel is badly decayed, between 26 and 28mm long and around 10mm deep (**Fig. 24b**), hence a little larger than Ringlemere all round; (Hardaker's stated length of 22mm does not correspond with two views in his drawings). It has two symmetrically placed pegholes of fine bore. The Winterbourne Stoke example is now lost (Annable and Simpson 1964, 60 no. 453), but fortunately Thurnam published a drawing from one of Hoare's unpublished plates (1871, 503 fig. 196). It appears as around 24mm long and 6mm deep, again highly comparable to the Ringlemere example (**Fig. 24c**). No peg holes are apparent in the engraving. The one surviving associated artefact is a simple flared cup with dot decoration, a form not unlike the squatter version in the Manton grave.

These three amber pommels belong to the main group of pommels post-dating *c.* 2000 BC and termed *long oval pommels with pronounced lips*; they mostly equate with Hardaker's group II and twelve examples are now known in bone (Needham forthcoming). The amber examples are not quite so long on the main axis as most bone ones, but a bone pommel from Narrowdale Hill, Staffordshire, is only 19.5mm long (Hardaker 1974, no. 9), while those from Irthlingborough, Northamptonshire, and Radwell I, Bedfordshire, may not have been much longer (Needham forthcoming). This shortening may simply be due to their being intended to furnish knives rather than daggers. It is suggested that pommels under 35mm long generally belong to knives and may in turn signify female graves (ibid). The Ringlemere pommel is likely to have been attached to a slender handle, not more than 12 x 6mm in cross section.

The remaining amber pommel known from Britain is the ornate and famous example (sadly destroyed) from Hameldon Down, Devon, which was inlaid with dozens of tiny gold studs (Hardaker 1974, no. 33, pl. IIe; Pearce 1983, pl. 128). This too is oval with a pronounced lip, in keeping with an early 2nd millennium date, but the oval is of broader proportions than the main group above. In shape it finds good parallels in the gold-covered wood(?) pommel from Ridgeway 7, Dorset, and the

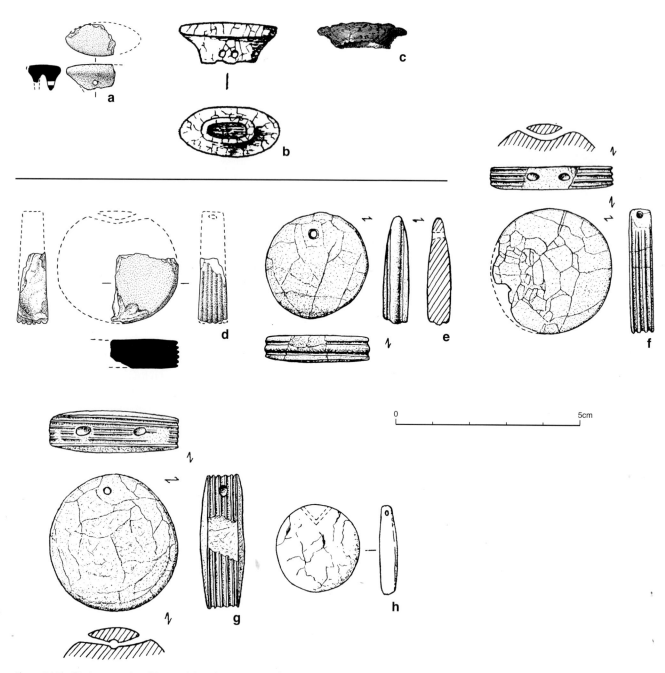

Figure 24 The Ringlemere amber objects and their closest parallels: a) Ringlemere; b) Manton Preshute G1a, Wiltshire (after Annable and Simpson 1964); c) Winterbourne Stoke G9, Wiltshire (after Thurnam 1871); d) Ringlemere; e-g) Kernonen-en-Plouvorn, Côtes d'Armor (after Briard 1970); h) Wilsford G7, Wiltshire (after Annable and Simpson 1964). Scale 100%

bone or ivory example from Grange, Co. Roscommon, Ireland (Hardaker 1974, fig. 7, pl.2). These were classified as group VI by Hardaker, but two others in that group are entirely different. An unpublished amber pommel from Liscahane, Co. Cork, excavated with fragments of Encrusted Urn by Barra Ó Donnabháin (Mary Cahill – pers. comm.), also belongs to this group; it is reconstructable to 40mm in length compared to 45–60mm for the other three. It has a double-socket mode of attachment very similar to the Grange example.

Oval pommels with pronounced lips occur in a good number of datable graves and span the earlier half of the 2nd millennium BC (Needham forthcoming). The very similar amber example from Manton comes from a grave group which is of classic Wessex I (Bush Barrow series) composition. Current dating of this assemblage is 1950/1900– 1750/1700 BC. The slightly larger bone example from a Collared Urn cremation at Irthlingborough, Northamptonshire, is radiocarbon dated (by the cremated bone) to 3520 ± 30 BP (GrA-19652/20156/20176

combined), calibrating to 1970–1740 BC. Four more graves yielding socketed bone pommels with pronounced lips have been dated to 3665 ± 45, 3590 ± 100, 3520 ± 30 and 3257 ± 80 BP (see Needham forthcoming for full details).

Pendant fragment
Condition
The original surfaces are lightly weathered, matt orangey-brown with incipient crazing and some more reflective orange patches. The two straighter edges are fractures – these and some chipped corners expose very dark orange glass-like amber and it is possible that some damage occurred during recovery. The weathered surface is shown to be extremely thin.

Form
Two faces are virtually flat and are parallel on one cross-sectional axis, but converge significantly on the orthogonal axis (**Fig.24d; Colour Pl. 4**). The original edge of the object is a very

neatly fashioned squared side engraved with five grooves. In plan the middle section follows an even curve of about 12mm radius, but this is flanked by straighter stretches; it appears not therefore to have come from a totally circular object. One of the straighter parts is at the thickest end and is most likely to be close to the base of the ornament on the assumption that the ornament would hang best if suspended from the slighter end. It may be that the outline is simply that of a disc which was not perfectly circular (see parallels below), but if so, it was rather asymmetrical given the care in execution evident; the alternatives are a sub-hexagonal or sub-pentagonal shape.

The grooves are of crisp V profile, their sloping walls retaining longitudinal scoremarks from the cutting instrument, perhaps a flint tool. Although neatly executed and regularly spaced, under magnification they do not exhibit constant profiles or widths to a high precision. The ribs left standing in between retain a flat crest, but those along the two outer angles are narrower, more rounded beadings.

Dimensions

Maximum dimension 24.5mm
Maximum intact thickness 7.9mm
Estimated thickness at base (before chipping) > 8.0mm
Minimum intact thickness 6.7mm
Estimated thickness at thinnest point of fragment (before chipping) c. 6.0mm
Groove width 0.4–0.8mm
Groove depth c. 0.2mm

Identification, parallels and dating

This is obviously an object of ornamental character, but the absence of any point of attachment makes its identification a little speculative. Nevertheless, there are sufficient points of comparison with other Early Bronze Age ornaments to suggest that this would have been from a disc-like object, presumably serving as a pendant. A variety of amber pendant and bead forms are known from Britain (Beck and Shennan 1991).

Circular amber discs with symmetrical profiles in all directions are a well known feature of just four Wessex 1 graves. Those at Manton Preshute G1a, Amesbury G44 and Wilsford G8 have gold bindings around the edges, leaving the centre as exposed amber. They have narrower edges than on the Ringlemere piece, but still carry edge grooves; they also have encircling grooves on their faces (Annable and Simpson 1964, nos 188-9, 195; Clarke et al. 1985, 109 fig. 4.32). An example from Wilsford G7 is plain and has no gold binding (**Fig. 24h**), in this respect seemingly similar to the Ringlemere one.

More specific parallels for the features on the Ringlemere piece can, however, be found among the 12 amber ornaments from the Armorican tomb of Kernonen, Côtes d'Armor (**Fig. 24e–g**; Briard 1970; Needham 2000b, 165 fig. 6.23). Here three rather thick discs of different sizes have squared edges which are broad enough, on the largest one, to carry five parallel grooves as at Ringlemere (**Fig. 24g**). The others have two and three grooves. Their diameters are 29, 34 and 37mm, the last being very close to that reconstructed for Ringlemere. The faces of the smallest Kernonen example (**Fig. 24e**) converge towards the point of suspension, but the other two are parallel-faced. The largest one, that otherwise most similar to the Ringlemere piece, has the symmetrical swollen profiles of the Wessex discs. The

Kernonen discs are not perfectly circular and it is therefore perhaps possible that the Ringlemere outline also derives from an imperfect circle.

The derivation of this disc form of pendant is uncertain, but one possible source of inspiration is the earlier 'pulley-rings'. These are open in the centre, but have a more-or-less broad annular band often carrying one or occasionally two edge grooves – for example, an unprovenanced example of shale or jet in Devizes Museum (Annable and Simpson 1964, 43 no. 133, 96 fig. 133). At 50mm diameter this is larger than the Ringlemere ornament is likely to have been, whereas the gold-bound amber discs are between 25 and 30mm diameter.

All three of the types discussed – the Wessex discs the pulley-rings and the Armorican discs – were most often suspended by means of a V-boring penetrating one side of the ornament. This is most likely therefore to have been the mode of suspension for the Ringlemere ornament, but two from Kernonen have a straight face-to-face perforation, in one case doubling up with a V-boring. While the pulley-rings are a feature of mature Beaker contexts, c. 2200–1950 BC, all the amber disc parallels cited here are datable again to Wessex 1 or the equivalent Armorican phase - Kernonen/Kerodou.

Prehistoric pottery
Grooved Ware
by Gillian Varndell

The bulk of the prehistoric pottery retrieved from the site to date is Late Neolithic Grooved Ware. The assemblage is of considerable size (over 5,000 sherds so far) and derives from pre-mound occupation. Grooved Ware pottery was recovered from cut features, the buried soil and from the turf mound. Some of the pits yielded very large sherds including the greater part of of a tub-shaped vessel (**Fig. 25.3**). Some sherds have burnt residues and one has produced a date from associated charcoal (see below). One vessel appears to be entirely fire-blackened.

A preliminary assessment was carried out after the first year's work, and an evaluation of the material excavated subsequently confirms the initial impression that this assemblage falls into the Clacton sub-style (Wainwright and Longworth 1971, 236ff). The range of decorative traits includes the use of wavy cordons occurring externally and on internal rim bevels (**Fig. 25.6**). Cordons are finger-pinched and not applied, and this sometimes manifests itself quite crudely when fingernails and tips are used to mould the cordon into a wavy shape. In some cases this technique produces raised lentoids forming a herringbone pattern between grooves or ridges. There are zones of nail impressions (Fig. 25.1), impressed circular pits and other impressions in staggered rows. Occasionally a solid round-sectioned tool has been used to create jabbed impressions. Grooved decoration includes opposed lines as well as one or more circumferential grooves. A minority of vessels appears to be fairly small and thin-walled with larger, thick-walled vessels in the majority. Jar and tub shapes predominate.

Most of the sherds range from moderately eroded to quite fresh. The bulk display bipartite colouration, red externally and black internally. There is little by way of filler other than grog although some vessels have sporadic large flint grits. Breaks may have a finely laminated appearance.

The regular association elsewhere in southern Britain of

Grooved Ware

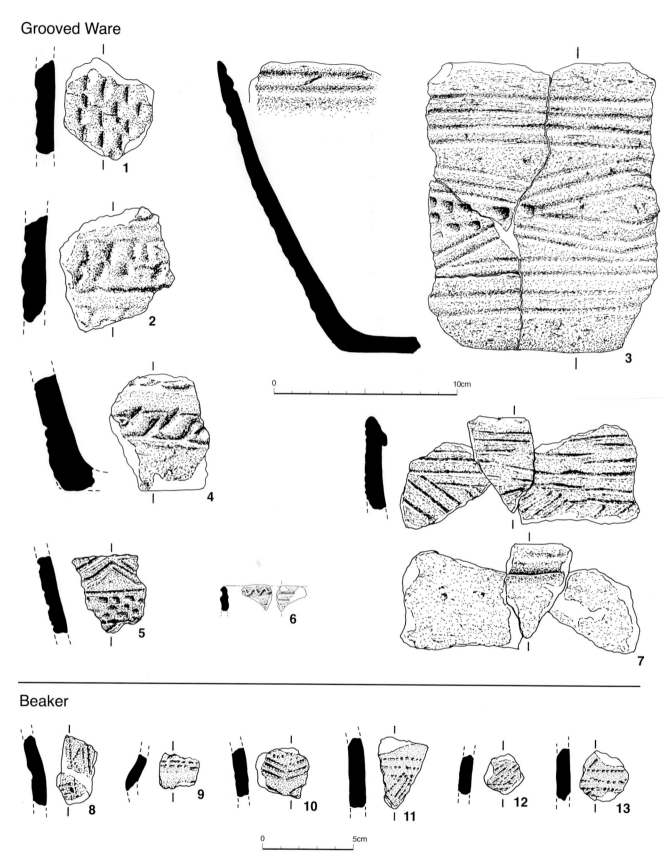

Figure 25 Selection of Grooved Ware and Beaker sherds from Ringlemere M1. Scale 50%

Grooved Ware with Neolithic ritual sites has posed the question as to whether its occurrence in some quantity under Ringlemere M1 is more than fortuitous. Clearly this exciting possibility requires much more excavation and analysis before we can venture an informed opinion but either way, some form of regular Late Neolithic activity must have occurred at Ringlemere.

Beaker pottery
by Stuart Needham

From preliminary inspection of the prehistoric pottery it is apparent that there is a small admixture of Beaker ware in both the turf mound and the pre-mound soil horizon. The quantity is very small by comparison with Grooved Ware, but will be significant in terms of the chronology of the sequence.

The Beaker sherds recognized so far are mainly fineware

thin-walled vessels, ranging from 4–9mm thick, and made in fine-sand fabrics with occasional to sparse grits of well crushed calcined flint. Colour is mainly two-tone with pale to mid grey core and buff to light orange exterior. A selection is shown in **Figure 25**. Decoration is predominantly by tooth-comb stamp with the probable addition of fine incised line. Although the sherds are mainly small to medium sized, several motif variations are already apparent. Most are probably based on horizontal filled/reserved zoning, sometimes with pendant triangle rows (**Fig. 25.11**), but departures include one with vertical panel division (**Fig. 25.8**; context 1209) and another with a weak zigzag field comprising a reserved band between multiple lines (**Fig. 25.10**; Context 1001/131 – mound).

The Beaker material is all rather weathered, partly because of the friable nature of the fabric, but taking into account sherd size as well, there is little to suggest this material was newly deposited at the time the turf mound was erected. With Beaker pottery first coming into use in Britain around 2500/2400 BC and some of the design elements unlikely before about 2250 BC

(Needham 2005), the Ringlemere assemblage suggests that the turf mound should date to the last quarter of the 3rd millennium BC at the earliest.

Flintwork
by Chris Butler

To date, well over 30,000 prehistoric worked flints have been recovered from the excavation of Ringlemere M1, with several thousand more from field-walking in the area. At this stage, only an assessment of the 12,000 flints from the initial field-walking and Trenches 1 and 2 has been carried out (**Table 2**) and the following report is based on the results of that study. It should be seen as an interim statement on the nature of the lithic material present on the site. Nevertheless, it is already clear that several different industries are represented by the flint assemblage. Six different types of raw material have been noted, most of which could be obtained as nodules in the vicinity of the site, or from other sources nearby.

Table 2 Details of the analysed flintwork from Ringlemere

	Fieldwalking	Trench 1	Trench 2	Total
Hard hammer-struck flakes	897	2928	1232	5057
Soft hammer-struck flakes	137	1317	88	1542
Hard hammer-struck blades	10	45	7	62
Soft hammer-struck blades	9	119	9	137
Soft hammer-struck bladelets	17	76	2	95
Bladelet fragments	9	112	4	125
Flake/blade fragments	306	2177	464	2947
Chips	6	479	58	543
Shattered pieces	53	420	128	601
Chunks	17	24	8	49
Axe thinning flakes	3	16	0	19
Core rejuvenation flakes	5	21	1	27
Crested blade	1	4	0	5
Core tablets	2	0	0	2
Single platform flake cores	53	44	23	120
Two platform flake cores	46	46	16	108
Multi platform flake cores	9	7	1	17
Single platform blade core	1	3	0	4
Single platform bladelet core	0	1	0	1
Discoidal core	2	2	3	7
Core fragments	4	29	8	41
Tested nodules	3	0	0	3
End scrapers	72	129	33	234
Side scrapers	24	26	8	58
End & side scrapers	19	37	0	56
Hollow scrapers	2	8	4	14
Button scrapers	2	5	0	7
Miscellaneous retouched pieces	16	2	1	19
Combination tools	6	4	1	11
Piercers	10	11	4	25
Awls	2	2	0	4
Notched flakes	17	5	1	23
Notched blade	1	1	0	2
Backed knives	3	3	0	6
Discoidal knife	0	1	0	1
Serrated flakes/blades	0	6	3	9
Burin	0	1	0	1
Truncated blades	0	3	0	3
Arrowheads	1	15	2	18
Fabricator	1	2	1	4
Tranchet adze	0	1	0	1
Tranchet adze sharpening flake	1	5	0	6
Misc. axe/adze fragment	0	3	0	3
Polished axe fragment	1	0	0	1
Chopper	1	1	0	2
Pick	3	1	1	5
Hammerstones	11	11	3	25
Cores re-used as hammerstones	18	4	2	24
Total	**1801**	**8157**	**2116**	**12074**

Mesolithic activity

There was a small group of residual Mesolithic material, making up less than 5% of the analysed assemblage. These pieces included bladelets, a tranchet adze, a number of tranchet adze-sharpening flakes, a pick and some flake implements. Despite the fact that there were bladelets and bladelet fragments in the assemblage, there is little evidence that microliths were being produced at the site. This seems typical for Mesolithic sites in east Kent (see above p. 8), which tend to have no microliths and instead have high proportions of tranchet adzes and adze-sharpening flakes (G. Halliwell and K. Parfitt pers comm.; Butler 2005, 118; Butler forthcoming). The mix of implement types would suggest the presence of a longer-stay camp site, rather than just a short-stay hunting or special-task site.

Early Neolithic activity

There was a component of the analysed assemblage that comprised soft and hard hammer-struck blade and long-flake debitage, much of which had prepared platforms. This material, which was mostly of one flint type, also includes a small number of cores typical of the Early Neolithic, with prepared platforms at right angles to one another, as well as some crested blades. Furthermore, Early Neolithic flintworking traits could be seen on a group of well-produced implements that included scrapers, backed knives, serrated flakes and a burin, together with other retouched pieces made on blades and long flakes.

In addition, a small leaf-shaped arrowhead was recovered from Trench 2. The type is primarily characteristic of the earlier Neolithic (Green 1984) and, taken together with other earlier material, seems to indicate an Early Neolithic phase of activity at the site, for which no associated features or pottery have yet been recognised. It may also be noted that a fragment of Neolithic ground stone axe of coarse-grained rock comes from the pre-mound topsoil in Trench 1. Further fragments of both flint and stone polished axeheads have come from subsequent excavations on the site (K. Parfitt – pers.comm.).

Late Neolithic and Bronze Age

Most of the excavated flint assemblage is of Late Neolithic character, possibly extending into the Early Bronze Age, and comes from the same range of contexts as the large collection of Grooved Ware pottery. It had a mixture of hard and soft hammer-struck debitage, with hard hammer-struck flakes predominating, together with flake cores and limited evidence of platform preparation. The large proportion of fragments, chips and shattered pieces found indicate that knapping and implement manufacture were very probably taking place on the site.

The implements include large numbers of finely retouched scrapers with abrupt retouch around the distal end and occasionally along one or more sides. One or two scrapers had invasive retouch around the distal end, and there were also a number of button scrapers. The latter is a Beaker/Early Bronze Age type. Amongst the other flake implements found were piercers, awls, notched pieces and knives, a polished discoidal knife and a number of combination tools, which are found in the Late Neolithic and Early Bronze Age. Sixteen later Neolithic transverse arrowheads were also found, together with a single Early Bronze Age barbed-and-tanged arrowhead. These arrowheads cover a broad span, at least c. 3000 to 2000 BC.

Transverse arrowheads are frequently found in association with Grooved Ware pottery (Wainwright and Longworth 1971, 257–9).

A number of pits under the barrow mound contained Neolithic flintwork and pottery (**Fig. 6**). Amongst these, pit F. 1004 produced six pieces of worked flint, comprising three rough hard hammer-struck flakes and three scrapers, one of which was broken. Pit F. 1006 contained 21 pieces of worked flint, which apart from the mostly hard hammer-struck debitage included five scrapers. Central L-shaped timber slot, F. 1099 (see above) produced 22 pieces of worked flint, including two end scrapers and a side scraper.

Pit complex F. 1046, near the centre of the enclosed area, contained a total of 229 pieces of worked flint. The debitage is predominantly hard hammer-struck with a large proportion of fragments. The implements include a number of end scrapers on blades or long flakes, some of which appear to have prepared platforms. An oblique arrowhead and two further retouched fragments which may be arrowheads, were also recovered from the pit. Some of this material is residual Mesolithic material, with other pieces, especially the long flake/blade scrapers, resembling the depositions in pits F. 1004 and F. 1006. The worked flints contained within these pits may be interpreted as special 'placed' deposits.

The flint assemblage contained within the make-up of the mound dates from the Late Neolithic to Early Bronze Age, with some residual Mesolithic and Early Neolithic components incorporated. Although there appears to be little overall difference between the debitage from the pre-mound topsoil and that from the mound, there is a tendency towards longer, almost blade-like flakes from the pre-mound topsoil. The implements from the pre-mound soil also tend to be Neolithic rather than Early Bronze Age. The initial ditch fill seems to have an assemblage that is broadly contemporary with the mound.

The final component of the analysed assemblage, seen in the modern plough-soil and also in the upper ditch fills, and therefore associated with later use of the site, is later Bronze Age material, comprising hard hammer-struck flakes and a few crude scrapers (Ford *et al.* 1984).

Conclusions

Overall then, the substantial flintwork assemblage recovered from the Ringlemere site includes material dating from the Mesolithic period through to the later Bronze Age. The main phase of activity is associated with the Late Neolithic and Early Bronze Age activity at the site, and a full analysis of the assemblage in due course will enable comparisons to be made with other sites of this period in Kent and elsewhere in southern Britain.

The excavations and field-walking have also yielded very large quantities of calcined flint (approaching 500 kg). Plotting the surface distribution indicates that the entire area is liberally covered with such material, with a marked concentration in the area of M1. A number of other minor concentrations occur further away from the mound implying extensive prehistoric activity across the area. A number of struck flakes which have been subsequently calcined are present which demonstrates that flint working and flint calcination were, at least in part, contemporaneous activities.

Wood remains
Identification of wood and charcoal remains associated with the central features and the cup
by Caroline Cartwright

Wood and charcoal samples recovered from four contexts were submitted for identification: those excavated archaeologically from contexts 1025, 1103 and 1104 and that retrieved by the finder with the gold cup. Standard techniques of wood identification usually require transverse, radial longitudinal and tangential longitudinal thin sections to be made of each wood sample. These thin sections, approximately 12–14 microns in thickness, are usually cut on a base-sledge microtome, and are then mounted on glass microscope slides and examined by transmitted light optical microscopy with darkfield and polarising capabilities and a range of objectives providing magnifications from x50 to x1000. However, these wood samples were far too dessicated and powdery to be thin sectioned, so they were examined using the fracture method and reflected light microscopy normal for charcoal, but under similar magnification. Each fragment of sufficient size was fractured by hand to expose the required transverse and longitudinal surfaces. Identification of the surviving diagnostic features was carried out according to standards laid down by the International Association of Wood Anatomists (IAWA), published by Wheeler *et al.* (1986) and Wheeler, Baas and Gasson (1989). For each wood sample, the key features were also compared with reference collection specimens and text descriptions.

The samples from the southern L-shaped slot F. 1102 (1103, 1104) included a mixture of charcoal, partially burnt and unburnt wood. In 1103 ('Samples 1–3') identifiable material was of *Quercus* sp. (oak), *Acer campestre* (field maple), *Corylus avellana* (hazel), *Buxus sempervirens* (box) and F*agus sylvatica* (beech). The first three species were found in all three conditions, the box as charcoal and the beech as partially burnt wood.

Context 1104 ('Sample 4') contained only tiny fragments of charcoal and partially burnt wood; those identifiable were *Quercus* sp. (oak), *Acer campestre* (field maple) and *Corylus avellana* (hazel). Also noted were soil pellets with dark, possibly mineral staining.

Under the binocular microscope many of the tiny fragments of unburnt wood from context 1025 appeared to be fragmenting in an irregularly 'prismatic' fashion. When sectioned for examination, these orange-brown fragments rapidly disintegrated into very fine powder, owing to their extremely desiccated state. Despite this condition, sufficient diagnostic features survived to enable the identification of the following three taxa: yew (*Taxus baccata*), field maple (*Acer campestre*) and beech (*Fagus sylvatica*). It is worth emphasising that none of the fragments in this batch is root material. *Acer campestre* was selected for radiocarbon dating (below).

The small sample of organic material found with the cup was received from the finder in two small self-seal bags. One bag contained very fine root filaments from modern cereal crops. The other had a few tiny fragments of unburnt wood which are possibly from *Acer campestre*, but which have a slightly darker colour and less 'prismatic' appearance than those excavated from context 1025. The difference in condition means that it is not certain from the taphonomic and anatomical evidence alone that they can be considered to be from the same context.

Assuming that the majority of the wood fragments from 1025, 1103 and 1104 are not modern or intrusive, it is worth noting the type of ecology which the identified taxa represent and some of the distinctive properties of the timber yielded.

The yew is a slow growing, long-lived evergreen tree which prefers chalky soils, often in the dense shade of oak woods. Yew timber is strong but elastic and is particularly well suited to the manufacture of archery bows. It is also used for tool handles, furniture veneers and firewood. The field maple is most commonly found in hedgerows, edges of woods or as understorey in woodlands. It is frequently associated with ash, hazel and oak on heavy calcareous soils. As it coppices strongly it is very suitable for hedges. Its wood is fine grained, but as it is seldom available in long lengths, its use is largely confined to small turned artefacts, marquetry and firewood. Beech trees grow well on chalk and limestone but are also tolerant of a wide range of soils and conditions. Large trees may produce building timber, although not generally suitable for outside use; instead the wood is mainly used for furniture, small turned artefacts and veneers. It is a particularly good source of firewood and charcoal.

Hazel (*Corylus avellana*) comprises deciduous shrubs and small trees, often found as understorey in oak woodlands. Hazel is frequently coppiced, providing long sticks, hurdles, thatching and spars. The wood is relatively fine grained and is useful for cask hoops, basketry and good firewood. Management of hazel woods not only ensures productive coppicing timber but also maximises the harvest of the nutritious nuts (when protected from large birds, squirrels and mice).

Oaks (*Quercus* spp.) are large, long-lived deciduous trees which will tolerate a range of soil pH and moisture conditions, including wet soil and dry clay. Oaks yield good all-purpose long lasting and durable timber, useful for building, furniture, firewood and charcoal. Coppicing of oak woodland produces stakes and poles for fencing.

The box tree (*Buxus sempervirens*) is an evergreen species that once formed part of woodlands which are now very rare. Its preferred habitat is on chalk and limestone slopes, sometimes with beech. Box timber is very hard, heavy and close-grained and is used for tool handles, precision instruments and decorative carving and turnery.

In conclusion, the wood and charcoal samples recovered from excavated contexts 1025, 1103 and 1104 at Ringlemere have been identified as typical southern England oak and beech wood components consisting of field maple (*Acer campestre*), hazel (*Corylus avellana*), oak (*Quercus* sp.), beech (*Fagus sylvatica*) and box (*Buxus sempervirens*).

Radiocarbon dates from the central structures
by Keith Parfitt and Stuart Needham

Since the excavation of monument M1 is ongoing, no systematic dating programme has yet been instigated. However, a few samples have been submitted for radiocarbon measurement in order to give some early indications on the chronology of the site sequence and particularly the central structures (**Table 3**).

Table 3: Radiocarbon and OSL dates for Ringlemere and Mill Hill, Deal

Site	Feature	Material	Date BP	Calibrated date (2-sigma) BC	Lab. ref.
Ringlemere	Pit F. 1321 – charcoal at interface of two layers	Charcoal – whitebeam (*Sorbus aria*) and box (*Buxus sempervirens*)	4170 ± 40	2890–2600	Beta-183862
Ringlemere	Buried soil 1020/103	Pot sherd (KF 49)	2530 ± 460 BC	2990–2070 (1-sigma)	OSL(Oxford)
Ringlemere	L-slot F. 1102, context 1103 sample 2	Unidentifiable charcoal flecks, 1.3g	3460 ± 40	1890–1680	Beta-180487
Ringlemere	L-slot F. 1102, context 1103 sample 3	Unidentifiable charcoal flecks, 1.5 g	1750 ± 40	AD 130–410	Beta-180488
Mill Hill	Pit SRD F. 428	Cow bone	4105 ± 45	2880–2500	OxA-7441
Mill Hill	Pit CRD F. 1	Sheep bone	4020 ± 60	2870–2450	OxA-7531

Beta-183862 gives an initial indication that at least some of the Grooved Ware activity on the site belongs to the first half of the 3rd millennium BC rather than the second half. Further samples will be dated in due course. Radiocarbon dates for Grooved Ware contexts at Mill Hill, Deal, are shown for comparison.

The decayed, unburnt woody material at the base of F. 1102, the southern L-shaped slot, was thought to be too degraded to allow the extraction of any suitable samples for radiocarbon dating. Small charcoal fragments, which occurred in the same deposit, provided an alternative. In the light of initial uncertainties about both the age and potential significance of this feature, it was decided that it would be worth attempting to get dates from this charcoal, accepting from the outset that the sample material was far from ideal. This in fact seems to be the case for the two results are somewhat unsatisfactory in being very divergent from one another. There can now be little doubt that sample Beta-180488 had been contaminated by later, intrusive organic matter. The Early Bronze Age date for sample Beta-180487 may be reliable but the possibility remains that, if intrusive organic matter accounts for the other measurement coming out late, it may also have infiltrated this one. Another sample , this time of unburnt wood fragments, was submitted from context 1025 in the stratigraphically later pit F. 1024. After rigorous pretreatment it failed to yield datable material (Groningen Laboratory – Van der Plicht, pers. comm.).

Chapter 5: Ringlemere and Ritual and Burial Landscapes of Kent

Keith Parfitt

Kent's lack of prehistoric monuments – the price of being the 'Garden of England'

The general lack of prehistoric field monuments across much of Kent has long been recognized, even though the rolling chalk downland of east Kent in particular has readily invited comparison with the similar landscapes of Sussex, Wessex and the Yorkshire Wolds, so rich in prehistoric remains. Yet prehistorians throughout the 19th and 20th centuries have been continually disappointed by the absence of comparable numbers of upstanding Neolithic and Bronze Age structures in this region (e.g. Woodruff 1874, 17; Champion 1982, 32; Barber 1997, 82). As a consequence, until recently, Kent has often been envisaged (sometimes almost subconsciously) as being less densely occupied during the prehistoric past than many other parts of southern Britain.

However, it is now quite clear that the paucity of visible ancient remains is very much the result of subsequent land-use. Thus, central to understanding the preservation, distribution and survival of local prehistoric field monuments is a thorough appreciation of the nature, extent and intensity of agricultural activity throughout the historic period, particularly over the last two or three centuries. In this context, the prehistoric complex now identified at Ringlemere effectively presents a microcosm of the situation across much of the county and serves to demonstrate that, even though there is often virtually nothing to be seen on the surface, with detailed investigation, there is still much of significance too be discovered below the fertile top-soil of the 'Garden of England'.

Potential Neolithic ceremonial enclosures and henge monuments in Kent

From the excavation evidence there would now seem to be two main periods in the prehistoric development of Ringlemere M1 (Chapter 2). In its earliest form, the monument appears to have constituted a Class 1 henge. Subsequently, the addition of a central mound transformed this monument into a barrow of large diameter, but not necessarily very high, which may or may not have served as a place of burial.

In Kent generally, henge monuments have remained elusive or controversial, thus making the new discoveries at Ringlemere of exceptional interest and importance. Other possible examples of henges and ceremonial enclosures, however, are now also beginning to be identified and it would anyway seem improbable that Ringlemere M1 was the only such monument that existed in prehistoric Kent.

Not far to the north-east of Ringlemere, at Richborough (**Fig. 26**), Paul Ashbee has recently noticed (Ashbee 2001, 86; 2005, 113) how William Stukeley's drawing of the Roman amphitheatre there (Stukeley 1776, 36.2d; reproduced in Ashbee 2001, fig. 5) has very much the appearance of a henge. He suggests a Roman adaptation of an earlier monument, similar to

the sequence known at Maumbury Rings, Dorchester (Bradley 1976). Moreover, a recent geophysical survey of the Richborough site has revealed two large enigmatic side-features which cannot be readily understood in the context of a Roman amphitheatre (Millett and Wilmott 2003, 190), perhaps further raising the possibility of an earlier monument here; only detailed excavation will resolve the issue.

Aerial reconnaissance across the county has revealed further possible henge sites. An assessment conducted by the RCHME in 1989 (unpublished) listed 11 air photograph sites in Kent that might represent henges, although only one of these seemed likely (RCHME 1989, list 18; Bewley, Crutchley and Grady 2004, 72). Of the potential sites noted, ten lie on the chalklands in the eastern-most part of the county, with no less than seven occurring on the Isle of Thanet, including two close to the excavated Lord of the Manor monument complex described below. Two more possible henge sites (refs KE 674.14.1, TR 2900 5260; KE 674.83.1, TR 3034 5422) lie on downland near Eastry, only a short distance to the south of Ringlemere (**Fig. 26**); site 674.83.1, about 45m across, is almost 3km away, with the much larger KE 674.14.1 cut through by Thornton Lane, some 4.4km distant. This latter site, of which just under half has been recorded by aerial photography, is of particular interest because of its apparent double ditch and large size, around 200m in diameter. Three round barrows have been previously recorded from the immediate area (see below) and one of these can now be seen to lie near the centre of the enclosure.

The clearest identifiable example of a henge monument, however, is located some 40km to the west of Ringlemere, at Bredgar near Sittingbourne. Here, the crop-mark of an apparent Class 2 henge has been recorded on high downland to the north of Trundle Wood (ref. KE 735.1.1, TQ 8847 5907). The monument is oval in outline, between 30 and 40m across, with opposed entrances on the south-east and north-west sides.

Further possible candidates for henges may exist among the 50 double and triple concentric ring-ditch sites that have also been noted on air photographs of the east Kent and Thanet chalklands (RCHME 1989, list 19). Excavation of several has now taken place, mostly on Thanet and although details of most have yet to be published in full, it is apparent that the bulk of them are complex monuments of multi-phased development. Evidence for internal features, re-cutting and replacing of the enclosing ditches, together with finds of Neolithic pottery and flintwork combine to show that most of the excavated examples are not straightforward Bronze Age round barrow sites. Indeed, it has been suggested that a number originated as Late Neolithic ceremonial enclosures, which were only later developed as burial sites and covered by a barrow mound, now invariable destroyed. Perkins (2004, 76) has termed such sites 'henge-barrows'.

On the southern side of the Isle of Thanet, about 10km

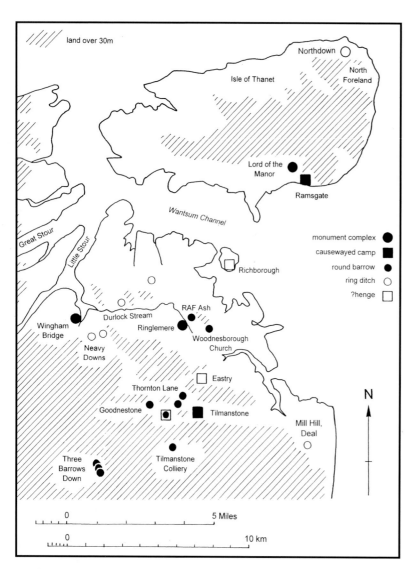

land over 30m

Northdown

North Foreland

Isle of Thanet

Lord of the Manor

Ramsgate

Wantsum Channel

Great Stour

Little Stour

monument complex
causewayed camp
round barrow
ring ditch
?henge

Richborough

RAF Ash

Durlock Stream

Wingham Bridge

Ringlemere

Woodnesborough Church

Neavy Downs

Eastry

Thornton Lane

Goodnestone

Tilmanstone

Mill Hill, Deal

N

Three Barrows Down

Tilmanstone Colliery

0   5 Miles

0   10 km

Figure 26 Map of north-east Kent showing location of principal prehistoric sites mentioned in the text

north-east of Ringlemere, a key site lies at the Lord of the Manor (Ozengell) crossroads (**Fig. 26**) where excavation of a complex, concentric triple ditched enclosure was undertaken in the 1970s (LOM Site I). Situated on a chalk ridge overlooking the sea and the Wantsum Channel, this monument was associated with a cluster of other ring-ditches. Two of the RCHME's possible henge sites lie nearby.

Analysis has suggested four phases of development to LOM Site I (Macpherson-Grant 1977). A circular outer ditch, unbroken by any obvious entrance causeway, was believed by the excavator to be the earliest feature and this enclosed an area about 24m in diameter, possibly with an internal bank. It was provisionally dated to the Late Neolithic period (Macpherson-Grant 1977, 15). During Phase 3, sometime in the Early Bronze Age, a grave containing two crouched inhumations was cut at the centre of this enclosure, surrounded by an inner ditch and probably covered by a small mound. Later, in Phase 4, further burials were added to the central barrow, which was then enlarged by material derived from a new penannular middle ditch, cut just inside the assumed position of the internal bank of the original Late Neolithic enclosure.

Further excavations on the site led to the suggestion that at least two of the other adjacent ring-ditches might also have originated as Late Neolithic enclosures (LOM Sites IID and III). Site IID consisted of a single penannular ring-ditch enclosing an area about 17m in diameter, with a broad entrance causeway on the south-western side. Internal features included post-settings

and a hearth, and later, a central crouched inhumation. The excavator believed that the monument had undergone three phases of development, the earliest dating to the Late Neolithic period (Macpherson-Grant 1980). Site III was another single ditched enclosure, with an internal diameter of almost 20m. It was provided with an entrance causeway on the south side and again appeared to have gone through several phases of development, with a central cremation burial contained within a Bronze Age Collared Urn, added during Phase 2 (Perkins 1980).

On the north side of Thanet, at Eastchurch Road, Northdown, Margate, the discovery of another large 'Neolithic ceremonial circle', perhaps subsequently re-used as an early Bronze Age burial site, awaits detailed publication, along with a group of adjacent barrow ring-ditches (**Fig. 26**; Rosa 1982, 18; John Willson pers. comm.).

Some distance to the west of Thanet, a possible Neolithic ceremonial circle has been identified above the valley of the River Medway on Holborough Hill, near Snodland (Grinsell 1992, Snodland 1). Here, a previously excavated, plough-damaged ring-ditch with an internal diameter of about 25m (Evison 1956) has, on the evidence of the pottery contained within its lower silts, recently been recognised as originating as a circular Neolithic enclosure (Harding 2003, 19). At the time of its investigation, it was assumed to be the remains of a simple Bronze Age round barrow. There was no surviving evidence for the presence of any primary burials, nor a barrow mound, although the prior existence of the latter was suspected by the excavator because, like Ringlemere, the monument had subsequently served as the focus for an Anglo-Saxon cemetery.

If the sequences proposed for these Lord of the Manor and other ring-ditch sites are fundamentally correct, the notion of Late Neolithic ceremonial circles which evolve during the Early Bronze Age into burial monuments marked by round barrows could mirror the sequence now interpreted for Ringlemere M1 (Chapter 2). Clearly, detailed publication of all the Thanet sites is urgently required before any more useful local comparisons can be made.

It seems likely that further and more secure henge monuments will be identified in Kent over the coming years, especially if the pace of fieldwork continues to increase at its present rate. Currently, however, Ringlemere M1 seems to be the most convincing classic henge within the county.

Bronze Age barrows and ring-ditches in east Kent

At some stage after its construction, the original henge enclosure at Ringlemere, with its central timber structure, was significantly modified by the addition of a mound to create what, in conventional archaeological terms, may be regarded as a round barrow, the last vestiges of which are still visible today. This general sequence may be broadly comparable with the smaller, less well-preserved 'henge-barrows' previously examined at the Lord of the Manor complex on Thanet (see above, this Chapter). At Ringlemere, the new barrow mound was surmounted by a centrally positioned timber façade, apparently intended either to replace or enhance the original timber 'cove' (Chapter 2).

Bronze Age round barrows represent the most common prehistoric monuments known in Kent and Ringlemere M1 in its later form can now be added to the list of surviving remains. During the early 1990s, in the last of his great surveys, Leslie Grinsell was able to detail about 170 round barrow sites in Kent overall (Grinsell 1992), of which half were concentrated in the eastern-most part of the county, mainly on the higher chalk downland to the south and west of Ringlemere. In constrast, few sites were known on the Tertiary and later clay and sand deposits that skirt the foot of the North Downs dip-slope (Ashbee and Dunning 1960, fig. 1;Grinsell 1992, fig. 1), though this is precisely the region where Ringlemere and another newly identified monument complex at nearby Wingham Bridge (detailed below) are located. Even as Grinsell, then 85 years old, was completing his long-planned Kent survey, it was becoming increasingly clear from the results of aerial photography that for every visible barrow mound in the county there were dozens of others that had been destroyed by ploughing. The unpublished 1989 RCHME study of crop-mark evidence across the county (see above) had already identified over 640 probable sites in Kent (RCHME 1989, lists 19–21).

Shortly after Grinsell's catalogue was published, Dave Perkins attempted a revised quantification of the numbers of levelled Kentish barrows. In 1995 he counted 739 potential round barrow sites in the county, recorded on air photographs (Perkins 2004, 76). As with the extant mounds, the distribution of these sites was very uneven, with three-quarters of them again lying in the eastern-most part of Kent. For the block of chalkland between Deal, Canterbury and Folkestone some 356 ring-ditch sites were noted, with another 315 spread across the

much smaller area of the adjacent Isle of Thanet. Adding Grinsell's figures for surviving mounds and newly discovered sites such as the Ringlemere and Wingham Bridge complexes, it now transpires that a total of over 900 probable round barrows is recorded from Kent. The average density of barrows on Thanet, an area intensively studied by Perkins for many years, seems to approach parts of prehistoric Wessex, at almost 4 sites per km^2. On the chalk downs of mainland Kent east of Canterbury, the density is lower at about 1.25 barrows per km^2. West of Canterbury, up to the south bank of the Thames and into the Weald, which together account for some four-fifths of the total area of the historic county of Kent, however, the number of recorded barrow sites remains very much smaller. At least in part, this will be due to the obscuring effects of woodland and soils less conducive to the formation of crop-marks, together with urban sprawl from London, rather than any genuine absence of prehistoric monuments. Even allowing for originally lower barrow densities in these regions compared to the eastern part of the county, the former presence of 2000 Bronze Age round barrows across Kent now seems very likely. Such a figure may be compared with the area of prehistoric Wessex, around four times larger than Kent, which has an estimated total of over 6,000 round barrows (Cunliffe 1993, 117).

Amongst the plough-eroded sites recorded on air photographs in Kent are examples with double and triple concentric ring-ditches, many of which are likely to represent complex sites with several phases of development. As noted above, some of these sites could even have originated as henge monuments. Also represented by crop-marks are clusters of half-a-dozen or occasionally more ring-ditches grouped together. From the available evidence, however, it would seem that the very large nucleated barrow cemeteries such as are famously known on the Wessex chalklands, are essentially absent from Kent (as in many other parts of the country). Surviving barrows on the Kentish chalklands most frequently occur singly or in pairs and very occasionally in groups of three or four (Ashbee and Dunning 1960, 48). Almost all are simple bowl barrows, invariably without a visible ditch. As far as can be determined from the surviving remains, the more elaborate forms of round barrow – the so-called 'Wessex fancy barrows' – are not present in any significant numbers in Kent (Grinsell 1992, 357), although extensive plough damage will have destroyed the relevant evidence at many sites. A saucer barrow has been preserved in Warren Wood at Crundale, near Ashford (Grinsell 1992, 357; Crundale 1). This has the remains of a bank set outside a still visible ditch which encloses an area about 18m in diameter (Kent SMR, TR 04 NE 26). It appears to be the only extant example of an embanked barrow surviving in east Kent, although we now also have the (limited) evidence for an outer bank at Ringlemere M1. Moreover, the evidence implying that the mound of M1 was never very high suggests that, in traditional field-worker's terms, this too might be regarded as a (large) saucer barrow.

Although examples of primary cremations and inhumations have been recorded, perhaps unsurprisingly, modern excavation of many heavily plough-damaged Kentish prehistoric barrow sites has failed to yield any contemporary burials and it must be that these have been previously destroyed. The discoveries under one upstanding barrow mound excavated in the 18th century by James Douglas, on Bay Hill at St Margaret's-at-Cliffe near Dover, demonstrates the potential nature of the problem.

This mound was found to contain the cremated remains of a child 'deposited exactly at the centre of the barrow on the surface of the native soil, without any excavation whatever, the mound of earth raised simply over it' (Douglas 1793, 120). Clearly, such a fragile burial deposit could not have survived on any heavily plough-eroded site.

It is difficult to document the destruction of the prehistoric round barrows of Kent at all closely but it seems likely that their erasure has been a continuous process over many centuries. Two of the three barrows situated below the North Downs scarp at the foot of Castle Hill, Folkestone, seem to have been under the plough by the Iron Age (Rady 1992) and comparable evidence for destruction in pre-Roman times is reported from the Lord of the Manor complex on Thanet (Perkins 2004, note 2). A number of other mounds, such as those at Holborough Hill, Snodland (see above); Mill Hill, Deal; Long Hill, Buckland and Bay Hill, St Margaret's must have survived as visible monuments until at least the 6th century AD, however, because they provided *foci* for early Anglo-Saxon inhumation cemeteries, as now also clearly seen for Ringlemere M1.

It seems likely that many prehistoric barrow sites had already been lost county-wide by the time of the first antiquarian interest in the region; thus Kent's early barrow diggers, most notably Bryan Faussett and James Douglas, working at the end of the 18th century, generally located and excavated mounds that were of Anglo-Saxon date, with just a few earlier monuments. Douglas opened a prehistoric mound not far from Ringlemere, somewhere on Shingleton Down, near Eastry, in 1782; it produced a central cremation in an urn (Douglas 1793, 160–1; Grinsell 1992, Eastry 3a). This may have been one of the mounds which still survive off Thornton Lane (see below).

About 6.5km to the south of Ringlemere, a barrow almost 9m in diameter and surrounded by a ditch was excavated ahead of its destruction by an extension to Tilmanstone Colliery in 1911 (Ashbee and Dunning 1960, 57; Grinsell 1992, Eythorne 2; **Fig. 26**). Situated on a chalk ridge-top, a detailed report on this site was never published. However, it would seem that an inhumation burial was discovered near the centre of the monument and, in a position not stated, a slotted incense cup was recovered (**Fig. 33.4**) but this has now been lost for many years (Jessup 1930, 122).

Several mounds off the chalkland, in the general vicinity of Ringlemere, were recorded by early antiquaries. Stukeley (1776) notes that 'there are a great number of large barrows about Sandwich, one at Winsborough [Woodnesborough] with a tree upon it...; between that and Sandwich [town] is another called Marvil hill' (Iter V, 126 footnote). Whilst travelling along the Roman road from Canterbury to Richborough, Stukeley had noted at Wingham '... a very large barrow, of Celtic make, by the road side, called the Mount: upon enquiry I found there were several more in the parish...' (Stukeley 1776, Iter V, 124: quoted in Grinsell 1992, 356; Ashbee 2001, 72; and see below; **Figs 2 & 27**).

The mound at Woodnesborough seems to have been just north of the parish church and is also described and illustrated by Hasted (Hasted 1800, 122; **Fig. 2**) but, like all the other mounds around Sandwich, it no longer survives. Situated on higher ground about 1.5km to the east, the Woodnesborough mound was probably visible from Ringlemere but a prehistoric

date for it cannot be demonstrated. Indeed, it could have been of natural origin, as could several of these other lost mounds. The barrow at Wingham, however, appears to have been recently re-discovered (see below, Wingham Bridge; **Fig. 27**), but now survives only as an eroded remnant of the monument Stukeley observed.

The combined results of geophysical survey and aerial photography have indicated that grouped around Ringlemere M1 there are at least nine other ring-ditches (monuments M2–M10), all of more modest proportions (**Figs 3 & 4**; Chapter 1). Many of these are likely to represent conventional round barrows now levelled by ploughing. Nevertheless, one (M5) is double-ditched, and the evidence from the geophysical survey suggests that some of the other lesser monuments could be complex or multi-phase structures; two may have causeways. Collectively, these monuments appear to constitute a nucleated barrow group, of a size not often encountered in Kent (see above). Ringlemere also stands out as being unusual for the substantial size of one of its monuments (M1) and the occurrence of rare and exotic items of gold and amber here. Together, these features mark out the Ringlemere complex as having an elevated status within the region during the Late Neolithic–Early Bronze Age. Lying on the slopes of the Durlock valley, however, this newly identified complex does follow a general pattern emerging nationally, in which Bronze Age barrow groups are being regularly identified in valley or head-of-valley locations, sited close to springs and streams (Woodward 2000, 73).

The top of the long ridge just to the north-east of the Ringlemere site (**Fig. 2**) represents another classic location for the positioning of Bronze Age round barrows, although nothing now survives here. Nevertheless, it is of relevance to note that immediately opposite the site, the summit of a short spur projecting into the valley and forming a local high-point, was once occupied by an artificial mound. This low circular mound was destroyed by the construction of RAF Ash just after the Second World War, but Ronald Jessup and O.G.S. Crawford had previously made an inspection of the site and believed it to represent a tumulus, even if re-used as the base for an 18th-century windmill (Davidson and Webster 1967, 4–5; **Fig. 2**).

Further west, ring-ditches known from aerial photographs imply the former presence of other round barrows on the higher ground adjacent to the Durlock valley (**Fig. 2**). North-west of Ash there is a large double ring-ditch (Kent SMR, TR 25 NE 35) which has yet to see any investigation. Some examination of a single ring-ditch on Neavy Downs south of Wingham was possible when it was cut through by a pipe trench in 1960 (Ogilvie 1977, 122; Grinsell 1992, Wingham 1). It appeared to be some 30m in diameter and was associated with a Beaker of Clarke's East Anglian type (Clarke 1970, Corpus no. 409), although the exact context of the vessel could not be determined.

On the chalklands to the south of Ringlemere, the closest recorded barrow sites are the three mounds situated off Thornton Lane near Eastry, about 4.4km away (Grinsell 1992, Eastry 1–3; **Fig. 26**). Unfortunately, these mounds are now almost ploughed-out but aerial photograph evidence suggests that they might be associated with a large henge enclosure (see above). Much better preserved is the single, 1.3m. high barrow surviving in woodland at Knowlton Park, Goodnestone (Grinsell

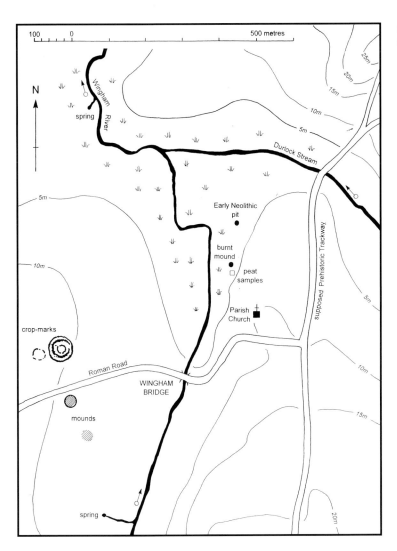

Figure 27 Plan of the Wingham Bridge prehistoric monument complex

1992, Goodnestone 1; **Fig. 26**), 4.5km to the south-west of Ringlemere. Locally, the finest barrow group lies in a wood on Three Barrows Down, Womenswold, some 8.5km to the south-west of Ringlemere (Grinsell 1992, Womenswold 1–3; **Fig. 26**).

Wingham Bridge – another local valley-side monument complex

A low mound recently observed by Grant Shand on the western outskirts of Wingham, some 5.7km to the west of Ringlemere, could well represent the last remnants of the large barrow previously recorded in this area by William Stukeley (see above) but now otherwise lost. Situated by the road-side near Wingham Bridge (NGR TR 236 572), the mound lies on the southern side of the present A257, Canterbury–Sandwich road, which is highly likely to have been the route that Stukeley followed to Richborough (**Fig. 27**).

The mound lies towards the bottom of a gentle slope which constitutes the western side of the valley of the Wingham river. It stands at an elevation of about 9m OD, just above springs which mark the source of the river. The subsoil here is head brickearth. An aerial photograph of the site provided by Kent County Council Heritage Conservation Group shows the faint outline of an enclosing ring-ditch, around 28m in diameter, leaving little doubt that this is the remains of a prehistoric barrow. Nor is this newly identified barrow an isolated feature because the remains of a second low mound are visible in the same field about 100m to the south, whilst a similar distance up-slope to the north, on the other side of the road, crop-marks

show another ring-ditch immediately adjacent to a larger, more complex triple concentric ditched circular monument (Kent SMR, TR 25 NW 65; **Fig. 27**).

About 400m to the north-east of Wingham Bridge, in the valley-bottom (**Fig. 27**), an Early Neolithic pit containing an important group of pottery and other artefacts, has been previously reported, together with a nearby spread of calcined flint and burning debris likely to be a prehistoric 'burnt mound' site (Greenfield 1960). Adjacent peat deposits were the ones sampled by Godwin to produce the important pollen diagrams previously noted above (Chapter 1).

On the opposite side of the valley of the Wingham River, about 1km south-east of the newly identified ring-ditches, lie Neavy Downs, with their possible Beaker barrow (**Fig. 2**), crossed by the modern B2046 which is believed to follow the line of a prehistoric trackway leading inland, southwards from the shores of the Wantsum Channel (**Fig. 27**). No doubt further investigations in the region of Wingham Bridge would be highly informative but already there seems to be enough evidence to suggest the presence of another Neolithic and Bronze Age centre of activity here.

Reconstructing Kent's lost ritual and burial landscapes

In Wessex and a number of other southern regions, ritual landscapes established in the Neolithic period apparently often continued into the Early Bronze Age, with round barrows frequently clustering around earlier, Neolithic monuments. We now appear to be glimpsing elements of a similar prehistoric pattern across the heavily ploughed landscape of east Kent and the Isle of Thanet. In addition to the newly identified monument complex at Ringlemere, another Neolithic-Bronze Age focus of activity would seem to be emerging close to the head-waters of the Wingham River, less than 6km further west. The valley-side location of the Wingham Bridge monument complex is indeed very reminiscent of Ringlemere and the relatively close proximity to these two sites, within the same valley system, may suggest that they were connected in some way.

Taken together, the evidence from Ringlemere and Wingham Bridge, along with the previously excavated ridge-top complex at the Lord of the Manor on Thanet, combines to suggest that there were a number of local Neolithic-Bronze Age ceremonial centres scattered across north-east Kent, on either side of the Wantsum Channel. Other discoveries help to reinforce the view that these were significant places. Thus, a Neolithic causewayed enclosure and part of a possible cursus monument have now been excavated within 1km of the Lord of the Manor complex (Dyson, Shand and Stevens 2000, 472; Shand 2001; **Fig. 26**) whilst two possible henge monuments are recorded on air photographs in the same region. Another probable causewayed enclosure has been noted on an air photograph near Tilmanstone, 4.5km to the south of Ringlemere (Oswald *et al.* 2001, 153 no.47) and only just over 1km east of the monuments off Thornton Lane, Eastry, which include round barrows and the possible henge enclosure (see above; **Fig. 26**).

Some distance further to the west, beyond our main area of concern in this discussion, another region which must be mentioned is the Medway valley, between Maidstone and Rochester. Here, the famous megalithic long barrows clustered in two groups on either side of the valley, have long been known (Holgate 1981). Now, with the recent discovery of a large Neolithic rectangular timber building at White Horse Stone not far from the Lower Kits Coty burial chamber, the identification of a possible new causewayed camp at Burham (Dyson, Shand and Stevens 2000, 472; Oswald *et al.* 2001, 152 no.44), along with the circular enclosure at Holborough (mentioned above), this region stands out as another one containing an important ritual Neolithic landscape, which is in need of extensive, detailed modern study.

Elsewhere in Kent, evidence for Neolithic long barrows remains comparatively scarce. The nearest upstanding remains to Ringlemere are represented by a group of three long mounds above the Stour valley, around 22km to the south-west (Parfitt 1998b). However, recent air photograph analysis again has identified a dozen potential new sites scattered across the Kentish chalklands (RCHME 1989, list 17; Bewley, Crutchley and Grady 2004, 72). Six of these sites lie within 11km of Ringlemere, further underlining the prehistoric landscape potential of the region.

Chapter 6: Precious Cups of the Early Bronze Age
Stuart Needham

History of discovery and study

The first record of a cup belonging to the group of 'precious cups' defined for the Early Bronze Age dates back to 1774; it was found at Stoborough in Dorset seven years earlier and was possibly made of shale (cat. no. 16). The piece has been lost since early the following century and cannot be attributed to this group with absolute certainty. However, the burial rite and monument, described in enlightened fashion for the time, is patently consistent with an Early Bronze Age date (Hutchins 1774, 26–7; Gough 1786, xlv–xlvi). Moreover, by interpreting Gough's drawing rather than the schematic reconstruction in Hutchins, the cup has much in common with the subsequent finds of carved cups. In tune with the state of knowledge of the time Gough ventured: 'There is no pretence for this having been the body of Edward the Martyr, AD 978, but it is highly probable that it belonged to some petty prince or chieftain of the Saxon or Danish times.'

The next cup to come to light was the amber one from Hove, 1856 (cat. no. 11). We are fortunate to have another fine description of the grave and its contents with a sober assessment of their parallels (Phillips 1856). Phillips was able to make a number of comparisons with barrow material published by Colt Hoare which was already being ascribed to the 'Bronze Period'.

Three more cups were discovered or brought to antiquarian attention in the late 1860s. Already at this time Smirke, Way, Hutchinson and Kirwan were noting similarities between the first few cups known despite the fact that three different materials were involved. Smirke (1867, 192–3) and Way (1867, 197), in the first publication of the Rillaton gold cup (cat. no. 2; 30 years after its discovery), likened it to the Hove amber version. Although Albert Way had '…great difficulty in suggesting a date… .' (ibid, 196), the associated bronze objects at the two sites, plus some other evidence from Cornwall and Scandinavia, led him '… to assign the relics to a remote period, when the use of that metal prevailed' (ibid). Way's further discussion of broader stylistic comparisons paid particular attention to corrugated objects, amongst them the Mold cape and the Cuxwold armlet, now linked together with the Rillaton and Ringlemere cups, *inter alia*, as part of an embossed tradition of goldworking (Needham 2000a).

Kirwan and Hutchinson were independently drawing a parallel between the newly excavated Farway shale cup (cat. no. 14, quickly followed by no. 15) and those from Rillaton and Hove (Kirwan 1867–8, 630–2; Hutchinson 1867–8). They both also drew attention to the earlier Stoborough find (above and cat. no. 16) thus bringing it in for consideration as a related vessel. Originally described as 'a small vessel of oak, of a black colour', Kirwan ventured that 'it is more probable… . that it may have been of the Kimmeridge shale of the district' (1867–8, 628). He went on to make some comparisons with certain ceramic cups, but these have stood the test of time less well.

Later in the 19th century a second amber cup was unearthed, from the Clandon barrow, Dorset (cat. no. 10). Although the excavation was not properly published until much later (Drew and Piggott 1936), Abercromby dealt with it and the other three cups known in shale or amber in his comprehensive treatment of Bronze Age pottery. He commented that they 'are remarkable as regards both material and form, and more especially as they seem to have been turned on a lathe like similar wooden cups from Denmark' (Abercromby 1912, 29). On this point of technology he was following Evans (1897, 446), rather than Thurnam (1871, 524) who inclined towards hand turning. Thurnam seems to have been the first to note the comparison with surviving wooden cups or bowls from the Danish waterlogged coffin burials, but we now know that these are a little later than the precious series under consideration. Another key feature of Abercromby's publication was the early use of photographs, thus providing us with the first published examples of the two Farway cups and that from Clandon (1912, pl. LXII fig. 3a, pl. LXXXI figs 260, 261).

The next thorough treatment was by R.S. Newall, occasioned by Salisbury and South Wiltshire Museum's acquisition of two shale cups (cat. nos 12 & 13) as part of the Job Edwards collection (Newall 1927–9). Sadly, the provenance of these two is effectively unknown; Newall concluded that 'probably Wiltshire' would be a safer description than the 'Amesbury neighbourhood' (ibid, 111) and we have followed his advice in even more tentative fashion here (possibly Wiltshire). By this time, the number of illustratable vessels in this series from England was eight. He listed but dismissed two other examples as of unknown form and date – from East Riding, Yorkshire, and Rempstone, Dorset. One of the Scandinavian wooden vessels (from Dragshoi) and ceramic cups from Swiss Lake sites were also mentioned, but are not now considered particularly relevant.

Piggott gave the shale and amber cups fairly brief discussion as part of his seminal formulation of the Wessex Culture, deferring to Newall (Piggott 1938, 82–3). However, he did make a rather pertinent suggestion regarding origins which was later to be taken up by Gerloff. Being at pains to find form parallels for the English precious cups and, moreover, given other evidence for links with the Aunjetitz world, Piggott wondered whether '…it may not be too fantastic to suggest connection with the handled cups of similar form characteristic of this phase' (1938, 83). He was of course referring to the many ceramic examples of the Aunjetitz and congener cultures. He also noted the silver sheet fragments from St Fiacre (cat. no. 9) which he alternatively described as from a cup or a bowl (ibid, 68, 100). Aveneau de la Grancière, the excavator in 1898, thought that the fragments were unreconstructable and were from a burnt *bronze* vessel (Aveneau de la Grancière 1898, 88, 93).

At some point after 1938 restoration of the Saint-Fiacre fragments was attempted in the Ashmolean Museum by mounting them on a wooden former of the shape envisaged. Although we offer here a modified reconstruction, this earlier attempt showed that they belonged to a cup-sized vessel.

Even though the complete Gölenkamp example had been found much earlier, in the 19th century, it was the discovery of the Fritzdorf gold vessel in 1954 that first made clear that similar precious cups could occur on the Continent (von Uslar 1955). Von Uslar showed that although not identical vessels, the Fritzdorf and Rillaton cups were strikingly similar in their handles and rivet fixings. A decade later Briard linked the lost gold object from Ploumilliau (cat. no. 6) to this precious cup series (Briard 1965, 76–7).

So by the time of Sabine Gerloff's important review of these cups in the early 70s (Gerloff 1975, 177–96), it was clear that an interrelated series could be identified stretching from Cornwall and Brittany in the west, to the middle Rhine in the east. Potential examples that she considered from more outlying locations – the Cuxwold ornament from Lincolnshire and the Caldas de Reyes cups from Pontevedra province, Spain – can be dismissed from this series for different reasons. The former can now be seen to be so similar to the Lockington armlets as to leave little doubt of a similar identification (an identification suggested by many scholars over time; Needham 2000a). The three handled cups in the Caldas de Reyes hoard are thick and heavy (between 540 and 640g), having been cast by the lost-wax method, and they are of rather different style from the series under consideration here (Armbruster 1996; 2000, 128–35, 201–2). The dating of the large Caldas de Reyes treasure has been much debated, but Armbruster points out that both the technology of the cups and the many associated massive-bar ornaments (arm- and neck-rings) are in keeping with a later Bronze Age date, rather than earlier.

Consolidation of a 'Rhineland' distribution came with the public appearance in 1974 of the Eschenz example, it having been unearthed much earlier in 1916 (Hardmeyer and Bürgi 1975). Coming from the head of the Rhine in the Alpine foreland, Eschenz indicated penetration of this precious cup series into the heart of Europe. The research it engendered also brought into the open the 19th-century find from Gölenkamp, near the German/Dutch border, a vessel with some significant similarities, but in many ways the most deviant of the whole group under discussion.

At about the time that Eschenz was published, Jacques Briard was excavating a second silver example from a tomb at Saint-Adrien (Briard 1978; Briard 1984, 134 fig. 83, 135 fig. 84, 225–6); this added further weight to the Armorican distribution (cat. no. 8). The only other related find we are aware of since is a cup published for the first time in 2001 (Wamser and Gebhard 2001) and said to be from Germany, but wholly lacking any contextual or historical information, a decidedly unfortunate situation given its potential importance (cat. no. 7).

For the sake of completeness, mention needs to be made of two small rim fragments of jet vessels or ornaments, both from Northumberland. The respective publishers have suggested they could come from vessels, but neither comes from a well-dated context. The fragment from Hebburn Moor is part of a surface collection made over many decades (Newbiggin 1941) and cannot necessarily be accepted as Bronze Age or even prehistoric. Its radius of curvature is not given. The second fragment was excavated by George Jobey from within a small double entrance enclosure (hengiform), where it was 'lying on the disturbed brash surface above bed-rock' (Jobey 1966, 37–42 fig. 15). The fragment is under 4cm long and 1.8cm deep with an estimated external diameter of 10cm; the wall thickens towards the rim which has a flat top and bulbous outer lip. Jobey was not confident that this was from a cup.

With the final addition of Ringlemere, the current distribution of Early Bronze Age precious cups is that shown in **Figure 28**. The intensity of the distribution along the southern coastal strip of England is striking, but may be enhanced by deposition and recovery factors relative to the opposite shores of France and Belgium. The Armorican finds also basically fall within 'coastal' zones, although Saint-Fiacre would seem to relate to the Morbihan coast facing the Bay of Biscay rather than to the Channel. At the east end of the distribution, the three provenanced finds are more inland, although two come from locations on the Rhine and the Gölenkamp example is not far distant from the Frisian coast (100km).

Comparative features of the cups

Before exploring further the contacts and transfer of influences implied by the precious cups, it is necessary to review the series and the extent to which they represent a single phenomenon, or ideal of style or usage. For Sabine Gerloff, an important common property was the biconical shape combined with a single handle (1975). Of course they are also united by being fairly small vessels, but size in itself cannot be a defining attribute since small vessels also occur among the ceramic repertoires of the north-west European Early Bronze Age.

The presence of a handle is similarly of limited value as a defining feature, not least because a minority of the precious cups actually lacks handles. Again, handles can occur on various types of ceramic pot in Britain (see below) and are standard on the aptly named vases á anses of Brittany, but they only systematically appear on cup-sized ceramics further inland in continental Europe (**Fig. 28**). In fact, Gerloff, developing an initial suggestion from Piggott (1938, 83), argued persuasively that many ceramic cups of the mature Early Bronze Age in the middle to upper Rhinelands – belonging to the Adlerberg and related cultures – offered good form parallels for some of the north-western precious ones (Gerloff 1975, 184). This connection remains significant, we believe, and deserves further exploration of transmission process and reason for imitation.

What has become clearer from our new study of the cups is that although there are many common features, not all examples conform in all key respects. Indeed, when examined on a trait by trait basis, there is a surprising amount of diversity (**Fig. 29**; **Tables 4 & 5**). No specific trait forms are universal and few are predominant among the series. This variability needs to be examined in relation to geography, chronology and material used.

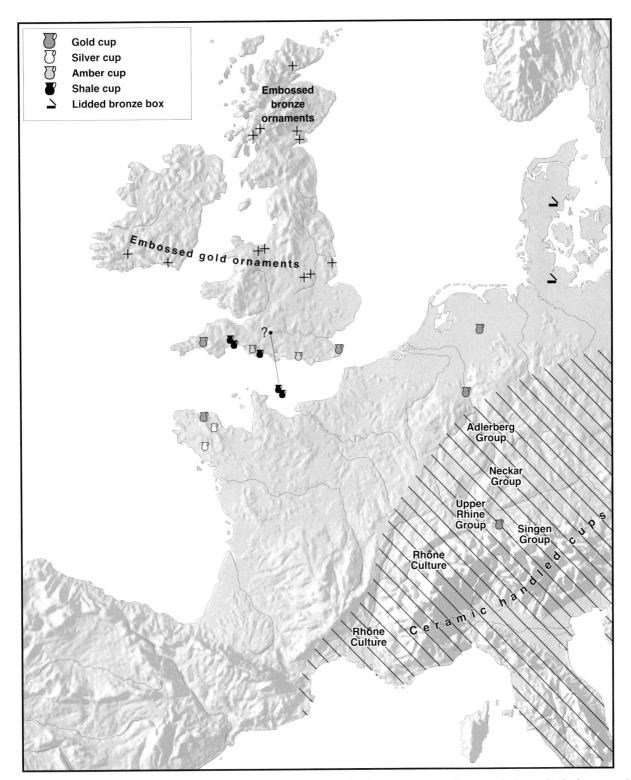

Figure 28 Map of recovery for north-west European Early Bronze Age precious cups. Also shown are the sources of inspiration for form and technology – ceramic handled cups and embossed sheet metalwork.

Gold

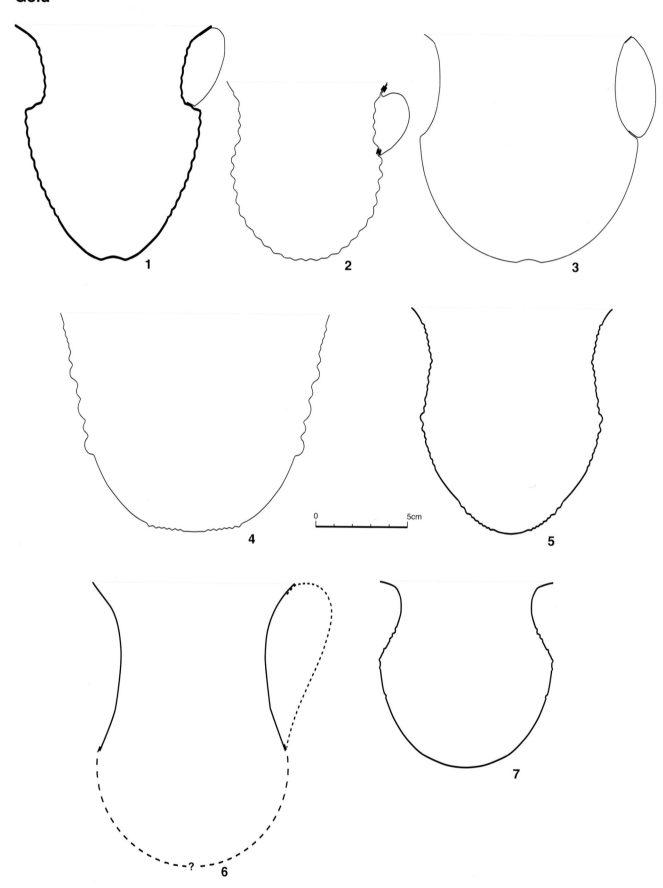

Figure 29 Comparative profiles of the precious cups (for full 'ideal reconstructions' see respective catalogue entries)

Silver

Amber

Shale

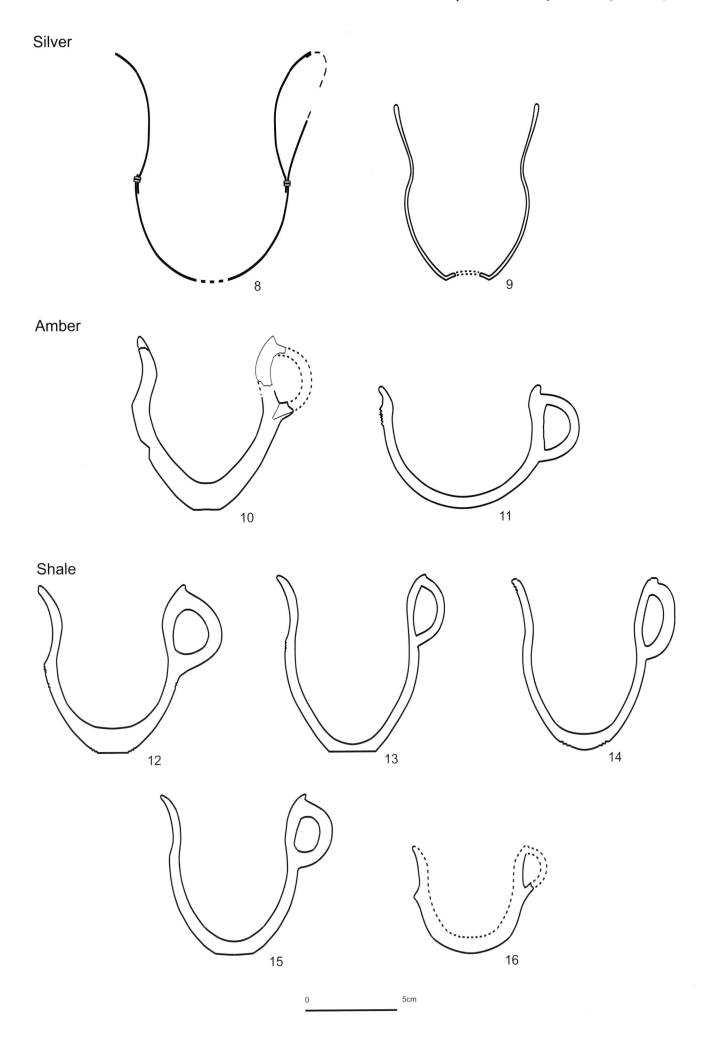

Table 4 Summary of principal dimensions of precious cups as reconstructed

Provenance	Height (mm)	Mouth diam.(mm)	Carination diam.(mm)	Weight (g)	Capacity (litres)
1. Ringlemere	123	109	96	184	0.60
2. Rillaton	95	85.5	77.5	77	0.36
3. Fritzdorf	121	116	122	221	0.91
4. Gölenkamp	116.5	149	-	255	1.31
5. Eschenz	118	110	98.5	136	0.69
6. Ploumilliau	>90	110	98	Lost	>0.52
7. No provenance	98	94	94	90	0.45
8. Saint-Adrien	122	106	86	Fragmentary	0.53
9. Saint-Fiacre	93	80	68	Fragmentary	0.31
10. Clandon	92	76	80	(115, as restored)	0.21
11. Hove	65	89	88.5	-	0.21
12. ?Wiltshire 1	88.5	80	73	Incomplete	0.20
13. ?Wiltshire 2	93	82	72	Incomplete	0.23
14. Farway 1	90	80	66.5	- 0.23	
15. Farway 2	85	77.5	69.5	Incomplete	0.18
16. Stoborough	55	65	60	Lost	0.08

Table 5 Summary of attribute variation for precious cups

Provenance	Cat. no.	Metal/ carved	1 or 2 part body	Grooves/ embossing[1]	Handle[2]	No. handle grooves	No. rivets	Washers[2]	Other handle grooves[3]	Body[4]	Mouth form[5]	Carin[6]	Base form[7]
Gölenkamp	4	M	1	C	a	-	-	-	-	S	3	0	2
No prov.	7	M	1	C	a	-	-	-	-	M	1	2	1
Eschenz	5	M	1	C	a	-	-	-	-	N	2	1	1
Rillaton	2	M	1	S	p	5	3	p	0	N	2	2	1
Ringlemere	1	M	1	S	p	3	4	p	0	N	1	3	3
Fritzdorf	3	M	1	0	p	3	4	p	0	M	2	3	3
St Fiacre	9	M	(1)	0	a	-	-	-	-	(N)	4	1	(3)
St Adrien	8	M	2	0	p	(0)	7	a	0	N	1	2	(1)
Ploumilliau	6	M	2	0	p	?	7	a?	-	-	2	-	-
Farway 1	14	C	1	C	p	2	-	-	0	N	3	1	1
Stoborough	16	C	(1)	C	(p)	-	-	-	-	S	(3?)	3	(1?)
Hove	11	C	1	S	p	5	-	-	T	S	3	2	1
Clandon	10	C	1	0 (S?)	p	(0)	-	-	-	M	3	2	2
?Wiltshire 1	12	C	1	S	p	3	-	-	TV	N	2	2	2
?Wiltshire 2	13	C	1	S	p	4	-	-	T	N	2	1	2
Farway 2	15	C	1	S	p	2	-	-	0	N	2	1	2

Key

-   N/A
1   0: none, S: simple design, C: complex design
2   a or p: absent or present respectively
3   0: absent, T: transverse, V: v-shaped
4   Body proportions – S: squat, M: medium, N: narrow
5   Mouth form – 1: very flared, 2: moderately flared, 3: slightly flared, 4: slightly convex
6   Carination – 0: none, 1: slight, 2: moderate, 3: strong
7   Base form – 1: rounded, 2: flat or near-flat, 3: omphalos

There is a surprising spectrum of capacities from as little as 0.08 l to 1.3 l (calculated from the estimated original profiles; **Table 4**). The main variation in capacity is straightforwardly explained by difference in materials. All of the carved cups of amber and shale have capacities under 0.25 l. Most form a tight group between about 0.18 and 0.23 l. The unavoidable thickness of the body of the carved cups severely reduces their capacity relative to a sheet metal vessel of comparable external dimensions. A second factor is that, for the amber ones in particular, size would have been limited by the block of raw material it was possible to obtain.

The metal cups all have capacities greater than 0.3 l but in a broad range extending to over a litre. The smallest estimated capacity, for Saint-Fiacre, is uncertain due to its very fragmentary state. Rillaton, Saint-Adrien and the unprovenanced cup fall between about 0.36 and 0.53 l; Ringlemere and Eschenz between about 0.60 and 0.7 l and

Ploumilliau would have been comparable if its lower body matched the shape of Saint-Adrien. The Fritzdorf vessel has a larger capacity of approaching a litre while Gölenkamp is larger still, primarily because it has no carination and the body continues to flare unchecked all the way to the rim.

The number of cups is small, but it is possible that there is a trend with larger capacities found in more easterly locations than the smaller ones. This can only be tested for the metal versions given the more restricted geographical occurrence of the carved cups. However, the four largest capacities (>0.65 l) come from Kent and the Rhineland group, with just the possible addition of Ploumilliau. Three of the smaller capacities (<0.5 l) are from Cornwall and Armorica; the fourth is the unprovenanced gold cup.

In terms of the underlying body form (ie ignoring initially corrugations and grooves), the strongly flared mouth of the Ringlemere cup is really only closely paralleled on the unprovenanced gold one and the St Adrien silver cup (nos 7–8; **Fig. 29**; **Table 5** – mouth form 1). The shoulder-like form of the carination is equally unusual, only Fritzdorf (no. 3) coming close. Other cups have moderate or indistinct carinations, with the exception of Gölenkamp (no. 4) which has no break at all in its flared profile. Fritzdorf also has a neat small omphalos, a feature otherwise only present at Saint-Fiacre, according to our new reconstruction. To isolate these three in this respect may, however, be a little artificial since most of the other cups also have a defined base roundel which, when not an omphalos, can be either a rib-encircled boss or a flattened circular surface, in either case of small diameter. Only the Hove cup (no. 11) certainly lacks any defined base feature, the fragmentary nature of Saint-Adrien (no. 8; **Fig. 47**) precluding certainty. Whether the bases are omphaloid, rounded or flat, they all basically give rise to cups that would have great difficulty standing unaided on a flat surface, especially when full of liquid; they are inherently 'unstable'.

Body proportions are rather variable through the series with two, and perhaps three, cups being particularly squat (Hove, Gölenkamp and Stoborough no. 16). However, the majority, at least eight cups including Ringlemere, have relatively slender proportions (carination diameter/height less than 0.82). There is no correlation between body proportions and geographical location.

Decoration of the body is generally fairly restrained and two main types correlate with the material employed. The corrugations seen on Ringlemere are a feature now uniting five gold cups, while the other four metal cups (two of gold, two silver) probably all had uncorrugated sheet bodies with decoration restricted to punched dot rows at the rim. In contrast, six out of the seven carved cups (amber and shale) carry narrow bands (or broader fields on one) of multiple incised grooves. These do not mimic the corrugations either in scale or coverage and yet this could have been achieved by a highly competent craftsman if desired. Indeed, it would appear that the Clandon cup (no. 10; **Fig. 49**), otherwise plain, was given a single crescentic groove on the lower body opposite the handle. Conversely, the metal versions could just as easily have been decorated with incised lines if directly copying the shale/amber versions. The implication is that these two decorative forms were for some reason integral to the respective materials, technologies or traditions of production. There was an accepted way of decorating a precious cup according to the material from which it was made.

The corrugations are in fact treated very differently on each cup on which they occur. Rillaton (no. 2; **Colour Pls 5–6**; **Fig. 41**) bears truly sinuous corrugations of fairly constant amplitude and depth until they get close to the base. In contrast, the corrugations meet in well defined, albeit obtuse, angles on Ringlemere to give a continuously cuspate profile; again there is only a little variation in amplitude. Gölenkamp (no. 4; **Colour Pl. 9**; **Fig. 43**) has two distinct grades: small sinuous corrugations in a band below the rim and concentrically on the base; much larger bulbous ribs on the main body separated by flat zones carrying boss rows. Two grades are also present on Eschenz (no. 5; **Colour Pl. 10**; **Fig. 44**), but the larger is represented by just a single prominent rib on the carination; it divides two fields of continuous small corrugations. It too has boss rows, but also totally novel components: panels of diagonal

ribs on the lower body and a single band of embossed cabling. Each element of the last is in the shape of a stretched out 'S'.

The unprovenanced, ?Germany cup (no. 7; **Fig. 46**) is similar to Eschenz in having a relatively elaborate embossed design employing ribs in different motifs. A limited number of narrow horizontal corrugations divide the body into registers. The lower two are filled respectively with alternating panels involving in both cases vertical ribs. The lowest register has intervening reserved triangles with a supplementary rib along the top border; in the register above, vertical-rib panels alternate with long oval, dot-lined grooves. The shoulder field is plain but for horizontal ribs, while the neck has yet another novel motif – a continuous double zigzag again executed as dot-lined grooves which spring from a horizontal double dot-groove just under the rim. This recalls the band of decoration inside the mouth of Farway 1 (no. 14; **Colour Pl. 13**; **Fig. 53**) and the single motif on top of the handle of ?Wiltshire 1 (no. 12; **Fig. 51**). However, it is also carried through onto the later flask like vessels from Villeneuve-Saint-Vistre, and Lienewitzer Forst (**Colour Pl. 14**; Springer 2003, 15–16 figs 7 & 8; Eluère 1982, 104–7 figs. 125–6, 159 fig. 158; Ellmers 2003). In fact, it is easy to see these latter vessels as the direct descendants of the Eschenz/ '?Germany' form of the early series, but now with the addition of the encircled boss motif (*Kreisbuckel*) which so critically marks out the later tradition of Bronze Age embossed gold (Gerloff 1995; Needham 2000a, 48).

The distinctive handles present on many of the Early Bronze Age cups have commanded much attention in the past. They are not universally present, however, and it is noteworthy that the three examples on which they are definitely absent are among the four furthest East in the overall distribution. This may be another point of significance in the heralding of the predominantly handle-free series of embossed gold vessels of the later stages of the Bronze Age in northern central Europe.

At least 11, and possibly 12, cups had handles, all four materials being represented. The handle evidently had not survived on the Ploumilliau piece (no. 6; **Fig. 45**), but seven rivet emplacements under the rim testify to its original existence. Of the remaining 10, or 11, at least 8 carry groove decoration running parallel with the convex sides. This is either incised on the carved materials or formed as narrow corrugations on the metal ones – Ringlemere included. The type of decoration on the Saint-Adrien handle (no. 8; **Fig. 47**) mentioned by Briard (1984, 225) is not described, while the surviving handle stumps of the Clandon amber cup (no. 10; **Fig. 49**) show no groove ends; normally they extend the whole length of the handle. Handle grooves occur as a band of between two and five on either side of the handle, with three being the most recurrent, as seen on Ringlemere, Fritzdorf (no. 3; **Fig. 42**) and the shale cup from ?Wiltshire 1 (no. 12; **Fig. 51**). Three of the carved cups also have horizontal grooves on the handle, usually at top and bottom thus forming a frame with the side bands, and one of these (?Wiltshire 1) has in addition the double-line 'V' motif suspended from the top.

The handles are all waisted to some degree, expanding top and bottom towards the body attachments. This 'hourglass' shape is in fact widespread on ceramic vessels which have handles from many periods and is presumably a general attempt to provide a stronger union with the body; such handles are separate components which are luted onto and/or plugged into the body. Where the precious metal cups have a handle, it too is attached, although in one case (Saint-Adrien, no. 8; **Fig. 47**) it is formed as an extension of the lower body portion and only needed attachment at the top. This is also likely to have been the construction used for Ploumilliau (no. 6; **Fig. 45**). The five metal handles were fixed by between three and seven rivet emplacements per end; perhaps significantly seven rivets occur on the two Breton handled cups, while fewer were used elsewhere: three at Rillaton (no. 2; **Fig. 41**), four at Ringlemere and Fritzdorf (no. 3; **Fig. 42**). It is only on these last three that rivet-washers survive and the closely matching diamond shape on Rillaton and Fritzdorf which has long attracted comment (von Uslar 1955) now extends to Ringlemere.

There is evidence for a handle on all of the extant carved cups although this is a tentative interpretation for Stoborough (see cat. no. 16) and this would have been shaped from an initial lug left on one side of the block being worked (Sloper 1989). Experience would quickly have taught the craftsmen that the waisted shape desired would naturally have arisen by cutting the sides of the lug to a trapezoid plan tapering away from the body (*contra* Sloper's fig. 1a). If cut thus as flat planes converging on one another outwards, the intersection of those planes with the curved handle profile would naturally result in the classic waisted shape in face view. The precise degree of waisting may have been less easy to predict while roughing out the blank and this makes it difficult to assess the significance of the spectrum of curvatures found. The strongest waist curvatures all occur on carved cups (Hove no. 11, ?Wiltshire 1 no. 12, Farway 2 no. 15; **Figs 50, 51 & 54**), with the Ringlemere handle being more intermediate.

There is one further decorative feature to be discussed – the occurrence of pointillé rows. These are subtle in their impact – sometimes to the point of being easily overlooked – and yet would seem to be of symbolic importance or an engrained part of a tradition, for they occur on virtually all of the metal cups. No evidence survives on the Saint-Fiacre fragments (no. 9; **Fig. 48**) and the feature is definitely absent from Gölenkamp (no. 4; **Fig. 43**). In every other example one or two horizontal rows occur just below the rim, although at Rillaton (no. 2; Kinnes 1994, A26) only a short row beside the handle exists. Normally, the rows are punched directly into the plain band below the rim, but on the Eschenz example (no. 5; **Fig. 44**) they have been set into the uppermost two grooves of the neck corrugations. This groove-set pointillé is echoed on the unprovenanced gold cup (no. 7; **Fig. 46**) – in its oval motifs as well as the V motifs suspended below the standard under-rim pointillé.

As relatively consistent as its presence is on the metal cups, such dot decoration is wholly absent from the carved cups. That their materials would not have lent themselves so readily to taking dot decoration may be a factor; nevertheless, some similar effect could surely have been achieved if this was really important to convey a certain message. It is noteworthy, for example, that contemporary spacer-plate beads of jet include dots in their decoration. We do therefore seem to have an unexplained feature which was important to the integrity of the gold and silver vessels, but not to that of the amber and shale ones. Dot decoration does have a long ancestry on sheet metalwork going back, in north-western Europe, to the earliest ornaments of the Copper Age (*c.* 2500–2150 BC; Taylor 1980, 22–4). While this ancestry does not in itself explain the meaning of the dots on the cups, it does give a strong line of continuity in the realm of prestige metalwork.

Dating evidence, sequence and origins

Seven of the 16 cups have associations that may help with relative dating; not all are necessarily closed associations and they are also weighted towards the west, five in England, two in Brittany. This makes it particularly difficult to ascertain the relationship with Adlerberg ceramic cups in the critical interaction zone of the Rhinelands (**Fig. 28**).

The two Armorican silver cups (nos 8 & 9) both come from tombs that contained relatively rich inventories. The possibility has been raised that in both cases these inventories were the product of more than one burial event spread over a long enough time for perceptible change to have occurred in classic grave goods (Needham 2000b). Both, however, are series 2 assemblages, where the last diagnostic accompaniments can be dated to the Kernonen-Kerodou phase, *c.* 1950–1750 BC. In the case of the well-excavated grave of Brun Bras at Saint-Adrien (no. 8), it seems almost certain (given the absence of a body) that the cup was among a small group of prestige items surrounding the latest interment in a coffin (Briard 1984, 56 fig. 33); a Trévérec type dagger is included and is considered diagnostic of Kernonen-Kerodou (Needham 2000b, 173). These are among the earliest demonstrable contexts for precious cups. A radiocarbon determination on an oak plank in the Brun Bras grave gave an even earlier date (3650 ± 35 BP; GrN-7176; 2140–1930 cal BC), but is potentially based on mature wood.

A specific context for the Ringlemere cup must remain unproven (see above), but even if not in closed association, it is likely to be significant that the cup and the two amber objects are the only Early Bronze Age artefacts recovered from the site so far (excluding Beaker material) and all were recovered from a limited area of the interior. Because the cup has certain similarities to that from Rillaton, it was at first assumed that they would be closely contemporary, datable to the period of Wessex 2. However, the detailed morphological and technical comparisons made above, plus the clear fact that precious cups had an overall currency of some three to four centuries, allow scope for reconsideration. The two amber objects at Ringlemere are best dated earlier, broadly contemporary with the Bush Barrow grave series of Wessex 1, *c.* 1950–1750/1700 BC. The pommel is best paralleled in the Manton grave, in Wessex (whose second cup is not of Aldbourne type characteristic of the succeeding phase – *contra* Taylor 2005, 316, 324, but instead a Longworth type 7, trunco-conic cup – Longworth 1984, 52), while the probable pendant has parallels in both Wessex and more specifically in the Kernonen tomb, eponymous to the contemporary phase in Armorica.

The Clandon amber cup (no. 10) is more certainly of this earlier phase. Although apparently not deposited as a classic grave group (Drew and Piggott 1936), it and a few other prestige objects were clearly part of a single depositional horizon trapped between the inner cairn and a later mound enlargement. The objects associated at this horizon are all acceptable as specific to the Bush Barrow/ Wessex 1 period (Gerloff 1975, 182).

Three British contexts are of the subsequent, Camerton-Snowshill grave series, *c.* 1750–1550 BC, a Camerton-Snowshill dagger being present in each case. The associated cups are of gold, amber and shale showing that varied materials coexisted.

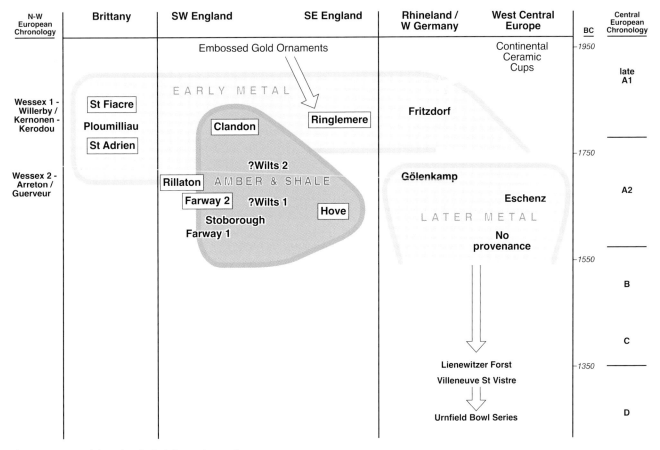

Figure 30 Suggested chronology for Early Bronze Age precious cups

At Rillaton (no. 2) the cist also contained other objects now lost, but no useful descriptions or depictions are known. At Farway 2 (no. 15) the dagger lay on charred material, the cup approximately 1m away; both were among the stones of the central cairn, but may not represent exactly the same depositional event. Finally, the Hove cup (no. 11) came from a closed grave group (**Colour Pl. 12**); not only is the dagger closely datable typologically, but so too is the developed style of battle-axe present – Roe's stage V Snowshill type (1966, 237). A perforated whetstone is less diagnostic in itself, but is a type primarily placed in graves during the Camerton-Snowshill phase (Wessex 2). A final piece of evidence from Hove is a radiocarbon date on remains of the coffin, 3190 ± 46 BP (BM-682; 1610–1310 cal BC); this is an early-run measurement and now looks a little on the young side.

With these fixed points and the evidence of feature comparisons between individual cups it is possible to venture a tentative chronology for the whole series (**Fig 30**). The Saint-Fiacre (no. 9) and Saint-Adrien (no. 8) cups are both plain-bodied, excepting under-rim pointillé; the third Breton, incomplete example (no. 6) matches in this respect and has the bipartite construction of the latter. It is thus also best placed in an early phase. Its associated gold spoon or ladle has a dot row outlining the handle, decoration recurrently found on early sheet goldwork from primary Beaker times on.

Clandon (no. 10) too, just across the Channel from Brittany, is essentially undecorated and this raises the likelihood that the remaining plain-bodied vessel, Fritzdorf (no. 3), is of an early phase. From an interpretive point of view this helps to make sense of the initial north-westwards transmission of the idea of handled, unstable cups from the middle Rhineland or beyond, where the ceramic versions abound. Fritzdorf's handle and its

fixing are of neat workmanship, whereas the body seems rather less proficient even allowing for later denting and distortion (**Colour Pl. 8**). The omphalos is neatly executed, but this would be a technically easier feat than obtaining good all-round shaping of the body.

Connections between Armorica and western central Europe are clearly attested at this date. Not only is there the general stylistic parallelism seen in the mutual adoption of long grooved daggers a little earlier (Quimperlé and Rumédon types in Armorica; Oder-Elbe types in northern Aunjetitz zone), there are four daggers at Singen (close to Eschenz) of Atlantic inspiration if not manufacture (Krause 1988; Gerloff 1993, 75 footnote 48) and, more poignantly, a Rhône-type dagger in the Saint-Fiacre assemblage (Needham 2000b, 164 fig. 6.6). One should also mention the Gaubickelheim hoard from the middle Rhine in which one dagger betrays some affinity with the Breton Quimperlé style (Hundt 1971; Needham 2000c, 40).

Ringlemere would thus stand out as the one early cup which was not plain-bodied; is this a problem? Certainly if Fritzdorf is early, we have an ideal model for the handle and its fixings, plus important similarities in profile, which leaves only the matter of the corrugated body. Embossed goldworking had already been developed to a highly proficient standard in central Britain by the years either side of 2000 BC, at this date employed for ribbed armlets (Needham 2000a) – so the technology and the ribbed style were already available by the time the idea of precious cups emerged in the lands flanking the Channel and the Rhine. Since these cups were for the most part individual interpretations, indeed individual creations by leading craftsmen at their respective points of gestation, it is eminently plausible that the conjunction of cup and embossing could have been made early on, as soon as these influences impinged on one another.

Arguments based on the technical sophistication involved can also be dismissed once it is appreciated that the Mold gold cape may date as early as the period in question or, if later, only a little later (Needham 2000a). There is no particular obstacle to an early date for the Ringlemere cup and nothing specific to push it later; it may be that it was indeed contemporary with the amber items from the site.

Rather than allowing Rillaton to drag down the date of Ringlemere, it may be that it would be worthwhile to consider whether Ringlemere should elevate the date of Rillaton. The context of Rillaton is as solidly dated as it can be in the absence of most of the grave group; Camerton-Snowshill daggers are still best interpreted as a later style than those in the Bush Barrow grave series, despite earlier debates on the subject. However, the Rillaton cup hardly seems to be in fine condition, especially when it is considered that unlike many of the other cups, it was protected from the weight of a mound by a stone cist. The difficulties of discriminating between ancient and more modern wear notwithstanding, the condition of the upper original rivet suggests that the cup was far from fresh when buried.

Thus far, we would suggest that an early phase of cups includes plain-bodied examples of gold (2), silver (2) and amber (1). One or both of the simple-ribbed gold cups may also belong this early. Three gold cups from west central Europe are the only remaining metal cups and are not dated by association. In all three the embossed decoration is more complex than on the British pieces. All three have no handle, thereby departing from the previous ideal. The design of Eschenz (no. 5; **Colour Pl. 10**) and, even more so, that of the unprovenanced cup (no. 7; **Fig. 46**) seem to be moving towards the earliest of the later Bronze Age vessel series of continental Europe. In particular, it is not hard to see the flasks from Villeneuve-Saint-Vistre and Lienewitzer Forst (**Colour Pl. 14**; Eluère 1982, 104–7 figs. 125–6, 159 fig. 158; Springer (ed) 2003, 293–7; Ellmers 2003), dated to around the 14th century BC, as being direct descendants of the style and technique, albeit once the new array of motifs appropriate to the later (Urnfield) series had become key design elements.

The final group to be discussed in terms of dating comprises the majority of the carved cups, excluding only Clandon which has been dealt with. The associations at Farway 2 (no. 15) and Hove (no. 11) are of the later phase – Camerton-Snowshill – and the others can be argued to belong here on stylistic cross-linking. All have horizontal groove bands, while the more complex motifs on Stoborough and Farway 1 have parallels with designs on late metal vessels. The vertical-to-diagonal hatching of the lower body of Stoborough (no. 16; **Fig. 55**) could represent the same theme as the diagonal-filled panels seen in a similar position at Eschenz (no. 5; **Fig. 44**), while Farway 1 (no. 14; **Colour Pl. 13**) shares with the unprovenanced cup (no. 7; **Fig. 46**) a row of deep pendant triangles, or zig-zags. The zig-zag is of course a commonly employed motif in decorating a variety of materials and was certainly frequently used on Beaker ceramics at an earlier date. However, the position on the two cups, descending from the rim, makes them strikingly similar, albeit that one is carved inside the mouth, the other is impressed from outside, creating ribs inside.

The single 'V' motif on the handle of the ?Wiltshire 1 vessel (no. 12; **Fig. 51**) may be linked less certainly to the continuous triangle row. Otherwise, the two ?Wiltshire vessels share with

Hove (no. 11; **Fig. 50**) transverse handle grooves, these additional to the edging groove bands present on the whole group, but apparently absent at Clandon (no. 10; **Fig. 49**).

Flattened bases link the two ?Wiltshire cups (nos 12 & 13; **Fig. 29**) and that from Farway 2 (no. 15) with the Gölenkamp late gold vessel (no. 4), but it also appears earlier at Clandon (no. 10). Another base form, the ringed-roundel, puts Farway 1 (no. 14) with the other later gold cups, Eschenz (no. 5) and unprovenanced (no. 7); indeed Rillaton (no. 2) as now reconstructed would have been a variant on this theme. Even the multiple rings on the flatter Gölenkamp base (**Fig. 43**) reflect a similar concern with neatly styled concentric design at the very bottom, where earlier some had neat omphaloi or were simply rounded. Farway 1 is unique among the carved cups in adopting this otherwise gold-focused design theme.

To summarise and simplify the complex interactions and chronology deduced above, it is possible to define three groups of precious cups (**Fig. 30**). Chronological primacy can be given to an *Early Metal Group* comprising six vessels of silver and gold. Rillaton may be a little later but otherwise these can be attributed to the period *c.* 1950–1750 BC (Kernonen-Kerodou/ Bush Barrow/ Reinecke A1b). They were initially inspired by the ceramic cups of west central Europe and the Rhône Culture which share in having single handles and frequently being unstable. Fritzdorf was pivotal typologically and geographically in this formulation of precious metal cups. Why this imitation should have occurred is discussed below. An alternative source of inspiration is feasible for the Breton cups, given the Rhône culture connections, but it seems highly unlikely that these two developments would have happened in isolation from one another. The inter-regional contacts traversing northern France mentioned above could easily have promoted parallel developments in certain spheres.

Cups of the *Carved Group* in amber and shale (seven vessels) were first developed during the early period as attested by the Clandon find, but the great majority thus far would seem to belong to the succeeding period, *c.* 1750–1550 BC (Camerton-Snowshill/ Reinecke A2–beginning B). Given the prevailing chronology and the fact that all are from southern England, it is most likely that they were a response to the early metal cups, rather than having been directly inspired by the ultimate ceramic prototypes.

Third is a *Later Metal Group* comprising just three cups with more complex embossing from west central Europe. These show the transfer of embossing skills *par excellence* to continental Europe (Needham 2000a, 46–8) and anticipate the vigorous uptake of embossing for fine gold vessels and the supreme status equipment represented by the crowns of west-central Europe (Schauer 1986 Springer 2003). In the design of these late metal cups a handle was usually not considered necessary and they were thus in some respects departing from the later British series. Nevertheless, there would appear to have been continuing connections at some level to account for certain shared features.

A chronological overlap is possible between the Later Metal Group and the four embossed vessels from Biha in Roumania, if we accept Mozsolics (1965–6, 10ff, 56–7, pls 4–10) dating of them to the Hajdúsámson period, *c.* 16th century BC. However, these are so utterly different in morphology and decoration that it is hard to see any connection to the north-west European series.

They are shallow bowls with squat necks, the neck formed of a single or double concave profile; the mouths on three turn out horizontally and the handle projects initially in line; the style and technology of the handles is totally distinct from our series and they may never have rejoined the body lower down (only one is complete); the main embossing on three of the Biha vessels is continuous vertical ribbing below the carination, each rib tapering towards the base. The base itself is in two cases plain, the third bears three concentric beaded ribs and the fourth a single annular rib, much as a foot-ring. This fourth vessel has curvilinear punched decoration in four zones and a row of simple hemispherical bosses along the centre line of the handle. The others have close set rows of smaller bosses at the carination, at the rim, or under the rim – the close setting of bosses creates the effect of beading.

A separate vessel, from a hoard at Biia, is different in being a deeper bowl with a contracting upper body before an out-turned mouth (Mozsolics 1965–6, 48–9, pl 12; Florescu 1971, 32–3 no. 110, pl.). Two opposed handles are long straps terminating in double spirals; again, these seem never to have rejoined the body. Decoration includes one register of a repeating inverted Y motif executed in dots and on the lower body three rows of hemispherical bosses amongst which are set symmetrically three *Kreisbuckel* motifs – a boss encircled by three rings. Bouzek (1985, 51–2) is doubtful that any of these Romanian vessels need be as early as Mozsolics argues. Her main argument rested on the spiral decoration on one of the Bihar examples, but Bouzek notes that such decoration continues later, while other features better place the vessels between Reinecke C and D (c. 14th–13th centuries BC.

A series of precious metal cups and vessels from the Aegean has often been called upon as the source of, or the stimulus for the north-western gold cups (eg Bouzek 1985, 51). There are now considerable chronological difficulties in deriving the north-western series from Mycenaean prototypes, and neither these nor earlier vessel styles represented in the Aegean and Anatolia (Segall 1938, 11–14 no. 1; Childe 1924; Hood 1956, 87–92; Catling 1964, among figs 17–21; Bouzek 1985, 50 fig. 19) have more than a superficial resemblance. Beyond sometimes being of precious metals, being vessels of small-ish capacity and having handles, no useful comparison can be made.

The fact that a bronze bowl, found at Dohnsen, north-west Germany, seems to be an import from the south does not alter the picture. Sprockhoff identified it as a Mycenaean vessel, datable at that time to about 1400 BC (Sprockhoff 1961). While that dating may now be revised backwards, this find yet again emphasises the morphological rift between north-western precious cups and those of the Aegean and south-east Europe. The Dohnsen bowl cannot be in any way responsible for the development of the north-western series, instead its presence in the far north strengthens the case that there was a growing interest in fine metal vessels in the north German area from the final Early Bronze Age onwards.

No good case then can be made for initial inspiration from the south-east; there is an enormous geographical and morphological gulf between Fritzdorf and the Romanian/Aegean cup zone, not to mention the chronological dislocation that now appears between the earliest cups in the two regions. If the south-east of Europe can no longer be understood to be the source of stimulus for the north-western

precious cups, then we do need to explain how the technology involved emerged indigenously. Sheet metalwork forms that were both fully three-dimensional and expertly embossed had in fact been mastered in northern and central Britain by 2000 BC, as already noted; the main products at that time were broad armlets (Needham 2000a; 2000c). With such background skills available, adaptation to produce cups, and indeed embossed cups, would have been no great technical leap forward.

However, we are left with something of a conundrum with respect to the hypothesised earliest cups. At first sight one might assume that the plain-bodied cups from Fritzdorf and Armorica would have emerged first, being technically easier to produce than embossed versions. And yet there is no evidence at all for the prior development of hollow-sheet-working skills in those regions. So a big question is whether they could have been coincidentally developed independent of British metalworking traditions. Given that sheet-metal cups of similar style appear on both sides of the Channel at about the same time, it seems more realistic to accept that all depended on a common pool of experience and specialist skills. This would suggest that there was a transfer of the required expertise across the Channel to allow the production of the Continental cups. But in this case, does it mean that the 'precious cup' had already been invented on British shores and, if so, were the first ones already embossed following in the wake of the armlets?

The resolution of our dataset, with only a small number of vessels represented, makes it impossible to determine where the fusion of the unstable cup form with hollow-sheet-metalworking techniques first occurred. The important point is that the fusion represents a cross-over of style-*cum*-function from one direction and technical expertise from the opposite direction and, moreover, that it took place in lands flanking the Channel and lower Rhine. If, as we argue below (Chapter 8), communities in this zone were united by certain common objectives, it rather diminishes the importance of isolating one side of the Channel or the other as the originator of the precious cup.

Manufacture of the carved cups

The one-piece cups of shale or amber have given rise to much discussion as to whether they were lathe turned (see Shepherd 1985 and Sloper 1989 for recent discussions of techniques of production). In-ground distortion of some cups and the need to restore others from sherds have made it impossible to be sure of precise dimensions. Usually, therefore, it is not possible to make a judgement on the basis of rotational symmetry. In all examples however, the handle has been carved out of the same block of raw material and must have started as a lug on the side of the roughed out vessel. Consequently, the late stages of shaping the exterior of the body could not have been achieved by a continuously rotational action since the handle lug would prevent rotation through 360° (a problem appreciated by Phillips as long ago as 1856).

Supporting evidence for hand-turning comes from the apparently undistorted Hove cup (no. 11; **Fig. 50**). Subtle profile variations and a variation of up to 2mm in mouth diameter are not what would be expected of proficient mechanical turning. On the other hand, this reasonable degree of symmetry, pleasing enough to the eye, would be readily achieved by careful hand cutting by an experienced craftsman (Thurnam 1871, 524).

During the early roughing out of the body a large projecting lug would have been left on one side to form the handle. As the body was nearing the desired shape, the lug could be refined. Most of the surviving handles seem to have been trimmed down so as to have a trapezoid shape in plan and a neat semi-circular or less protuberant C-shape in side view. The orthogonal intersection of these two profiles naturally gives rise to the attractive waisted shape that the handles all present in face view (as discussed above). In the case of the ?Wiltshire 1 vessel (no. 12; **Fig. 51**), the handle is of the same basic form, but the plan view is modified so that the sides of the trapeze are gently concave rather than straight.

After shaping the outer surface of the handle, its perforation could be tackled. Obviously the greater restriction on tool angles could lead to a cruder finish inside the handle, while the fact that it was less visible might also have encouraged a less fine finish being applied. Theoretically, the interior profile of the body itself could have been turned full circle on a pole lathe with a centering device, ie a pivot-hole, on the inside. Since there is no sign of any such hole in the bases of the cups, the last part of the interior would have to have been removed manually; evidence for toolmarks has been noted inside the Hove cup (no. 11). Whatever technique was used for hollowing out the interior of the vessel, this would have best been done secondarily, once the desired external profiles had been attained.

Relationships to local pottery

The point has already been made that one of the unifying characteristics of the precious cups is their inability to stand on a surface unaided. The peculiarity of this feature is highlighted by the fact that contemporary ceramic vessels from the regions concerned always have flat bases that allow them to stand freely. Nevertheless, some thought still needs to be given to potential relationships with indigenous pottery in the relevant regions.

Handles, although never standard attachments on British vessels of this age, occur repeatedly on a wide variety of forms (Manby 2004). They are certainly occasionally found as early as Beaker period 2 (c. 2250–1950 BC), that is preceding the appearance of the handled precious cups. The Dunnichen Beaker bowl, Angus (Coutts 1971, 46 no. 83, 49; Manby 2004, fig. 79.2) is associated with a flat riveted bronze dagger of this period; few other bowls are known with handles and their restricted distribution has led to the nomenclature *Dorset bowls* (Clarke 1970, nos 1028, 1033, 1035; Manby 2004, 216 fig. 72).

A complete form contrast is provided by the collared vessel from the secondary grave at Gravelly Guy, Oxfordshire (Cleal 2004), associated with a radiocarbon date calibrated to 2150–1920 BC (2-sigma). This is classified as a Beaker and joins some 15 other handled Beakers in having more or less pronounced 'collars' formed by wall thickening, under-rim cordon, or in-turned mouth (Clarke 1970, 412, 415–6). The decorative designs on at least some of these would place them in the same period, but others are probably a little later. This series merges into handled Beakers which are of tankard form (Clarke 1970, 413–4).

Food Vessels too can occasionally have loop handles, as distinct from the frequently perforated lugs on Yorkshire Vases (Manby 2004). The vessels in question vary in form and decorative design, although cord impression is the dominant technique, as found more generally in this potting tradition.

Manby agrees with Clarke that the application of handles on Food Vessels probably copied handled Beakers and that these in turn were imitating wooden prototypes (Manby 2004, 231, 234).

One handled vessel, classified alternatively as a Beaker or a Food Vessel, must be singled out for detailed treatment – that from Balmuick, Perthshire (eg Clarke *et al.* 1985, 116–8 fig. 4.49, 282–3). Its profile of continuous horizontal grooves with intervening ribs has frequently been compared with the Rillaton cup in particular and other precious cups in general. The comparison does not stand up to scrutiny (Manby 2004, 236) especially now that it is established that Rillaton had no flat base whereas Balmuick has a broad flat one. In the absence of the corrugated gold cups, Balmuick would not have attracted undue attention and certainly would not have evoked metal prototypes. The handle is decorated throughout with horizontal impressed grooves quite unlike the designs on the precious cup handles. The body is otherwise unremarkable – a mid-carinated Beaker form with a typical under-rim cordon and All-Over ornamentation. The execution of the latter makes no attempt to simulate the undulating topography of the corrugated cups.

Strap, or ribbon handles are proportionally much better represented on the Trevisker Urns of the south-west than any other Early Bronze Age pottery (Patchett 1944; 1950). Again, some of these are more like perforated lugs. In addition to the three handled Beaker bowls from Dorset, the far south of Britain has also yielded at least three more individual vessels of relatively small size (**Fig. 31**). The first is a cup from Denzell Downs, Cornwall, associated with a cremation burial (**Fig. 31a**); it is about 94mm high with a simple flared profile rising from a rounded foot (Abercromby 1912, 92, pl. 22 no. 301; Patchett 1944, 27 fig. 5; 1950, fig. I). Patchett (1944, 26–7) likened its stabbed decoration within lozenge frames to that of Aldbourne cups; while there may indeed be a relationship, the cup is not of Aldbourne type and is currently unique.

The second is from an inhumation grave at Collingbourne Ducis G16, Wiltshire (**Fig. 31b**), and has a profile not dissimilar from the Denzell Down example, but is undecorated and has a more obvious flat base with a vestigial carination above mid-height (Annable and Simpson 1964, 63 no. 499, 117 fig. 499). It is also of similar size, 90mm high, but the handle is smaller, being confined to the upper body. Both of these cups are squat relative to most of the precious cups, but it is possible that they do represent a ceramic response to them, particularly the late Hove and Stoborough versions.

The third example is more distinctive still; it is from Gallibury Down, Isle of Wight (**Fig. 31c**), associated with two enlarged Food Vessels containing a cremation (Tomalin 1988, 219) and now three separate radiocarbon dates – one on charcoal and two on cremated bone (Needham forthcoming). The handled Gallibury vessel is a very globular jar 135mm tall. The handle was broken off in antiquity, but the vessel was kept in use (Tomalin 1988, 208–9). It is of a high-quality ware with a reddish slip and in some respects this too might be regarded as a 'precious cup'. The radiocarbon dating (2050–1900 BC) suggests it was deposited late in Beaker period 2 and thus precedes the group under discussion. The decoration is simple and of widely used motifs, so, given chronological antecedence, one should not press comparisons too far. This vessel comes, like all the British precious cups, from south coastal strip of England, but it differs from them in having a stable flat base.

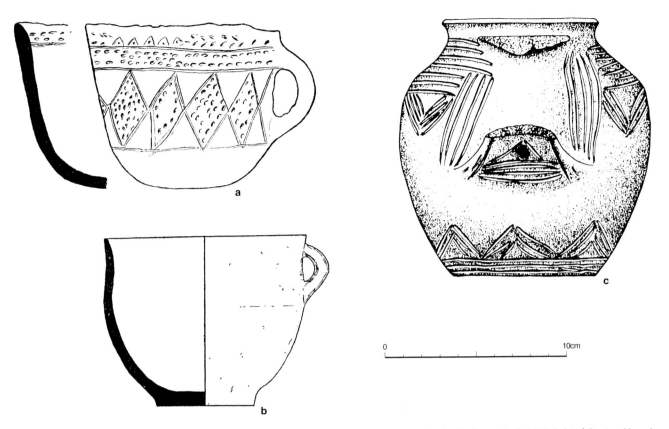

Figure 31 Small ceramic vessels with handles from Britain: a) Denzell Downs, Cornwall (after Patchett 1950); b) Collingbourne Ducis G16, Wiltshire (after Annable and Simpson 1964); c) Gallibury Down grave H, Isle of Wight (after Tomalin 1988). Scale 50%

Tomalin recognised that the Gallibury vessel reflects a ceramic tradition alien to the region, and found the best comparisons in the Armorican *Vases à Anse* series. But he also appreciated that it did not entirely conform to that series and concluded that it may have been manufactured in the Channel Islands, rather than on the Armorican peninsula. At the very least on current evidence we can say that the Gallibury vessel is individual and that it relates to a trans-Channel style, further points that may herald the ensuing precious cup series.

The high frequency of handled pottery in the Armorican Early Bronze Age is well known. Briard believed that the addition of handles was due to central European influence (1984, 118). This would give a more general background to the specific links between those two regions noted above and could offer a context for the parallel adoption of the handled biconical cup form. Unfortunately, there is little useful dating evidence for the origins of the *Vases à Anse* (Briard 1984, 113 ff, 192; Needham 2000b, 152, 165–7), but the Gallibury dates would point to an early evolution of the style, by the beginning of the 2nd millennium BC.

The profiles of the Armorican *Vases à Anse* are typically carinated, but unlike the precious cups, the carination tends to be placed high and is often strong, leading to a sharply contracted mouth. They do not therefore, even vaguely, look like enlarged versions of the cups. Conceivably more relevant are occasional pots with a single handle and moderate carination at around mid-height, as at Hellen à Cléder and Juno Bella à Berrien (Briard 1984, 117 fig. 67.1, 123 fig. 72.1) and again much further east at Etaples, Pas-de-Calais (Blanchet 1984, 131 fig. 56.1). Without chronological information it is hard to speculate on their precise relationship to the Armorican precious cups, let alone the wider group.

It remains to consider the handle-less small ceramic vessels

which are broadly contemporary. These are the 'incense cups' or 'pygmy cups' frequently found as accessory vessels in British graves. There is much variation in form, not yet fully explored by any modern classification (Abercromby 1912). Such vessels are characterised above all by small capacities and relatively squat bodies. They frequently occur in a grave in association with a larger pot, most usually a cremation urn and this context suggests they could have played a regular part in the rituals attending the funeral. The accompanying pot is most often, but by no means universally, a Collared Urn. That they are not simply domestic drinking cups is clear from the fact that many have perforations or slits in their walls.

Incense cups probably appeared at about the same time as the cremation urns they accompany, towards the end of the 3rd millennium BC, and they then continue to the end of the Early Bronze Age making them broadly coeval with the precious cups. Incense cups are found the length and breadth of the country, a point which only goes to highlight the restricted distribution of the precious cups. They are not, however, exclusive of one another; indeed one type – the slotted incense cup – may be a complementary part of the cultural system employing the precious cups.

Slotted incense cups are sometimes thought of as a 'Wessex' type, but in geographical terms this is not the case (**Fig. 32**; Ashbee 1967, 31). Taking together Longworth's groups B and E (1983), characterised by rectangular to narrow linear slots, only two come from the Wessex heartland with another two from south Dorset (**Fig. 33**). In addition, a related cup with broad oval perforations comes from Great Shefford, Berkshire (**Fig. 33.13**); it has the cord decoration found on virtually all of the slotted group. This is a thin distribution given the over-representation of excavated graves in the region. In reality these cups show essentially a south coast distribution, with one in the Upper

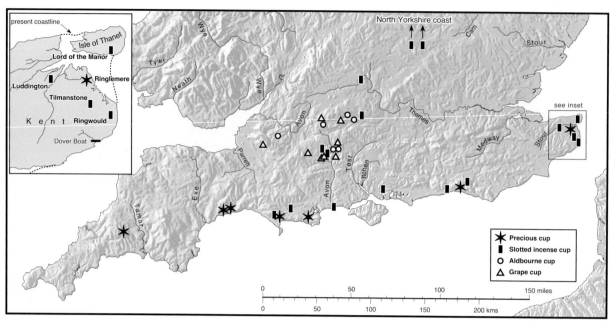

Figure 32 Map of recovery for precious cups in southern Britain in relation to incense cups of selected types – slotted, grape and Aldbourne

Thames valley and two near the coast of North Yorkshire, one of which is in any case a hybrid (**Fig. 33.14;** Longworth 1983, 67, 69 fig. 20).

As many as four slotted cups occur in east Kent (Parfitt and Champion 2004, 270), the strongest cluster anywhere; Ringlemere lies amidst them (**Figs 32 & 33.1–4**). Two examples come from central Sussex, close to Hove, and one is from Portsdown, overlooking Portsmouth Harbour and the Solent. The next following westward is from Hengistbury Head, a grave group that we shall see is pivotal in the passage of amber from the east into Wessex and, furthermore, has express links with one central Wessex grave group containing such a slotted cup – Wilsford G8. Finally along the south coast are examples from Burleston, east Dorset, lying between the Clandon and Stoborough precious cup finds, and one from the Clandon barrow itself (Cowie in Clarke *et al.* 1985, 274–5; Ann Woodward – pers. comm.). Precious cup and slotted incense cup were not, however, together at Clandon; while the incense cup was found deliberately broken and scattered under an internal flint cairn, the amber cup was one of the objects distributed on top of that cairn (**Fig. 34**); they clearly belonged to separate depositional

events (Drew and Piggott 1936, 19, pl. I).

A cultural distinction between a south coast zone and inland Wessex is further emphasised by consideration of two highly specialised incense cup forms – grape cups and Aldbourne cups (**Fig. 32**). These have a distribution confined to Wiltshire and immediately adjoining areas (Abercromby 1912, 25–7, types 1 and 2), which includes the more recent find from Charnham Lane, Berkshire (Ford 1991).

In distributional terms, then, it can be seen that there are strong links between slotted cups and the precious cups. They may belong to different aspects of a single ritual system prevailing in the southern coastal areas. The Wessex heartland features instead the other specialised incense cup forms discussed and as yet there is no secure evidence that it took in precious cups and their attendant rituals. The function of the incense cups is far from settled (Gibson 2004), although Woodward concludes that 'the cups seem to have been designed specifically for the controlled burning of substances'(2000, 114; see also Parker Pearson 2003, 20). One thing is certain; unlike the precious cups, most incense cups are ill-suited to holding liquid.

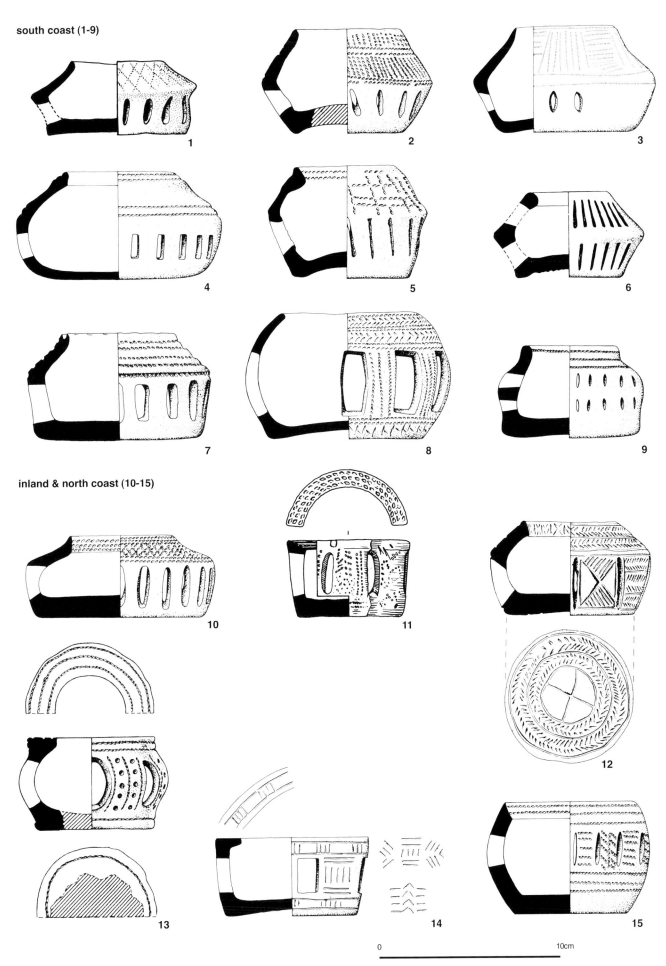

south coast (1-9)

inland & north coast (10-15)

0   10cm

Figure 33 Slotted incense cups (after Longworth 1983; Perkins 1980, and Green and Rollo-Smith 1984): 1) Lord of the Manor, Kent; 2) Luddington Wood, Kent; 3) Ringwould, Kent; 4) Tilmanstone, Kent; 5) Clayton Hill, Sussex; 6) Lancing, Sussex; 7) Portsdown, Hampshire; 8) Hengistbury Head, Hampshire; 9) Burleston 3A, Dorset; 10) Wilsford G8, Wiltshire; 11) Shrewton 5c, Wiltshire; 12) Stanton Harcourt, Oxfordshire; 13) Great Shefford, Berkshire; 14) near West Ayton Moor, North Yorkshire; 15) Comboots, Scalby, North Yorkshire. Scale 50%

Chapter 7: Precious Cups: Concept, Context and Custodianship

Stuart Needham

Diversity as a diagnostic property

It should be clear from the inter-comparisons made above that there is no homogeneous class of precious cup in north-west Europe. Despite the recurrence of a number of features, no one feature is ubiquitous and they can occur in different combinations (**Table 5**). There may be a case for greater internal homogeneity among the shale cups, but only if we exclude the lost Stoborough vessel (no. 16). Otherwise, variability is certainly found within each material sub-group. The two silver cups are, insofar as their fragmentary condition allows to be known, of different form and different construction. The two amber vessels are also of very distinct forms and, while their respective proportions might have been strongly conditioned by the shape of the raw material block available (large blocks of amber would be hard to come by in southern England), this does not account for significant stylistic differences which could have been mitigated if so desired.

The same is true for the gold cups; despite the similarity of the handles and rivet-washers on three of them, body forms are all individual. Even the superficial similarity between the Ringlemere and Rillaton cups dissolves under more careful scrutiny in terms both of manufacture and the final form achieved. Ringlemere's accentuated shoulder and well-flared mouth contrast with the more graceful profile of Rillaton (no. 2); the corrugations are executed in a quite different manner, and they have different overall proportions, capacities and metal thickness. A further point of difference is extremely revealing in relation to craftsmanship. Whereas the Ringlemere and Fritzdorf (no. 3) handles have both tab ends tucked inwards, making the second stage of fixing rather tricky, on the Rillaton vessel an easier option was chosen for the upper, presumably second-attached handle tab. This technologically significant difference has only come to light with the discovery by Jane Marchand of the 1837 watercolour sketch of the Rillaton cup (cat. entry no. 2).

The eclecticism seen in detailed attributes could in part stem from the smallness of the sample recovered. Supposing on this hypothesis that precious cups were actually far more common in circulation than is currently apparent from the archaeological record, then any standardisation of sub-groups within the whole population may be yet to reveal itself. Even so, we cannot avoid the conclusion that the extant cups are not the products of regularised workmanship closely replicating an ideal pattern. Instead of slavish imitation, each seems to have its own individual qualities; indeed the range of properties can be extended by those intrinsic to the material, as yet not discussed (see for example Thurnam 1871, 517–24): warmth or coolness of feel, lustre, light reflection or transmission, electrostatics, feel of the rim to the lips – aspects which would affect the feel of the object and the ways it could be projected as something very different and special relative to contemporary material culture and, moreover, unique even among its peer group.

Lack of standardisation is important to our appreciation of both the dissemination process and the centralisation or dispersion of production. The general idea inherent in these precious cups, and perhaps also in their usage, appears to have been transmitted over a sizeable area, but not as a result of distribution from a restricted production zone, nor as the wholesale transmission of very particular technical skills and stylistic requirements. It would seem likely then that the really important attributes were not precise form and material, but instead a combination of the generic form, the fact that the material was exotic, the quality and individuality of the craftsmanship. In the social context of the Early Bronze Age it is rather unlikely that the convergence of these attributes in a single class of object occurred simply as a result of aesthetic whim, and much more probable that what bound them together was a widely accepted notion of what social role the cups performed.

The context of use

It will have become very apparent that even the flat-based cups, just five examples, were not well suited to standing on a flat surface unaided. This would be especially the case when full of liquid. Indeed on two of these five the 'flat' base is actually slightly convex. The round based varieties would have required a receptacle in order to remain upright. It is possible to invoke specially cut hollows in tables or alternatively, special stands in which to set the vessel. If such stands existed, they must have been of organic materials. They too would have been special equipment tied specifically to the precious cup, given that contemporary ceramics in north-west Europe were flat based. However, no annular wear traces were observed on lower bodies to support the idea of regular rubbing against a stand.

Rather than suppose that we are missing a vital component due to its non-survival archaeologically, it might be worth exploring an alternative proposition – that the cups were never intended to stand on a surface at the critical stage of use. For example, a pattern of use that involved periodic but brief service for the enactment of certain rites fits better with our understanding of the ritual nature of Early Bronze Age society than does the assumption that these were vessels for everyday use by high-status individuals.

The association of some cups with an individual of eminence in a grave could be ambiguous in this regard. The temptation may be to follow traditional interpretation which relates quality, quantity and rarity of grave goods as reflections of the relative 'wealth' and thus status of the interred. Subsequent interpretations have begun to weaken this dogma, by introducing debate on the role of the mourners, the need to effect appropriate transfer of authority after the death of a leader, and the need to reference ancestral claims, which was

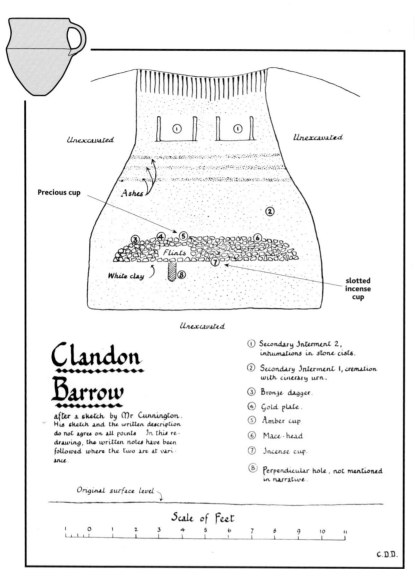

Figure 34 Section of the Clandon barrow, Dorset (after Drew and Piggott 1936)

Unexcavated

Unexcavated

Precious cup

Ashes

slotted
incense
cup

Flints

White clay

Unexcavated

Clandon

Barrow

after a sketch by Mr Cunnington.
His sketch and the written description
do not agree on all points In this re-
drawing, the written notes have been
followed where the two are at vari-
ance.

① Secondary Interment 2,
 inhumations in stone cists.
② Secondary Interment 1, cremation
 with cinerary urn.
③ Bronze dagger.
④ Gold plate.
⑤ Amber cup.
⑥ Mace-head.
⑦ Incense cup.
⑧ Perpendicular hole, not mentioned
 in narrative.

Original surface level

Scale of Feet

0 1 2 3 4 5 6 7 8 9 10 11

C.D.D.

achieved in various ways (eg Barrett 1988; Woodward 2000). The fact that important personages occasionally had a precious cup placed with them (at Saint-Fiacre (no. 9), Saint-Adrien (no. 8), Rillaton (no. 2), Farway 1 (no. 14), Stoborough (no. 16), Hove (no. 11) and perhaps originally others) could above all signify that these were the members of society that held the necessary spiritual authority to have custody of the vessels and put them to use. It is intriguing that in three cases the association with a deceased person is ambiguous or 'detached': the cup was a little removed from the interment at Farway 2 (no. 15); fine 'grave goods' were apparently scattered across the inner cairn at Clandon (no. 10) without obvious skeletal remains (**Fig. 34**); the Gölenkamp cup (no. 4) was in a mound but may not have accompanied a burial; and finally, it is ▓▓▓▓▓ certain that there was a grave group as such at Ringlemere either. Indeed, if anything, the deposition of the amber pendant and, probably, the gold cup in the top of the turf mound recalls the stratigraphic position of the Clandon finery.

Whatever their final context of deposition, it seems that some of these cups at least had a prior use-life; they were not made especially for the grave. Wear traces can be very fickle, especially on materials that have deteriorated, but something was noted on four of the carefully inspected vessels (details in the catalogue). The Farway 1 (no. 14) and ?Wiltshire 1 (no. 12) shale cups show traces of wear under the top curve of the handle, these are suggestive of long-term suspension from a

thong. A little wear has been deduced for Ringlemere – it would seem that repeated cleaning/polishing has led to the more exposed angles around rim and rivet washers becoming rounded. Some sets of striations on the body, although not obtrusive, also seem to result from coarser abrasion than the finishing. In the case of the Rillaton cup (no. 2), little certainty can be ventured because of treatment post-discovery; however, it does seem likely that the inner upper rivet emplacements had suffered wear before deposition and if this is a valid deduction it would imply wear of the interior and the rim more generally.

It seems likely that for most of their use-life the cups were simply in store or on display. Since it is not certain that the sheet metal handles would have been strong enough to support the vessel when full of liquid, the handle's main purpose may have been to suspend them by thong from a belt or from a beam or hook in a building. Alternatively, they could be stood on their rim, a clear signal that they were currently 'not in service'. Suspension about the person brings to mind somewhat parallel small vessels from Scandinavia. Just two bronze 'boxes' are known from this period (Scandinavian Late Neolithic B) and, distinct though they are in design and perhaps function (Vandkilde 1988), they do share with the north-western series several common characteristics: small capacity, instability, the use of a material exotic to the region, high craftsmanship and individuality in design (location shown in Fig. 28).

If the ▓▓▓▓▓ contexts of deposition a▓▓▓▓▓ sites are

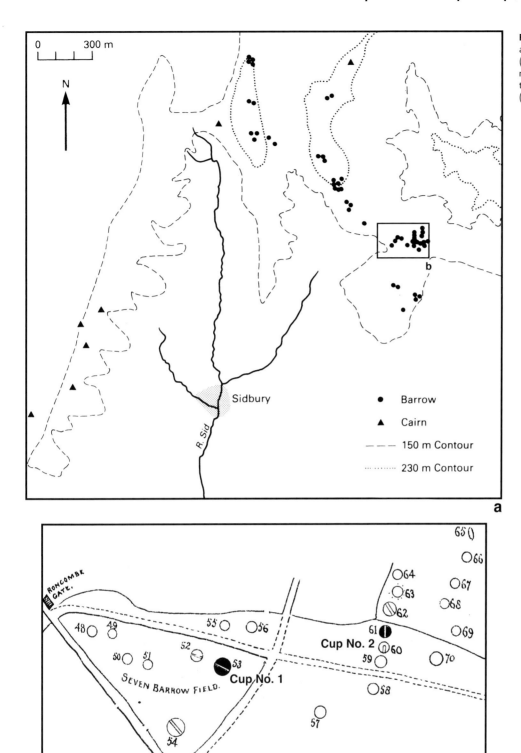

Figure 35 Barrows and cairns around the head of the Sid valley (after Todd 1987), and the nucleated group which yielded the two Farway shale cups, nos 14–15 (after Hutchinson 1880)

significant (see also Needham 1988a; Needham 2001), this could suggest that the cups had an active role at burial sites beyond simply their interment with a deceased person. It seems eminently plausible that one of their main uses involved funerary rites at the ritual complexes prior to the interment of the dead. We might also conjecture their use in ancestor rites where no specific act of burial was taking place. Ringlemere could well be pertinent here, the cup coming from within a sizable monument in which the scale of the enclosing ditch with

its northerly entrance may have been as important as the height of the mound, or more so. Indeed, this monument seems to be the focal point of a fairly large monument complex (**Fig. 3**), one of the largest yet known from Kent, and which invites comparison with the familiar agglomerated 'cemeteries' of Wessex and some other regions.

Likewise at Farway Down, the two cups (nos 14 & 15) come from a large spread of barrows which includes some tighter clusters (**Fig. 35**; Hutchinson 1880, fig. opp. 124). Cup no. 1 was from one of the largest mounds locally, almost 30m across and 2.5m high; several mounds spread away from it mainly westwards. The mound of cup no. 2 did not seem to stand out in terms of size, but it lies in the middle of a tight linear arrangement of seven barrows aligned roughly north-south; a similar row of six runs parallel to the east. Nevertheless, it is significant that these cups come from a remarkable concentration of barrows and cairns on the plateaux and ridges around the head of the small Sid valley at Sidbury. The mounds include a wide variety of structural forms and Fox found much to link the complex to Wessex (Fox 1948; Todd 1987, 144).

The Rillaton cairn, on the east side of Bodmin Moor, is more isolated with just a single second cairn adjacent to it. It may not be without coincidence, however, that it lies only 500m NNE of the three closely set stone circles of The Hurlers (**Fig. 36**; Johnson and Rose 1994, 45 fig.). A similar distance in the opposite direction (NNW) is the undated enclosure complex of Stowe's Pound, at the north end of which stand two large cairns. Two more lie to the south of The Hurlers. On Craddock Moor, a kilometre and more to the west of Rillaton, a much denser distribution of prehistoric remains has been identified dominated by many hut foundations, field systems, clearance and small cairns, as well as a few larger cairns. Ann Woodward has noted that the larger cairns in this landscape are preferentially distributed between the settlements and Stowe's Pound and tend to occupy prominent positions (2000, 60).

The Clandon barrow would appear to be even more isolated than Rillaton at first sight; there is no rich monument complex in evidence immediately around it (Grinsell 1959, 152 Winterborne St Martin 31). It is not situated on the highest ground locally, but nevertheless occupies a prominent knoll which gave it great inter-visibility with a number of key sites and landmarks in the region (Woodward and Woodward 1996, 278). Indeed, the substantial height of this mound, as well as that of the Lanceborough barrow not far to the east, significantly enhanced view-sheds and the two may have been connected together in a system deliberately exploiting explicit oversight of a domain (Woodward 2000, 142). Ann Woodward sees the ash layers recorded by Cunnington in the upper mound at Clandon (**Fig. 34**) as being the residues of bonfires lit to reinforce the position of dominance (ibid, 140).

If we are right to deduce that the cups were not used with a stand and, equally, to assume that they were for holding a liquid, then it intriguingly constrains their mode of use. The cup would need to remain in the hand while it still contained liquid. Two main alternatives present themselves, one based on the liquid being for consumption, the other that it was a libation.

If for consumption, the draught could have been 'downed in one', or if drunk more sedately over a period it was kept in hand by the master of ceremonies or passed from hand to hand among a select band of initiates. In either case, such a setting gives a strong presumption that the liquid concerned had very particular properties – narcotic or hallucinogenic (Sherratt 1991; 1995; see also Woodward 2000, 113). Just as plausible would be the use of this special vessel for libations at particular ceremonies, for example, the collecting and pouring of blood

from an animal sacrifice. Or again, was the cup in fact a dipper for the dispensing of liquid, the act of which served to endow the dispensed liquid with special favour?

A relevant feature of the Ringlemere cup and, to a lesser extent the Fritzdorf one, is the pronounced shoulder which would tend to trap the last of the liquid as it was poured out. This would have inhibited steady draining for whatever purpose, but if designed with a functional aim it could have been to retain a small portion, perhaps dregs or a draught for the gods?

Experiment by Geoff Halliwell (Dover Archaeological Group) with a full-sized replica of the Ringlemere cup has demonstrated that it serves entirely adequately as a drinking vessel. A brew of tea was used to simulate a prehistoric beverage which could have contained unwanted dregs at the bottom. When drinking, the tea leaves were largely prevented from reaching the lips by the corrugations and, more importantly, the shoulder on the vessel. With a pure liquid, around 20ml is held back by the shoulder.

Custodians of the cups

The assumption that the cups were 'owned' by a powerful person also merits further examination. The grave associations would seem to demonstrate an attachment to an individual, but this may not constitute 'ownership' in the way we understand it in the modern world. Even a sacred communal object has to fall under the responsibility of one or more guardians, or custodians (Godelier 1999).

The practice of placing objects with the dead was endemic in the Early Bronze Age and the objects were very diverse, ranging from the most basic of flint or bone tools to the real finery of the time. Choice of objects was guided by rules which allowed expression of an individual identity, regardless of whether that identity was literally representative of the person or in part a construct. Given the prevailing preoccupations of the age, it should not seem surprising that some of the precious cups ultimately came to accompany their custodians to the grave. There are various reasons why even a precious cup with a central ritual role might have been committed to the grave. It may have been deemed to have served its time among mortals and be due for service in the Otherworld. Or maybe the cup was damaged to the point that it was felt necessary to replace it with another. Alternatively, the particular custodian may have had an unusually strong association with the cup – perhaps he or she arrived with it from another community.

If we are right in inferring that the cups served a central role in certain ritual rites, it places them among the shamanistic gear that Ann Woodward has argued to be present amongst Early Bronze Age grave goods (Woodward 2000; 2002). Such equipment is vital to facilitate communication with gods and spirits, but it is essentially held in trust for the benefit of the community. Our conclusion is that the precious cup is more likely to have been connected to an individual by virtue of its highly specialised role, which entailed highly specialised knowledge, than to have been the accoutrement of a person simply because of the status he or she held. On this basis the Early Bronze Age precious cup would be more analogous to the religious chalice than to the kingly goblet.

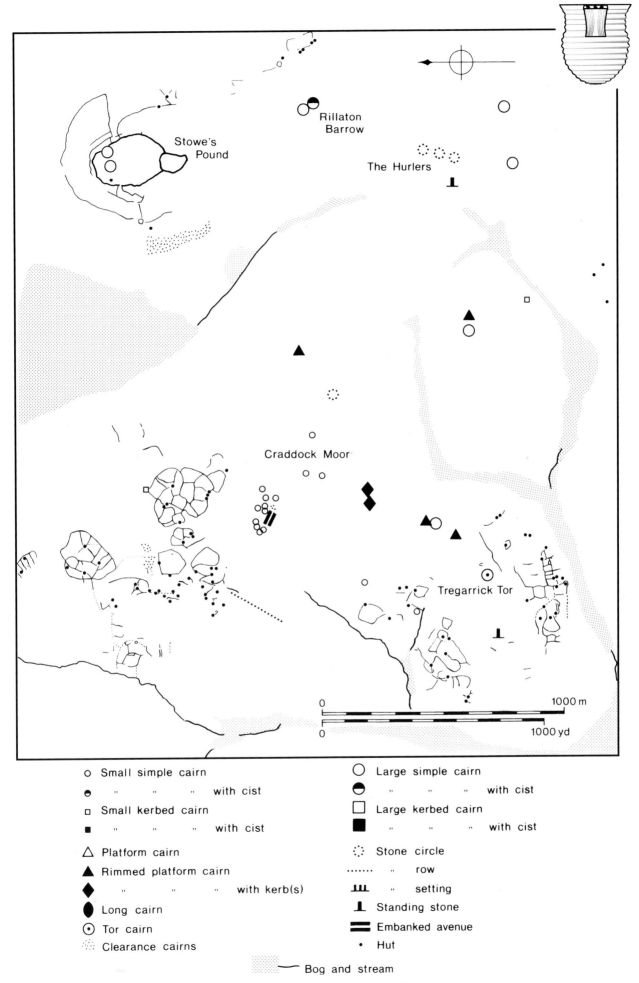

Stowe's Pound

Rillaton Barrow

The Hurlers

Craddock Moor

Tregarrick Tor

0   1000 m

0   1000 yd

○ Small simple cairn	◯ Large simple cairn
◓ " " " with cist	◖ " " " with cist
▫ Small kerbed cairn	▢ Large kerbed cairn
▪ " " " with cist	■ " " " with cist
△ Platform cairn	⬡ Stone circle
▲ Rimmed platform cairn	⋯⋯⋯ " row
◆ " " " with kerb(s)	⊔⊔ " setting
⬤ Long cairn	⟂ Standing stone
⊙ Tor cairn	▬▬ Embanked avenue
⋰ Clearance cairns	• Hut

Bog and stream

Figure 36 Monuments on Bodmin Moor in the area of the Rillaton barrow (after Johnson and Rose 1994)

Chapter 8: Networks of Contact, Exchange and Meaning; the Beginning of the Channel Bronze Age
Stuart Needham

In geographical terms alone, the Ringlemere cup is pivotal. Its location extends the string of finds along the coastal strip of southern England and, moreover, fills a 'gap' between these western finds and those across the North Sea, in or close to the Rhinelands (**Figs 28 & 32**). Such a pattern is often viewed literally, the respective finds seen to be marking out routes of trade or contact. But the end-points of the individual life histories of such treasured items as the cups are unlikely to represent straightforwardly a fall-out pattern from the primary communication routes. This is emphasised by the observations made above that the cups have individual qualities, sometimes even betraying individual craftsmanship. The cups themselves have not been exchanged over distance from limited production sites (although clearly some displacement during their use-lives is possible), instead it is the core idea associated with them that has been relatively mobile within a specific geographical sphere.

If the key unifying factor for the cups is their function, is it possible that function too was inherited from the putative ceramic prototypes? Possible, yes; but the fact that unstable handled cups were frequent in the cultures to the south and east (**Fig. 28**) makes it hard to envisage an identical function to that for our precious cups. The ceramic versions lacking flat bases (which in fact merge into those with flat bases) would be subject to similar constraints in use, and this may have been a key feature that commended the form to north-western communities: instability gave them an element of functional exclusivity. Beyond this, however, it seems more likely that in the process of transmission the specific role of the precious cups derived from specific regional needs.

What might that regional need be? It was far from ubiquitous in north-west Europe and yet recurrent in the Channel-Rhine-Frisian zone for three or more centuries. One striking feature is the close proximity of virtually all of the cups to their respective coast-lines or the Rhine and it would be easy to link them directly to exchange activity. However, I have already argued that the cups were not themselves the object of exchange, so what other link might there be? One possibility is that the specialised role envisaged above for the cups was intimately involved in servicing a specialised communication network focussing on the waterways of the Channel-Rhine-Frisian Coast axis. Propitiatory rites of some sort would almost inevitably accompany hazardous maritime travel and it may be that the cups and their particular mode of use were quickly adopted across the whole zone as a unified response to common dangers experienced by the Channel-bordering communities who were beginning to engage more in maritime contacts.

It has long been appreciated that the early part of the 2nd millennium BC was a time of growing inter-connections on a continental scale. Links between southern Britain and mainland regions such as Armorica, west central Europe and southern Scandinavia were on the increase, although not necessarily prolific in terms of exchanged goods. Recent re-evaluation of the oft-claimed close connections between southern Britain and Armorica in the early precious cups phase (Bush Barrow/Willerby) suggests that they may have been overstated; certainly whatever the nature of the contact it did not lead to any sort of cultural unity between the two regions (Needham 2000b). Small numbers of continentally made daggers and pins were brought across to Britain and several decorated British low-flanged axes were transported outwards, mainly in an easterly direction (most recently considered by O'Connor and Cowie 2001 and Jockenhövel 2004). But in most respects the cultures on either side of the Channel were still 'insular'. Much of the amber found in the west also belongs to this period, but even though the raw material must have been transported most if not all of the object production seems to have been local (Beck and Shennan 1991).

By the second phase of our cups (c. 1750–1500 BC), early Trevisker and early Deverel-Rimbury Wares, along with Arreton and early Acton metalwork, all have strong parallel traditions on the southern shores. Indeed, Trevisker Ware, although primarily a south-west English tradition, has also been found in Kent (Isle of Thanet), Pas-de-Calais and the island of Ile Tatihou off the Normandy coast (Gibson *et al.* 1997). Hilversum pottery in the Netherlands also has strong echoes of the more western ceramic traditions, particularly Biconical Urns. Of relevance in this context is the Biconical Urn from Wouldham, Kent, in a grave now radiocarbon dated to 3435 ± 40 BP and 3380 ± 50 BP on cremated bone giving a mean of 3414 ± 31 BP; 1750–1640 cal BC (1-sigma; Cruse and Harrison 1983; John Cruse pers. comm.). By this stage bronze of continental origin was coming into southern Britain on a more significant scale than hitherto (Northover 1982; Rohl and Needham 1998, 179). Precious cups and the network they reflect therefore catch the opening up of a newly constituted set of cultural relations which tied together communities in southern Britain, northern France and the Low Countries (but not further up the Rhine) to some degree for the rest of the Bronze Age.

The latter half of the Early Bronze Age is in this respect the beginning of what might be termed the *Channel Bronze Age*, populated by Clark's *people of La Manche* (Clark 2004b, 7). Parallelism in metalwork traditions on the two sides of the Channel throughout the Middle and Late Bronze Ages has been well appreciated since at least the 1960s (eg Briard 1965; Burgess 1968). Subsequently, this has found support in other material in the archaeological record, but the question as to what exactly in social and cultural terms these commonalities represent must await further discussion elsewhere.

One thing that will have become clear from the above discussion is that the Wessex core zone played relatively little part in these developments. Instead, we can suggest that it was southern areas outside the Wessex core that contrived or monopolised the special Channel-Rhine-Frisian zone relationship. This relationship has been explored to explain why the 'Wessex culture' – in the narrow and more useful definition – became ever more isolated towards the end of the Early Bronze Age (Barrett and Bradley 1980, 59–64, 85–90). In this respect, it is unhelpful to think of the precious cups as being an integral part of a Wessex-inspired grave phenomenon; instead they represent different ritual processes emanating from another sphere and only marginally impinging on Wessex-specific rites (cf. Ashbee and Dunning 1960). This emphasises that we should be cautious of assuming that the two Salisbury Museum cups were found in the Wessex heartland, until such time as documentary evidence of their provenance comes to light.

This south coast/Wessex differentiation can be more fully characterised by looking at other contemporary material. One key material is amber, which is present as fine objects in both regions and, moreover, in most regions where precious cups occur. Something must be said first on whether the immediate source of the western amber objects was southern Scandinavia or the eastern coast of Britain. Not only has the latter region been recorded historically as yielding a regular supply of amber nodules washed up on the beaches, but on occasion these could be blocks of some size (Taylor 1980, 45; Shepherd 1985, 204; Beck and Shennan 1991, 17) – perhaps even large enough for the cups? Shepherd saw no reason why both the east coast and Baltic sources could not have been exploited (1985, 210), while Beck and Shennan make the point that any Baltic-type amber objects found inland in Britain would have been of a non-local material, even if from the east coast (1991, 27). The fact that an egg-sized lump of raw amber has been found at East Coulston on the northern edge of Salisbury Plain (Thomas 2005, 217), even if contemporary with Early Bronze Age usage, does not favour one conclusion over the other; instead, it would merely go to emphasise Beck and Shennan's conclusion (1991, 63) that raw material was imported for local manufacture. This point certainly applies to the few finds from Armorica as well.

In fact, having considered patterns of amber exploitation over a wider area of Europe, Beck and Shennan (1991) concluded that most of the British Early Bronze Age amber would have come from beyond the North Sea. The lack of any concentration of worked amber along the east coast is one factor arguing against this being the primary source; Shennan's proportional analysis shows that amber is much rarer in explored East Anglian graves than in those of Wessex (Beck and Shennan 1991, 77). It seems unlikely that the material was valued less along the east coast; it would still have been a scarce resource and the Little Cressingham find in particular illustrates association with a pre-eminent individual (Clarke *et al.* 1985, 275–6). One possibility is that initial acquaintance with amber from the east coast was merely the trigger to generate an appetite for this exotic substance, particularly once there was a desire in Wessex to imitate the complex northern jet necklaces with spacer plates. Against this background one can speculate that a desire grew to venture farther afield to procure the raw material.

Shennan's thorough evaluation of British prehistoric amber highlighted that all the more complex pieces belonged to the Early Bronze Age (*post* Bell Beaker) and deduced clearly that they were crafted in the west – Britain and Armorica – rather than close to the Jutish/Baltic sources (Beck and Shennan 1991,

63). He envisaged the high-level craftsmen being attached to, or circulating among, high-ranking individuals in the areas where the rich burials occur, such as Wessex or Brittany (ibid, 64). However, he was also clear that although Wessex, and especially Wiltshire, have yielded most of the amber-associated burials, the region is not pre-eminent in respect to quantities of amber per grave. Nor does it have a disproportionate representation of 'special types' – defined as spacer-plates, fancy pendants, pommels and cups (ibid, 80-1). Some graves rich in amber lie outside Wessex. A revised distribution of amber finds dating specifically to the first half of the 2nd millennium BC is shown in **Figure 37**.

There is no evident fall-off in the distribution of amber away from the south coast and yet neither is there a single prime centre for amber finds. Instead, Shennan observes that the distribution is patchy with a number of concentrations, some clearly relating to established ritual centres. In fact only three or four graves in Wessex contain enough beads along with a set of spacer plates to have formed a spacer-plate crescentic necklace (Woodward 2002, 1043–4); the usually smaller quantities of amber beads in grave groups may sometimes have been residual portions of necklaces which had circulated and suffered losses or been split up over a long period of time. In relation to the presumed zone of entry along the south coast, Shennan ventured that Hengistbury Head, whence comes a Wessex I grave group with, *inter alia*, a slotted incense cup, was 'a point where exotic items such as amber were introduced' (ibid, 84–5).

Most innovative, however, was Shennan's assessment of the raison d'être for the 'trade' in amber, drawing upon Helms' ideas on the potential cosmological references made by the material. Helms had previously pointed out that amber can easily be seen in the perspective of elite acquisition of esoteric knowledge – 'indeed the temptation to do so is virtually irresistible given the strange properties of the material and the unusual nature of its source in the sea' (Helms 1988, 129). This latter 'property' of amber may have seemed to the mariners of our maritime exchange network to be an especially pertinent connection.

Despite his extremely well-balanced evaluation for the most part, Shennan's conclusion placed too much emphasis on the Wessex-specific associations for Early Bronze Age amber. It is true that Wessex was able to procure a good share of amber due to its prominent spiritual legacy (**Fig. 37**; Beck and Shennan 1991, 72 fig. 6.1), but the control exercised by the southern coastal communities allowed them to monopolise at least some of the prize blocks of amber, especially those suitable for carving out a cup. Indeed, when larger blocks were available, careful working might create primary off-cuts of sufficient size to manufacture small objects, notably beads. The Hammeldon amber pommel and the two amber bracer-ornaments from Armorican tombs would also have each required a modest sized block. It is, moreover, the cups and pommels that Shepherd sees as requiring the 'most exacting and lengthy process' in their manufacture (1985, 212).

In considering relative densities of finds, we should never overlook the incontrovertible over-representation of Wessex distributions due to historical factors. The fact that amber has turned up at Ringlemere, just the second find of Early Bronze Age amber from Kent, may be telling in this regard. It is also of interest that northern France, a zone incredibly poor in excavated Early Bronze Age burials, has yielded a large domed

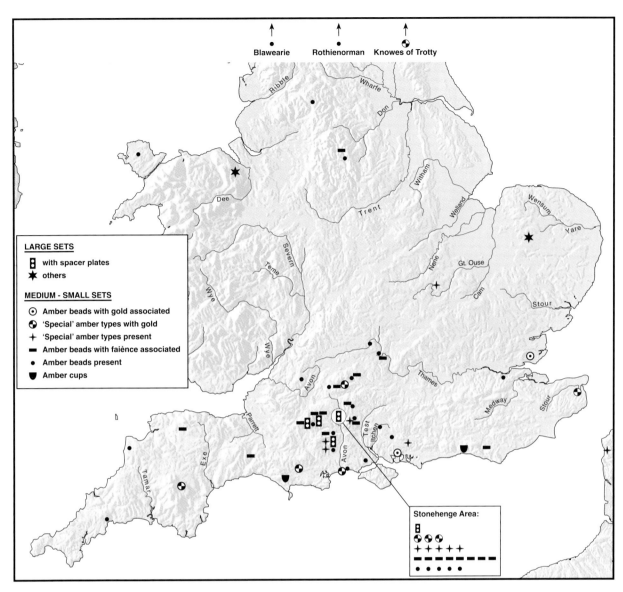

Figure 37 Map of recovery for amber finds dating to the mature Early Bronze Age, *c.* 1950–1500 BC (data from Beck and Shennan 1991, with additions and modifications).

button of amber, from Wimereux, Pas-de-Calais, just across the Straits of Dover (**Fig. 37**); Blanchet was unsure whether it was of Beaker date or full Early Bronze Age (Blanchet 1984, 95 fig. 42), but the latter seems more likely on the British parallels.

Looking eastwards along our maritime axis, it transpires that there is also a remarkable concentration of Bronze Age amber finds in the south-east of Drenthe province, Holland (around Emmen) – a combination of necklaces (including beads of other materials) found in graves and bog hoards (Butler 1990, 48). This cluster lies just 25km away from the Gölenkamp cup's findspot (no. 4) in the Spöllberg domain of Germany, which juts into Holland in this stretch of the border.

Although the possible date range suggested by Butler for these amber finds is broad, *c.* 19th–12th centuries BC, it spans the date of the cup. The find dated earliest in the sequence is the famous necklace from Exloërmond, which includes a mixture of amber, faience, tin and bronze beads and pendants. Two of the amber ornaments are trapezoid pendants with just rare parallels: eight in the Kernonen grave already discussed in relation to the Ringlemere pendant, one from Wilsford G7 and a surface find from Holland (Butler 1990, 54).

There are also two important contemporary finds to the south-west of Spöllberg, again just across the Dutch border. One

is a grave group with amber beads, bronze wire ornaments and a bronze cone (?button cover), the other a probable warrior's grave of the Sögel/Wohlde phase (*c.* 1700–1500 BC; Butler 1990, 76–8 no. 13, 84–6 no. 15). The striking absence of relevant finds in the Spöllberg itself must surely have something to do with poor recovery rates on the German side of the border.

The implications of the Drenthe amber cluster is that the region was able to procure amber objects over a longish passage of time (though perhaps less than seven centuries) and, moreover, that there was continuity in given practices of necklace deposition. The source of the amber may not have been far distant, since it can be collected on the Frisian coast to the north and even inland in glacial moraine deposits (Butler 1990, 52; Brongers and Woltering 1978, 104–7). We should not therefore presuppose that amber would be regarded as exotic and valuable as it evidently was further west. Nevertheless, it is hard to resist the conclusion that amber consumption and use of precious cups were again connected in this small zone straddling the Dutch/German border and that this community shared some of the key values evident among the Channel coast communities even though it was not coastal.

Amongst other materials relevant to our Channel-Rhine-Frisian network are the decorated tin-bronze axes of British/

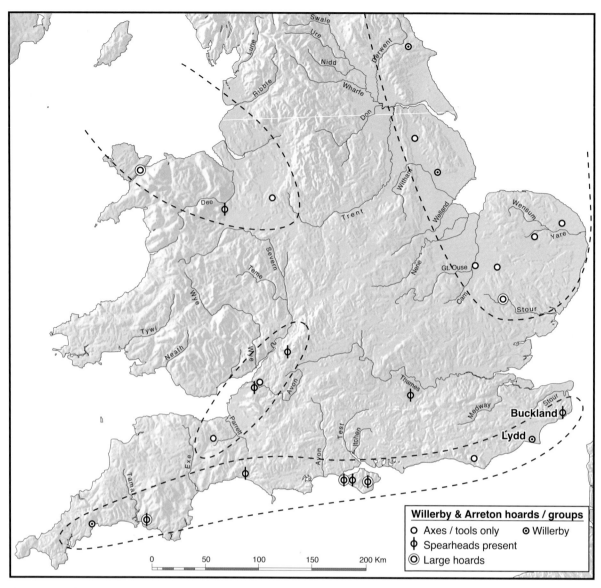

Figure 38 Map of recovery for hoards and other possible associations of Willerby and Arreton stage metalwork in southern Britain, c. 1950–1550 BC. Regional groups are suggested by the dashed outlines.

Irish origin so well known from southern Scandinavia and northern central Europe (Megaw and Hardy 1938; Butler 1963). The probable hoard of five from the coast at Lydd, Kent (**Fig. 38**), implies that sufficient were in circulation in the far south by the Willerby stage to allow the permanent deposition of 'surplus', a situation which would certainly lend itself to their distribution to the lands beyond the sea (Needham 1988b). The tin content and frequently also the patterns of decoration of British axes would have made them unusual if not mysterious and the deposition of one in the large Dieskau 2 hoard in Saxo-Thuringia (von Brunn 1959) perhaps testifies to the high regard in which it was held.

The occurrence of multiple-axe deposits of Willerby stage in near-coastal locations (Willerby, Trenovissick, Lydd) gives a foretaste of the distribution of the more numerous Arreton stage hoards (**Fig.38**). Of interest to us among three or four regional groups is that spread along the south coast; no fewer than seven hoards between Devon and Kent, that from Buckland, Dover, lying just 15km south of Ringlemere. Five more hoards occur south of the Thames-Severn line, four of them lying little inland from the Severn estuary. Looking at the types present in these hoards – now no longer simply axes – there proves to be another

highly significant connection eastwards along our maritime network. Nine of 12 of these southern hoards contain one or more bronze spearheads, a totally new type in the British metalwork repertoire. By constrast, of nine hoards in north Wales and its Marches and in eastern England, only one contains a spearhead (Ebnal). The inclusion of spearheads in most of the southern deposits is not a reflection of the introduction of the type *per se*, for single finds also occur further north. The real significance of this pattern seen in the associations probably lies more in the regional adoption of a custom of hoard deposition which involved spearheads for the first time, perhaps following continental precedents. This would appear to be another direct outcome of the Channel-Rhine-Frisian sphere of interaction.

Unalloyed tin may well also have played a part of these exchanges, but we need to be careful not to overstate its role. Undoubtedly some tin passed east to the Continent; it was used purely ornamentally as studding on the Bargeroosterveld knife pommel and for the tubular segmented beads in the Exloërmond necklace (Clarke *et al.* 1985, 148 fig. 4.82, 313; Sheridan and Shortland 2004, 267, ill. 21.32). If some tin was also supplied for addition to central European copper, there is no sign of a significant impact before Reinecke A2 (Pare 2000, 18–20) and at this stage it is most likely that the massive amount of tin required to convert the prodigious central European copper production into bronze was largely based on sources within the region. The true role of western tin and the alloyed bronze objects it made possible may thus have been to stimulate an interest in alloying further east.

Looking further at reverse flows, east to west, it is probable that early in the period concerned here, around the 19th century BC, faience was introduced to Britain from central Europe (Sheridan 2004, 265–6). While it is not yet clear if more than occasional British finds are actual imports, it is now established from typology and composition that the majority must be of indigenous production, so the key transfer was one of specialist technological knowledge rather than manufactured objects. Locally, it is significant that four faience beads accompanied a cremation burial under a barrow at Ringwould overlooking the Channel between Dover and Deal (Woodruff 1874, 24; Grinsell 1992, Ringwould-with-Kingsdown 1). The same burial contained an incense cup of the highly pertinent slotted type discussed above (**Fig. 33.3**).

Other influences seen in the west drew on the far east of the Channel-Rhine-Frisian axis. Although no Aunjetitz axes as such have been found in Britain, a number of Arreton flanged axes show distinct aspects of style which are best seen as derived from them (Needham 1979, 278–80). The best examples come from coastal areas or not far inland: Ramsgate, on the Isle of Thanet in Kent; Plymstock, Devon; Abbeville, Somme (**Fig. 39**). A second, squat style of axe within the Arreton repertoire has been linked to axes in north-west Germany (ibid, 275–6; see also Kibbert 1980, type Oldendorf). Without the privileged axis of connections under discussion the geographical distance between the Arreton and Aunjetitz-Baltic spheres would make explanation of these similarities difficult. But yet other, more specific links drive home the reality of a connection along this east-west axis.

One is the Aunjetitz-inspired ribbed armlet from a grave at Shorncote, Gloucestershire (Needham 2000c, 37; Barclay and Glass 1995), but more intriguing are the halberd pendants found in three southern English graves. These are miniaturised imitations of the magnificent metal-shafted halberds of the northern Aunjetitz zone (Piggott 1973; Needham 2000a, 51; Wüstemann 1995) and can have no practical significance other than proclaiming some distant link. They must again be locally manufactured, but represent an alien type and incorporate materials drawn from afar, including amber from the same direction. One of the halberd pendants is from a grave on the coast at Hengistbury Head, Hampshire; the other two from close to Stonehenge. These have been interpreted as prime examples of cosmologically-driven acquisition of materials and 'knowledge' (Needham 2000a, 51; 2000b, 187), but could they also have a more immediate significance? The graves contain a rich array of fine ornamental gear and are thought to be those of women. It may not be inconceivable that these were elite marriage partners drawn from the far east for whom the halberd pendants were a symbol of their homelands. One of the individuals (Wilsford G8) was also accompanied by a torc pendant, thought to be imitating the abundant copper ingot-torcs of central Europe.

These particular grave groups raise another highly significant connection in relation to Ringlemere. Among the finery in the Manton Preshute grave is also one of the two amber pommels which most closely parallel that from Ringlemere. Both this grave and that from Wilsford G8 contain the gold-bound amber discs that relate to the Ringlemere pendant fragment (Annable and Simpson 1964, 100-1 figs). These important cross-linking finds illustrate that although there are very significant differences between the communities of the Wessex heartland and the coastal zone, they were nevertheless engaged in a socio-economic relationship which was probably of a symbiotic nature.

There is no need to say much about the mechanics of our network here. With the very recent full publications relating to the Dover Bronze Age boat (Clark (ed) 2004a, 2004b), there is a wealth of detail about the practicalities of early sea-faring and the capabilities of the sewn-plank boats that continue to appear in the British Bronze and Early Iron Age. For our purposes, suffice it to say that much opinion is in favour of vessels such as those at Dover and Ferriby being fit for sea-going travel in the clement conditions that early mariners will always have sought (if not always found). It would also appear from finds to date, that this new way of constructing boats emerged during the first three centuries of the 2nd millennium (Wright 2004). We can therefore see them as a specialised artefact being developed, just as the cups, for the conduct of certain inter-regional relations which were becoming desirable for the acquisition of exotic materials and knowledge. As Clark says (2004a, 321) 'even today, the vessels that negotiate the dangerous and alien sea away from the security of land can still excite a relationship that transcends the rational'.

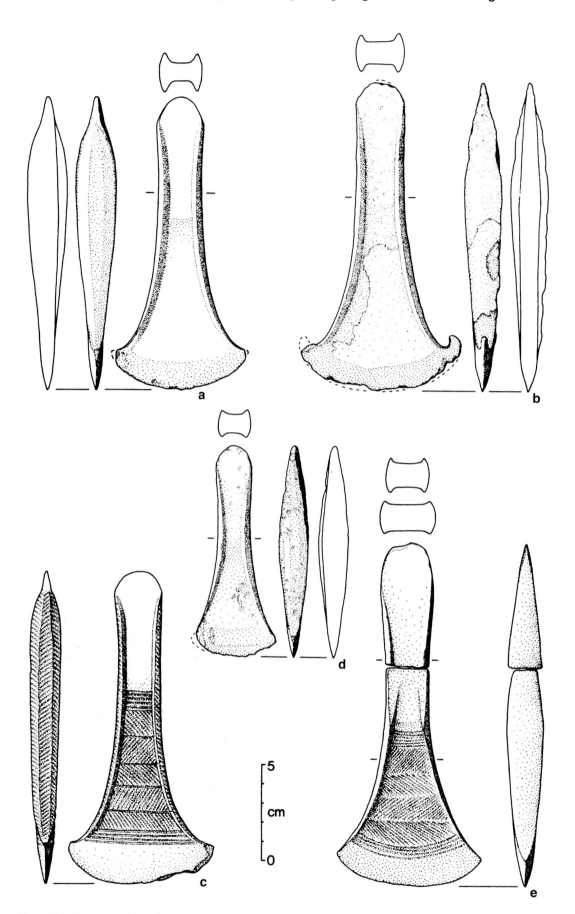

Figure 39 Aunjetitz-inspired flanged axes in the west and two eastern parallels: a) Plymstock hoard, Devon; b) Abbeville, Somme; c) Ramsgate, Kent (after Bronze Implements Index); d) Neuenheiligen hoard, Upper Saxony; e) Aebelnaes, Seeland, Denmark (after Aner and Kersten 1976, 189 no 1318). Scale 50%

Conclusions

The precious cups, then, relate to a *specific* maritime contact network, not to maritime connections in general nor, indeed, to exchange in general. Although exchanges of materials, objects, skills, knowledge, artisans and marriage partners are likely to have been among the driving forces behind its creation, the network represented a sphere of more exclusive interaction which worked independently of other spheres which bound other sets of communities together. Inevitable and regular exchanges inland in Britain did not carry the precious cup concept with them. Similarly, the long eastern coasts of Britain reveal no equivalent artefact type (discounting the fragments from Northumberland – Chapter 6) and yet the Ferriby boats attest to water-borne contact there in the Early Bronze Age (Wright 2004; Wright *et al.* 2001). The cups belong therefore to one particular network operating with its own particular ideological and organisational framework. The east coast of Britain must have had one or more different networks with different preoccupations, objectives and sanctions. Prominent in that network, whether by land or sea, was the widespread distribution of Whitby jet (Shepherd 1982; Sheridan and Davis 2002). By contrast the distribution map for Early Bronze Age amber (**Fig. 37**) shows only a handful of finds north of the Wash.

The precious cups have therefore helped us to identify a specific mechanism within the otherwise generalised evidence for cross-Channel and cross-North Sea exchange. They mark out a set of sea-faring communities who shared a common understanding of how to engage in such ventures and what propitiatory precautions to take. Through that understanding they were able to maintain more exclusive rights to the network and thus ensure the acquisition of exotics for cosmological purposes (Needham 2000b). This was of multidirectional benefit. The amber so prized at this time in southern England and, to a lesser extent, Armorica was actively procured as raw material from the shores of the North Sea (or beyond in the Baltic) for working locally. This may suggest that, once the medium for transmission could be constructed, it was the western communities who were proactive in procurement, rather than simply receptive to available 'traded' goods.

Conversely, the decorated bronze axes of western origin, once they became known in the east, may have been actively sought for their special aesthetic and magical properties rather than any functional advantage. Tin was valued in the east, at least in part, as a novel and scarce decorative medium.

The hypothesis of the ritual servicing of a maritime exchange network seems to make sense of these extraordinarily unusual and highly crafted objects – the precious cups – which are both comparable to one another and yet individually 'singular' (*sensu* Kopytoff 1986, 73–7; see also Fontijn 2001). Their singular nature stems from the need to produce something which is highly special and community specific – the sacred object of the group (Godelier 1999). Their comparability stems from a common acceptance of the role these vessels needed to play in ensuring the success of a new venture in fostering inter-regional elite interactions. The communities participating in the network understood the need for some commonalities in order to assure their membership of the club, but this did not necessarily mean that all aspects of their respective cultures were similar or became so. Nevertheless, precious cups can be seen to stand at a turning point in the cultural constitution of cross-Channel relations.

What has emerged from the fieldwork around the gold cup's findspot at Ringlemere – a sizeable monument, a major monument complex surrounding that, and fine artefacts of another exotic material, amber – can on the surface appear to be in emulation of the comparable complexes in Wessex. It may be that the regionally large complexes here and at Broad Down, Devon, do reflect some influence from that direction; an active engagement between Wessex and the southern coastal zone is not in doubt. However, our analysis of artefacts contemporary with the precious cups shows that far from the coastal zone simply emulating a Wessex-led ideology, it was developing its own novel and distinctive character featuring, above all, regionally specific rituals connected to maritime exchange. Perhaps initially stimulated by a desire in Wessex to add amber to its ritual riches, the coastal communities began to look ever more to and across the sea to satisfy certain social needs. But this new outlook on the part of the coastal communities was to last and proved to have a profound effect on the longer-term development of Bronze Age culture in north-west Europe.

Chapter 9: Catalogue of Early Bronze Age Precious Cups in North-West Europe

Stuart Needham and Gill Varndell

GOLD CUPS

1. Ringlemere, Woodnesborough, Kent, England

British Museum 2003 5-1 1.

Figs 22 & 40, Pls. 3–12, Colour Pls 1–3

Described fully in Chapter 3

Dimensions

Body

Estimated original height	123mm
Estimated height of lower body to shoulder	78mm
Estimated diameter of rim	109mm
Estimated diameter of top rib (no 19)	84.5mm
Estimated diameter of shoulder (rib 11)	96mm
Estimated diameter of crest of bottom rib	64.5mm
Diameter at base of bottom rib	58.5–62.5mm (→60.5)
Diameter omphalos	12mm
Linear surface distance from rim to carination	58mm (excluding rib/cusp detail)
Horizontal breadth of shoulder	10mm
Depth omphalos	2.0mm
Thickness at rim	0.8–0.9mm
Weight	183.7g

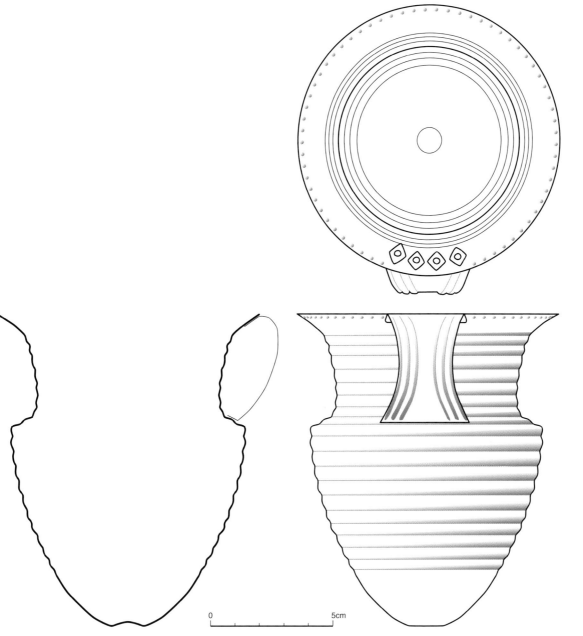

Figure 40 Ideal reconstruction of the Ringlemere gold cup. Scale 67%. [cat. no. 1]

Handle

Surface length (excluding tabs)	52mm
Minimum width	21.8mm
Maximum width (upper tab)	37.5mm
Thickness of handle edge	c. 0.3mm
Breadth of groove/rib bands	8–8.5mm
Length of top rivets	c. 3.3mm
Diameter of rivet heads	3.0–3.5mm
Length internal washers	9.5–10mm
Width internal washers	7–8mm
Length external washers	8–9.5mm
Width external washers	7mm
Distance between internal washers and rim	1.3–2.9mm
Gaps between internal washers	1.0–2.0mm

Punched dot decoration

62 dots	
Negative imprint diameter	c. 0.7mm
Positive boss diameter	1.0–1.2mm
Distance from rim	c. 1.5mm

---

2. Rillaton, Cornwall, England

British Museum (on loan from the Crown).
Fig. 41, Colour Pls 5–7

Context and circumstances

The Rillaton gold cup was found in 1837 during stone-robbing by workmen of a cairn on Bodmin Moor, Liskeard, Cornwall. A cist at the edge of the mound and above the old ground surface contained decayed human bones (taken by Gerloff to be cremated), the cup, a bronze dagger, a pot, a 'rivet', pieces of 'ivory', and a few 'glass beads'. The last are usually presumed to be faience beads. All but the cup and broken dagger (Type Camerton; Gerloff 1975, 107) are lost. The primary published account is Smirke's (1867), 30 years after the event; in it he notes the probability that the cup was inside a larger pottery vessel with a covering stone; the pot was broken when being disengaged from the stone. All this information derives from the workmen's accounts.

Recently a letter has come to light in the West Devon Records Office in Plymouth from Phipps Hornby to Henry Woollacombe, a Plymouth antiquarian (papers 710/772 – Jane Marchand pers. comm.; Colour Pl. 7). It was written a few days after the discovery, noting that the cup had been found within a ceramic vessel, and lying with it 'a skeleton a sword and a spearhead'. An accompanying sketch of the cup clearly shows a rounded base (Colour Pl. 6). The cairn was on Duchy land and the contents were thus the property of William IV, who died in that year. Hawkes published an account of the subsequent history of the cup insofar as it can be reconstructed (Hawkes 1983). In summary, Queen Victoria and Prince Albert had the cup and dagger in their Swiss Cottage private museum in the grounds of Osborne House; after Victoria's death it was transferred to Marlborough House. George V had it taken to Buckingham Palace where it was kept in his private apartments. The dagger remained at Osborne, wrongly labelled, and was identified by 'the Matron' soon after the death of George V. Hawkes trawled the Swiss Cottage for the missing items in 1936 to no avail. The cup and dagger remain on permanent loan to the British Museum.

Condition

Because of its protection within a stone-lined cist, and apparently also within a pottery vessel, the Rillaton cup has not suffered the gross crushing or distortion seen in some others. Nevertheless, it has had a long history out of the ground and there is a fair amount of damage which could be a combination of both ancient and modern. Post-discovery polishing has left all the high zones of the corrugated topography very bright, while the recesses between retain reddish patina to a variable extent. Inside the mouth and neck polishing is similarly thorough and this has severely rounded the *in situ* rivet and its washer, but it diminishes downwards, as shown by increasing traces of the patina. Some zones, such as close to the rim, are associated with relatively coarse striations (under magnification) and look heavily worn by this polishing; the rim is rounded with tiny scrapes. If earlier use-wear contributed to the wear, which is possible, unfortunately this cannot now be demonstrated. Surface reduction would account for the sudden changes in dot diameter in the pointillé row at the top of the uppermost rib, if these have been truncated and were originally struck to varying depths.

There is a long tear descending from the rim almost to the carination and several shorter ones trapped within the body, all on an approximately vertical axis. Minor buckles and many fine stress cracks frequently border these splits. Elsewhere there are linear zones with similar stress fractures which have not split open. The body generally bears many small dents and buckles.

The handle is in similar condition with transverse instead of vertical cracks; one at least (at its base) ran all the way across. It has also been altered at the top and soldered at both upper and lower fixings as part of a 19th-century (pre-1867) restoration. It now appears, on the evidence of both the watercolour sketch contemporary with the discovery and renewed inspection of the cup, that the handle has been restored wrongly. The watercolour shows the upper handle approaching the vessel at the level of the uppermost rib, not at the rim as currently restored; the tab was then bent upwards to be riveted to the plain band between rim and rib. The upper handle had at some point, probably after discovery, been ripped away from the body; this had left one rivet still clasping a small fragment of the tab *in situ*. That fragment shows an extremely thin edge along the top which would have been the original position of the tab's terminal, running virtually level with the rim. The lower, broken edge of the in situ tab fragment takes a diagonal line which would in fact be joined by the line of the break on the major part of the tab remaining attached to the handle if this were to be turned back upwards, as originally orientated.

The major tab portion likewise has a fine end (now pointing downwards). Because of a tear, it is probably now barely joined to the handle, but the tear has been filled with solder. The two rivets and washers that grip this portion are indeed modern brass (XRF analyses), as implied by the incorrect orientation of the tab. We cannot now know how damaged the original fixings were, but whatever may have remained *in situ* was obviously removed in order to re-attach the upper handle. The bending of the tab through about 180° may have involved some working; this probably accounts for the slightly puckered nature of a 3–4mm band of the handle alongside the rim. Re-attachment also gave rise to several distinctive scratches and gougings on the body surface around the upper rivet line.

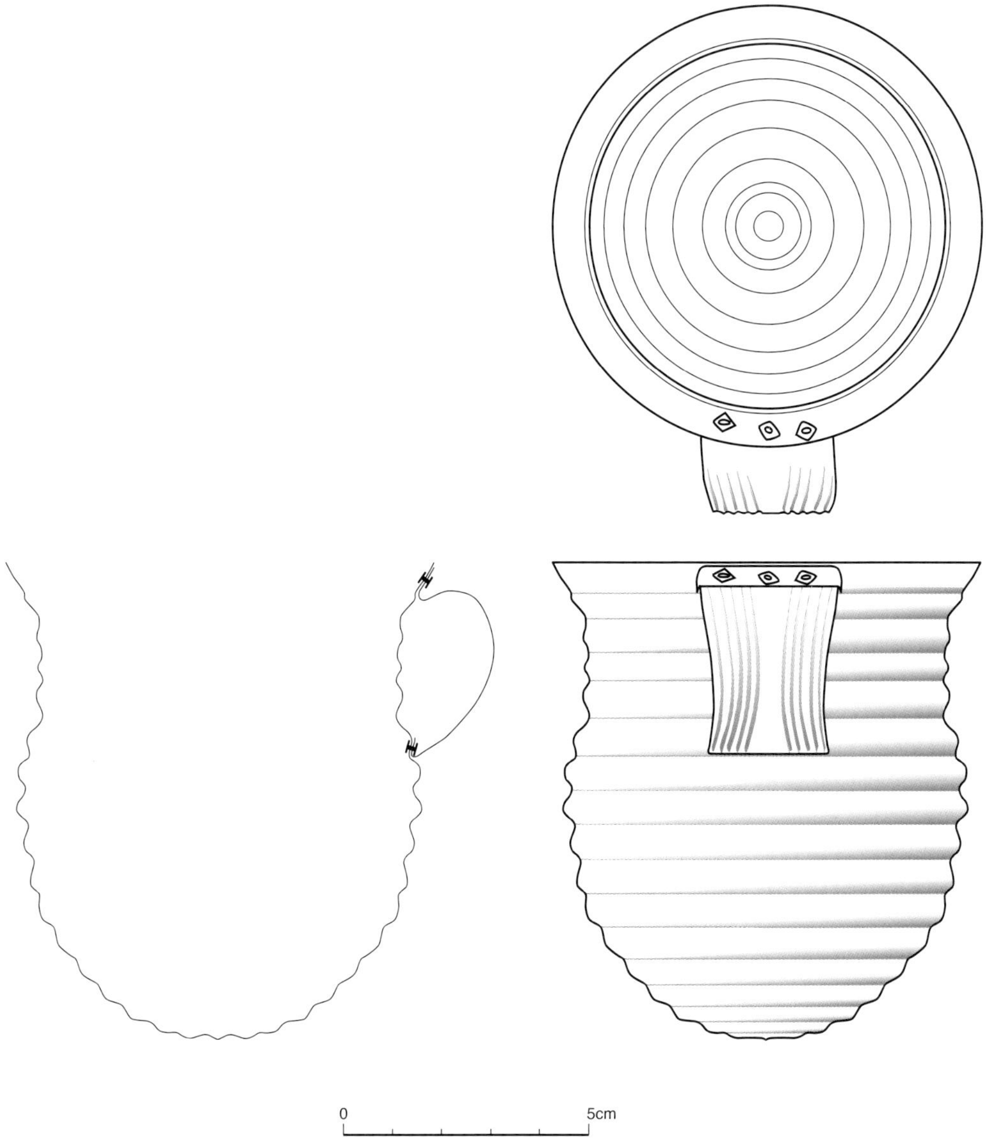

Figure 41 Ideal reconstruction of the Rillaton gold cup. Scale 67%. [cat. no. 2]

The handle had evidently at some stage torn totally away from its lower tab – the latter remains *in situ* with all three original rivets and their washers. Detachment could easily account for small distortions in the body close by and a tear alongside the right-hand end of the tab. A small corner is also missing from the handle side of the break. In order to re-attach it, the handle has been slightly overlapped with the upturned stump from the tab and the gap filled with solder. There are coarse grinding marks running alongside this join and cutting through reddish patina, probably preparing the surface for keying the solder.

The sides of the handle have mini-crimping, denting and burring at intervals and there is too much interference to assess ancient wear. There are, however, two tiny perforations pierced more or less symmetrically through the lower part of the handle which appear to be ancient, for there is no bright metal around them. As often with ancient piercings through sheet metal, the metal around has simply been allowed to split radially where it will, the intervening flaps being pushed inwards. Later the flaps were partially pressed back to close up the holes. They would have been up to 1mm in diameter when open. The handle furrows have been reamed out to varying degrees; on the right side the tool used tends to have left angular edges which interrupt a previously sinuous profile.

An equally important alteration can be shown in the form of

the base. There has long been a suspicion that the roughly flattened base is the product of alteration for there are irregularities of various kinds (described below). This has recently found confirmation from the contemporary watercolour sketch. While not precise in every detail – in particular the overall proportions are wrong – this depiction shows the curve of the lower body continuing all the way from rib 11 at the carination to rib 1. It gives the appearance of a flat base inside rib 1, but this could be due to the slightly oblique angle of view. By the time Smirke published a woodcut in 1867 (Smirke 1867), the cup evidently had a flattish base beneath rib 4. This is more-or-less the case today, but in fact circumferential changes in the damaged profile mean that the rib currently acting as 'footring' varies between ribs 3 and 5; Smirke's illustrator may have schematised the situation to make the cup look neat and undamaged. Indeed, just as the earlier watercolour showed the cup a little too fat in the body, this woodcut portrayed it a little too narrow.

In reassessing the nature of distortion in the base zone, an open mind has been kept as to whether the contemporary artist had partly worked from memory and misrepresented the lower body. He had faithfully represented the number of ribs – 16 – and, although the body is shown too fat, he does recognise that there is something of an angle in the profile at rib 11, ie a carination. He also has the handle attached at the correct points of the profile. It seems unlikely then that the draughtsman mis-represented the lower body to the point that a flattened base inside rib 4 was shown as continuing the rounded profile above. This is strongly supported by examination of the cup itself.

Today the area inside rib 4 is belled upwards – superficially as an omphalos. While a broad omphalos seems to be a feature of the Saint-Fiacre cup, at Rillaton it is associated with other features that suggest another explanation. Firstly, the average plane of the smaller ribs inside is tilted relative to the 'footring' formed by rib 4. Secondly, ribs 4, 5 and one side of 6 have pronounced lobate profiles which are not consistent all round and, indeed, the spatial relationship between these three ribs varies since they fluctuate from the horizontal plane. Thirdly, the character of ribs 1–3 and to some extent 4, is very different from the rest – they are sharply cuspate mouldings rather than the sinuous corrugations of the body. While this distinction could have been a deliberate design feature, this is unlikely because of the poor attention to regularity contrasting with the corrugations. Ribs 1–3 show irregularities in height and sharpness, while there are intermittent subtle angles around their otherwise circular circuits. All of these features can be explained as resulting from forces of tension created during compression of a previously cupped base into the rigid frame created by higher ribs. On this hypothesis the lowest ribs would originally also have been sinuous, but became compressed into ridges. Some of the tension created during compression was relieved by pushing the base right through to form the superficial omphalos.

Description

Working from the conclusions drawn above and the early watercolour, the original form can be reconstructed thus. All ribs were in fact part of a continuously corrugated profile, unlike the cusping ones on the Ringlemere vessel. Their amplitude decreased towards the base, as would be natural and easiest for the craftsman to achieve as the body diameter became progressively smaller. The small zone of 9mm diameter within rib 1 is not securely reconstructed; the current small boss (about 5mm diameter) is rather irregular in shape, but may be distorted by the forces exerted during compression. It is not impossible, however, that this boss is entirely secondary.

Despite the uninterrupted corrugations, the craftsman has been able to give the cup a gently carinated profile in aggregate very similar to many of the parallels; the median line of the profile has the break of angle falling at rib 11. The lower body exhibits a steady convex curve, the upper one a gentle concave curve narrowest at ribs 13 an 14 and expanding upwards to the rim more than downwards to the carination. Only the top 6mm of the wall beneath the rim is free of corrugations. The rim is currently rather rounded, but may once have been more flat-topped.

Aside from the corrugations, the only body decoration is a short stretch of faint and enigmatic pointillé in two rows just below the rim to the right of the handle (Kinnes 1994, A26; Needham 2000a, 41 fig. 13). A longer row of 31 dots extends for 25mm, sited at the crease between uppermost rib and rim band. Immediately below at the handle end is a very short second row of six dots. All are very fine, but under magnification they vary in diameter from 0.1–0.35mm and in detailed shape from oval to round to sub-triangular. It is possible that these have been

somewhat truncated by heavy wear/polishing. While this process might account for the total removal of some dots, ie those originally most shallow, the fact that there is no trace of dots anywhere else around the circumference, makes it unlikely that the extant stretch was ever part of a continuous dot row such as seen on most other metal vessels.

The handle is gently waisted in face view, expanding marginally less towards the bottom than the top. The curved sides are outlined by sets of five grooves, between which only a narrow hourglass-shaped panel remains plain. The grooves were originally formed as sinuous corrugations; the cycle of oscillation was not quite complete for the outermost ones. The top of each groove ends in a neat arch apparently undamaged by the reworking just above; the bases are obscured by the reattachment to the lower fixng. Sharp turns at top and bottom of the handle create short tabs which are riveted to the body. Currently both tabs turn inwards, but, as described above, the upper junction is incorrectly restored and the tab originally turned upwards after the handle met the body at the top of the top rib. The early illustration shows the handle to bell up a little from the upper fixing, before curving round to the lower one. However, this could already have been pushed in towards the body wall and our ideal reconstruction (**Fig. 41**) offers a more bulbous profile with a more horizontal top.

The lower fixings are all *in situ*, three rivets in a line, as is one of the upper rivets. All have lozenge-shaped washers inside and out, the former aligned vertically, the latter horizontally because of the confined space given by the tabs.

Dimensions
Body

Present maximum height (rim to rib 4)	84mm
Estimated original height	95mm
Diameter of rim	84–87mm (→85.5mm)
Diameter of neck (rib 14)	68.5–73mm (→70.5mm)
Diameter rib 12	72.3–73mm (→72.5mm)
Diameter carination (rib 11)	76.5–79mm (→77.5mm)
Diameter rib 8	72.5–73.5mm (→73mm)
Diameter rib 6	56–63.5mm (→60mm)
Diameter rib 4	41.5–42.5mm (→42mm)
Diameter rib 3	31.5–32.5mm (→32mm)
Diameter rib 2	19.5–21mm (→20mm)
Diameter rib 1	9.5–11mm (→10mm)
Thickness rim	0.3–0.5mm
Thickness body (crack above carination)	0.1–0.15mm
Weight	76.6g

Handle

Maximum extant width of handle top	25.3mm
Maximum extant width handle bottom	24.5mm
Minimum width	21.1mm
Surface length (excluding tabs)	c. 48mm
Thickness	0.1–0.2mm
Internal rivet-head diameters	c. 2.0mm
External rivet-head diameters	c. 2.5mm
Rivet lengths	c. 2.2–2.5mm
Measurable rivet washers: lengths	4.9–5.5mm
widths	3.5–4.2mm

Composition

Body: silver *c.* 10 %, copper 0.7 %, tin 0.2 %, antimony trace
Handle: silver *c.* 25 %, copper 0.38 %, tin 0.082 %, nickel trace
(Hartmann 1982, 100 tables 6 & 7, Au 3113, 3114)

Manufacture, wear

The original handle arrangement, although not known on any of the parallels, would certainly have made the fixing of the upper tab easier. The lower one would be riveted in place first, then the handle bent round with its upper tab already bent upwards. The upper riveting could be done before the handle was manipulated into the desired profile, thereby giving more access to the outer rivet heads.

Of the original rivets, only the inner head of the upper one shows significant wear. A possible combination of modern and ancient wear has burnished the head almost seamlessly into the washer, and heavily rounded off the latter. If this has occurred entirely since discovery, it must have happened in the very early years before restoration, for otherwise one would expect to see more rounding of the modern rivets alongside. It seems more likely that at least part of the marked wear evident is indeed ancient and due to repeated cleaning of this very exposed location just inside the flaring mouth.

The external head of this upper rivet has fairly crisp edges and is proud of the washer which itself has crisp corners and angles. This contrasts sharply with its inner head. The external head therefore escaped significant denudation in both the 19th century and antiquity. This is not entirely surprising as it would have occupied an acute angle between rim and upper handle, even though not tucked beneath the handle. A further ancient feature here is the occurrence of striations in varied directions across the washer, for they must precede insertion of the rivet.

The three original rivet/washer emplacements in the lower row exhibit similar lack of appreciable rounding both internally and externally. These, however, occupy zones that may not have experienced cleaning (ancient or modern) as regularly or thoroughly as other areas.

3. Fritzdorf, Rhein-Sieg Kreis, Nordrhein-Westfalen, Germany

Rheinisches Landesmuseum, Bonn. Description based on von Uslar 1955 plus inspection through glass case.
Fig. 42, Colour Pl. 8

Context and circumstances

The cup from Fritzdorf was found in 1954 inside a pottery vessel. Gerloff (1975, 190) states that this was found under a stone but there is no mention of the stone in von Uslar's account (1955). The discovery was made during turnip-digging and the ceramic vessel was destroyed; only a few sherds remain. Investigation of the surrounding ground surface revealed no more material; the region had produced few prehistoric finds.

Condition

The vessel is complete and the only significant damage is a limited tear into the rim opposite the handle. Nearby, a stretch of rim is rather crinkly, while there are lots of minor dents and buckles across the surface of the body.

Description

The overall form is rather squat, a near hemispherical lower body being surmounted by a concave necked upper part of lesser depth. The roundedness of the lower body is interrupted only by a neat small central omphalos. The profile of the carination is a little variable around the vessel. Where least damaged by denting, to the right of the handle, it appears as a fairly well defined angle; elsewhere the angularity, if originally present, has been smoothed. The neck profile is not an even curve; instead there is a tighter curve low down which generally creates a sloping shoulder down to the carination. Locally (opposite the handle) this is more accentuated by the hint of a crease separating shoulder from neck. Similarly at the top of the neck the curvature becomes stronger as it flares to the rim. The mouth stands at an angle of about 45°.

The handle is a ribbon of sheet metal, symmetrically waisted in face view with gracefully curved sides. The latter are each outlined by bands of three grooves which are in fact neat corrugations of the metal such that they appear in opposite relief on the under side. The handle edges are thin. In profile the handle has a rather slack curvature keeping it relatively close to the body wall. The two end tabs are turned sharply inwards to align with the respective parts of the wall for attachment. These sharp turns give rise to a straight fold which does not match the curve of the rim and carination respectively; hence, while the handle's corners are set close to rim or carination, respectively, in the middle they are 2–3mm adrift. The handle tabs have a straight end with rounded corners.

Attachment to the body is by means of a row of four rivets top and bottom, each rivet clasping a washer both internally and externally. The washers are of a consistent rather rounded diamond shape, but while those under the handle are all horizontally set because of the limited space available, on the inside of the vessel the lower row is horizontal and the upper aligned vertically. Visible rivet heads show minor cracks and irregularities around their lips, undoubtedly formed during clenching.

Two rows of dots have been punched from the outside immediately below the rim. The rows are not entirely parallel to the rim, and the dot spacing is not especially regular. There are 105 dots in the upper row and 95 or 96 in the lower row, being variably aligned with or staggered from the former. The dots cease at the handle and the rows curl up a fraction indicating that this decoration was executed after the handle was fixed.

Dimensions

Body

Height	121mm
Diameter of rim	116mm
Diameter of carination	122mm
Diameter of omphalos	14mm
Rim thickness	0.6mm
Wall thickness	c. 0.3mm
Weight	221g

Handle

Width handle feet	37mm (upper), 36mm (lower)
Width handle waist	20mm
Rivet head diameters	2.5–4mm
Washer dimensions	9 x 7mm

Composition

Silver c. 12 %, copper 0.22 %, tin 0.006 %, nickel not detected (Hartmann 1970, 100 table 10, Au 1262)

Manufacture, wear

No evidence recorded.

Figure 42 Ideal reconstruction of the Fritzdorf gold cup. Scale 67%. [cat. no. 3]

4. Gölenkamp, Kr. Grafschaft Bentheim, Niedersachsen, Germany

Private collection (Schloss Burgsteinfurt). Studied by kind permission of the owner whilst on loan to the Germanischen Nationalmuseum, Nürnberg.
Fig. 43, Colour Pl. 9

Context and circumstances

In 1840 a gold vessel was found during sand extraction on the Spöllberg at Gölenkamp. It had been placed as a cover on a ceramic vessel which does not survive (Fröhlich 1992). There had been eight burial mounds at Gölenkamp; mound 1 – considered to be the likely findspot for the cup – was dug into at some time before 1877 and about a third of it removed. A Dr. Müller completed the excavation in 1877, fully demolishing the mound. Mention was made of an urn beneath a large stone, charcoal and cremated bone.

Condition

Generally the vessel has retained its original shape with only minor disfigurements. However, while the ribbed parts have suffered limited denting due to their rigidity, the plain lower wall shows copious denting which becomes progressively worse lower down. The wall meets the flattish base in a rough and variable obtuse angle; immediately inside is a variably sharp groove before the neat concentric base ribs. It is considered that the 'base angle' and internal groove are largely the products of distortion, the body having been compressed a little at this point of the profile. However, since there is no evidence of gross distortion of the base itself (just minor dimpling of the central roundel), it would appear that its current very slightly convex form is original.

The rim exhibits minor crimping all round and there is a 35mm stretch with a more ragged indent.

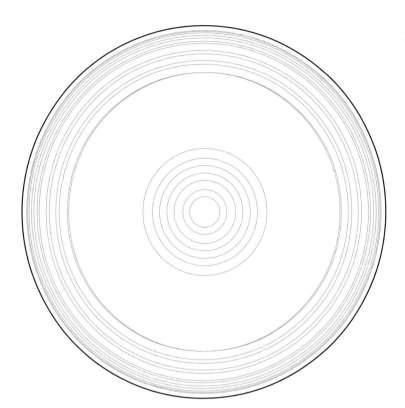

Figure 43 Ideal reconstruction of the Gölenkamp gold cup. Scale 67%. [cat. no. 4]

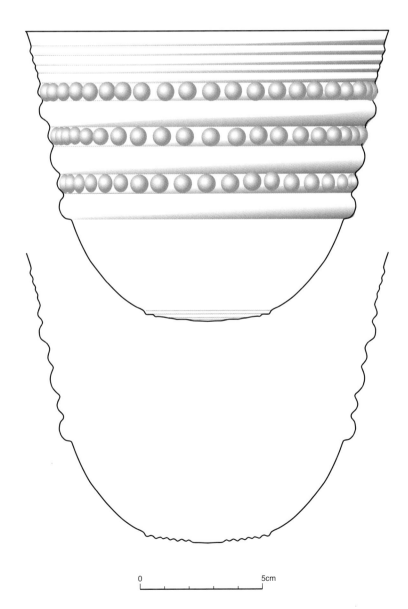

0 ⊢──────────── 5cm

Description

A slightly convex base comprises a central roundel and six encircling ribs. The first five are of similar dimensions, up to 0.5mm in amplitude each, but the outermost one is larger, even when measured from the internal groove. The best reconstruction of the lower wall has it springing from outside the sixth rib initially at a wide angle, but rapidly and smoothly curving upwards. It meets the first rib in a crisp angle at about one-third of the height of the body. Three stout horizontal ribs alternate with boss rows and this is capped off with a band of four corrugations of similar amplitude to the basal ones. The stout ribs are all of neat hemispherical profile, but vary in detailed dimensions; average widths are between 9.5–10mm, while the height of the lowest rib, up to 3.8mm, contrasts with the other two, up to 2.5mm. The bosses are sub-conical and are also more consistent from row to row with typical diameters of 7mm in the uppermost and 8mm in the others. Because of the contracting circumference of the vessel the number of bosses accommodated falls from 54 at the top to 46 and then 41. They are mainly near-contiguous and one pair in the top row is particularly tightly set.

Dimensions

Present height	114.5mm
Estimated original height	116.5mm
Diameter of mouth	147.2 x 151.2 (→149mm)
Diameter beneath lowest wall rib	c. 112.5–114mm
Diameter outside outer base rib	53mm
Diameter of base roundel	15.5mm
Thickness at rim	0.4–0.5mm
Weight	255g

Composition

Silver c. 24 %, copper 0.46 %, tin 0.077 %, nickel c. 0.03 % (Hartmann 1970, 108 table 14, Au 1756)

Manufacture, wear

The angles flanking the stout body ribs have been given extra definition by punching from the outside – linear tool-marks can be seen. This appears to have been done at a late stage for the punching tends to impinge on the boss edges top and bottom.

The insides of the bosses have a 'double-action' profile with a deeper indent at the centre of the shallow cone. The deeper part is actually consistently off-centre downwards and this is very likely due to having been struck by an obliquely set narrower punch coming in from above the rim opposite. It is possible this was a secondary action to the initial basic formation of the conical bosses to give them better definition.

5. Eschenz, Kanton Thurgau, Switzerland

Museum des Kantons Thurgau, Frauenfeld. Studied with the permission of Jost Bürgi whilst on loan to the Germanisches Nationalmuseum, Nürnberg.
Fig. 44, Colour Pl. 10

Context and circumstances

The gold vessel from Eschenz was found in 1916 during railway construction; it entered a private collection where it went unnoticed until 1974, when it was given to the Museum of the Canton of Thurgau (Menghin and Schauer 1983, 71). Hardmeyer and Bürgi (1975) noted that no accompanying objects had been observed. The Eschenz region is at the outflow of the Untersee into the upper Rhine.

Condition

Generally the body is in good condition, but it is suggested that the currently flattened base zone, containing up to seven corrugations, is a result of subsequent pressure. The micro-topography of the corrugations in this zone is rather erratic and some of the amplitudes between crest and furrow have been exaggerated by the compression of an overall curved profile into a flattened plane. Inside the smallest definite rib, there is an area of complex topography about 18mm in diameter (Hardmeyer and Bürgi 1975, 112 abb. 6; Bürgi and Kinnes 1975, pl. IX lower). Although it includes some roughly concentric raised rings, they bifurcate and have lateral spurs; on balance it is thought more likely that these have arisen from the compression of a plain well-domed surface.

There has also been a tiny amount of compression in the neck causing the narrowing of greater or lesser parts of two adjacent furrows. Slight undulations in the line of the rim, as seen in profile, are associated with buckling. There are other localised elements of damage that have disfigured and occasionally obliterated embossed features.

Description

Since there is no evidence for a flat base, the lower body would have described a graceful parabolic curve interrupted just above the mid-point by a gentle, but distinct change of angle. This carination is in fact emphasised by a rib. Above, the neck has a gentle concave curve expanding towards a moderately out-turned mouth.

The convex basal roundel was enclosed by a zone of six small corrugations. These are now much distorted, but were probably fairly regular in their execution and spacing. Immediately above is a single row of 33 sub-conical bosses, each around 3.7mm in diameter and up to 0.8mm in relief. Their tops tend to be slightly flattened and one has been double-struck.

A single rib divides this lower boss row from a deep field comprising four panels of diagonal ribs. The latter are 2–3.5mm broad and form continuous corrugations within their near-rectangular frames. The vertical divisions between panels are broader ribs, 4–6.5mm wide and generally tapering downwards, and are further defined by small flanking furrows. The latter tend to have a shallow V-profile with a crease along the bottom.

Between these hatched panels and the carination a neatly cabled rib is underlined by three plain ribs and topped with a fourth. The individual 'twists' of the cable have a subtle S shape and are 3–3.5mm broad. Next, at the carination, there is a more pronounced rib with a row of bosses both above and below. The rib is rounded in profile where well preserved, 5.5mm broad and up to 2.3mm in relief. The flanking boss rows are different from one another: the lower one has 45 sub-conical bosses which are mostly contiguous, 5.5–6mm in diameter and up to 1.3mm high; the upper one has as many as 83 smaller hemispherical bosses, again contiguous, 4mm in diameter and at most 0.5mm in relief. The boss counts given include one and two respectively where damage has effectively erased bosses, as well as two unusually closely set in the lower row. There is also a double-struck boss there.

The neck is less complicated in design, the morphology being simply a continuous sequence of 12 corrugations.

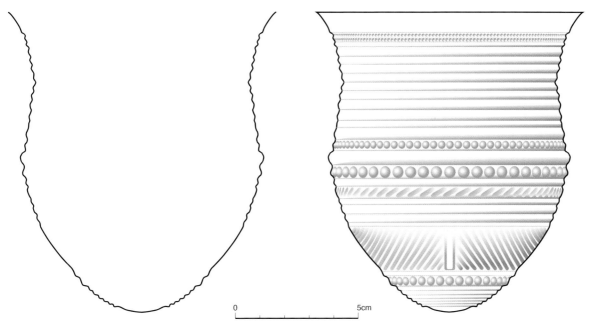

Figure 44 Ideal reconstruction of the Eschenz gold cup. Scale 67%. [cat. no. 5]

However, the top two grooves have rows of punched dots along them and are a little narrower than the others, perhaps as a result of the punching having deepened the groove. Although fairly evenly spaced, the dots appear to have been individually punched with a circular, slightly domed tool point. Under magnification spacing is not especially regular and they are not especially well aligned. Dot positions in one row are not in phase with those in the other; indeed, while spacing is mainly between 4–4.5 dots per centimetre in the upper row, it is between 5–5.5 in the lower.

Finally, at the mouth is the only plain band on the whole vessel, around 10mm deep. At its base, immediately above the dotted grooves, there is an inconsistent and extremely light crease. The rim is flat-topped with minor facets. The metal at the neck is seen (through small tears) to be much thinner than at the rim.

Dimensions

Present height	111mm
Estimated original height	118mm
Diameter of rim	110mm
Diameter of neck	c. 90mm
Diameter of carination	97–100mm (→98.5)
Present diameter of flattened base	43.5mm
Diameter of rib encircling original base roundel	22mm
Thickness of rim	0.8–0.9mm
Weight	136g

Composition

Silver 25%, copper 0.45%, tin 0.02% (Hartmann 1982, 100 table 7, Au 4902)

Manufacture, wear

No evidence was noted.

6. Lan ar Croaz, Ploumilliau, Côtes d'Armor, France

Lost; description based on Anonymous 1886

Fig. 45

Context and circumstances

The gold vessel portion from Lan ar Croaz was found in the mid-19th century and melted down soon afterwards; only a drawing of the portion survives (Eluère 1982, 102 fig 122). A gold spoon was discovered at the same time and acquired by the Bibliothèque Nationale. The find circumstances and exact provenance are far from clear (Briard 1965, 76), though Briard (1984, 223) notes that the find was made in 1840 'near' the tumulus of Le Roudoulu, and admits the possibility that the objects might have come from a burial.

Condition

Apparently the upper half of a two-part vessel. The depiction shows no obvious damage to this portion.

Description

The upper body had a smooth concave profile, the curvature evidently increasing towards a well out-turned rim. A row of close-set fine dots is shown immediately beneath the rim, presumably representing pointillé ornament. This is interrupted on the far side by a row of seven larger features which can be interpreted as rivet heads for securing a handle, as seen on some of the other metal cups. It is possible that these represent both rivets and washers, but if so the latter are small and seemingly round.

The bottom edge is apparently neatly fashioned and is angled inward relative to the main profile. The flange thereby created is deep enough to accommodate a row of rivet holes, 13 of which are depicted. The lower body would therefore have been a separate piece of metal joined immediately below a carination by rivets, a construction otherwise only known on the Saint-Adrien silver cup. Briard recognised the strong similarity between these two examples (1984, 134–6). The handle could have been a third separate component, riveted to the body at both ends. However, the analogy with Saint-Adrien allows an

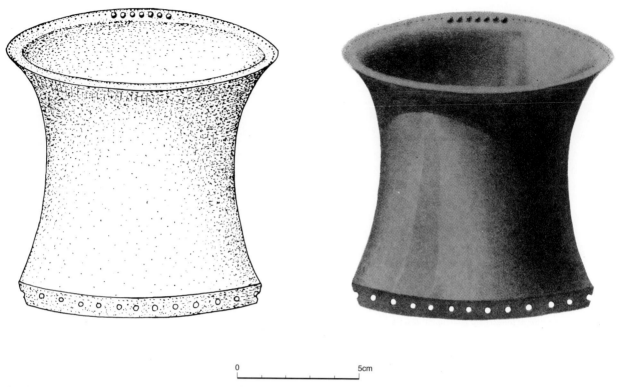

Figure 45 The Ploumilliau gold cup, upper body only (after Briard 1984, 134 fig. 83.4 and Eluère 1982, 102 fig. 122). Scale 67%. [cat. no. 6]

alternative possibility in which the handle would have been a linear extension drawn out from one side of the lower body, thus requiring fixing only at its top end, close to the rim. That such a lower component could be achieved is demonstrated not only by the Saint-Adrien parallel, but also by the associated spoon or ladle at Ploumilliau itself (Eluère 1982, 103 fig. 123). Other than the obvious fact that its bowl is elliptical rather than round, this object would have closely resembled the form of the cup's lower body plus handle prior to assembly.

Dimensions
Height of portion   *c.* 90mm
Maximum diameter (rim)   *c.* 110mm

Manufacture, wear
None known.

7. No provenance ('South Germany')
Private collection (Switzerland). Description and drawing based on Wamser and Gebhard 2001.
Fig. 46

Context and circumstances
This cup came to attention relatively recently when it was displayed in the Museum für Vor- und Frühgeschichte, Munich in 2002 in the context of a special exhibition, *Gold: Magie Mythos Macht*. At the time of writing it is in a private collection; its provenance is unknown but said to be South German.

Condition
There appears to be no loss, but there is a significant amount of buckling around the rim and part is crushed downward a little. The lower body also shows denting and a small degree of distortion, but the major part of the body appears to have suffered little damage.

Description
The lower body is strongly convex, curving in to a rounded base. If the base is flattened at all, this must be confined to the small central roundel which is encircled by concentric rilling, or corrugations. Approximately half-way up the vessel the profile angles at a moderate carination emphasised by a double corrugation with a third corrugation immediately above. The wall contracts gently and steadily to the neck, this part being occupied first by a shallow plain zone then by three more corrugations. Above, the body evidently flared strongly towards the rim, even allowing for some exaggeration caused by later pressure. Currently the rim, which is thin and simple, fluctuates around the horizontal.

The concentric corrugations already described with the addition of a single one a little below the carination divide the wall into four registers, three of which contain more elaborate decoration. The deep basal register has four broad vertical bands of vertical rills. These leave blank triangular fields in between as the body expands; each triangle is topped by a single horizontal rill. The register above is shallow and occupies the girth of the vessel. Positioned directly above each of the rilled bands below is an elongate oval motif, defined by a groove into which dots have been punched. The intervening gaps are filled with vertical rills, these therefore being offset from the comparable panels below.

The uppermost decorative register, from neck to rim, employs yet different motifs, but again utilising pointillé rows. Immediately under the rim are two delicate rows punched from the outside. Suspended from this are perhaps 16 pendant triangles, the double dot rows here being set in double grooves.

There is no evidence for a former handle.

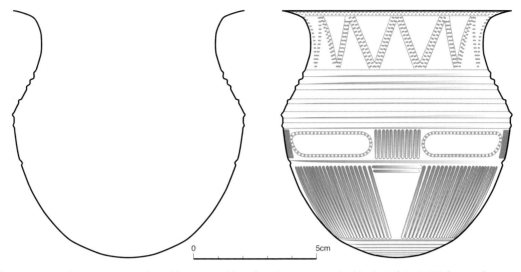

Figure 46 Ideal reconstruction of the unprovenanced, possibly German gold cup (based on Wamser and Gebhard 2001). Scale 67%. [cat. no. 7]

Dimensions

Present height	*c.* 98mm
Maximum diameter (carination)	*c.* 94mm
Weight	*c.* 90g

Manufacture, wear

Nothing known.

SILVER CUPS

8. Brun Bras, Saint-Adrien, Côtes d'Armor, France

Laboratoire d'Anthropologie, Université de Rennes. Description and drawing based on Briard 1978, Briard 1984 and Clarke *et al.* 1985.

Fig. 47, colour Pl. 11

Context and circumstances

A number of fragments of a silver cup came from the tumulus of Brun-Bras, Saint-Adrien. The cup was restored sufficiently to obtain a profile (Briard 1984, 134 fig. 83 1–3, 225–6). The tumulus was excavated in 1974; it comprised a barrow with a central cairn over a wooden mortuary structure set in subsoil. Traces of a wooden box or coffin were found against the north wall; the cup is thought to have lain near the head of the corpse which had totally decayed. The grave assemblage included 20 flint arrowheads, a bronze flat axe and a dagger of which the hilt had been decorated with tiny gold nails; 5 small gold roundels (probably 6 originally) may have decorated the hilt or blade. A second dagger lay outside the coffin. A date of *c.* 2160–1920 cal. BC (at 2 sigma) was obtained from oak charcoal from the coffin or from the surviving lining of the mortuary structure; this may be a little early (Needham 2000b, 160).

Condition

Very corroded and fragmented vessel, now reconstructed; about 50% missing. More than half of the handle is also lacking; this is the upper part including the riveted fixing to the mouth.

Description

Enough survives to be confident of its shape and its construction from two portions. The lower body is hemispherical with no indication of any flattened area or omphalos, although this might conceivably be on a missing fragment. It terminates at a horizontal 'rim' which externally overlaps the upper body to allow riveting. At this junction the upper portion has an angled flange thus creating a moderate carination; the lower body projects just beyond the overlap.

The rivets are washer-less and are not entirely regular in spacing or alignment. They continue across the base of the

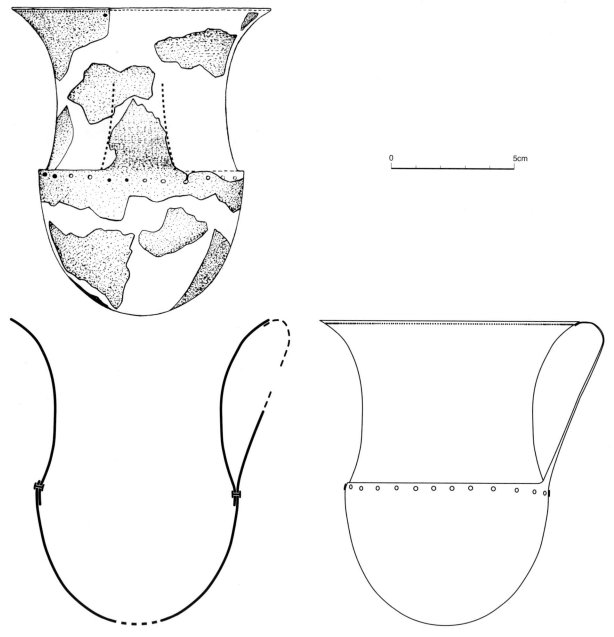

Figure 47 Ideal reconstruction of the Brun Bras, Saint-Adrien silver cup. Scale 67%. [cat. no. 8]

handle which is a strip drawn out from the metal of the lower body. In profile the handle diverges slightly from the line of the body below; its shape is otherwise uncertain due to poor condition. One rivet emplacement appears to survive on a rim fragment where the handle would originally have been fixed.

The upper body has a continuously curving profile, accentuating towards a well flared mouth. Immediately below the simple rim is a row of very fine pointillé. Briard also mentions that there are traces of such decoration on the handle (1984, 225; also Clarke *et al.* 1985, 310), but the lay-out is not shown.

Dimensions

Reconstructed height	122mm
Reconstructed rim diameter	106mm
Reconstructed neck diameter	70mm
Reconstructed carination diameter	86mm
Thickness	*c.* 1mm

Manufacture, wear

Nothing known.

9. Saint-Fiacre, Melrand, Morbihan, France

Ashmolean Museum, Oxford: 1926.147

Fig. 48

Context and circumstances

The tumulus at Saint-Fiacre-en-Melrand produced fragments of a silver vessel when excavated in 1897 (Aveneau de la Grancière 1898). The surviving plan is not very detailed (a schematic version is published by Needham 2000b, 173 fig 13). The tomb was a dry stone chamber covered by a granite slab; the wood-lined floor rested on a paved area laid on the old ground surface (Briard 1984, 292). Associated with the cup was a rich assemblage: a *Vollgriffdolch* (Rhône type), the blades of some nine more daggers, two bronze axes, two bronze arrowheads and an amber bracer-ornament, as well as a number of small gold-wire nails undoubtedly from a dagger hilt. No skeletal remains survived, but it has recently been suggested that these may represent accumulation from a few successive burials rather than a single grave group (Needham 2000b, 168–76).

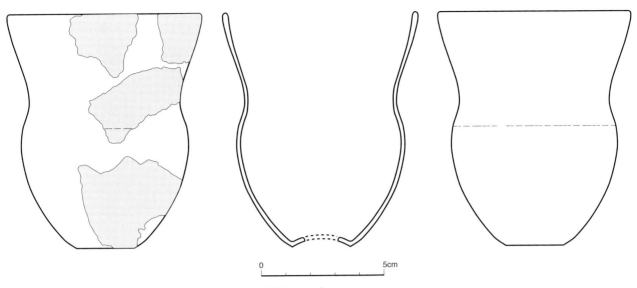

Figure 48 Ideal reconstruction of the Saint-Fiacre silver cup. Scale 67%. [cat. no. 9]

Condition

The vessel is represented by a number of small fragments of sheet silver, virtually none joining one another; six larger ones are useful for reconstruction. Some fragments are thin without significant corrosion, others are thickened locally by lamination and extrusions. At the time of excavation, Aveneau de la Grancière (1898, 88, 93) thought the fragments to be bronze which had totally lost its patina. He attributed this to the action of fire despite the fact that no associated objects had been burnt. He noted that the fragments disintegrated at the slightest touch and were too broken up for reconstruction. Historically, whilst in the care of the Ashmolean Museum, they have been attached to a wooden core shaped to the form the cup was thought to take. However, renewed study suggests an alternative shape.

Description

The former reconstruction has a sub-conical lower body with rounded base, a sloped shoulder above a rounded carination, and a moderately flared upper body from neck to rim. The strong shoulder depended on a fragment with one edge turned through about 70° (and actually quite angular). However, there is another fragment with a much more subtle bend in profile, c. 30°, and the stronger bend is associated with a curvature far too tight to easily be accommodated at the carination. Assuming neither of these is distorted significantly, they come from different parts of the vessel and are best accommodated at carination and base respectively.

The longer profile springing from the strong bend representing the foot is convex and must belong to a sub-conical lower body. The best angle for the latter suggests that the base itself was raised internally, creating an omphalos. The lower wall rises thence in a gentle convex curve to a weak carination perhaps half-way up the profile. Very little of the carination itself survives, but the adjoining wall above is clearly concave. Contraction to the neck would have been limited before curving outward to a modestly flared mouth. Three fragments are likely to be rim sherds; that in the best condition thickens gradually towards the rim, although there is some minor lamination associated at the top. The flared mouth appears to have had marginal convexity. Away from the rim, the wall is of constant thickness.

There is no sign of a handle, but that could be due to the high degree of loss.

Dimensions

Reconstructed height	c. 93mm
Reconstructed rim diameter	c. 80mm
Reconstructed neck diameter	c. 62mm
Reconstructed carination diameter	c. 68mm
Reconstructed foot diameter	c. 25mm
Rim thickness (?corrosion thickened)	2.5mm
Wall thickness	c. 1–1.5mm

Manufacture, wear

Nothing observed.

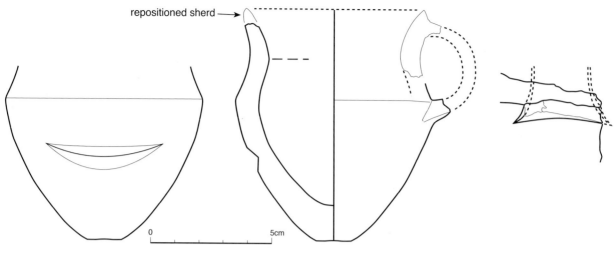

repositioned sherd →

Figure 49 Ideal reconstruction of the Clandon amber cup. Scale 67%. [cat. no. 10]

AMBER CUPS

10. Clandon barrow, Martinstown, Dorset, England

Dorset County Museum, Dorchester.
Fig. 49

Context and circumstances

This amber vessel was found in 1882 in a barrow opened by
Cunnington at Clandon (Winterborne St. Martin 31; Grinsell
1959). Drew and Piggott in their 1936 review of Cunnington's
unpublished records note that his written account and his sketch
do not always tally. The barrow stood 18½ feet (5.7m) high and
Cunninton's trench struck a shallow flint 'cairn' at 7 feet (2.15m)
down (**Fig. 34**). Scattered over this were a bronze dagger (of
Gerloff's Armorico-British B, Cressingham type), a gold lozenge
plaque, and a shale macehead with jet and gold stud fittings.
The amber cup was in fragments, 'scattered amongst the flints
and spread over a surface of two feet' (Cunnington's record,
quoted in Drew and Piggott 1936, 19). An accessory cup was in
scattered pieces beneath the cairn at a level still well above the
old ground surface. A Collared Urn, crushed and resting on a
'thin stratum of ashes and small flints', was found 'at six feet
from the centre surface and a foot from the flints' (ie a foot from
the flint cairn). ▮▮▮▮▮▮▮▮ cremated or otherwise,
appears to have been recorded in any firm association with the
amber cup and the other artifacts scattered over the cairn and
this has invited comparison with other ▮▮▮▮▮▮ deposits of
valuables a▮▮▮▮▮ sites (Needham 1988a, 241; Woodward 2000,
105).

Condition

The surface is corroded to a very matt orangey-brown colour
and appears lustreless under reflected light. Nevertheless, when
light is shone through it from the inside the original amber is
still semi-translucent. There are small pock-scars, but otherwise
the surface is largely smooth polished despite much fine crazing.

The sherds recovered represent roughly 75% of the original
vessel and they survive in an early restoration. A significant
portion of the upper body and rim is lacking and only two
limited parts are filled in order to attach or secure the projecting
rim sherds. There are also three tiny areas of infill on the upper
body and three more, larger ones where sherds are missing in
the more complete lower body. Some of these areas of infill are
shown as unshaded zones in a pencil sketch in the Cunnington
archive. This sketch would have been done by Cunnington's
daughter, Alice, not long after excavation, showing that the
current restoration is equally early, except for an extension to
one of the upper pieces of infill to give added support to a rim
sherd.

The early sketch shows two sherds apparently reaching the
rim; this is also the case in the photograph in Abercromby's
great corpus (Abercromby 1912, pl.LXII, 3a) and the 1936-
published drawing (Drew and Piggott 1936, pl. II,3). One rim
fragment, that bearing the upper stump of the handle, has since
become detached. The second has also suffered attrition since
these early depictions, such that virtually the whole of its top
edge has been chipped to expose fresh amber.

Description

Sherds are generally well aligned in the restoration and the
restored diameter more-or-less correct. However, the attached
rim sherd seems to be mis-positioned, being set both too high
and tangentially skewed. Shallow flakes have been detached
since excavation from either side of the join between the still
mounted rim sherd and that below. Without dismantling, the
relative position of the sherd can only be ascertained by
reference to a diffuse internal bevel inside the neck. Other
original sherds extend to 30mm above the carination before
fracture and the best estimate regarding the near-rim sherd is
that it would have extended a further 6mm. On this basis, with
the lower body height unchanged at around 56mm, the overall
height would be 92mm rather than the 100mm of the current
restoration. The upper handle sherd, when attached to the
restored vessel, was separated from the main profile by a piece
of infill; it too possesses a thickening in profile which, when
aligned with that on other neck sherds, confirms the lower
overall height.

Original stretches of profile across the carination are all
broadly similar, with convex curve beneath and concave above,
but they vary in detail. This variation alone might suggest that
the cup was not lathe turned. Indeed, just to the left of the
handle, the carination turns down slightly from the horizontal.
The small flat base is neatly circular and surrounded by a
slightly rounded angle; its plane is not quite parallel to that
through the carination.

The basal stump of the handle survives on one side

immediately beneath the carination, but projects at most 5mm before the fracture, which is 5mm thick. Virtually all of the handle/body junction is present (extant width 36mm), the underside being a graceful concave line terminating at an acute angle with the left-hand side. The opposite end is clipped by a fracture, the sherd beyond being missing. The upper handle stump is highly damaged and only a little of its upper surface is original. This projects from the body at an obtuse angle just 4mm below a strongly-tapered rim.

Opposite the handle and below the carination is a shallow crescentic notch which does not penetrate more than about half way through the wall (unlike a larger damage notch below). There is a fracture line running along this notch and part of the wall above is now a restored portion. At first sight the notch appeared to be the result of another misalignment of conjoining sherds. However, the original internal surfaces are flush and the notch would seem to be an integral feature of the cup, at least in its final phase.

The lower facet of the notch, where intact, has a very smooth surface with a crisp basal edge. Towards the left it has been progressively removed by a fracture showing resonance-shatter. The upper facet grades more smoothly into the profile above. The cup was obviously susceptible to breaking along this line because the wall was thinner. The notch may be a result of working out a flaw in the amber or a mistake during production. However, the fact that it is symmetrical and diametrically opposite the handle encourages the possibility that it is an intended part of the design. A tiny dimple, 4mm in diameter and half removed by cracking and spalling, lies 10mm below the carination to the left of the notch. It is neat and smooth, but rather insignificant.

Dimensions

Body

Height as currently restored	100mm
Estimated original height	92mm
Estimated diameter of rim	76mm
Estimated diameter of neck	69mm
Estimated diameter of carination	80mm
Diameter of flat base	13.5mm
Thickness close to rim	4.2mm
Thickness at internal bevel	7.2–8.3mm
Thickness at carination	9.0–9.8mm
Thickness of base (centre)	c. 13.5mm
Weight (incomplete; parts infilled)	120g

Handle

Maximum depth of lower handle attachment	8mm
Minimum thickness of handle stumps – lower: 5mm, upper: 5.5mm	
Width of handle base	≥36mm

Composition
Amber of Baltic origin (Beck and Shennan 1991, 38 GB 29).

Manufacture, wear
Striations are visible on the internal surfaces, especially at the neck. They are generally circumferential but can also be oblique.

There are some exposed fractures with interesting damage characteristics. The vertically aligned side of one neck sherd shows a clean smooth-sheared break, apparently ancient since it is weathered. Perpendicular from its base, running above the handle stump, is a hinge fracture, also ancient. There is another short vertically sheared stretch approaching the rim. One end of

the handle fracture is unevenly shattered (?modern) but the long run is mostly smooth-sheared and weathered with resonance-shatter along its upper edge.

A similar resonance-shatter runs along a hinge fracture on the lower side of an intriguing crescent shaped (unrestored) gap in the lower body. Most of this fracture is smooth and not far off perpendicular to the wall's thickness, but the hinge scar has spalled a further 3–4mm from the exterior surface. The upper edge of this crescentic gap also features a narrow hinge scar, the two strongly suggestive of pressure exerted from above on one or two occasions. The two fractures converge into a single line which then runs vertically through the carination and upper body.

---

11. Hove barrow, West Sussex, England
Brighton & Hove Museums R 5643.1
Fig. 50, Colour Pl. 12

Context and circumstances
Some years before 1856 an approach road to Hove railway station was cut through a mound, but nothing was recorded at that point. There was further removal of earth in 1856 to make a garden; at the centre of the remnant mound and about 9 feet (2.75m) down an oak coffin was struck, aligned approximately E–W (Phillips 1856). All but a knot crumbled away. Within the earth contained in the coffin were found some fragments of 'carious bone, apparently charred'; in the central area of the coffin were an amber cup, a stone battleaxe, a perforated whetstone and a dagger, 'as if … they had rested on the breast of the body' (according to one of the workmen). The coffin lay on natural yellow clay; the mound comprised 'surface earth and rubbish thrown up together'. The remains of the bones, coffin and mound were carted off to the garden. All the first-hand information came to Phillips via the workmen and the clerk of works of the estate where the tumulus stood. The finds were presented to Brighton Museum by Baron Goldsmid. A radiocarbon date was subsequently obtained from the remaining coffin fragment of 3190 ± 46 BP; 1610–1310 cal BC at 2 sigma (BM-682).

Condition
The cup is generally in very good condition. The handle was broken in three places, probably at the time of excavation, and the central part would seem to have become entirely detached. This has been refixed, but some adjoining chips are missing. The rim has six detached chips, two of which survive reattached to the body. Of the others, one has left a fresh surface, but the others are matt, weathered and probably ancient. A small spall has been detached from the base just off-centre. Two linear fissures at oblique angles in the wall (visible externally and internally) peter out into solid amber and must be flaws in the raw material, but have not obviously led to any perforation of the wall.

Description
Most of the body is close to hemispherical in form and of constant thickness. However, the short upper body has different profiles inside and out for the groove band, neck and rim. The neck is hollowed and just 9mm deep. It is recessed relative to the band carrying grooves immediately below as is the lower body.

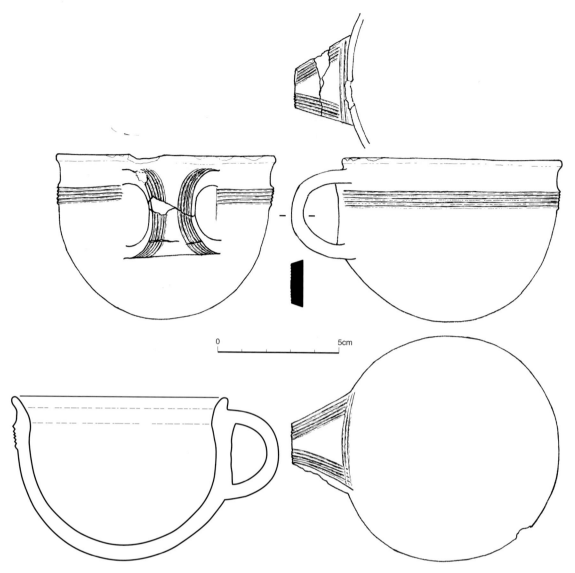

Figure 50 Drawing of the Hove amber cup. Scale 67%. [cat. no. 11]

The groove band is thus around 1mm proud of the flanking surfaces and is 9mm deep, but the five 'V'-section grooves have been inscribed close together so as to effectively create a corrugated profile on a miniature scale.

The rim is slightly out-turned, its lip having both a flat vertical exterior (3–3.5mm deep) and a flat narrow top (2–2.5mm wide). The wall thickens internally towards a pair of very diffuse horizontal bevels at the neck (approximately 8 and 13mm below rim), before belling out a little into the main vessel.

The handle contracts from the feet to the middle giving strongly curved sides, viewed face on. However, from the top view it can be seen that the sides are actually planar cut-lines, tapering from the body outwards. After the initial cut, the flat sides of the handle were further trimmed so as to angle them in slightly towards the internal edge; this lessened the trapezoidality of the cross-section. The interior is neatly hollowed and the handle of fairly constant thickness (5–6mm). The part of the body wall straddled by the handle is thicker than elsewhere being flush with the raised groove band. This under-handle zone is gently curved and meets the walls to either side in a diffuse bevel. The handle has groove decoration to match that around the girth, a set of five grooves outlining either side. At the feet, just before they join the vessel wall, the design is closed off by transverse double-grooves, scored rather more

heavily. That on the underside splays into three grooves at one end, perhaps due to an error during the cutting. In places the end grooves overlap the side ones.

Dimensions
Body
Height	65mm
Diameter of rim	87.5–89.5mm (extremes at *c.* 45° to one another)
Thickness close to rim	*c.* 3mm
Thickness at internal bevel	*c.* 7mm
Thickness of base (centre)	*c.* 6.5mm

Handle
Depth of handle	35mm
Width of handle feet	40mm (both)

Manufacture, wear
The flattened rim top conforms well to a plane, suggesting final grinding on a large flat block. Virtually all the exterior is extremely smooth and even, but the under-handle zone has slight undulations. There are numerous more-or-less circumferential fine striations on the lip, neck and just under the groove band, and others on the handle sides, but they are less evident on the lower body. This could be due to a finer finish or additional use-wear. Parts of the lower body retain vestiges of

clawed tool-marks otherwise ground away; they are presumably relics from an earlier stage of coarse shaping. The inside of the vessel has diffuse but macroscopically visible scallop-like tool-marks on random alignments. Localised striations occur within the decorative grooves, being dependent on the detailed morphology of the pointed instrument used. The grooves do not follow a perfectly straight line and hence the space between any two varies from a sharp ridge to a narrow flat band. There is no obvious wear on the underside of the handle.

The body, although extremely well shaped, is not exactly circular; diameters vary between 87.5 and 89.5mm. Taken in conjunction with the absence of any centering feature at the base, this argues for production by hand-turning rather than lathe-turning. The projection for the handle, being part of the same block, would anyway be an obstacle to continuous rotational trimming or grinding of the exterior surface.

To the right of the handle a short sharp vertical incision descends from the upper handle foot and partially intersects the ends of the grooves on the body. Given its position and alignment, it is highly likely to be a slight overcut into the body during final trimming of the right-hand side of the handle lug.

SHALE CUPS

12. ?Wiltshire 1, England
Salisbury & South Wiltshire Museum 191.
Fig. 51

Context and circumstances
Newall's original publication of this pair of cups (nos 12 & 13; Newall 1927–29) made it clear that there was no record of their provenance. The assumption that they could have come from the Amesbury district relies entirely on that being the area of residence of the previous owner, Job Edwards. Without any documentation, the assumption that they were found near Amesbury, or indeed in the county, should be treated very circumspectly. No documented finds of precious cups come from so far inland in southern England.

It is intriguing that Edwards managed to obtain or excavate two unrecorded cups. It is extremely improbable that they would have come from two independent sites, in both cases being unreported finds. It might be inferred that these were either together in a single deposit, or that they were in two closely related contexts, recalling the two shale cups from two barrows on Broad Down, Farway (nos 14 & 15 below).

Condition
Restored, with missing portions filled; these include much of the upper body and a narrow strip running diagonally through lower body. Only about one-third of the rim is extant, but virtually the whole of the handle survives unbroken. In addition to the base of the handle, about one-sixth of the circumference of the carination remains (to its left). The main fractures and fissures on the body and base follow the bedding planes of the shale and it is probable that there has been some distortion of the vessel.

The internal surface is a little crazed but mainly in fair condition to show its original smooth-polished finish.

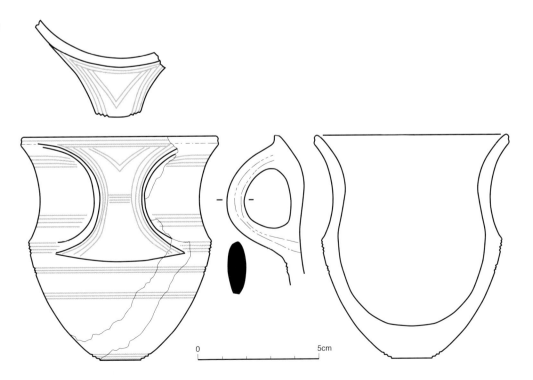

Figure 51 Ideal reconstruction of the ?Wiltshire 1 cup. Scale 67%. [cat. no. 12]

0 _____ 5cm

Description

The intact rim shows curvature varying between about 75 and 85mm diameter indicating an elliptic or asymmetric shape. The flatter side is alongside the stout handle, where there is no cracking from distortion. The loss of the greater part of the rim, however, makes it difficult to assess the degree to which non-circularity was original. Again, at the carination the wall immediately below the handle is less tightly curved than the segment alongside.

In profile the carination is moderate and crisp externally, sitting immediately above a groove band and running directly into the inner edges of the handle. However, this is not echoed in the inner profile which is instead a sinuous curve rising from a rounded bottom; this results in a thinner wall just above the carination than below. There is also a gentle thickening of the wall around the middle of the neck before it tapers to about 4mm at the rim. The rim itself is gently out-turned and is double-beaded externally due to an encircling groove in the middle. The top is rounded. The inner profile is not exactly concentric with the outer one, so the wall is thinner to one side of the lower body.

The base is flat inside the innermost groove at the foot of the wall. It is not co-planar with the rim, the planes diverging by around 3°.

The handle is a dominant feature on this cup, being large relative to the body. It also has some subtly curving lines. The sides, as seen from the top, are slightly concave rather than the more usual straight sides of a trapeze; moreover, they splay out to broad feet which run seamlessly into the curves of rim and carination respectively. The cross-section is markedly elliptical, modified by narrow flattened sides which are non-parallel. The outer surface becomes flat as it approaches and joins the rim, but retains its strong convexity at the lower body junction.

In addition to the single groove at the lip, the body carries six bands of horizontal grooves, the upper three comprising four grooves each, the lower three, three grooves each. The spacing of these bands is very deliberately unequal; in particular, the design leaves broader plain zones around the centre of the neck and on the lowest part of the body above the foot grooves.

Triple-groove bands outline the sides of the handle and at the top they join a transverse double-groove in acute angles. The latter suspends a double-groove 'V' motif which neatly occupies the upper part of the reserved central field. Below, four horizontal grooves traverse the narrowest point.

Dimensions

Body

Height	88.5mm
Depth of neck	41.5mm
Estimated diameter of rim	c. 80mm
Estimated diameter of carination	c. 73mm
Diameter, innermost groove at base	18.3mm
Thickness of wall (above base)	4–6mm
Thickness of base	12.5mm

Handle

Minimum width of handle	19.5mm
Width of handle feet (reconstructed)	c. 56mm (upper), c. 52mm (lower)
Handle thickness	7.5mm

Composition

Non-jet (Bussell *et al*. 1981, 31)

Manufacture, wear

There are no apparent wear traces on or above the base, but part of the surface is in extremely poor condition resulting in the disappearance of the basal grooves for half their circuit. The handle has possible wear in the form of a worn patch on the left side under-edge; opposite this on the right side is a slight notch which could have resulted from either differential wear or the working out of a flaw or mistake. Slight undulations in the bottom of the interior may be vestiges of original tool-marks rather than features of distortion, but generally it presents a well polished surface. The inside of the handle is also smooth-finished, but there are residual minor undulations. Groove profiles are neat but shallow V's with rounded bases.

---

13. ?Wiltshire 2, England

Salisbury & South Wiltshire Museum 192.
Fig. 52

Context and circumstances

As above for no 12.

Condition

The whole of the lower body is present, but only about half of the upper body. Only a small part of the missing portion, which extends from under the handle well to the left, is restored. Fracture lines in the shale generally form an orthogonal pattern. The vessel is extremely distorted and, although the base itself retains circularity, even the lower body has become elliptical.

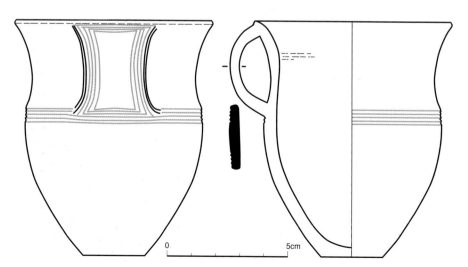

Figure 52 Ideal reconstruction of the ?Wiltshire 2 cup. Scale 67%. [cat. no. 13]

0   5cm

There are three fracture lines right across the handle, which is now restored. The base angle has spalled away around one third of its circumference.

Description

The base is neat and smooth, but (currently) not perfectly flat. There is a crisp angle to the lower wall which rises in a bowed profile of constant thickness to a weak carination externally. A gently concave neck then leads to a moderately flared mouth with a simple rounded rim. Internally the neck thickens to a neat but weak bevel (c. 13mm down), below which a steady curve runs all the way to the rounded bottom.

The handle is a fairly thin ribbon of near rectangular section with slight bowing of the external face. In profile it describes less than a semi-circle. From the top it exhibits a near trapezoid shape.

The body has a single band of four grooves placed immediately beneath the carination. While three of these grooves continue uninterrupted beneath the handle, the uppermost one butts up to its thin, ungrooved sides. The face of the handle is totally framed by groove bands just inside the edges. Four grooves outline the curved sides and three cross at top and bottom; the latter join the inner three of the sides to form an enclosure of waisted rectangular shape.

Dimensions

Body

Present height	90–96mm
Estimated original height	92–93mm
Rim diameter	c. 60 x 105mm(→82mm)
Neck diameter	c. 44 x 91mm (→67–68mm)
Carination diameter	52 x 91.5mm (→72mm)
Base diameter	25mm
Rim thickness	c. 2mm
Thickness at internal bevel	4–5mm
Minimum thickness of neck	3–3.5mm
Thickness of carination	4.5–5.5mm
Thickness of base	3.5mm

Handle

Width of handle feet	33 (upper), 34mm (lower)
Minimum handle width	25.7mm

Composition

Non-jet (Bussell et al. 1981, 13)

Manufacture, wear

Despite the extensive hairline cracking, much of the surface presents a polished sheen. No wear traces were noted on the body or the underside of the handle, which is in poor condition. The angles between the inner handle surface and the wall are for the most part very crisp, showing good attention to finishing the perforation.

---

14. Broad Down barrow 53, Farway 1, Devon, England

Exeter Museum 290
Fig. 53, Colour Pl. 13

Context and circumstances

Two shale cups were found in barrows on Broad Down, Farway (barrows 53 and 61). The first was found in 1868 during excavations instigated by the Devonshire Association for the Advancement of Science, Literature and Art (Kirwan 1868). Kirwan's account describes a barrow thrown up over a pyre; the cup was found immediately above a central cremation deposit of burnt bone on a bed of charcoal, itself on top of an area of flint paving with signs of in situ burning; beneath was the old ground surface which appeared to have been dug away by a few inches to level the pyre site (Kirwan 1868, 307, fig. 1). There were no other finds.

Condition

The cup is complete, but highly distorted from lateral pressure in the ground. The basal boss is still perfectly circular due to its rigid structure, but the body becomes progressively more elliptical towards the rim. That this is not the original shape is indicated by the eccentric position of the handle, situated on neither of the axes of the ellipse. Unsurprisingly the vessel is extensively cracked, yet none of the fissures have opened up significantly. The dominant ones follow the bedding planes of the material, vertical or steeply diagonal on the vessel, but there is also a finer web of crazing in patches. One large portion extending from the rim to below the carination is entirely isolated by a major crack and has probably been detached in the past and restored.

Description

The base is domed with no flat area at all and the profile curves upwards towards the maximum girth which is gently rounded

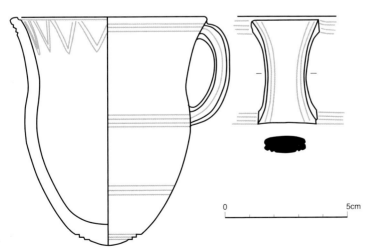

Figure 53 Ideal reconstruction of the Broad Down, Farway 1 shale cup. Scale 67%. [cat. no. 14]

0   5cm

rather than carinated. Above the belly, there is a small constriction emphasised by the slightest of creases, before the neck expands modestly outwards to the rim. The inner profile mirrors the outer one for virtually the whole depth and the wall only becomes thicker at the very base.

The rim undulates a little, although perhaps partly due to the distortion. It has a flattish top with rounded angles internally and externally. On the inside it is emphasised by a single horizontal groove, from which hang 16 pendant V-motifs, each comprising a double groove. Four sets of body grooves decorate the exterior and, although widely spaced, they are not evenly spaced. The band at the belly comprises four grooves, those above (at rim) and below (on the lower body) comprise three, while that encircling the base roundel has just two. The upper two bands butt up to the feet of the handle and one groove from each set continues onto the side of the handle as a single linking groove. Adjacent grooves at top and bottom respectively just run out onto the handle side, while the basal belly groove continues across thereby defining the handle base. The outer face of the handle has a simple double groove outlining the curved sides for their whole length.

The handle is strap like, but of swollen rectangular section and is relatively slack in profile. In face view it is gently waisted and broader at the top than the bottom.

Dimensions

Body

Height (maximum)	90mm
Rim diameter	71.2 x 88.3 (→80mm)
Neck diameter	57 x 70.5 (→64mm)
Belly diameter	62.4 x 70.8mm (→66.5mm)
Diameter of top basal groove	24.0 x 24.0mm
Thickness at rim	3.8mm
Thickness of walls	c. 4mm
Thickness of base	8.5mm

Handle

Handle depth	41mm
Width of handle feet	27mm (upper), 24mm (lower)
Minimum handle width	16.7mm
Minimum handle thickness	6.5mm

Manufacture, wear

Despite the extensive cracking, the intervening surfaces retain a beautiful high polish. Where striations are discernible, they tend to be very fine, although there are some coarser ones under the handle and elsewhere. Inside the lower body rotary grinding marks are clear, but these change to a vertical orientation inside the belly and up to the mouth. There is a whitish stain (rather

than accretion) inside the base that has linear elements aligned with the grain – presumably reflecting differential absorption.

The decorative grooves generally have broad V profiles with rounded bases, but the internal ones seem crisper and also bear traces of whitish material (?soil or deliberate infill). There is the slight suggestion of greater rounding of the under edges of the handle on either side at the top which might reflect wear from, for example, thong suspension.

15. Broad Down barrow 61, Farway 2, Devon, England
Exeter Museum A344
Fig. 54

Context and circumstances

The second Farway cup, found by Kirwan in 1870, is from a barrow covering a cairn of stones over a collapsed cist, in which were 'burnt bones on the bark of a tree' and a dagger of Gerloff's Type Camerton in several pieces (Gerloff 1975, 106–7). The cup was found about 3 feet (0.92m) from the bones 'in a compact mass of stones' (Newall 1927–9, 116). Hutchinson's account (1880) of the excavation, at which he was not present, is sketchy. The burial may be interpreted as a cremation in a tree-trunk coffin, but it is intriguing that the cup seems not to have accompanied the main deposit.

Condition

Most of the vessel is present, but about 20% of the rim is lacking. Damage to the rim seems to have occurred between Kirwan's 1870 publication and that of Hutchinson (1880, 136–7). The whole surface is extremely laminated on a horizontal plane giving a fragile appearance. Very small patches of polished surface survive. Like Farway cup 1 the shape changes from circular in the lower body to elliptical at the mouth, but the degree of distortion is considerably less on this cup. This time the handle lines up with the long axis of the ellipse. The rim lies on a plane rather skewed to that of base and shoulder, this likely to be due to differential shrinkage. There is a crack across the handle high up; some chips have become detached and are missing at one end.

Description

Although the base is a small circle defined by a distinct if obtuse angle, it is very slightly convex rather than perfectly flat. This should not be due to alteration given that the lower body seems to have escaped distortion. It is possible that there was an encircling groove round the base, but condition precludes

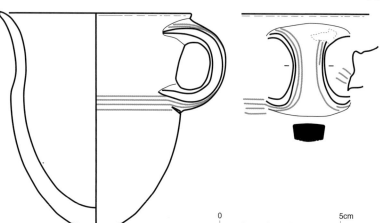

Figure 54 Ideal reconstruction of the Broad Down, Farway 2 shale cup. Scale 67%. [cat. no. 15]

0   5cm

certainty.

The wall rises in a graceful convex curve with the slightest inflection at the middle creating a weak carination; above is a small contraction into the gently hollowed neck. The mouth appears to have been moderately expanded and tapers to a thin rounded rim. Internally the profile is smoothly sinuous from the rounded base to the mouth, and this gives rise to some variation in wall thickness, slightly thicker towards the base and marginally thinner low in the neck.

Despite its poor surface condition, it would seem that the body was decorated with only one set of grooves, a band of four immediately beneath the carination. Because of the crescentic shape given to the handle feet, it was possible for the craftsman to continue the middle pair of grooves onto the external face of the handle; with a subtle change in direction they sweep round and upwards to outline the sides.

With the bowed feet and a pronounced waist, the handle has a strongly peltate shape in face view. In profile it is more-or-less semi-circular and in cross-section sub-rectangular with well bowed faces; the sides are fairly flat and taper out as they reach the feet.

Dimensions

Body

Average present height	c. 82mm
Estimated original height	c. 85mm
Rim diameter	73.5 x 81mm (→77.5mm)
Neck diameter	60 x 70mm (→65mm)
Carination diameter	67.5 x 72 (→69.5mm)
Lower body diameter (12mm from base)	45 x 45mm
Base diameter	20 x 20mm
Thickness at rim	2mm
Thickness of walls	4–7mm
Thickness of base	7mm

Handle

Handle depth	37mm
Width of handle feet	c. 35mm (both)
Minimum handle width	12.5mm
Minimum handle thickness	6.5mm

Manufacture, wear

Condition is too poor for fine evidence to survive. However, in the neck immediately to the right of the handle is a set of three short parallel strokes set diagonally which may be ancient tool marks.

SHALE or WOODEN CUP

16. Stoborough 'King Barrow', Dorset, England

Lost (in Richard Gough's possession around 1787). Description and drawing based on Hutchins 1774 and Gough 1786 (account also fully given in Ashbee 1960, 86)

Fig. 55

Context and circumstances

The possible shale cup from King Barrow, Stoborough (formerly Stowborough), was found when a 100 ft wide (30.75m) and 12 ft high (3.7m) barrow was opened in 1767 during construction of a turnpike road. It entered the possession of R. Gough later in the 18th century and is now lost. The first published account was by Hutchins (1774) where the cup is figured as an imagined reconstruction. The drawing which appears in Gough (1786) shows the cup in its broken and distorted state. At the time the cup was described as being made of wood and Hutchins favoured oak. By the date of Hutchins' third edition (1861) it was '*formerly* in the possession of Mr Gough' (current authors' italics) and by the time Clift (1908) pronounces it to be 'a lathe-turned cup of Kimmeridge shale' its whereabouts was unknown. Its reassessment as shale (for example by a Dr. Wake Smart, mentioned in Kirwan's account of the first Farway vessel (1868, 299) when it had already vanished from view, is probably surmise, but may be correct.

The burial context of the cup is fairly well described for the time: central in the mound, it comprised an enormous oak trunk coffin about 10 ft long (3.1m) and 4 ft (1.25m) wide, resting on the old ground surface and covered by a turf mound, 'in some of which the heath was not perished'. The skeletal remains were

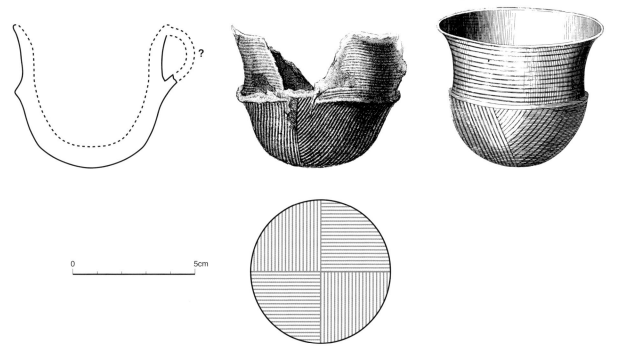

0   5cm

Figure 55 Ideal reconstruction of the Stoborough shale(?) cup with the two early depictions it is based upon (after Gough 1786 (middle) and Hutchins 1774 (right)). Scale 67%. [cat. no. 16]

partial, 'unburnt, black and soft … and all had been wrapped up in a large covering, composed of several skins, some as thin as parchments, others much thicker, especially where the hair remained, which shewed they were deer skins.' The material was well enough preserved for 'seams and stitches' to be visible and it was thought to have wrapped around the body 'several times'. Inside 'the bones were compressed flat in a lump, and cemented together by a glutinous matter, perhaps the moisture of the body. On unfolding the wrapper, a disagreeable smell was perceived, such as is usual at the first opening of a vault' (Hutchins 1774).

The vessel was found at the south-east end, perhaps near the head, but no skull was identified. The only other grave good was a small piece of 'gold lace' which remains a puzzle. This was published by Bury Palliser in her *History of Lace* (1911, 4, fig 1). It was accepted by her as gold lace 'of the old lozenge pattern, that most ancient and universal of all designs, again found depicted on the coats of ancient Danes, where the borders are edged with an open or net-work of the same pattern.' It was blackened when found but the original account is firm that 'bits of wire plainly appeared in it'. It is hard to find an Early Bronze Age gold type that matches the description given, but another possibility is that this was a highly eroded thin bronze object, so eaten in an acidic environment that it appeared as 'lacework'. Despite this difficulty, there can be little doubt that the burial described conforms to Early Bronze Age traditions.

Condition

One of two early drawings (Gough 1786) shows the vessel apparently realistically and incomplete in the upper body (**Fig. 55 centre**); around 70% of the vessel is depicted. Even Hutchins had acknowledged that it was 'much broken' (1774, 25). There is also surface spalling in evidence which had clearly disrupted the decoration locally and there are hints of distortion; indeed, it was described as 'compressed' and the dimensions of the mouth given as 3 inches by 2.

Description

The following description and our own reconstruction drawing (**Fig. 55**) are based on Gough's 1786 engraving, rather than the earliest published drawing, in Hutchins 1774, which shows a complete and perfect looking vessel and may be taken to be a hypothetical restoration of its original form. The illustration given by Gerloff (1975, pl. 57P) is a more embellished rendering of the latter.

The lower body is near to hemispherical with no indication for any flattening of the base. About halfway up the vessel it expands into a protuberant carination, which is met above by a concave upper body. The dimensions given in the early accounts suggest that the rim and carination would have had similar diameters and the mouth was thus lightly flared.

The upper body is shown covered with twenty horizontal lines, described as "hatched" and made "with a graving tool" (Hutchins), while similar grooves on the lower body are separated into panels (?four quadrants) and instead aligned vertically to diagonally. At the vertical panel junction shown, the lines to the left are vertical and to the right, diagonal. This could actually be a natural consequence of starting the decoration at a panel boundary and keeping each line roughly parallel to the previous one. As they progressed round the quarter sphere, the lines would thus become more and more skewed to the vertical (see **Fig. 55**).

There is no suggestion in the early accounts that the cup had a handle, but Gough's depiction shows a curious discontinuity in the line of the carination immediately above the panel junction in the lower decoration ; the lower design actually projects a little higher here before being interrupted by a broad and thin break. This surface seems to overlap and be situated in front of the broken edges of the upper body and gives every impression of being the stump of a missing handle. That the handle is not otherwise in evidence would be explained by the trapezoid gap in the upper body at this point.

Dimensions

Reported height	'two inches'
Estimated original height	*c.* 55mm
Reported rim diameter	"three inches by two" (→*c.*65mm)
Wall thickness (? upper body, where broken)	'two tenths of an inch', *c.* 5 mm
Width of possible handle stump	?19mm

Composition

'A small wooden vessel, much broken and comprest' – Gough 1786, xlv. 'A small vessel of oak, of a black colour' – Hutchins 1774, 25. Conceivably in fact shale or a similar material (Kirwan 1867–8, 628).

Manufacture, wear

Nothing known.

Bibliography

Abercromby, J. 1912. *A Study of the Bronze Age Pottery of Great Britain and Ireland and its Associated Grave Goods.* Oxford: Clarendon Press.

Alexander, J., Ozanne, P.C. and Ozanne, A. 1960. Report on the Investigation of a Round Barrow on Arreton Down, Isle of Wight. *Proceedings of the Prehistoric Society* 26, 263–302.

Aner, E. and Kersten, K. 1976. *Die Funde der Älteren Bronzezeit des nordischen Kreises in Dänemark, Schleswig-Holstein und Niedersachsen: Band II, Holboek, Soro und Praesto Amter.* Copenhagen & Neumunster.

Annable, F.K. and Simpson, D.A. 1964. *Guide Catalogue of the Neolithic and Bronze Age Collections in Devizes Museum.* Devizes.

Anonymous 1886. *Trésors archéologiques de l'Armorique occidentale.* Rennes: Société d'Emulation des Côtes-du-Nord.

Armbruster, B. 1996. Zu den technologischen Aspekten der Goldfunde aus dem bronzezeitlichen Schatz von Caldas de Reyes (Prov. Pontevedra). *Madrider Mitteilungen* 37, 60–73.

Armbruster, B. 2000. *Goldschmiedekunst und Bronzetecnik: Studien zum Metallhandwerk der Atlantische Bronzezeit auf der Iberischen Halbinsel.* Montagnac: Monographies Instrumentum no. 15.

Ashbee, P. 1960. *The Bronze Age Round Barrow in Britain.* London: Phoenix.

Ashbee, P. 1967. The Wessex grave. In A. Corney, A prehistoric and Anglo-Saxon burial ground, Ports Down, Portsmouth. *Proceedings of the Hampshire Field Club and Archaeology Society* 24, 20–41.

Ashbee, P. 2001. William Stukeley's Kentish Studies of Roman and Other Remains. *Archaeologia Cantiana* 121, 61–100.

Ashbee, P. 2005. *Kent in Prehistoric Times.* Stroud: Tempus.

Ashbee. P. and Dunning, G.C. 1960. The Round Barrows of East Kent. *Archaeologia Cantiana* 74, 48–57.

Ashmore, P.J. 2000. A list of archaeological radiocarbon dates. *Discovery and Excavation in Scotland* 1, 122–8.

Ashmore, P. J. 2001. A list of archaeological radiocarbon dates. *Discovery and Excavation in Scotland* 2, 122–8.

Askew, P. 2001. Area 330 (Zone 1) Whitehill Barrow (ARC WHR 99) Archaeological Post-excavation Assessment Report (Channel Tunnel Rail Link, InfoWorks Document Reference 004/EZR/SMUSE/00047-AA; Museum of London Archaeology Service).

Atkinson, R.J.C., Piggott, C.M. and Sandars, N.K. 1951. *Excavations at Dorchester, Oxon.* Oxford: Ashmolean Museum.

Aveneau de la Grancière, P. 1898. Fouille du tumulus à enceinte semi-circulaire de Saint-Fiacre-en Melrand (Morbihan), *Bulletin de la Société Polymathique du Morbihan*, 81–95.

Bamford, H. 1985. *Briar Hill, Excavation 1974–1978.* Northampton Development Corporation Archaeological Monograph 3.

Barber, M. 1997. Landscape, the Neolithic and Kent. In P. Topping (ed.) 1997, 77–85.

Barclay, A. and Glass, H. 1995. Excavations of Neolithic and Bronze Age ring-ditches, Shorncote Quarry, Somerford Keynes, Gloucestershire. *Transactions of the Bristol and Gloucestershire Archaeological Society* 113, 21–60.

Barclay, A., Gray, M. and Lambrick, G. 1995. *Excavation at the Devil's Quoits, Stanton Harcourt, Oxfordshire, 1972–3 and 1988.* Oxford: University Committee for Archaeology; Thames Valley Landscapes: the Windrush Valley vol. 3.

Barclay, G. 1983. Sites of the third millennium BC to the first millennium AD at North Mains, Strathallan, Perthshire. *Proceedings of the Society of Antiquaries of Scotland* 113, 122–281.

Barclay, G. 1999. Cairnpapple revisited: 1948–1998. *Proceedings of the Prehistoric Society* 65, 17–46.

Barclay, G. and Russell-White, C. J. 1993. Excavation in the ceremonial complex of the fourth to second millennia BC at Balfarg/Balbirnie, Glenrothes, Fife. *Proceedings of the Society of Antiquaries of Scotland* 123, 43–210.

Barnatt, J. 1990. *The Henges, Stone Circles and Ringcairns of the Peak District.* Sheffield University, Department of Archaeology and Prehistory. Sheffield Archaeological Monographs 1.

Barrett, J. 1988. The living the dead and the ancestors; Neolithic and Early Bronze Age mortuary practices. In J. Barrett and I. Kinnes (eds) 1988, *The Archaeology of Context in the Neolithic and Bronze Age: Recent Trends.* Sheffield: University of Sheffield, Department of Archaeology, 30–41.

Barrett, J. and Bradley, R. (eds) 1980. *Settlement and Society in the British Later Bronze Age.* Oxford: British Archaeological Reports British Series 83 (2 vols.).

Barrett, J., Bradley, R. and Green, M. 1991. *Landscape, Monuments and Society: the Prehistory of Cranborne Chase.* Cambridge University Press.

Beck, C. and Shennan, S. 1991. *Amber in Prehistoric Britain.* Oxford: Oxbow Monograph 8.

Bewley, B., Crutchley, S. and Grady, D. 2004. Aerial survey and its contribution to understanding the Neolithic of the South East. In J. Cotton and D. Field (eds) *Towards a New Stone Age; Aspects of the Neolithic in South-East England.* York: CBA Research Report 137.

Birchenough, A. 2004. One man and a Magnetometer: A geophysical investigation into the extent and morphology of monument construction at Ringlemere Farm, Woodnesborough, Kent. (Unpublished undergraduate dissertation submitted to Bournemouth University, April 2004).

Blanchet, J-C. 1984. *Les Premiers Metallurgistes en Picardie et dans le Nord de la France.* Paris: Mémoires de la Société Préhistorique Française 17.

Bouzek, J. 1985. *The Aegean, Anatolia and Europe: Cultural Interactions in the Second Millennium BC.* Göteborg: Studies in Mediterrannean Archaeology 29.

Bowman, S.G.E., Ambers, J.C. and Leese, M.N. 1990. Re-evaluation of British Museum radiocarbon dates issued between 1980 and 1984. *Radiocarbon* 32, 59–79.

Bradley, R. 1976. Maumbury Rings, Dorchester: the excavations of 1908–1913. *Archaeologia* 105, 1–97.

Bradley, R. 1993. *Altering the Earth: the Origins of Monuments in Britain and Continental Europe.* Edinburgh: Society of Antiquaries of Scotland Monograph Series no 8.

Bradley, R. 1998a. Stone circles and passage graves – a contested relationship. In A. Gibson and D. Simpson (eds) *Prehistoric Ritual and Religion: Essays in Honour of Aubrey Burl.* Stroud: Sutton, 2–13.

Bradley, R. 1998b. *The Significance of Monuments: on the Shaping of Human Experience in Neolithic and Bronze Age Europe.* London: Routledge.

Briard, J. 1965. *Les Dépôts Bretons et l'Age du Bronze Atlantique.* Rennes: Université de Rennes.

Briard, J. 1970. Un tumulus du Bronze Ancien, Kernonen en Pouvorn (Finistère). *L'Anthropologie* 74, 5–55.

Briard, J. 1978. Das Silbergefäss von Saint-Adrien, Côtes-du-Nord. *Archäoligisches Korrespondenzblatt*, 13–20.

Briard, J. 1984. *Les Tumulus d'Armorique.* Paris: L' Age du Bronze en France 3.

Brongers, J. and Woltering, P. 1978. *De Prehistorie van Nederland, economisch, technologisch.* Harlem.

Burgess, C.B. 1968. The later Bronze Age in the British Isles and north-western France. *Archaeological Journal* 125, 1–45.

Bürgi, J. and Kinnes, I. 1975. A gold beaker from Switzerland. *Antiquity* 49, 132–133.

Burl, H.A.W. 1969. Henges: internal structures and regional groups. *Archaeological Journal* 126, 1–28.

Burl, H.A.W. 1976. *The Stone Circles of the British Isles.* Newhaven and London: Yale University Press.

Burl, H.A.W. 1979. *Prehistoric Avebury.* New Haven and London: Yale University Press.

Burl, H.A.W. 1988. Coves: structural enigmas of the Neolithic. *Wiltshire*

Archaeological Magazine 82, 1–18.

Bussell, G.D., Pollard, A.M. and Baird, D.C. 1981. The characterisation of Early Bronze Age jet and jet-like material by X-Ray Fluorescence. *Wiltshire Archaeological Magazine* 76, 27–32.

Butler, C. forthcoming. The Flintwork. In *A Mesolithic site at Finglesham, Kent*.

Butler, C. 2005. *Prehistoric Flintwork*. Stroud: Tempus.

Butler, J.J. 1963. Bronze Age Connections across the North Sea. A study in prehistoric trade and industrial relations between the British Isles, the Netherlands, North Germany and Scandinavia, c. 1700–700 BC. *Palaeohistoria* 9.

Butler, J.J. 1990. Bronze Age metal and amber in the Netherlands (I). *Palaeohistoria* 32, 47–110.

Catling, H.W. 1964. *Cypriot Bronzework in the Mycenaean World*. Oxford: Clarendon Press.

Chadwick, A. and Pollard, J. 2005. A ring-cairn and Beaker burial at Gray Hill, Llanfair Discoed, Monmouthshire. *PAST* no. 50, 11–14.

Champion, T. 1980. Settlement and Environment Later Bronze Age Kent. In J. Barrett and R. Bradley (eds), 223–46.

Champion, T. 1982. The Bronze Age in Kent. In P.E. Leach (ed.) *Archaeology in Kent to AD 1500*. London: CBA Research Rep. no. 48, 31–9.

Childe, V.G. 1924. A gold vase of Early Helladic type. *Journal of Hellenic Studies* 44, 163–5.

Clare, T. 1986. Towards a reappraisal of henge monuments. *Proceedings of the Prehistoric Society* 52, 281–316.

Clark, P. (ed.), 2004a. *The Dover Bronze Age Boat*. Swindon: English Heritage.

Clark, P. (ed.), 2004b. *The Dover Bronze Age Boat in Context: Society and Water Transport in Prehistoric Europe*. Oxford: Oxbow Books.

Clarke, D., Cowie, T. and Foxon, A. 1985. *Symbols of Power at the Time of Stonehenge*. Edinburgh: HMSO.

Clarke, D.L. 1970. *Beaker Pottery of Britain and Ireland*. 2 vols. Cambridge University Press.

Cleal, R. 2004. Neolithic and Bronze Age pottery. In G. Lambrick and T. Allen, *Gravelly Guy, Stanton Harcourt: the Development of a Prehistoric and Romano-British Community*. Oxford Archaeological Unit, Thames Valley Landscapes Monograph 21, 65–82.

Cleal, R. and MacSween, A. 1999. *Grooved Ware in Britain and Ireland*. Oxford: Neolithic Studies Group Seminar Papers 3.

Cleal, R.M.J., Walker, K.E. and Montague R., 1995. *Stonehenge in its Landscape: Twentieth Century Excavations*. London: English Heritage Monograph 10.

Clift, J. 1908. Wareham. *Journal of the British Archaeological Association* (new series) 14, 19–20.

Coutts, H. 1971. *Tayside before History: a guide-catalogue of the Collection of Antiquities in Dundee Museum*. Dundee Museum and Art Gallery Publication, Catalogue no. 1.

Craw, J.H. 1930–1. Further excavations of cairns at Poltalloch, Argyll. *Proceedings of the Society of Antiquaries of Scotland* 65, 269–280.

Cruse, R.J. and Harrison, A.C. 1983. Excavation at Hill Road, Wouldham. *Archaeologia Cantiana* 99, 81–108.

Cunliffe, B.W. 1968. *Fifth Report on the excavations at the Roman Fort at Richborough Castle*. London: Society of Antiquaries Research Report 23, 1–41.

Cunliffe, B.W. 1993. *Wessex to A.D. 1000*. London and New York: Longman.

Cunnington, M.E. 1907–8. Notes on the opening of a Bronze Age barrow at Manton near Marlborough. *Wiltshire Archaeological Magazine* 35, 1–20.

David, A., Cole, M., Horsley, T., Linford, P. and Martin, L. 2004. A rival to Stonehenge? Geophysical survey at Stanton Drew, England. *Antiquity* 78, 341–58.

Davidson, H.R.E. and Webster, L. 1967. The Anglo-Saxon burial at Coombe (Woodnesborough), Kent. *Medieval Archaeology* 11, 1–41.

Douglas, J. 1793. *Nenia Britannica: a Sepulchral History of Great Britain from the earliest period to its general conversion*. London.

Drew, C.D. and Piggott, S. 1936. Two Bronze Age barrows, excavated by Mr Edward Cunnington. *Proceedings of the Dorset Natural History and Archaeological Society* 58, 18–25.

Dyson, L., Shand, G. and Stevens, S. 2000. Causewayed Enclosures. *Current Archaeology* 168, 470–2.

Ellmers, D. 2003. Die Aussagen der Goldschatzfunde von Langendorf, Eberswalde und Lienewitzer Forst zur Nutzung des Geswässernetzes zwischen Elbe und Oder. In T. Springer (ed.) *Gold und Kult der Bronzezeit*. Nürnberg: Germanisches Nationalmuseum, 162–74.

Eluère, C. 1982. *Les Ors Préhistoriques*. Paris: L' Age du Bronze en France 2.

Eogan, G. and Roche, H. 1997. *Excavations at Knowth, 2: Settlement and Ritual Sites of the Fourth and Fifth Millennia BC*. Dublin: Royal Irish Academy.

Evans, C. 1988. Acts of enclosure: a consideration of concentrically-organised causewayed enclosures. In J.C. Barrett and I.A. Kinnes (eds), 85–96.

Evans, J. 1897. *Ancient Stone Implements of Great Britain*. London: Longmans.

Everitt, A.M. 1986. *Continuity and Colonisation: the evolution of Kentish Settlement*. Leicester University Press.

Evison, V. 1956. An Anglo-Saxon cemetery at Holborough, Kent. *Archaeologia Cantiana* 70, 84–141.

Florescu, R. 1971. Notes on the history of ornamentation in antiquity. In *Treasures from Romania: a special exhibition held at the British Museum, January – March 1971*. London: British Museum Publications, 16–34.

Fontijn, D. 2001. Rethinking ceremonial dirks of the Plougrescant-Ommerschans type – some thoughts on the structure of metalwork exchange. In W.H. Metz, B.L. Beek and H. Streegstra (eds) *Patina: Essays presented to Jay Jordan Butler*. Groningen (privately published), 263–80.

Ford, S., Bradley, R., Hawkes, J. and Fisher, P. 1984. Flint-working in the Metal Age. *Oxford Journal of Archaeology* 3, 157–73.

Ford. S. 1991. An Early Bronze Age pit circle form Charnham Lane, Hungerford, Berkshire. *Proceedings of the Prehistoric Society* 57, 179–81.

Fox, A. 1948. The Broad Down (Farway) necropolis and the Wessex culture in Devon. *Proceedings of the Devon Archaeological Exploration Society* 4, 1–19.

Fox C. 1959. *Life and Death in the Bronze Age*. London: Routledge & Kegan Paul.

Frantz, J.H. and Schorsch, D. 1990. Egyptian Red Gold. *Archeomaterials* 4, 133–52.

Fröhlich, S. 1992. *Das Grabhügelfeld auf dem Spöllberg, Gemeinde Gölenkamp, Landkreis Bentheim. Fundstelle des goldenen Bechers*. Bramsche.

Gale, R. 2003. Potential radio-carbon sample from L-shaped feature (F. 1103). In K. Parfitt 2003b.

Gerloff, S. 1975. *The Early Bronze Age Daggers in Great Britain, and a reconsideration of the Wessex Culture*. Munich: Prähistorische Bronzefunde VI, 2.

Gerloff, S. 1993. Zu Fragen mittelmeerländischer Kontakte und absoluter Chronologie der Frühbronzezeit in Mittel- und Westeuropa. *Praehistorische Zeitschrift* 68, 58–102.

Gerloff, S. 1995. Bronzezeitliche Goldblechkronen aus Westeuropa. In A. Jockenhövel (ed.) *Festshrift für Hermann Müller-Karpe zum 70. Geburtstag*. Bonn.

Gibson, A. 1998. *Stonehenge and Timber Circles*. Stroud: Tempus.

Gibson, A. 2004. Small, but perfectly formed? Some observations on the Bronze Age cups of Scotland. In A. Gibson and A. Sheridan (eds) 2004, 270–88.

Gibson, A. and Sheridan, A. (eds), 2004. *From Sickles to Circles: Britain and Ireland at the Time of Stonehenge*. Stroud: Tempus.

Gibson, A., Macpherson-Grant, N. and Stewart, I. 1997. A Cornish vessel from farthest Kent. *Antiquity* 71, 438–41.

Gillings, M. and Pollard, J. 2004. *Avebury*. London: Duckworth.

Godelier, M. 1999. *The Enigma of the Gift*. University of Chicago Press. (Original French edition, 1996).

Godwin, H. 1962. Vegetational History of the Kentish Chalk Downs as seen at Wingham and Frogholt. *Veröffentlichung des Geobotanisches Institut (Zurich)* 37, 83–99.

Gough, R. 1786. *Sepulchral Monuments of Great Britain I*. London.

Gray, H. St G. 1903. On the excavations at Arbor Low, 1901–1902. *Archaeologia* 58, 461–98.

Green, C. and Rollo-Smith, S. 1984. The excavation of eighteen round barrows near Shrewton, Wiltshire. *Proceedings of the Prehistoric Society* 50, 255–318.

Green, S. 1984. Flint Arrowheads: Typology and Interpretation. *Lithics* 5, 19–39.

Greenfield, E. 1960. A Neolithic Pit and other Finds from Wingham, East Kent. *Archaeologia Cantiana* 74, 58–72.

Grinsell, L.V. 1959. *Dorset Barrows*. Dorchester: Dorset Natural History and Archaeology Society.

Grinsell, L.V. 1992. The Bronze Age Round Barrows of Kent. *Proceedings of the Prehistoric Society* 58, 355–84.

Halliwell, G. and Parfitt, K. 1985. The Prehistoric Land Surface in the

Lydden Valley: an Initial Report. *Kent Archaeological Review* 82, 39–43.

Hardaker, R. 1974. *Early Bronze Age Dagger Pommels from Great Britain and Ireland*. Oxford: British Archaeological Reports (British Series) 3.

Harding, A.F. and Lee, G.E. 1987. *Henge Monuments and Related Sites of Great Britain*. Oxford: British Archaeological Reports (British Series) 175.

Harding, J. 2003. *Henge Monuments of the British Isles*. Stroud: Tempus.

Hardmeyer, B. and Bürgi, J., 1975. Der Goldbecher von Eschenz. *Zeitschrift für Schweizerische Archäologie und Kunstgeschichte* 32, 109–20.

Hart, C.R. 1981. *The North Derbyshire Archaeological Survey to A.D. 1500*. Chesterfield: North Derbyshire Archaeological Trust.

Hartmann, A. 1970. *Prähistorische Goldfunde aus Europa*. Mainz: Römisch-Germanisches Zentralmuseum; Studien zu den Anfängen der Metallurgie, 3.

Hartmann, A. 1982. *Prähistorische Goldfunde aus Europa II*. Mainz: Römisch-Germanisches Zentralmuseum; Studien zu den Anfängen der Metallurgie, 5.

Hartwell, B. 1998. The Ballynahatty Complex. In A. Gibson and D. Simpson (eds) *Prehistoric Ritual and Religion: Essays in Honour of Aubrey Burl*. Stroud: Sutton, 32–44.

Hasted, E. 1800. *The History and Topographical Survey of the County of Kent*, Canterbury: Bristow (reprinted Canterbury, 1972).

Hawkes, C.F.C. 1983. The Rillaton gold cup. *Antiquity* 57, 124–125.

Healy, F. 1997. Site 3. Flagstones. In R.J.C. Smith, F. Healy, M.J. Allen, E.L. Morris and P.J. Woodward (eds) *Excavations along the Route of the Dorchester By-pass, Dorset, 1986–8*. Salisbury: Wessex Archaeology Report no. 11, 27–48.

Heathcote, J. 2003. Geoarchaeological assessment of buried soil, mound material and ditch deposits. In K. Parfitt 2003b.

Helms, M.W. 1988. *Ulysses' Sail*. Princeton: Princeton University Press.

Helms, M.W. 1993. *Craft and the Kingly Ideal: Art, Trade, and Power*. Austin: University of Texas.

Hemp, W.J. 1930. The chambered cairn of Bryn Celli Ddu. *Archaeologia* 80, 179–214.

Holgate, R. 1988. *Neolithic Settlement of the Thames Basin*. Oxford: British Archaeological Reports (British Series) 194.

Holgate, R. 1981. The Medway Megaliths and Neolithic Kent. *Archaeologia Cantiana* 97, 221–234.

Hood, M.S.F. 1956. Another warrior-grave at Ayios Ioannis near Knossos. *Annual of the British School at Athens* 51, 81–99.

Hoskins, R. 1995. Mesolithic axe found near Goodnestone. *Kent Archaeological Review* 121, 8–9

Hundt, H-J. 1971. Der Dolchhort von Gau-Bickelheim in Rheinhessen. *Jahrbuch des Römisch-Germanischen Zentralmuseums Mainz* 18, 1–50.

Hutchins, J. 1774. *The History and Antiquities of the County of Dorset I*. London: Bowyer & Nichols.

Hutchinson, P.O. 1867–8. Some account of discoveries made in the opening of tumuli at Farway between Sidmouth and Honiton. *Proceedings of the Society of Antiquaries of London* (2nd ser.) 4, 159–61.

Hutchinson, P.O. 1880. Second Report of the Barrow Committee: Report of barrows near Sidmouth. *Reports and Transactions of the Devonshire Association for the Advancement of Science, Literature and Art* 12, 122–151.

Jessup, R. F. 1930. *The Archaeology of Kent*. London: Methuen.

Jobey, G. 1966. Excavations on palisaded settlements and cairnfields at Alnham, Northumberland. *Archaeologia Aeliana* 44, 5–48.

Jockenhövel, A. 2004. Von West nach Ost? Zur Genese der Frühbronzezeit Mitteleuropas. In H. Roche, E. Grogan, J. Bradley, J. Coles and B. Raftery (eds) *From Megaliths to Metal: Essays in Honour of George Eogan*. Oxford: Oxbow Books, 155–167.

Johnson, N. and Rose, P. 1994. *Bodmin Moor: an Archaeological Survey, vol. 1: The Human Landscape to c. 1800*. Truro: Cornwall Archaeological Unit.

Kibbert, K. 1980. *Die Äxte und Beile im mittleren Westdeutschland I*. Munich: Prähistorische Bronzefunde IX, 10.

Kinnes, I.A. 1994. *Beaker and Early Bronze Age Grave Groups*. London: British Museum Publications, British Bronze Age Metalwork, A17-30.

Kirwan, R. 1867–8. Memoir of the examination of three barrows at Broad Down, Farway, near Honiton. *Reports and Transactions of the Devon Association for the Advancement of Science, Literature and Art* 2:2, 619–649.

Kirwan, R. 1868. Sepulchral barrows at Broad Down, near Honiton, and an unique cup of bituminous shale there found. *Archaeological Journal* 25, 290–311.

Kopytoff, I. 1986. The cultural biography of things: commoditization as a process. In A. Appadurai (ed.) *The Social Life of Things*. Cambridge University Press, 64–91.

Krause, R. 1988. *Die endneolithischen und frühbronzezeitlichen Grabfunde auf der Nordstatterrasse von Singen am Hohentweil*. Stuttgart: Landesdenkmalamt Baden-Württemberg.

Lawson Finch, M. and Garrett, S.R. 2003. *The East Kent Railway*. (2 vols) Usk: Oakwood Press.

Longworth, I.H. 1979. The Neolithic and Bronze Age pottery. In G. Wainwright 1979, 75–124.

Longworth, I. H. 1983. The Whinny Liggate perforated wall cup and its affinities. In A.O'Connor and D.V. Clarke (eds) *From the Stone Age to the 'Forty-Five: Studies presented to R.B.K. Stevenson*. Edinburgh: John Donald, 65–86.

Longworth, I.H. 1984. *Collared Urns of the Bronze Age in Britain and Ireland*. Cambridge University Press.

Lynch, F. 1969. The megalithic tombs of north Wales. In T.G.E. Powell (ed.) *Megalithic Enquiries in the West of Britain: a Liverpool Symposium*. Liverpool University Press, 107–148.

Lynch, F. and Musson C. 2001. A prehistoric and early medieval complex at Llandegai, near Bangor, North Wales. *Archaeologia Cambrensis* 150, 17–142.

Macpherson-Grant, N. 1977. *The Excavation of a Neolithic/Bronze Age Site at Lord of the Manor, Haine Road, Ramsgate*. Isle of Thanet Archaeological Unit Publication No. 1 (privately printed, not dated).

Macpherson-Grant, N. 1980. Lord of the Manor – Site 2. *The Isle of Thanet Archaeological Unit Interim Excavation Reports 1977–1980* (privately printed, Thanet).

Manby, T.G. 2004. Food Vessels with handles. In A. Gibson and A. Sheridan (eds) 2004, 215–42.

Martin, L. 2003. Woodnesborough, Kent, Report on Geophysical Surveys January 2002. In K. Parfitt 2003b.

Meaney, A. 1964. *A Gazetteer of Early Anglo-Saxon Burial Sites*. London: George Allen and Unwin.

Megaw, B.R.S. and Hardy, E.M. 1938. British decorated axes and their diffusion during the earlier part of the Bronze Age. *Proceedings of the Prehistoric Society* 4, 272–307.

Menghin, W. and Schauer, P. 1983. *Der Goldkegel von Ezelsdorf: Kultgerät der späten Bronzezeit*. Nürnberg: Germanisches Nationalmuseum.

Mercer, R. 1981. The excavation of a late Neolithic henge-type enclosure at Balfarg, Markinch, Fife, Scotland, 1977-78. *Proceedings of the Society of Antiquaries of Scotland* 111, 63-171.

Mercer, R. 1990. *Causewayed Enclosures*. Princes Risborough: Shire.

Mercer, R., Barclay, G.J., Jordan, D. and Russell-White, C.J. 1988. The Neolithic henge-type enclosure at Balfarg: a reassessment of the evidence for an incomplete ditch circuit. *Proceedings of the Society of Antiquaries of Scotland* 118, 61–7.

Millett, M. and Wilmott, T. 2003. Rethinking Richborough. In P. Wilson (ed.) *The Archaeology of Roman Towns. Studies in honour of John S. Wacher*. Oxford: Oxbow Books, 184-94.

Moszolics, A. 1965–6. Goldfunde des Depotfundhorizontes von Hajdúsámson. *Bericht der Römisch-Germanischen Kommission* 46/47, 1–76.

Needham, S.P. 1979. The extent of foreign influence on Early Bronze Age axe development in southern Britain. In M. Ryan (ed.) *The Origins of Metallurgy in Atlantic Europe: proceedings of the fifth Atlantic Colloquium, Dublin, 1978*. Dublin: Stationery Office, 265-93.

Needham, S.P. 1988a. Selective deposition in the British Early Bronze Age. *World Archaeology* 20, 229–248.

Needham, S.P. 1988b. A group of Early Bronze Age axes from Lydd. In J.Eddison and C.Green (eds), *Romney Marsh: Evolution, Occupation, Reclamation*. Oxford University Committee for Archaeology Monograph 24, 77–82.

Needham, S.P. 2000a. The development of embossed goldwork in Bronze Age Europe. *Antiquaries Journal* 80, 27–65.

Needham, S.P. 2000b. Power pulses across a cultural divide: cosmologically driven exchange between Armorica and Wessex. *Proceedings of the Prehistoric Society* 66, 151–207.

Needham, S.P. 2000c. The gold and copper metalwork. In G.Hughes, *The Lockington Gold Hoard: an Early Bronze Age barrow cemetery at Lockington, Leicestershire*. Oxford: Oxbow Books, 23–46.

Needham, S.P. 2001. When expediency broaches ritual intention: the flow of metal between systemic and buried domains. *Journal of the Royal Anthropological Institute* 7, 275–98.

Needham, S.P. 2005. Transforming Beaker Culture in north-west Europe: proceses of fusion and fission. *Proceedings of the Prehistoric Society* 71, 171–217.

Bibliography

Needham, S.P. forthcoming. The dagger and pommel from Barrow 1. In F. Healy and J. Harding (eds) *Prehistoric Raunds*.

Newall, R.S. 1927–29. Two shale cups of the Early Bronze Age and other similar cups. *Wiltshire Archaeological Magazine* 44, 111–17.

Newbiggin, N. 1941. A collection of prehistoric material from Hebburn Moor, Northumberland. *Archaeologia Aeliana* (4th series) 19, 104–16.

Northover, J.P. 1982. The exploration of the long-distance movement of bronze in Bronze and Early Iron Age Europe. *Bulletin of the London Institute of Archaeology* 19, 45–72.

O'Connor, B. and Cowie, T. 2001. Scottish connections: some recent finds of Early Bronze Age decorated axes from Scotland. In W.H. Metz, B.L. van Beek and H. Steegstra (eds), *Patina: Essays presented to Jay Jordan Butler*. Groningen (Privately published), 207–30.

Ogilvie, J.D. 1977. The Stourmouth – Adisham water-main. *Archaeologia Cantiana* 93, 91–124.

Ogilvie, J.D. 1981. A Mesolithic adze from Goodnestone. *Kent Archaeological Review* 66, 144.

Ogilvie, J.D. 1982. The Hammill ritual shaft. *Archaeologia Cantiana* 98, 145–66.

Ogilvie, J. D. 1983. A Mesolithic adze from Sandwich. *Kent Archaeological Review* 71, 14–15.

Oswald, A., Dyer, C. and Barber, M., 2001. *The Creation of Monuments: Neolithic Causewayed Enclosures of the British Isles*. Swindon: English Heritage.

Palliser, B. 1911. *History of Lace*. New York: Charles Schribner's Sons.

Pare, C. 2000. Bronze and the Bronze Age. In C.F.E. Pare (ed.) *Metals make the World go round: the Supply and Circulation of Metals in Europe*. Oxford: Oxbow Books, 1–38.

Parfitt, K. 1998a. Some radio-carbon dates for prehistoric east Kent. *Archaeologia Cantiana* 118, 376–380.

Parfitt, K. 1998b. Neolithic earthen long-barrows in east Kent: a review. *Kent Archaeological Review* 131, 15–21.

Parfitt, K. 2001. The Woodnesborough cup – report on a site-visit. (Unpublished Canterbury Archaeological Trust report, November 2001).

Parfitt, K. 2003a. Bronze Age discoveries at Ringlemere Farm, Woodnesborough. *Archaeologia Cantiana* 123, 390–391.

Parfitt, K. 2003b. Ringlemere Farm, Woodnesborough, Kent, spring 2002: assessment report and updated project design. (Unpublished Canterbury Archaeological Trust archive report submitted to English Heritage, May 2003).

Parfitt, K. 2004. A round barrow near Haynes Farm, Eythorne. *Archaeologia Cantiana* 124, 397–415.

Parfitt, K. 2005. Rare Early Iron-Age brooch: Ringlemere Farm, Woodnesborough. *Archaeologia Cantiana* 125, 382–384.

Parfitt, K., Allen, T. and Rady, J. 1997. Whitfield-Eastry by-pass. *Canterbury's Archaeology 1995–1996* (Canterbury Archaeological Trust 20th Annual Report), 28–33.

Parfitt, K. and Brugmann, B. 1997. *The Anglo-Saxon Cemetery on Mill Hill, Deal, Kent*. London: Society for Medieval Archaeology Monograph Series No.14.

Parfitt, K. and Champion, T. 2004. The boat in its cultural setting. In P. Clark (ed.) 2004a, 264–275.

Parfitt, K. and Halliwell, G. 1983. A Mesolithic site at Finglesham. *Kent Archaeological Review* 72, 29–32.

Parfitt, K. and Halliwell, G. 1988. Thermoluminescence dates for two prehistoric sites in east Kent. *Kent Archaeological Review* 94, 79–80.

Parfitt, K. and Needham, S. 2004. Ringlemere: The nature of the gold cup monument. *PAST* no. 46, 1–2.

Parker Pearson, M. 2003. Food, Identity and Culture: an introduction and overview. In M. Parker Pearson (ed.) *Food, Culture and Identity in the Neolithic and Early Bronze Age*. Oxford: British Archaeological Reports (International Series) 1117, 1–30.

Patchett, F.M. 1944. Cornish Bronze Age pottery: part I. *Archaeological Journal* 101, 17–49.

Patchett, F.M. 1950. Cornish Bronze Age pottery: part II. *Archaeological Journal* 107, 44–65.

Pearce, S.M. 1983. *The Bronze Age Metalwork of South Western Britain*. (2 vols) Oxford: British Archaeological Reports (British Series) 120.

Perkins, D.R.J. 1980. Site 3 and Site 4 – Lord of the Manor (Ozengell) Ramsgate. *The Isle of Thanet Archaeological Unit Interim Excavation Reports 1977–1980* (privately printed, Thanet), 13–20.

Perkins, D.R.J. 2004. Oval barrows on Thanet. In J. Cotton and D. Field (eds) *Towards a New Stone Age; aspects of the Neolithic in south-east England*. York: CBA Research Rep. 137, 76–81.

Perkins, D.R.J., Macpherson-Grant, N. and Healey, E. 1994. Monkton Court Farm evaluation, 1992. *Archaeologia Cantiana* 124, 237–316.

Phillips, B. 1856. Untitled communication. *Archaeological Journal* 13, 183–4.

Piggott, S. 1938. The Early Bronze Age in Wessex. *Proceedings of the Prehistoric Society* 4, 52–106.

Piggott, S. 1947–8. The excavations at Cairnpapple Hill, West Lothian, 1947–48. *Proceedings of the Society of Antiquaries of Scotland* 82, 68–123.

Piggott, S. 1973. *A History of Wiltshire, vol. 1, part 2*. London: Victoria History of the Counties of England.

Piggott, S. and Piggott, C.M. 1939. Stone and earth circles in Dorset. *Antiquity* 13, 138–158.

Pitts, M. 2000. *Hengeworld*. London: Century.

Pitts, M. (ed.), 2002. Exceptional Bronze Age gold find in Kent. *Current Archaeology* no. 179, 452.

Pollard, J. 1992. The Sanctuary, Overton Hill, Wiltshire: a re-examination. *Proceedings of the Prehistoric Society* 58, 213–26.

Pollard, J. 1995a. Inscribing space: formal deposition at the Later Neolithic monument of Woodhenge, Wiltshire. *Proceedings of the Prehistoric Society* 61, 137–56.

Pollard, J. 1995b. The Durrington 68 timber circle: a forgotten Late Neolithic monument. *Wiltshire Archaeological Magazine* 89, 122–5.

Pryor, F. and French, C. 1985. *Archaeology and Environment in the Lower Welland Valley*. East Anglian Archaeology 27.

Rady, J. 1992. Castle Hill, Folkestone (F. 72). *Canterbury's Archaeology 1991–1992*, (Canterbury Archaeological Trust 16th Annual Report), 25–27.

RCAHM Scotland 1988. *An Inventory of the Monuments of Argyll, Volume 6: Mid Argyll and Cowal, Prehistoric and Early Historic Monuments*. Glasgow: HMSO.

RCHME 1952. *An Inventory of the Historical Monuments in Dorset, Volume I: West*. London: HMSO.

RCHME 1989. The classification of cropmarks in Kent. A report for the Monuments Protection Programme. (Unpublished RCHME internal report, July 1989).

Richards, C. 2005. *Dwelling among the Monuments: the Neolithic Village of Barnhouse, Maeshowe Passage Grave and surrounding Monuments at Stenness, Orkney*. Cambridge: McDonald Institute Monograph.

Richards, J. 1990. *The Stonehenge Environs Project*. London: English Heritage Archaeological Report 16.

Richardson, A. 2005. *The Anglo-Saxon Cemeteries of Kent*. (2 vols) Oxford: British Archaeological Reports, (British Series) 391.

Ritchie, J.N.G. 1975–6. The Stones of Stenness, Orkney. *Proceedings of the Society of Antiquaries of Scotland* 107, 1–60.

Roe, F.E.S. 1966. The battle-axe series in Britain. *Proceedings of the Prehistoric Society* 32, 199–245.

Rohl, B and Needham, S. 1998. *The Circulation of Metal in the British Bronze Age: the Application of Lead Isotope Analysis*. London: British Museum Occasional Paper 102.

Rosa, C. (ed.) 1982. *Kent Archaeology 1972–1882*. Dover: Kent Archaeological Rescue Unit.

Schauer, P. 1986. *Die Goldblechkegel der Bronzezeit: ein Beitrag zur Kulturverbindung zwischen Orient und Mitteleuropa*. Bonn: Römisch-Germanisches Zentralmuseums Mainz, Monograph 8.

Segall, B. 1938. *Katalog der Goldschmiede-Arbeiten*. Athens: Museum Benaki.

Shand, G. 2001. Ramsgate Harbour Approach Road. *Canterbury's Archaeology 1998–1999* (Canterbury Archaeological Trust 23rd Annual Report), 18–22.

Shepherd, I.A.G. 1982. Comparative background: the assemblage. In T. Watkins, The excavation of an Early Bronze Age cemetery at Barn's Farm, Dalgety, Fife. *Proceedings of the Society of Antiquaries of Scotland* 112, 129–32.

Shepherd, I.A.G. 1985. Jet and Amber. In D.V. Clarke, T.G. Cowie and A. Foxon (eds) *Symbols of Power at the Time of Stonehenge*. Edinburgh: HMSO, 204–16.

Shepherd, I.A.G. and Barclay, G.J. (eds) 2004. *Scotland in Ancient Europe: the Neolithic and Early Bronze Age of Scotland in their European Context*. Edinburgh: Society of Antiquaries of Scotland.

Sheridan, A. 2004. Going round in circles? Understanding the Irish Grooved Ware 'complex' in its wider context. In H. Roche, E. Grogan, J. Bradley, J. Coles and B. Raftery (eds) *From Megaliths to Metal: Essays in Honour of George Eogan*. Oxford: Oxbow, 26–37.

Sheridan, A. and Davis, M. 2002. Investigating jet and jet-like artefacts from prehistoric Scotland: the National Museums of Scotland project. *Antiquity* 76, 812–25.

Sheridan, A. and Shortland, A. 2004. '…beads which have given rise to so much dogmatism, controversy and rash speculation': faience in Early

Bronze Age Britain and Ireland. In I.A.G. Shepherd and G.J. Barclay (eds) 2004, 263–79.

Sherratt, A.G. 1991. Sacred and Profane Substances: the ritual use of narcotics in later Neolithic Europe. In P. Garwood, D. Jennings, R. Skeates and J. Toms (eds) *Sacred and Profane*. Oxford: Oxford University Committee for Archaeology Monograph no. 32, 50–64.

Sherratt, A. G. 1995. Introduction: 'Peculiar Substances', and chapter 1, 'Alcohol and its alternatives: symbol and substance in pre-industrial cultures'. In J. Goodman, P. E. Lovejoy and A. G. Sherratt (eds), *Consuming Habits: Drugs in History and Anthropology*. London: Routledge, 1–46.

Sloper, D. 1989. The experimental production of a replica of an Early Bronze Age shale cup from Farway Down. *Proceedings of the Devon Archaeological Society* 47, 113–116.

Smirke, E. 1867. Some account of the discovery of a gold cup in a barrow in Cornwall, AD 1837. *Archaeological Journal* 24, 189–95.

Smith, I.F. 1965. *Windmill Hill and Avebury: Excavations by Alexander Keiller, 1925–1939*. Oxford: Clarendon.

Springer, T. (ed.), 2003. *Gold und Kult der Bronzezeit*. Nürnberg: Germanisches Nationalmuseum.

Springer, T. 2003. Gold und Kult der Bronzezeit. In T. Springer (ed.), 11–34.

Sprockhoff, E. 1961. Eine mykenische Bronzetasse von Dohnsen, Kreis Celle. *Germania* 39, 11–22.

Stukeley, W. 1776. *Itinerarium Curiosum*. (2nd ed.) London.

Taylor, J.J. 1980. *Bronze Age goldwork of the British Isles*. Cambridge University Press.

Taylor, J.J. 2005. The work of the Wessex master goldsmith: its implications. *Wiltshire Archaeological Magazine* 98, 316–26.

Thomas, N. 2005. *Snail Down, Wiltshire: the Bronze Age Barrow Cemetery and Related Earthworks*. Devizes: Wiltshire Archaeological and Natural History Society Monograph no 3.

Thurnam, J. 1871. On ancient British barrows, especially those of Wiltshire and the adjoining counties (part II, round barrows). *Archaeologia* 43, 285–552.

Todd, M. 1987. *The South West to AD 1000*. London: Longman.

Tomalin, D. 1988. Armorican vases à anses and their occurrence in southern Britain. *Proceedings of the Prehistoric Society* 54, 203–21.

Topping, P. 1992. The Penrith henges: a survey by the Royal Commission on the Historical Monuments of England. *Proceedings of the Prehistoric Society* 58, 249–64.

Topping, P. (ed.) 1997. *Neolithic Landscapes*. Neolithic Studies Group Seminar Papers 2. Oxford: Oxbow Monograph 86.

Vandkilde, H. 1988. A Late Neolithic hoard with objects of bronze and gold from Skeldal, central Jutland. *Journal of Danish Archaeology* 7, 115–35.

von Brunn, W.A. 1959. *Die Hortfunde der frühen Bronzezeit aus Sachsen-Anhalt, Sachsen und Thüringen*. Berlin: Deutsche Akademie der Wissenschaften zu Berlin Schriften der Sektion für Vor- und Frühgeschichte, Band 7.

von Uslar, R. 1955. Der Goldbecher von Fritzdorf bei Bonn. *Germania* 33, 319–23.

Wainwright, G.J. 1979. *Mount Pleasant, Dorset: Excavations 1970–1971*. London: Society of Antiquaries Research Report 37.

Wainwright, G.J. and Longworth, I.H. 1971. *Durrington Walls: Excavations 1966–1968*. London: Society of Antiquaries Research Report 29.

Wamser, L. and Gebhard, R. 2001. *Gold, Magie, Mythos, Macht: Gold der Alten und Neuen Welt*. Stuttgart: Arnoldsche.

Way, A. 1867. Supplementary notices, relating to a gold cup found in a sepulchral cist near the Cheese-wring, and also to some other gold relics in Cornwall. *Archaeological Journal* 24, 195–202.

Wheeler, E.A., Baas, P. and Gasson, P (eds) 1989. IAWA list of microscopic features for hardwood identification. *International Association of Wood Anatomists Bulletin* 10, 219–332.

Wheeler, E.A., Pearson, R.G., LaPasha, C.A., Zack, T. and Hatley, W. 1986. *Computer-aided Wood Identification*. North Carolina Agriculture Research Service Bulletin no 474.

Whittle, A. 1997. *Sacred Mound, Holy Rings: Silbury Hill and the West Kennet Palisade Enclosures: a Later Neolithic Complex in North Wiltshire*. Oxford: Oxbow Monograph 74.

Woodruff, C.H. 1874. On Celtic Tumuli in East Kent. *Archaeologia Cantiana* 9, 16–30.

Woodward, A. 2000. *British Barrows: a Matter of Life and Death*. Stroud: Tempus.

Woodward, A. 2002. Beads and Beakers: heirlooms and relics in the British Early Bronze Age. *Antiquity* 76, 1040–7.

Woodward, A.B. and Woodward, P.J. 1996. The topography of some barrow cemeteries in Bronze Age Wessex. *Proceedings of the Prehistoric Society* 62, 275–91.

Wright, E.V. 2004. Affinities and differences. In P. Clark (ed.) 2004a, 256–63.

Wright, E.V., Hedges, R.E.M., Bayliss, A. and Van de Noort, R. 2001. New AMS radiocarbon dates for the North Ferriby boats – a contribution to dating prehistoric seafaring in northwestern Europe. *Antiquity* 75, 726–34.

Wüstemann, H. 1995. *Die Dolche und Stabdolche in Ostdeutschland*. Stuttgart: Prähistorische Bronzefunde VI, 8.

Colour Plate 1 Heavily dented face of the cup

Colour Plate 2 Opposite face of the cup with crushed handle

Colour Plate 3 Virtual restoration of the Ringlemere cup by Stephen Crummy

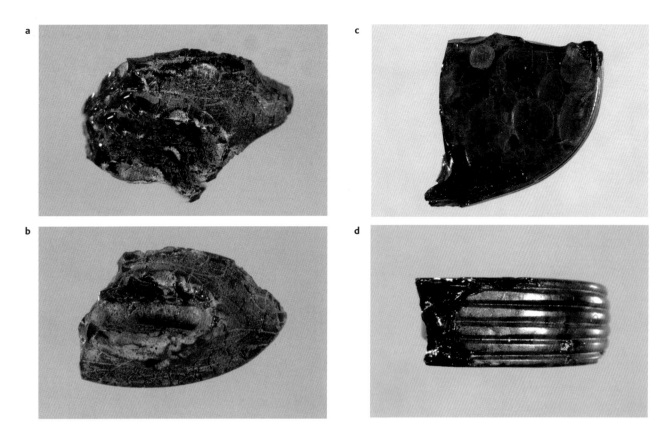

Colour Plate 4 Ringlemere amber objects: a) and b) pommel fragment, c) and d) pendant fragment

Colour Plate 5 The Rillaton cup, published with permission of the Royal Collection Trust

Colour Plate 6 Charles Hamilton Smith's watercolour of the Rillaton cup, 1837. © Plymouth & West Devon Record Office, with permission of Jim Woollcombe

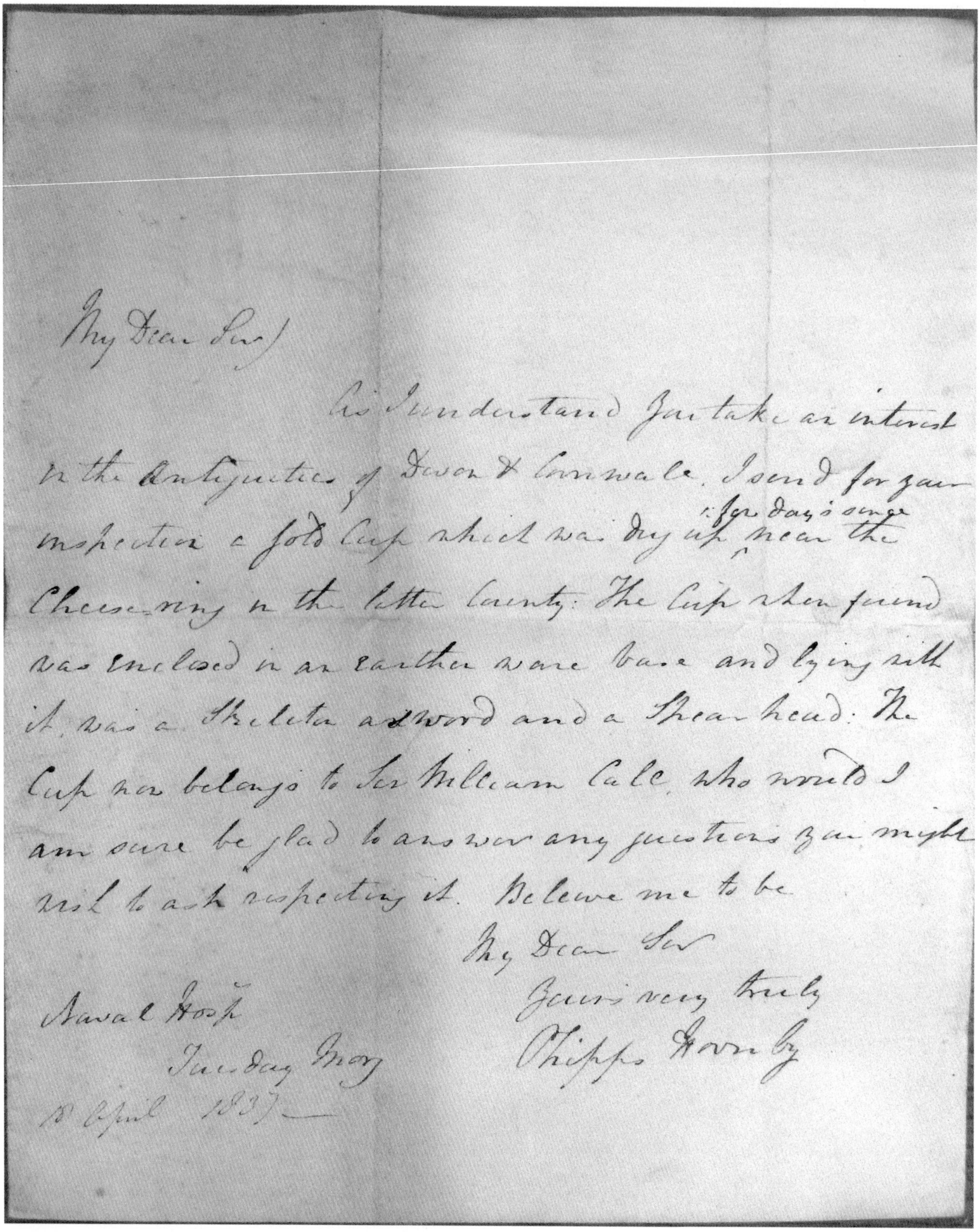

My Dear Sir,

As I understand you take an interest in the Antiquities of Devon & Cornwall, I send for your inspection a gold Cup which was dug up a few days since near the Cheesewring in the latter County. The Cup when found was enclosed in an earthen ware vase and lying with it, was a Skeleton a sword and a Spear head. The Cup now belongs to Sir William Call, who would I am sure be glad to answer any questions you might wish to ask respecting it. Believe me to be

My Dear Sir

Yours very truly

Phipps Hornby

Naval Hosp

Tuesday Morg

18 April 1837

Colour Plate 7 Letter of 18 April 1837 from Phipps Hornby to Henry Woollcombe about the Rillaton discovery. © Plymouth & West Devon Record Office, with permission of Jim Woollcombe

Colour Plate 8 The Fritzdorf cup. © Rheinisches Landesmuseum, Bonn

Colour Plate 9 The Gölenkamp cup. © Germanisches National Museum, with permission of Earl Bentheim

Colour Plate 10 The Eschenz cup. © Amt für Archäologie das Kantons Thurgau, Frauenfeld

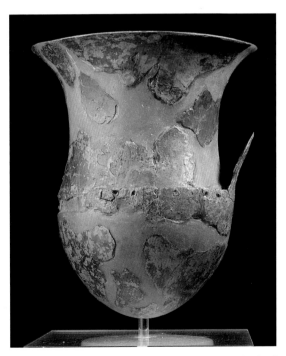

Colour Plate 11 The Saint Adrien cup. © National Museums of Scotland, with permission of the Laboratoire d'Anthropologie, Université de Rennes

Colour Plate 12 The Hove cup and its grave group. © National Museums of Scotland, with permission of the Royal Pavilion, Libraries & Museums, Brighton & Hove

Colour Plate 13 The Farway 1 cup. © National Museums of Scotland, with permission of the Royal Albert Memorial Museum, Exeter

Colour Plate 14 The gold flasks and associated objects from Villeneuve-Saint-Vistre, Marne, France. © La Réunion des Musées Nationaux, Paris

Amber
Gold
light
shape
float
water
handle
ladle

Mirror
   can't see anything
51.
Case VN numbered   Nope !!
item 2   bottom
PE. 2003, 0501.1   right

Item 1
Rillaton
loan
Royal Collection

Button shaped bar ++

5.3
nope multiple
numbers
Pulborough
PE 1953, 0211.1

unindex hinge 49
    grooved 43   Hint24 3

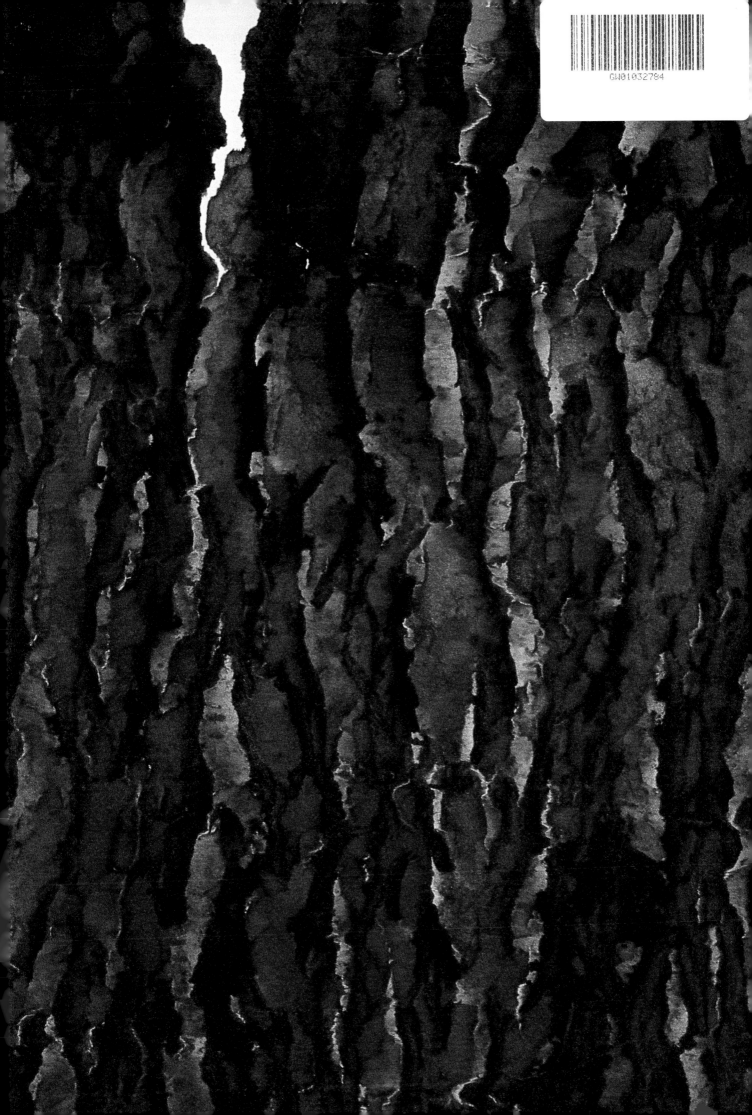

THE NEW ART OF INDONESIAN COOKING
Times Editions
422 Thomson Road, Singapore 1129

© Detlef Skrobanek, Jakarta Hilton International Hotel
Suzanne Charlé, Gerald Gay, Times Editions
1988

First published in Great Britain in 1988 by
Ward Lock Limited, 8 Clifford Street, London WIX IRB,
an Egmont Company

ISBN: 0 7063 6707 3

Printed in Singapore

T H E · N E W · A R T · O F

INDONESIAN COOKING

THE · NEW · ART · OF

INDONESIAN COOKING

RECIPES BY
DETLEF SKROBANEK

INTRODUCED BY
SUZANNE CHARLÉ

PHOTOGRAPHED BY
GERALD GAY

EDITED BY
JULIA ROLES

FOREWORD

I am happy to write this foreword to *The New Art of Indonesian Cooking*, the first book to be written on modern Indonesian cuisine.

I was glad to encourage the experiment undertaken by the Jakarta Hilton to launch a novel presentation of the richly varied food eaten by Indonesians, in a manner acceptable to a non-Indonesian audience in a modern setting. It would solve a problem I had been confronted with as Indonesian foreign minister hosting foreign dignitaries at official functions. At the same time, I saw it as an excellent opportunity to raise Indonesian food to the level of a cuisine comparable with that of China and France. I remember the numerous trial lunches and dinners the experiment went through before the new cuisine was formally launched by the Jarkarta Hilton. I consider myself fortunate to have been part of the process of developing this new Indonesian cuisine.

I am a believer in the universal community transcending national boundaries and I believe that beautiful things like music, art and dance, know no boundaries. Food is another area in which nations can learn from each other, and those involved in the culinary arts will readily adopt the best techniques available to achieve the optimum results. I view this as indicative of a wider movement, which I think is inevitable in this modern world with increased communication and people adventuring more and more across boundaries in a spirit of discovery, education and cultural exchange.

Dr. Mochtar Kusuma-Atmadja

PREFACE

When I first came to Indonesia in 1983 to work at the International Hilton Hotel in Jakarta, I expected Indonesian cuisine to be rich in flavours and spices but I did not anticipate the tremendous variety of fish and other seafood, poultry, vegetables and fruit. I was also intrigued by the uses and combinations of various aromatic grasses, leaves, roots and rhizomes.

The hotel already served the traditional *rijstaafel*, or rice table, an almost overwhelming array of dozens of dishes from all over the archipelago. But such a buffet-style feast does not lend itself to formal occasions. Why not take a new approach, using the same ingredients, but cooking the food in a lighter, healthier manner, and serving the meal course-by-course, with particular emphasis on a presentation which would appeal to more cosmopolitan tastes? A core group of twelve Indonesian chefs and I started work on dishes which would be Indonesian in character but which would also reflect the refinements in cooking techniques and artistic presentation developed in the finest European and American kitchens.

We spent months gathering as much information as possible. We visited fish, vegetable and spice markets in and out of Jakarta. Here we found long, slender bundles of lemon grass, elegant in appearance and fragrance; and dark brown pods of tamarind piled high next to blocks of its sour, sticky pulp. Makeshift tables buckled under the weight of huge jars of strongly aromatic *terasi*, *tempe* and *tauco*, the fermented pastes of shrimps and soya beans. Beyond were mounds of turmeric, galangal and ginger. Women in brightly coloured sarongs sang out the prices of fruits — some, such as papaya and mango, already familiar items in the West; others virtual strangers.

Then the real work began — applying modern cooking methods to what is essentially a village cuisine. We started to create our own recipes, and as our repertoire grew, so did the level of enthusiasm both in the kitchen and in the dining room. We created over 500 recipes, a selection of which is included in this book. Some are essentially variations of traditional village dishes, others take an old recipe and combine it with something new to Indonesia, while many are entirely new creations.

This is not a separate cuisine; we are not reinventing the wheel. It is simply our belief that Indonesian cuisine, as one of the great cuisines in the world, should have its epicurean dishes as well as its everyday fare. Cooks who are looking for traditional Indonesian recipes will not find them here, but should instead refer to some of the cookbooks already available. Nor is this a definitive work. This book represents only the start of a modern Indonesian cuisine that will evolve side-by-side with the traditional.

To all our readers, we wish *selamat makan* — good eating.

Detlef Skrobanek

CONTENTS

In this book we present a new approach to Indonesian cuisine, uniting traditional Indonesian ingredients and flavours with modern Western cooking and presentation techniques.

Indonesian cooking has been affected by many different influences — Chinese, Indian, Arab, Dutch, Portuguese — and the spices and herbs upon which these countries made, and lost, vast fortunes still grow here in abundance: nutmeg, cloves, pepper, cinnamon, cumin and more. The ethnic diversity of the nation's population, the fifth largest in the world, is almost inconceivable; there are 25 different languages and literally hundreds of dialects. More than 13,000 islands stretch, east to west, over 4,800 kilometres of sea, some little more than shifting sandbars, others the sites of ancient kingdoms. Here is Sumatra, where men still hunt wild boar in the jungles; and Java, where others risk their lives scaling high cliffs above the Indian Ocean in search of nests for bird's nest soup. Here, too, the lush island of Bali, where rice terraces wreathe mountains and people make offerings to Dewi Sri, the goddess of rice and fertility; and Sulawesi, famed for its fishermen and sailors who were once the fierce pirates of these waters.

Despite all this diversity and the abundance of local ingredients, Indonesian cooking has remained essentially a village cuisine. For the most part, it is done over open fires with lots of oil and little attention to presentation. This book presents a more elegant, refined version of this cuisine, one that appeals to Western tastes and that can be served at the most formal occasions; a happy meeting of East and West.

Indonesian Cuisine, Old and New

Although the presentation of the dishes in this book bears little resemblance to the Dutch *rijstaafel* or the Indonesian feast called the *selamatan*, the basic principles of cooking are the same as they have been for centuries. Both old and new cuisines use the same excellent and diverse ingredients, and create the same complex combinations of flavours. The philosophy of balance so important in a traditional Indonesian meal is equally important in this new cuisine. For every sweet taste there is something sour or salty; for every hot spice there is something cool and refreshing. Marinades pervade both the old and new cuisines, some brushed on just before cooking, others used for hours. No dairy products are used in traditional Indonesian cooking and very few in the new. Coconut milk, peanuts, candlenuts and mixtures of leaves and spices have always been used as binding agents instead of butter and flour.

There are, of course, differences: the principles of *nouvelle cuisine* have been applied to this traditional fare and affect mainly the presentation and cooking

Left: Rice terraces in Bali.
Right: An Indonesian sailing boat or *prahu*.

The only differences in ingredients are the omission of coconut oil for cooking as it burns quickly and tends to turn rancid, the use of dairy products in a very few instances, and the occasional decrease in the amount of hot spices. Over the centuries, spices — particularly ginger, pepper and chilies — have been used in large quantities, in part for taste and in part because they were believed to act as preservatives. To this day, chilies are often measured not by the piece, but by the handful. Such generous use of hot spices tends to alter or overpower the natural flavours of meat, fish and poultry. In some of the recipes in this book, the hot spiciness is reduced to let the flavours of the basic ingredients come through; in other instances, particularly in the sauces, the original fire of the chilies and other hot spices has been retained. In all cases, the cook should try the recipe and, if desired, gradually increase the number of chilies. For those who wish to make the dishes hotter at the table in the traditional Indonesian manner, we have included some *sambal* recipes in the Basics, Sambals and Sauces chapter.

Rice recipes are not included in this book, but it is assumed that plain rice will be served as an accompaniment to most of the hot dishes.

Connoisseurs of traditional Indonesian food may also note the absence here of *krupuk* (the rice wafer described by writer Aldous Huxley as "a queer kind of unleavened bread") and of *emping* (a cracker made from melinjo nuts). They are essential to traditional Indonesian meals, but not to the new — serve them only if you wish.

techniques. The Indonesian cook usually prepares meals in advance, leaving food out on the table under protective baskets for members of the family to eat as and when they are ready. In village life, families rarely sit down and eat together. Even at feasts, food is served in bowls or on large platters placed on a table. Celebrants help themselves, heaping plates with food — rice, chicken, meat, fish and poultry, vegetables, salads, pickles, spicy *sambals* and prawn-flavoured wafers called *krupuk*. Such banquets are grand, festive occasions, sometimes bewildering in their array of tastes, textures, and colours.

This book suggests a more Western approach to serving. One course is presented after another, dishes meant to be hot are served hot, cold dishes are served cold (another departure from traditional cuisine, which developed before refrigeration and gas and electric ovens were available).

The range of cooking methods has also been expanded to make the food lighter and healthier. Traditionally, Indonesian food is *goreng, goreng, goreng* — fried, fried and fried again. The *nouvelle* approach employs other techniques, including poaching, grilling, roasting, baking and sautéing.

Left: Traditional Indonesian cooking is essentially a village cuisine.
Right: A colourful *krupuk* stall.

9

The Search for the Spice Islands

Indonesia was home to some of the earth's earliest men. The remains of "Java man", found in the valley of Solo, indicate that the area was already inhabited by a primitive form of man by about 300,000 B.C. Much later, perhaps around 10,000 B.C., bands of hunters arrived from other parts of Asia. Some tribes simply hunted for their food and gathered fruits and vegetables, a way of life that is still practised by the hunter-gatherers living in the forests and jungles of Kalimantan, Irian Jaya and other remote parts of Indonesia. Other groups established highly complex rice cultures, evident to this day in the elaborate rice terraces of Java and Bali.

Life, however, was destined to change, for these tropical islands lay at the strategic crossroads of two great civilizations — China and India. The Chinese were early traders here. They brought with them porcelain dishes and huge ceramic jars, some of which can still be found throughout the islands. They carried back cloves and other produce of the islands. Some traders never returned home but instead established their own communities throughout the archipelago.

Today, Chinese influence is readily apparent in the cuisine of the islands; almost every village of any size has a Chinese restaurant, and every household kitchen has its *wajan*, or *wok*. The use of beansprouts, soya sauce and other soya-based products is widespread, not only in Chinese dishes, but traditional Indonesian recipes as well.

Perhaps the single largest early external influence, however, came from across the Indian Ocean. Indian traders and priests sailed to the islands, bringing two great religions — Hinduism and Buddhism. For more than 700 years, mighty Hindu and Buddhist empires ruled much of the archipelago until the Majapahit Empire collapsed in the fifteenth century under the onslaught of a new and powerful Islamic state in Java. Only in Bali did the Hindu gods find a safe and enduring home.

Arab traders had roamed these islands for many centuries before the fall of the Hindu empire and it was through these traders that Islam was first introduced to the islands. It is no coincidence that the sites established by Arab spice traders as major trading ports are, to this day, areas in which Orthodox Islam thrives. For generations, these Arab merchants managed to keep secret their trade

Hindu (left) and Buddhist (right) images bear witness to the powerful influences from India.

routes and sources of supply, duping European trading partners with fantastic fictions of winged monsters guarding remote forests of cinnamon, and false accounts of the spices' origins.

The Arabs' hold on the spice trade was finally broken, not by any great war but, in large measure, by the publication at the turn of the fourteenth century of a single book — Marco Polo's account of his 26-year journey through China and Asia. His tales of gold, jewels and spices sparked the imaginations and appetites of European kings, merchants and navigators. Christopher Columbus' copy of Polo's book was dog-eared and filled with marginalia. In fact, the explorer was searching for the Indies, indeed believed that he had found them, when he discovered the New World.

The Portuguese were the first among the European powers to arrive in the "Eastern Islands" in 1498. The British sailed these waters as well. But it was the Dutch who colonized the islands, slowly gaining control until, by the turn of the twentieth century, virtually the entire archipelago was under their flag. In 1945, Indonesia declared its independence, though Dutch influence still lingers in the nation's cuisine and in other aspects of life. Many of the Dutch settlers had tried to recreate the Netherlands in these tropical islands: they constructed canals, built homes with white stucco walls and red-tiled roofs, and planted familiar crops in their gardens: tomatoes, potatoes, string-beans, carrots, cauliflowers, cabbages — produce which modern Indonesia now exports to other Southeast Asian nations.

A Tropical Treasurehouse

Certainly the most important aspect of Indonesian cuisine, whether traditional or modern, is the use of a vast and exotic array of spices, herbs, fruits, vegetables, grasses, roots, fish and seafood. These tropical islands, straddling the equator, have been generously endowed by nature. "No region on earth can boast an equal abundance and variety of indigenous fruits," wrote an early nineteenth century naturalist, who went on to give equal praise to the rest of the region's plant and sea life. Since the first traders set foot on these islands, the history of the archipelago and the lives of its people have been integrally linked with the production of these raw materials.

Nutmeg ○ Looking at a map, it's hard to imagine that islands so tiny could once have had world powers fighting over them. Six coral and volcanic islands of the Banda Archipelago, a stretch of the Moluccas lying in the Banda Sea southwest of Irian Jaya, were the original Nutmeg Islands where the sweet spice was harvested in the well-tended gardens, and traded to Chinese, Javanese, Bugis and Arabs.

In the early seventeenth century the Portuguese began making annual voyages from Malacca to fetch cargoes of nutmeg and mace. The Dutch arrived soon after and claimed Banda as their own — their first acquisition in the East Indies. By 1650, the Dutch had banished the Portuguese and had raised the price of nutmeg by reducing supply. The lovely islands became tropical gold mines — in Amsterdam the nutmeg was worth hundreds of times the amount paid in Banda Neira.

Like other Dutch spice monopolies, the nutmeg monopoly collapsed in the early nineteenth century and Banda was soon all but forgotten. Now, most of Banda's gardens, highly praised for their beauty by the original Portuguese explorers, are in disrepair. The old mansions of the Dutch merchants and officials are decaying and tumbling down. The huge trees that shaded the main street were cut down years ago for firewood. The main industry of the island, it would seem, is catering to the few tourists who come to explore other gardens — those of coral in the clear sea.

But if Banda's nutmeg gardens are not faring so well, other areas growing *buah pala* — specifically Ambon and north Sulawesi — seem to be thriving. In these areas, just about everyone grows some

The waters surrounding the Indonesian archipelago provide plentiful supplies of varied fish and seafood.

pala, and visitors soon become accustomed to seeing nutmeg and mace drying in the sun and to smelling the hot perfume of the spice.

On the tree, the nutmeg looks something like a peach. As it ripens, it opens to show a woody pit inside, swathed with a coral-red net. The net is mace and inside the dark, purple-brown shell is the nutmeg kernel. The tree fruits continuously throughout the year, and the farmer usually harvests about four times, either knocking the fruits down with a stick, or climbing up the tree and pulling them off. In a good year, a twenty-year-old tree will produce about 2,000 fruits. Before being packed for export, the nutmegs are graded by colour (the paler seeds are immature and undesirable), size and sound. With unconscious grace the women sorters take the nutmegs between their fingers and clack them together. A high-grade nutmeg sings with a high pitch, a lesser quality is flat and the lowest grade has no resonance at all.

Cloves ○ The search for the source of cloves, along with nutmeg and mace, the other spices indigenous to the Moluccas, was at the very heart of the Age of Exploration. It also occasioned battles, bloodshed and treachery.

Chinese traders had been sailing to these eastern islands since the third century B.C. — according to court documents, subjects were required to sweeten their breath with cloves before speaking to the Emperor. However, it was not until the Portuguese arrived in 1512 in Ternate and Tidore — two tiny volcanic islands that were then the primary source of the world's supply of cloves — that the Europeans actually traded directly with the "Spice Islands". Some explorers, including Ferdinand Magellan who crossed the Pacific in 1521 under the Spanish flag, died in the attempt. Others were successful and were rewarded with titles and riches when they returned to Europe.

The Portuguese were at first welcomed by the king of Ternate but they met his greetings with plunder and oppression. The Dutch, who managed to drive the Portuguese out in the early seventeenth century, destroyed the clove trees on all islands but Ambon in order to limit supply and thus raise prices in Europe. Eventually, they lost the monopoly, thanks in part to the wiles of the governor of Ile de France (now Mauritius) named, as fate would have it, Monsieur Poivre. In 1770 he arranged to have clove tree seedlings smuggled out of the Dutch East Indies and soon clove plantations were established in French possessions.

Indonesia remains one of the world's largest producers of cloves, or *cengkeh*. But the country is also the world's largest consumer. Every year, the nation uses over half the world's supply in the manufacture of *kreteks*, the distinctively-scented clove cigarettes.

Meeting this overwhelming demand has meant prosperity for the Minahasa district of north Sulawesi — now Indonesia's premier clove-producing area — and in particular for Sonder, a charming town of white and pastel houses lying in the shadow of the volcano *Gunung Lengkoan*, where gardens of *cengkeh* were planted in the 1800s after the Dutch abandoned their "Ambon-only" policy.

From June to September, the town's 15,000 residents, plus 10,000 workers from outside the area, harvest the cloves, which are the trees' young flower buds. The first of the elegant, conical

Top: A tile on an old Dutch house shows the nutmeg flower, and peach-like fruit, opening to reveal the red net of mace swathed around the pit.
Bottom: Nutmegs being sorted and graded.

evergreens to be picked grow in rows near the shore; as the weeks progress, the rosy-hued buds etch the tree tops at successively higher altitudes, and the pickers climb the slopes of the volcano until, approaching the peak, they sleep overnight in the gardens, so no time is wasted. If they don't pick the *cengkeh* just at the right time, before the bud has opened, it is worthless.

Ambon, too, still produces cloves. The farmers treat their trees much like members of the family, knowing the age of each one and how much it will yield. "The tree is like a woman," says one farmer, "the better care you take of her, the more you appreciate her, the better she will produce." He explains, "Before the tree flowers, when it is 'pregnant', you can't disturb it; you must leave it alone, like a pregnant woman. You dare not make much noise or the buds will fall off. Just as when you expect a baby, you must watch and take care so the baby is healthy."

Cinnamon ○ The cinnamon trees with their sweet, near-magical bark, grew on the highest mountain peaks near Arabia. Giant birds used the twigs to build their nests, and the only way to get the twigs was to tempt the birds with huge chunks of meat that were so heavy that the nests would crumble when the birds settled down to feast. Herodotus the fifth century B.C. Greek historian had learnt this story from the Arab traders who told it to justify the high prices charged for cinnamon.

The story was, of course, a myth created by Arab traders to keep the true locations of the cinnamon trees a secret from their customers. For the trade was a valuable one, for which generations of men had risked their lives. According to one historian, J. I. Miller, as early as the second millenium B.C., traders may have sailed in primitive outrigger canoes from Indonesia to Madagascar, along what he calls the Cinnamon Route, so that the cinnamon could be transported along the east African coast to the Nile Valley where the ancient Egyptians paid high prices for the spice.

Eventually the sources of *Cinnamomum zeylanicum* (Sri Lanka) and its close relative *Cinnamomum cassia* (Indonesia), known as false or bastard cinnamon, were discovered, and European traders scurried to secure great quantities of them. Cinnamon and cassia were among the spices Vasco da Gama brought to the Portuguese king in 1501, after his successful voyage to India. And when the *Victoria*

arrived in Spain in 1522 — the only ship of five to complete Ferdinand Magellan's ill-fated but financially rewarding westward circumnavigation — her captain was presented with a coat of arms that included two cinnamon sticks, three nutmegs and twelve cloves.

Today Sri Lanka, the Seychelles and the Malagasy Republic produce most of the world's cinnamon, while Indonesia accounts for 90 per cent of the world's cassia. (Most of what is called cinnamon in the United States is actually cassia; in Europe, true cinnamon is preferred.)

Padang, on the west coast of Sumatra, exports most of Indonesia's cassia. It is a pleasant city, its port crowded with ships waiting for their cargoes of spices, its warehouses overflowing with piles of the sweet-smelling, red-brown bark of *kayu manis* — literally, sweet wood. In the Padang area alone there are probably about 8,000,000 cassia trees, though most are quite young. Many fine old trees were cut down when prices fell in the late 1960s and early '70s and were replaced by coffee and clove trees. Until the *kayu manis* tree is eight years old, it has little economic value since the bark has a low volatile oil content and no flavour, but by the

Detlef Skrobanek (left) peeling the sweet-smelling bark from the trunk of a *kayu manis* tree.

Pepper ○ Today, pepper is the world's most important and one of the most common of spices, and much of that pepper comes from Indonesia. But for many centuries, pepper was regarded as a rare and valuable commodity; in the thirteenth century, peppercorns were counted out one-by-one in Europe as payment for taxes, rents and other debts. The seas surrounding Java, Sumatra and Borneo were alive with adventurers from Portugal, England and the Netherlands, all in search of pepper. Wrote Joseph Conrad, "For a bag of pepper they would cut each other's throats without hesitation and would forswear their soul." After the collapse of the Dutch East India Company, the United States got into the world pepper trade. Schooners from Salem, Massachusetts, made the formidable round trip, braving pirates and storms at sea; their precious cargoes the foundations of the fortunes of the young nation's first millionaires.

Growing good pepper, though easier than growing cloves, is a relatively lengthy process. Shade trees must first be planted as supports for the pepper vines, and the earth must be weeded and turned with manure. For the first three to four years, the vine must be constantly pruned, and it is only in the fifth year that it will produce clusters of berries. If properly tended, a mature vine will produce for about twenty years, yielding about five kilograms a year. Unlike Indonesia's vast coconut plantations, most pepper fields are 200-square-metre plots with about 3,000 vines that are owned and tended by single families.

The colour of the pepper depends primarily on when the berries are harvested and how they are processed. In the south Sumatran province of Lampung, men climb narrow ladders to pick the berries while the skins are still green, just before turning red. After the berries have been picked, they are spread out on mats, with the skins intact, and laid in the sun for five to six days, until they dry to small black peppercorns. At harvest time, the narrow lanes of the villages look as if they are paved with pepper, and the air is tangy with the pungent smell.

For white pepper, the berries are fully mature when picked, then packed in burlap bags and soaked in water for about eight days, to loosen the outer skin. Workers trample the berries, until the skins fall off, and then lay them in the sun to dry until the berry turns white.

tenth year, a mild flavour exists and the tree will yield about eight kilograms of cassia, the highest grade coming from the trunk, the rest from the branches. The quality of the cassia improves as the amount of oil increases, until the tree is 30 years old, when it can yield as much as 100 kilograms. Unfortunately, there are virtually no such trees left around Padang, according to one young spice merchant. Nor are there likely to be any in future.

"Even today, when the price is high, you'll see farmers cutting the trees too early," says the spice merchant. "They should wait 20 to 25 years. But that's a long time. If they need money for their children to go to school, they cut the trees. If they need money for a wedding, they cut the trees. But the trees are too young, the quality is not high, so the price goes down.

Most of the old trees that do remain are found in an area called Kerinci, where the trees grow wild on rugged mountains shrouded in mists. Only the most determined men will attempt to harvest the wood, for they have to cut through dense forests and struggle up steep mountainsides not unlike those described by the Arab traders hundreds of years ago.

Sticks of the "near-magical" cassia or cinnamon bark for which generations of men risked their lives.

Coconuts ○ It is impossible to overrate the importance of the coconut to the lives of most Indonesians. The tall, graceful trees line the shores of virtually every island, houses are built with the wood of the palm and roofs are thatched with its leaves. Coconut meat is processed into oil, the husks used as kindling. The wealth of a village is, in part, measured by the number of coconut palms within its limits, and villagers often play down the size of their coconut groves to keep the taxman at bay. So precious are the coconut palms in the dry eastern islands of Nusa Tenggara that they are protected by law from being cut down as they provide the islanders with food and liquid during periods of drought.

Without the coconut, Indonesian cuisine, whether traditional or modern, would not exist. The coconut is an essential in all its many guises: the *kelapa muda*, or young coconut, with its translucent flesh and refreshing coconut water; the *kelapa setengah tua*, or ripe coconut, with its drier flesh which can be grated and roasted for use as a topping for main dishes and desserts; and most important of all, *santan* or coconut milk, made from water pressed through grated coconut flesh, and used in many dishes.

Chilies ○ Anyone who has tasted Indonesian cooking knows how vital chilies are to the cuisine, despite the fact that the capsicum family is not indigenous to the islands but transplanted from the New World centuries ago by the Portuguese. The chili, sometimes known in the West as the chili pepper or hot pepper, is omnipresent in sauces,

soups, main dishes and even salads, all over the archipelago. One island, just west of Bali, is actually called Lombok, which means chili or pepper. The burning sensation experienced when eating chilies is caused by capsaicin, a crystalline substance that is found. in varying amounts in different varieties, ranging from the rather large and mild *cabe lombok*, to the searing *cabe rawit*, or tiny bird's eye chili. Indonesian housewives serve diced *cabe rawit* in sweet soya sauce at the table to be used as a seasoning, and many Indonesians enjoy dipping the explosively hot, tiny chilies in salt and simply eating them whole!

Not surprisingly, Indonesians have a number of legends and stories about the chili pepper. One, a sort of spicy Cinderella variation, concerns a selfish, vain girl by the name of Cabe Lombok, and her hardworking stepsister, Cabe Rawit. One day, when Cabe Rawit was washing clothes by the river, an old woman gave her a watermelon. Her greedy stepmother tried to snatch it from her but it fell to the ground, spilling out gold and jewels. Cabe Lombok was sent by her mother to get another watermelon from the old woman but when this split open, out slithered spiders and snakes.

Left: A heavy load of freshly harvested coconuts.
Right: The chili seller with her piles of chilies, shallots and garlic is
a common sight in Indonesian markets.

Fruits ○ Visitors to Indonesia never fail to be impressed with the abundance of fruit on the islands. A respected nineteenth century English naturalist, Alfred Russel Wallace, wrote: "The banks of the Sarawak River are everywhere covered with fruit trees, which supply the Dyaks with a great deal of their food. The Mangosteen, Langsat, Rambutan, Jack, Jambou and Belimbing are all abundant; but the most abundant and most esteemed is the Durian." Despite its offensive smell, this was, he proclaimed, "the king of fruits ... In fact to eat Durians is a new sensation, worth a voyage to the East to experience."

Nowadays it is not uncommon to see "No smelly fruits in the rooms" included in the lists of rules on Indonesian hotel room doors. A strange restriction to Westerners, but not so in Indonesia, where the durian — that huge, high-smelling, highly praised fruit — is perhaps one of the favourite desserts.

Even less exotic fruits are surprising in their variations. There are some forty varieties of mangoes growing in these islands and over a hundred kinds of bananas. In fact, of the many plants growing in Indonesia, the banana is perhaps one of the most varied in its uses, and most households have some growing in the yard. They require little cultivation, bear fruit in eight to fifteen months, then die, but are soon followed by suckers growing from the rhizome. The leaves are used as wrapping for bundles of food, as colourful and easily replaced plates, and as baking dishes that impart a special flavour to food. The banana leaf often serves as a handy umbrella during unexpected downpours. In Bali, a banana plant in full bloom is tied to small shrines in preparation for cremations. In Java, the same inflorescence hung on an entrance gate signifies a wedding in the home.

Fish and Seafood ○ Literally hundreds of varieties of fish and crustaceans make their homes in the deep seas and shallow coral gardens of Indonesia. Such bounty attracts fishermen from all over the world, as it has for centuries. After the coastal waters of New England had been fished out, nineteenth century American whaling ships made their way to the eastern seas of Indonesia, and today huge Japanese trawlers ply the waters.

But there are also the traditional fishing boats. In Bali, brightly coloured *jukung* outrigger canoes line the beaches, the wildly painted "eyes" on the bows on constant lookout for dangers lurking in the deep (or perhaps for a stray tourist interested in being taken for a sail). Ujung Padang, the capital city of Sulawesi, is the centre for the archipelago's traditional sailing craft. Every day, hundreds of tiny outriggers set out from the harbour, their black sails dark triangles on the golden waters.

Further north, singing magic songs that they believe attract only the female fish, fishermen search for the flying fish with its precious roe. This musical persuasion works well for the fishermen. During the dry season, from May to August, nearly 150 boats sail the seas in search of the flying fish. The men of one small village have done this for many generations but it is only recently that the female fish have been sought for their roe. In the past the fish were sold and the roe was given away in the village, or thrown out. Now it is the roe which commands the high prices in fashionable gourmet emporiums and *sushi* bars in major cities worldwide, and the villagers eat only the fish.

Left: Strong-smelling but highly prized durians are often sold by the roadside to be taken by country people as gifts for city relatives.
Right: Fishing boats return at dawn to unload their catch.

Rice ○ Indonesians can't live without rice or, if they do, they do so unhappily. The word *nasi*, or cooked rice, is also often used to mean "eating" and "food", the implication being that rice will form the central part of the meal. Three colours of rice are grown in Indonesia — white, red and black — as well as glutinous varieties. The Javanese are quick to claim that the finest rice in the world is grown in Cianjur, which is known as the rice bowl of Indonesia, while the Balinese are equally certain that their traditional rice, *beras* Bali, is the best.

Rice is, in fact, deified on many islands. The Bataks in northern Sumatra, near the volcanic Lake Toba, call the rice soul "tondi"; the Toradja of Sulawesi give the rice soul the same name as the human soul — "tawuna". The Minangkabau, according to one anthropologist, go as far as to have rules proscribing humans' conduct toward rice. It is forbidden to take off one's shirt in the ricefield or to swear, for fear the rice might become ashamed and lose its perfume and taste. In Bali, Dewi Sri, the rice mother, is worshipped regularly, and her image can be seen in the form of small doll-like figures of rice stalks that are taken to the fields at harvest, and decorate the handsome,

steep-roofed barns. (Rice barns have been the inspiration for the design of many of the island's thatch-roofed tourist bungalows — a source of many laughs for the Balinese, who find it humorous that tourists rather than grain are stored in the structures.)

In Bali the government has introduced new strains of rice which produce higher yields and also require shorter growing periods. But, in many cases, these shorter growing periods have meant a change in the times for planting and harvesting, and thus the ceremonies for the gods. Whether this has disturbed the deities, no one can tell, but residents still talk of a disaster some years ago when the old schedules were ignored, and the crops failed. Regardless of new systems, the Balinese calendar is still consulted for propitious times to plant, and offerings made on the appropriate days. Around Ubud, the artistic centre of Bali, the farmers plant in August, as they always have, so that the rice flowers during October, a very holy month. Gusti Pekak, a man who has spent his life studying rice and growing it, explains: "This way, when the gods come down from the mountains, they can enjoy the view of the rice."

Working in the rice fields (left) and storing the harvested rice in thatch-roofed barns (right)

17

The rice likes to be sung to, Gusti Pekak notes. One bamboo instrument, the *tluktak*, makes a sound much like its name. It is just a length of bamboo on a hinge that catches the running water, fills up, then drops the water to the next level. As it swings up to catch more water, the hollow end hits a stone and makes a lovely sound, *tluktak*. "You hear the sound and you know that the water is still flowing as it should," says Gusti Pekak, who likes the sound of the *tluktak* to lull him to sleep in his simple hut in the fields. "Away from the streets, high in the rice terraces, they are like a chorus. But only the bravest farmers will have them," he adds. "The witches of black magic also like the sound, and will come to dance in the fields."

Like many Balinese farmers, Gusti Pekak appreciates the increased yields, but he doesn't really like the new rice: "It has no grace, no beauty. It is nothing to me. It is what you call a cash crop; it is good only for paying for cigarettes and electricity. But *beras Bali* is the rice for gods and for men. When you see it in the field, it is lovely, the heavy heads bent, like men with much wisdom. The new rice stands up straight, empty headed. And its taste...."

Leaves, Grasses and Ferns ◦ The islands of Indonesia are a botanical treasure-trove and the cooking reflects this bounty. First and foremost among the grasses used is *sereh*, or lemon grass, which imparts a beautiful, lemony fragrance to dishes. Dozens of leaves are used in cooking — long bean leaves, red pumpkin leaves, cassava leaves, and *pakis* (the delicate head of a wild fern) are some of the better known. Leaves and grasses are used as vegetables as well as spices, in main dishes, soups and salads. Most give flavour, some impart fragrance, others are used only to add colour and to dress up a dish.

This diverse and plentiful plant life is also a main theme in the islands' artistic life. The elaborately chiselled panels of the great temple of Borobodur and the carved wooden gates of traditional Javanese homes and palaces are alive with the flowers of the hills, the fruits of the markets. The many and varied weavings and *batiks* of the islands also feature patterns based on nature. Some are woven by hand from cotton dyed with roots and vegetables. Others, called *songket*, are made of silk or gold thread on silk or cotton grounds.

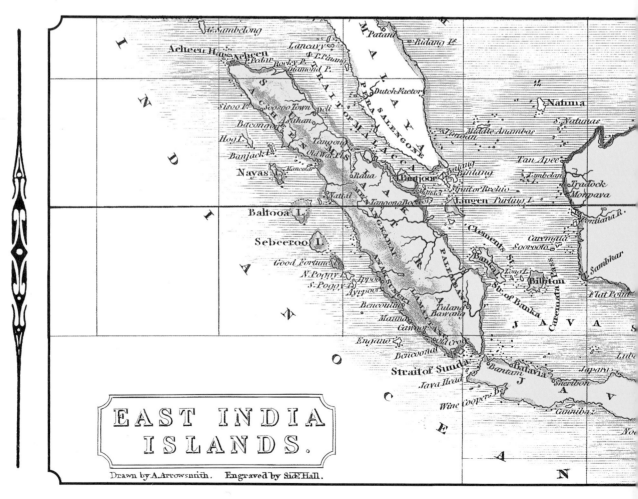

EAST INDIA ISLANDS.

Drawn by A. Arrowsmith.   Engraved by Sid.Y Hall.

Bird's Nest ∘ Every May, on a date prescribed by the Javanese calendar, the villagers of Karang-bolong hold a special ceremony to ask God for a bountiful harvest. For a day and a night, everyone joins in. Men dance in trance, families make special prayers, and a *wayang kulit*, or shadow puppet play, is performed.

When the signs are right, the men go to Karangbolong (which literally means "rock of holes"), a massive cliff jutting into the Indian Ocean. For this is not a harvest of rice or corn, but the harvest of the delicate white nests of the swiftlet. Like their fathers, and their fathers' fathers before them, the men carefully lower themselves down by ropes, dangling precariously over deep chasms, to the caves where the small swiftlets nest. There they gather the nests, gently scooping them off the walls, making sure not to disturb nests with eggs or young birds. Then comes the long, danger-ous ascent to the top of the cliff while hundreds of metres below, huge waves pound against the dark rocks and — according to local legend — the goddess of the south seas, Nyai Roro Kidul, waits to claim another victim.

The tiny white nests are built by the birds at mating time by weaving long, glue-like strands of secretion from their salivary glands. The nests, shaped like teacups cut in half, are attached to the walls of the caves. Brittle as spun glass when dry, the nests become translucent when cooked and form a gelatinous, spaghetti-like mass, which is rather tasteless to the novice. But to Chinese aficionados, the bird's nest is an almost magical food, a source of longevity, wisdom and virility for men, or beauty for women, as well as a restorative of the body and mind.

With such a reputation, it is not surprising that the nests are in great demand. Indonesia reports exports of almost 60,000 kilograms, an arresting statistic considering that there are approximately 110 nests to each kilogram. In the nineteenth century, the value of these nests in China was estimated as being weight for weight equal with silver. Today, the prices are closer to those of gold, and middlemen are very secretive about their sources of supply, and their delivery dates. Accord-ing to one dealer, "Thieves know the value of the nests. It's as if they're spun from gold."

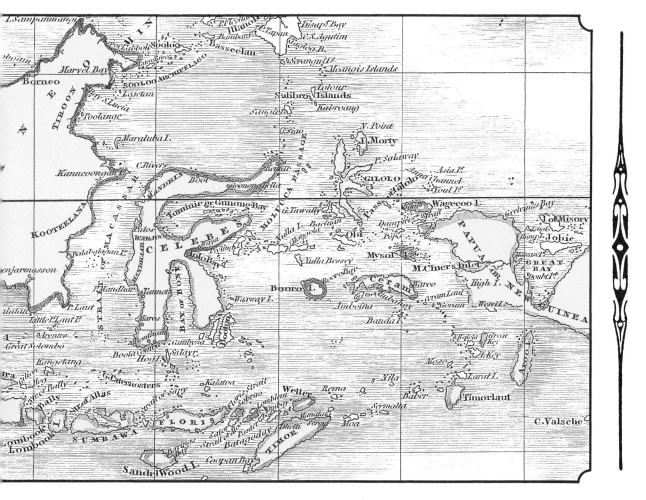

BASICS, SAMBALS AND SAUCES

In this section, we have compiled useful kitchen notes as well as information about some of the ingredients central to Indonesian cuisine: coconut milk (*santan*), chili juice and tamarind water. Also included are recipes for beef, chicken, fish and lamb stocks, direndam (a marinade for beef, veal and poultry), sugar syrup, *sambals* that may be served as side dishes, and sauces which form a vital part of most dishes in this book. Descriptions of spices, herbs, fruits, vegetables, and flavourings which are purchased ready-prepared are given in the glossary.

BASICS

KITCHEN NOTES

On Substitutions ○ Thanks to good transportation, increased interest in Asian foods and growing Asian populations in Western countries, most "Indonesian" ingredients mentioned in the book are easily found, usually in Asian food stores. There are also mail-order catalogues specializing in Asian herbs, spices and other foodstuffs. These sources are often advertised in food magazines.

Changes in the leaves, spices and herbs will actually affect the taste of the dish, but in the glossary we have suggested possible substitutions whenever they exist. Unfortunately there are certain items for which there are no counterparts. If you are unable to obtain a certain leaf or herb and no alternative is given, it is best to drop it from the recipe. This will make a difference to the flavour, but the recipe will still work.

On the Complete Kitchen ○ Most of the utensils required for new Indonesian cooking are more than likely already present in a well-equipped kitchen: several different sizes of frying pans, a roasting pan, stockpots, a steamer, sieve, ladle, piping bag, blender or food processor and some good knives. If you plan to make fresh coconut milk, you will need a grater for the coconut meat. A stone pestle and mortar is useful for crushing spices and herbs but otherwise the ingredients can be finely chopped by hand or in a blender.

On Cooking ○ Ingredients have been listed in the metric system in order to provide the greatest accuracy. Cooks more comfortable with American or Imperial equivalents should refer to the conversion charts at the end of the book.

All of the recipes have been carefully measured and tested. However the recipes are not dicta, nor is cooking an exact science; food should please chef and guests alike and the measurements in the recipes may be changed to suit individual tastes.

Oven temperatures may vary from one oven to another; it is always best, when first cooking a new recipe, to monitor the progress.

On Shortcuts and Timesavers ○ Unless otherwise indicated, stay away from ready-prepared ingredients; the time saved is not worth the flavour lost.

Generally it is best to prepare sauces the day the meal is to be served, but if you simply must make some preparations a day in advance it is better to chop and prepare the ingredients — this step usually involves the most time and labour — rather than to make the entire sauce. These chopped ingredients may be refrigerated for a day or two. Any extra cooked sauce may be kept in the refrigerator for two days, or frozen.

On Serving ○ At the risk of stating the obvious, the dishes in this book should be served Western style: hot foods should be served hot and cold dishes, cold.

Indonesians do not traditionally drink wines with their meals. If you wish to serve them, you will need to experiment matching the wine to the dish. This can be tricky because of the complexity of the sauces and flavours. Generally speaking, white wines go well with Indonesian food. Beer may also be served — its bitterness always complements spicy foods.

Many excellent teas come from Indonesia and are well suited to the food, as long as the tea selected is not too fruity or scented. A simple black or green tea is best. Do not serve sugared drinks as their sweetness will overlay the taste of the dishes.

COCONUT MILK

Coconut milk, or *santan*, is indispensable to Indonesian cooking. Used as a flavouring and also as a thickening agent for sauces, it is produced by mixing grated coconut flesh with water and squeezing it until the thick oily sap has been dissolved. It should not be confused with — nor substituted by — the liquid that is found in the young green coconut, which is coconut water. There are three ways to make coconut milk.

Fresh Coconut Santan ○ Made fresh from coconuts, this is always the best coconut milk in terms of colour, taste and texture, but it is also the most time consuming to make.

To prepare, grate the flesh of a mature coconut (approximately 250-300 g of flesh) into a bowl. Add 300 ml warm water and squeeze well until the water has extracted the juice from the flesh and turned white. Strain the liquid through a sieve, then squeeze the flesh a bit more to extract the remaining juice. This yields about 375 ml *santan*. This is the first squeezing and produces the best coconut milk. The process can be repeated with the same coconut flesh once or twice more, but each squeezing will yield successively thinner *santan*.

Dried Coconut Santan ○ The second best coconut milk after fresh, its taste is sweeter than fresh coconut milk and the colour is whiter. In order to achieve a flavour similar to that produced by the use of fresh *santan*, increase the amount of spices called for in the relevant recipe.

To prepare, place 300 g dehydrated grated coconut in a bowl. Cover with 750 ml warm water and let it soak for 10 minutes. Squeeze the coconut flesh, then strain the liquid and squeeze the flesh a bit more. As with fresh grated coconut, the process can be repeated once or twice. This yields 375 ml.

Coconut Cream Santan ∘ This coconut milk, produced from commercially packaged canned or frozen coconut cream, is recommended only if a *santan* cannot be made from fresh or dried grated coconut. It is a very fatty coconut milk, with a slightly coarse texture and very little natural sweetness. Its bright white colour will make sauces much lighter in colour than those based on the two other types of *santan*. If using coconut cream *santan* in a savoury dish, be sure to increase the quantity of spices used in the recipe. This type of *santan* should really only be used in desserts, and even then be sure to buy the unsweetened variety of coconut cream — the heavily sweetened kind will alter a recipe too much.

To make the *santan*, empty 125 g coconut cream, canned or frozen, into a bowl, add 500 ml warm water and stir with a whisk until smooth. Yields about 500 ml.

How to Store Coconut Milk ∘ *Santan* does not keep well and should be used within 24-30 hours of being made. It must be stored in a refrigerator. It may thicken like cream, but when heated it returns to its original state. *Santan* can be frozen and, if properly sealed, will keep for several months. Before using refrigerated or freshly made *santan*, stir well, mixing the cream and the water. Unless otherwise stated in the recipe, add the *santan* just before completing the dish. If you intend to refrigerate or freeze food, it should not contain *santan* unless the dish has been cooked long enough for the *santan* to have been thoroughly absorbed.

CHILI JUICE

Chili juice, either red or green, is used in marinades and sauces to give them a hot spiciness. Red chili juice (made from red chilies) tends to be hotter in taste than green chili juice (made from green chilies), and both may be stored in a refrigerator for up to 10 days. Commercially pre-packaged chili sauce is totally different and cannot be used as a substitute.

1 kg red or green chilies
1 litre water
30 ml white vinegar
30 g salt

1 Wash and clean the chilies, being sure to discard the stems. Do not remove the seeds from the pods since they add the spiciness to the juice.
2 Combine the chilies with the water, white vinegar and salt in a saucepan. Bring to the boil, then reduce the heat and let it simmer for 20 minutes.
3 Drain off half of the liquid and pour the other half with the chilies into a blender and purée until smooth.
4 Remove from the blender and strain through a fine sieve before storing in a refrigerator. The juice should be thin like water. If it is thick, add a little more water until the desired consistency is achieved. Yields 1 litre.

TAMARIND WATER

Tamarind water is used in some sauces and soups, imparting a sour but pleasant taste. The basic ingredient is tamarind pulp, which is readily available in Asian or health food shops.

125 g tamarind pulp
1 litre water

1 Cut the tamarind pulp into pieces.
2 Place the pieces in a saucepan, together with the water.
3 Bring to the boil, stirring constantly with a wooden spoon. In 5 minutes, the tamarind pieces should have disintegrated.
4 Strain the liquid through a sieve into a bowl, making sure to squeeze the pulp in the liquid to extract all its essence.
5 Let the liquid cool before storing in a refrigerator, where it can be kept for a week. Yields 1 litre.

DIRENDAM

This is a marinade that can be used for beef, veal and poultry.

30 ml peanut oil
20 g shallots (bawang merah), peeled, finely diced
10 g garlic, peeled, finely diced
5 g greater galangal, peeled, finely diced
30 g candlenuts, ground
1 salam leaf
1 lemon grass stalk, finely diced
2 g turmeric powder
30 g sugar
salt

1 Combine all the ingredients in a bowl and mix vigorously with a whisk. Let the marinade sit for approximately 1 hour, then discard the salam leaf.
2 Brush the marinade on both sides of the meat and let it marinate in the refrigerator for 8-12 hours before cooking the meat.

SUGAR SYRUP

This is one of the basic requirements for some of the recipes in the Desserts chapter. It can be made in advance and it keeps well for several days in the refrigerator.

500 ml water
500 g white sugar

1 Combine the ingredients in a saucepan. Bring the mixture to the boil and let it simmer for 8-10 minutes.
2 Withdraw the pan from the heat and strain the liquid through cheesecloth. Let the syrup cool completely before using. Yields 900 ml.

BEEF STOCK

Although commercially prepared stocks are available, try not to use them as they tend to be overly seasoned, particularly with salt, and will obscure the flavours of the dishes in which they are used. It is better to take a little extra time and make your own stock. The excess can be stored in the refrigerator for up to 4 days, or they can be frozen.

> 4 litres water
> 1 kg beef bones, chopped into 2-cm pieces
> 30 ml vegetable oil
> 100 g leeks, peeled, chopped
> 100 g onions, peeled, chopped
> 50 g shallots (bawang merah), peeled, chopped
> 4 salam leaves
> 2 lemon grass stalks, crushed
> 2 garlic cloves, peeled
> 30 g salt

1   Place half of the water together with the chopped bones in a stockpot and bring to the boil. Use a perforated ladle to remove the scum floating on the surface. Drain off the water.
2   In another stockpot, heat the oil.
3   Sauté the leeks, onions, shallots, salam leaves, lemon grass and garlic for 2-3 minutes without browning.
4   Add the bones and the remaining water to the pot. Bring the water to simmering point and season with salt.
5   Let the stock simmer for approximately 2½-3 hours on a very low heat, constantly removing the scum which appears on the surface.
6   Strain the stock through a very fine sieve or cheesecloth into a bowl. Let it cool at room temperature before storing in a refrigerator.

CHICKEN STOCK

Follow the same procedure used for preparing beef stock, but replace the beef bones with chicken bones and let the stock simmer for only 45 minutes.

FISH STOCK

> 30 ml vegetable oil
> 100 g leeks, peeled, chopped
> 100 g onions, peeled, chopped
> 50 g shallots (bawang merah), peeled, chopped
> 2 salam leaves
> 2 lemon grass stalks, crushed
> 1 kg fish bones or fish meat trimmings
> 1.5 litres water
> 6 g coriander leaves with stems
> 15 g salt

1   Heat the oil in a stockpot. Sauté the leeks, onions, shallots, salam leaves and lemon grass for 2-3 minutes without letting them brown.
2   Add the fish bones and continue to sauté for 2 minutes more.
3   Add the water and the coriander leaves to the pot. Season with the salt and bring the water to the boil.
4   Reduce the heat and simmer at low heat for 45 minutes. Constantly scoop off the scum which forms on the surface.
5   Strain the stock through a fine sieve or cheesecloth and let it cool before storing it.

LAMB STOCK

> 30 ml peanut oil
> 400 g lamb bones, cut into 2-cm pieces
> 1 x 50-60 g onion, peeled, diced
> 5 x 2 g garlic cloves, crushed
> 20 g greater galangal, diced
> 10 g ginger, diced
> 3 lemon grass stalks, crushed
> 4 salam leaves
> 50 g leeks, diced (use only the bottom part)
> 100 g tomatoes, diced
> 30 ml white vinegar
> 1 tablespoon black peppercorns, crushed
> 2 litres water
> salt

1   Heat the oil in a stockpot. Add the lamb bones and sauté, stirring constantly, until the bones are light brown.
2   Add in the onion, garlic, greater galangal, ginger, lemon grass, salam leaves and leeks and continue to sauté for 4-5 minutes.
3   Add in the tomatoes, vinegar, peppercorns and water. Bring the stock to the boil, then reduce the heat. Let it simmer for approximately 2 hours or until the liquid is reduced by half. While simmering, constantly skim off all surfacing scum in order to produce a clear stock.
4   Remove the pot from the heat. Strain the stock through a fine sieve or cheesecloth.
5   Let it cool at room temperature before storing in a refrigerator.

Some of the ingredients essential to these basic recipes are shown opposite. They are (from left to right, top to bottom): garlic, shallots (bawang merah), tamarind pods, lemon grass stalks, green chilies, red chilies, turmeric roots, leeks.

SAMBALS

At a typical Indonesian feast, many types of *sambals* are served as side dishes. In this book, *sambals* are used in sauces and as toppings for very hot dishes, but can also be accompaniments. Some *sambals* are cooked, others uncooked. All use ground or blended chilies as their base, with additions of shallots, garlic, gingers, tomatoes, sugar, spices, lime juice and salt.

SAMBAL BAWANG MERAH

Served uncooked, this sour, hot *sambal* makes a good relish to accompany grilled or roasted fish, poultry or beef dishes.

    150 g red chilies, seeded, cut into half lengthwise, sliced finely
    300 g shallots (bawang merah), peeled, sliced
    50 g garlic, peeled, finely diced
    60 ml freshly squeezed lime or lemon juice
    5 g salt

1   Mix all the ingredients in a bowl, seasoning with the salt.
2   Let the mixture sit in the refrigerator for 2 hours before using it. If a hotter sambal is preferred, let it sit overnight in the refrigerator.

SAMBAL TERASI

Dried shrimps should really be used in this recipe, but if there are none available, then fresh, shelled shrimps or baby prawns may be substituted, resulting in a milder-tasting *sambal*.

    45 ml vegetable oil
    80 g shallots (bawang merah), peeled, finely diced
    20 g garlic, peeled, finely diced
    100 g red chilies, stems removed
    30 g shrimp paste
    15 g lemon grass stalk, finely sliced
    5 g greater galangal, finely diced
    30 g brown sugar (gula Jawa)
    50 g dried shrimps
    salt

1   Heat the oil in a saucepan and sauté the shallots and garlic, stirring constantly, until the ingredients have browned.
2   Add in the chilies, shrimp paste, lemon grass, greater galangal and brown sugar, and continue sautéing for 2 minutes more.
3   Mix in the dried shrimps and season lightly with the salt.
4   Reduce the heat and let the mixture cook slowly for 10-15 minutes, stirring constantly. Remove from the heat, pour into a blender and purée until fine.
5   Let the sambal cool at room temperature before storing in a refrigerator.

SAMBAL TOMATO

Use ripe and full-flavoured tomatoes when preparing this *sambal* to ensure it is as tasty as possible.

    30 ml vegetable oil
    50 g shallots (bawang merah), peeled, finely diced
    20 g garlic, peeled, finely diced
    250 g tomatoes, chopped
    60 ml red chili juice (see page 23)
    10 g shrimp paste
    1 tablespoon brown sugar (gula Jawa)
    salt

1   Heat the oil in a saucepan and sauté the shallots and garlic for 2 minutes until light brown.
2   Add the tomatoes, chili juice, shrimp paste and brown sugar. Season lightly with the salt.
3   Bring the mixture to the boil for 15 minutes, stirring frequently.
4   Pour the hot liquid into a blender and purée until smooth. Let the sambal cool at room temperature before storing in a refrigerator.

SAMBAL MAKASSAR

As with all other cooked *sambals*, this *sambal* should be a thick paste. To thicken a thin *sambal*, pour the mixture back into the saucepan and cook over low heat until it is thick.

    125 ml water
    150 g red chilies, stems removed
    2 tomatoes, quartered
    30 ml vegetable oil
    40 g shallots (bawang merah), peeled — 20 g finely diced;
        20 g sliced, deep-fried until crisp
    5 g garlic, peeled, finely sliced
    2 g shrimp paste
    30 ml freshly squeezed lime or lemon juice
    salt

1   Pour the water into a saucepan, then add in the chilies and tomatoes. Boil for 5 minutes and drain off the water.
2   Using a stone mortar and pestle, grind the chilies and tomatoes into a purée. Set the mixture aside.
3   Heat the oil in a frying pan. Sauté the diced shallots and the garlic for 1 minute.
4   Add in the shrimp paste and sauté for another minute, until the shrimp paste has been thoroughly mixed in.
5   Add in the tomato and chili purée and continue to sauté over low heat for 5 minutes more.
6   Drop the fried shallots into the mixture, pour in the lime or lemon juice and season lightly with salt. (Use salt sparingly as the shrimp paste is already salty.) Sauté for a further 3 minutes. Remove from the heat and purée the mixture in a blender.
7   Put the sambal in a bowl and let it cool at room temperature. When storing in a refrigerator, be sure to seal it properly.

SAUCES

As in most cuisines, sauces play an important role in Indonesian cooking. The sauces are as varied as the spices used in making them, and they are as pleasing to the eye as to the tastebuds. Feel free to experiment using the different sauces given in this chapter with a variety of the dishes in other chapters. Most may be used to accompany fish, poultry, lamb, beef or pork. They may also be served hot or cold since nearly all are prepared with a coconut-milk base. Sauces which should be served hot or cold only are noted in the specific recipe, and sauces which are normally served with a particular dish are given with that recipe and not in this general sauce chapter.

Tips for Successful Sauces
- When using fresh chilies, be sure to seed them; the seeds release oils during the cooking process which cause the sauce to be fiery hot in taste. If you use bird's eye chilies (*cabe rawit*), start with only a small quantity and add 1 g more at a time if required, tasting and adjusting as you go along.
- When using chili juice, increase the amount by 1 teaspoon at a time should you require the sauce to be more fiery and more spicy.
- After coconut milk, candlenuts are the strongest binding agents used in preparing these sauces. Use only the amount indicated in the recipes; usually 20-30 g is sufficient to bind 500 ml of liquid. For a thinner sauce, decrease the amount of candlenuts.
- In most of the sauce recipes, the amount of salt has not been specified. Since various herbs, spices, leaves and rhizomes are used, salt should be added only sparingly.
- In the case of spices like nutmeg and coriander where the amount is not specified, a pinch is usually sufficient.
- In some instances, there is no weight indication for leaves, but rather cup measures are used because leaves are very light in weight.
- Coconut milk tempers the fire of the chilies. Therefore, in order to reduce the fieriness while maintaining the balance of the spiciness of the sauce, increase the amount of coconut milk 1 teaspoon at a time. You may also use stocks or simply use less than the amount of chilies or spices specified in the recipe, and then gradually add until the desired result is achieved.

Saus Bumbu Bajak
SPICY BAJAK SAUCE

This is a new Bajak Sauce for poultry and meats that is based on a traditional fiery *sambal*.

> 30 ml peanut oil
> 40 g shallots (*bawang merah*), peeled, finely diced
> 5 g garlic, peeled, finely diced
> 1 lemon grass stalk, crushed
> 2 salam leaves
> 10 g tamarind pulp
> 40 g candlenuts, ground
> 100 g tomatoes, peeled, seeded, diced
> 5 g white sugar
> 250 ml red chili juice (see page 23)
> 375 ml coconut milk (see page 22)
> salt

1 Heat the oil in a saucepan and sauté the shallots, garlic, lemon grass and salam leaves for 3-4 minutes in the oil without letting them colour.
2 Stir in the tamarind pulp and candlenuts, and continue sautéing for another 4 minutes.
3 Add in the tomatoes, sugar, chili juice, coconut milk and salt. Bring the mixture to the boil, reduce the heat and simmer until the sauce starts to thicken, approximately 10 minutes.
4 Remove the pan from the heat; discard the lemon grass and salam leaves.
5 Pour the sauce into a blender and purée until smooth, approximately 3-4 minutes. Yields 500 ml.

Saus Bali
BALI SAUCE

This sauce should be served chilled.

> 20 ml peanut oil
> 80 g red chilies, seeded, finely diced
> 10 g green chilies, seeded, diced
> 20 g lemon grass stalk, diced
> 10 g garlic, peeled, diced
> 40 g tomatoes, peeled, seeded, diced
> 500 ml coconut milk (see page 22)
> 10 g coriander powder
> 10 g shrimp paste
> 10 g brown sugar (gula Jawa)

1 Heat the peanut oil in a pan and sauté the chilies, lemon grass, garlic and tomatoes in the oil until golden brown.
2 Add the coconut milk, coriander, shrimp paste and brown sugar, and boil for 8-10 minutes, stirring slowly, until the sauce has thickened slightly.
3 Remove the pan from the heat and pour the contents into a blender. Purée until smooth, then chill. Yields 625 ml.

CHILI BASIL SAUCE

Saus Kemangi
CHILI BASIL SAUCE

Kemangi, the local sweet basil, is perhaps one of the most widely used leaves in Indonesian cuisine. It is found raw and cooked in salads, stews and sauces.

> 30 ml vegetable oil
> 30 g shallots (bawang merah), peeled, finely diced
> 10 g garlic, peeled, finely diced
> 40 g sweet basil leaves (kemangi), chopped
> 30 g candlenuts, ground
> 30 ml green chili juice (see page 23)
> 30 ml white vinegar
> 375 ml coconut milk (see page 22)
> 15 g turmeric root, finely diced
> salt
> 10 g sweet basil leaves

1 Heat the vegetable oil in a saucepan and sauté the shallots and garlic for 2 minutes in the hot oil.
2 Add in the chopped basil leaves and sauté for another minute.
3 Add the candlenuts and continue to sauté for 2 minutes more.
4 Pour in the chili juice, vinegar and coconut milk. Sprinkle in the turmeric and season with salt. Bring to the boil.
5 Reduce the heat and simmer for approximately 8 minutes, stirring constantly.
6 Pour the mixture into a blender and process the sauce until it is smooth.
7 Pour the sauce back into a saucepan, add in the whole basil leaves and serve hot. Yields 375 ml.

Saus Ubi Jalar
SWEET POTATO SAUCE

Although sweet potatoes are not used in traditional sauces, they are favourite snacks — boiled, fried or served with brown sugar. This new sauce is particularly good with lamb, and can also be served with beef. The chili juice makes a good counterbalance to the sweetness of the potatoes.

> 15 ml peanut oil
> 30 g shallots (bawang merah), peeled, finely diced
> 10 g garlic, peeled, finely diced
> 5 g ginger, peeled, finely diced
> 2 g coriander leaves, finely chopped
> 5 g turmeric root, finely chopped
> 1 lemon grass stalk, crushed
> 30 g brown sugar (gula Jawa)
> 100 g sweet potatoes, diced, blanched
> 30 ml tamarind water (see page 23)
> 60 ml red chili juice (see page 23)
> 250 ml chicken stock (see page 24)
> 90 ml coconut milk (see page 22)
> salt

1 Heat the oil in a pan and sauté the shallots and garlic in the hot oil for 1 minute until light brown.
2 Add the ginger, coriander, turmeric, lemon grass, brown sugar and sweet potatoes. Continue to sauté for 2 minutes.
3 Pour in the tamarind water, chili juice, chicken stock and coconut milk. Season with salt and bring to the boil. Reduce the heat and let the mixture simmer for approximately 10 minutes, stirring frequently.
4 Remove the pan from the heat and discard the lemon grass.
5 Pour the mixture into a blender and process until smooth, approximately 2-3 minutes. Serve hot. Yields 500 ml.

SWEET POTATO SAUCE

Saus Kacang
PEANUT SAUCE

Although peanut sauce can be found all over the archipelago, most people agree that the classic peanut sauces originate in Bali and central Java.

> 250 g raw peanuts, shelled, skinned
> 30 ml peanut oil
> 20 g shallots (bawang merah), peeled, finely diced
> 10 g garlic, peeled, finely diced
> 40 g red chilies, seeded, diced
> 15 g brown sugar (gula Jawa)
> 20 g tamarind pulp
> 2 kaffir lime leaves
> 1 lemon grass stalk, crushed
> 375 ml water
> salt

1 Deep-fry the peanuts at 375°C until they are light brown, approximately 5-8 minutes. Then grind the peanuts finely in a meat or coffee grinder. Set aside.
2 Heat the peanut oil in a saucepan and sauté the shallots, garlic and chilies for 2-3 minutes without colouring.
3 Stir in the brown sugar and tamarind pulp. Add in the lime leaves and lemon grass, and continue to sauté for 2 minutes more.
4 Mix in the ground peanuts and sauté an additional 2 minutes.
5 Pour in the water and season with salt. Bring the mixture to the boil, reduce the heat and simmer, stirring constantly, for approximately 10 minutes.
6 Remove the pan from the heat. Discard the lemon grass and lime leaves.
7 Pour the sauce into a blender and blend at medium speed for 2-4 minutes, until the sauce becomes a smooth, thick paste. Yields 625 ml.

Saus Labu Merah
PUMPKIN SAUCE

This hot sour sauce can be used to accompany veal, pork, beef, chicken and fish. It should be served hot.

> 30 ml peanut oil
> 40 g shallots (bawang merah), peeled, finely diced
> 20 g garlic, peeled, finely diced
> 5 g ginger, peeled, finely diced
> 1 lemon grass stalk, crushed
> 2 salam leaves
> 2 g anise seeds
> 30 ml tamarind water (see page 23)
> 45 ml red chili juice (see page 23)
> 250 ml coconut milk (see page 22)
> 125 ml chicken stock (see page 24)
> 150 g ripe pumpkin, boiled until soft — 8-12 minutes
> salt

1 Heat the peanut oil in a saucepan and sauté the shallots and garlic for 2-3 minutes in the hot oil until light brown.
2 Add the ginger, lemon grass and salam leaves. Continue to sauté for another 2 minutes.
3 Add the anise, tamarind water, chili juice and coconut milk. Pour in the chicken stock and bring to the boil. Reduce the heat and let the mixture simmer for 3-4 minutes. Stir it frequently.
4 Add in the pumpkin and season with salt. Continue to cook for approximately 8 minutes.
5 Remove the pan from the heat and discard the lemon grass and salam leaves.
6 Pour the mixture into a blender and process for 2-3 minutes until smooth. Yields 500 ml.

PEANUT SAUCE

Saus Tauge Pedas

SPICY BEANSPROUT SAUCE

The beansprout is usually associated with Chinese cooking. In Indonesia, however, after centuries of Chinese influence and trade, the beansprout is one of the most commonly used vegetables. Serve this sauce hot with fish and seafood.

30 ml peanut oil
30 g shallots (bawang merah), peeled, finely diced
10 g garlic, peeled, finely diced
50 g red chilies, seeded, finely diced
10 g greater galangal, peeled, finely diced
10 g lemon grass stalk, finely diced
375 ml coconut milk (see page 22)
100 g beansprouts, cleaned
salt

1 Heat the peanut oil in a saucepan. Add in the shallots, garlic and chilies and sauté until light brown.
2 Stir in the greater galangal and lemon grass, and continue to sauté for 2 minutes more.
3 Pour in the coconut milk and bring the mixture to the boil, then turn down the heat.
4 Add the beansprouts, season with salt and simmer for 10 minutes, stirring frequently.
5 Remove the pan from the heat and serve the sauce hot. Yields 500 ml.

Saus Cabe Hijau

GREEN CHILI SAUCE

This is a pleasantly mild chili sauce.

30 ml peanut oil
20 g shallots (bawang merah), peeled, finely diced
10 g garlic, peeled, finely diced
10 g greater galangal, peeled, finely diced
10 g ginger, peeled, finely diced
1 lemon grass stalk, crushed
3 salam leaves
10 g shrimp paste
2 tomatoes, chopped
250 g green chilies, seeded, diced
375 ml coconut milk (see page 22)

1 Heat the peanut oil in a saucepan. Add the shallots, garlic, greater galangal, ginger, lemon grass and salam leaves, and sauté until the ingredients are light brown.
2 Add in the shrimp paste, tomatoes and green chilies, and sauté for a further 2-3 minutes.
3 Pour in the coconut milk, bring the mixture to the boil and simmer for approximately 5 minutes, stirring gently until the sauce thickens.
4 Remove from the heat and discard the lemon grass and salam leaves.
5 Pour the sauce into a blender and blend for 2-4 minutes until smooth. Yields 625 ml.

Saus Rujak

RUJAK SAUCE

Central Java is the home of the *rujak*, a salad of assorted fresh fruits with a dressing made of *gula Jawa* and chili juice. This is our version of the *rujak* sauce — a syrupy delight for raw fruit and vegetable salads, or a mixture of the two.

200 g brown sugar (gula Jawa)
100 ml lukewarm water
40 g red chilies, finely diced
15 g tamarind pulp
125 ml red chili juice (see page 23)

1 In a saucepan, dissolve the brown sugar in the lukewarm water until the mixture is completely smooth.
2 Add in the remaining ingredients and mix well.
3 Bring the mixture to the boil, then reduce the heat and simmer for approximately 8 minutes.
4 Remove the pan from the heat and let the sauce cool completely before using. Yields 375 ml.

Saus Pesmol

PESMOL SAUCE

This is one of the most important sauces in Java, and virtually everyone has a different idea as to what constitutes the perfect pesmol. Coconut milk and turmeric, however, are always included, and the taste is always sweet and sour.

30 ml peanut oil
30 g shallots (bawang merah), peeled, finely chopped
10 g garlic, peeled, finely chopped
40 g tomatoes, chopped
20 g red chilies, cleaned, seeded, finely chopped
20 g ginger, peeled, chopped
20 g greater galangal, peeled, chopped
1 lemon grass stalk, crushed
1 g turmeric root, finely diced
500 ml coconut milk (see page 22)
10 g white sugar
10 ml white vinegar

1 Heat the oil in a saucepan and sauté the next 7 ingredients for 3-5 minutes until light brown.
2 Sprinkle in the turmeric root and continue to sauté for another 2 minutes.
3 Add in the coconut milk and sugar. Bring to the boil and let it simmer for about 8 minutes until the sauce begins to thicken. Stir occasionally.
4 Add in the vinegar and continue to simmer for an additional 3 minutes.
5 Remove the pan from the heat. Put the sauce in a blender and blend until smooth. Remove and keep warm. Yields 500 ml.

Saus Madu dan Cabe Merah

HONEY CHILI SAUCE

This is a spicy, sweet sauce for grilled or roast chicken and veal. It is served hot.

> 15 ml peanut oil
> 30 g shallots (bawang merah), peeled, finely diced
> 10 g garlic, peeled, finely diced
> coriander powder
> 15 ml lemon juice
> 185 ml red chili juice (see page 23)
> 30 ml tamarind water (see page 23)
> 90 ml honey
> 165 ml water
> salt

1 Heat the peanut oil in a saucepan. Add the shallots and garlic and sauté for 1 minute until light brown.
2 Add in the coriander powder and continue to sauté for an additional minute.
3 Pour in the remaining ingredients, seasoning with salt. Bring to the boil. Reduce the heat and simmer, stirring frequently, until the sauce thickens, approximately 10 minutes.
4 Remove from the heat and serve hot. Yields 500 ml.

Saus Pecel

SWEET SPICY PECEL SAUCE

Pecel — cooked vegetables served with a peanut sauce — originally came from east Java. *Kencur,* or lesser galangal, and the brown palm sugar, *gula Jawa,* give the sauce its distinctive flavour.

> 15 ml peanut oil
> 30 g shallots (bawang merah), peeled, finely diced
> 10 g garlic, peeled, finely diced
> 5 g lesser galangal, peeled, finely diced
> 50 g peanuts, deep-fried, chopped
> 30 g brown sugar (gula Jawa)
> 30 ml tamarind water (see page 23)
> 60 ml red chili juice (see page 23)
> 10 ml dark sweet soya sauce
> 375 ml water
> salt

1 Heat the peanut oil in a saucepan and sauté the shallots, garlic, lesser galangal and peanuts for 2-3 minutes.
2 Add in the brown sugar, tamarind water and chili juice. Stir in the sweet soya sauce and then pour in the water. Season with the salt. Bring the mixture to the boil, reduce the heat and simmer for 8 minutes, stirring from time to time.
3 Remove the pan from the heat and pour the mixture into a blender. Run the machine for 2 minutes until the sauce is smooth.
4 Serve warm with meat, or cold with vegetables. Yields 500 ml.

Saus Setup Banyuwangi

BANYUWANGI SAUCE

This sauce takes its name from a city in east Java, where the recipes frequently call for the use of coconut milk. The light fieriness of this sauce harmonizes well with the sweet basil.

> 15 ml peanut oil
> 40 g shallots (bawang merah), finely diced
> 10 g garlic, finely diced
> 40 g red chilies, seeded, finely diced
> 40 g green chilies, seeded, finely diced
> 15 sweet basil leaves (kemangi), finely chopped
> 250 ml coconut milk (see page 22)
> 10 g sweet basil leaves

1 Heat the peanut oil in a frying pan. Sauté the shallots, garlic and chilies in the oil for 3-5 minutes without browning.
2 Add in the chopped basil leaves and coconut milk. Bring the mixture to the boil, reduce the heat and simmer for 10 minutes.
3 Pour the sauce into a blender and blend for 2-3 minutes at high speed until smooth.
4 Remove the sauce from the blender and pour it back into the saucepan. Stir in the whole basil leaves. Yields 250 ml.

Saus Pala

NUTMEG SAUCE

Despite the small amount of nutmeg used in the recipe, this sauce has a strong nutmeg flavour and should go well with poultry and gamebird dishes.

> 15 ml peanut oil
> 250 g chicken bones
> 10 g garlic, peeled, coarsely chopped
> 30 g shallots, peeled, coarsely chopped
> 10 g ginger, peeled, chopped
> 2 salam leaves
> 50 ml dark sweet soya sauce
> 3 g nutmeg powder
> 500 ml chicken stock (see page 24)
> salt

1 Heat the peanut oil in a frying pan and sauté the chicken bones in the hot oil over high heat until they are light brown.
2 Add the garlic, shallots, ginger and salam leaves, and sauté until they are dark brown.
3 Pour in the sweet soya sauce, nutmeg and chicken stock, and season with salt. Turn down the heat and let the mixture simmer for 20 minutes.
4 Remove the pan from the heat and strain the sauce through a fine sieve. Yields 500 ml.

SPICY BEANSPROUT SAUCE

SWEET SPICY PECEL SAUCE

GREEN CHILI SAUCE

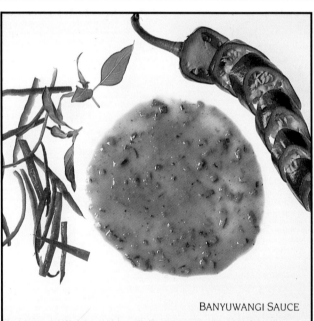

BANYUWANGI SAUCE

PESMOL SAUCE

NUTMEG SAUCE

Opor Sauce

Red Kidney Bean Sauce

Pineapple Coconut Sauce

Sour Turmeric Sauce

Spiced Soya Sauce

Papaya Sauce

Saus Opor

OPOR SAUCE

This sweet sauce is found almost everywhere in Java and Sumatra, and no ceremony would be complete without a dish using it.

> 30 ml peanut oil
> 50 g shallots (bawang merah), peeled, finely diced
> 5 g garlic, peeled, finely diced
> 20 g candlenuts, ground
> 5 g ginger, peeled, chopped
> 5 g greater galangal, peeled, chopped
> 1 salam leaf
> 500 ml coconut milk (see page 22)
> 250 ml chicken stock (see page 24)
> salt

1 Heat the peanut oil in a saucepan and sauté the shallots, garlic, candlenuts, ginger, greater galangal and salam leaf for 5 minutes without browning.
2 Add in the coconut milk and chicken stock and bring the mixture to the boil.
3 Reduce the heat and simmer until the sauce starts to thicken, approximately 8-10 minutes. Season with salt.
4 Remove the pan from the heat and discard the salam leaf.
5 Pour the sauce into a blender and process for 2-3 minutes until smooth. Serve hot. Yields 750 ml.

Saus Nanas Opor

PINEAPPLE COCONUT SAUCE

> 30 ml coconut oil
> 50 g shallots (bawang merah), peeled, finely diced
> 10 g garlic, peeled, finely diced
> 10 g greater galangal, peeled, finely diced
> 10 g lemon grass stalk, finely diced
> 1 salam leaf
> 5 coriander leaves
> 5 g anise seed
> 20 g candlenuts, ground
> 130 g pineapple, diced
> 375 ml coconut milk (see page 22)
> salt

1 Heat the coconut oil in a saucepan and sauté the next 6 ingredients in the oil for 2 minutes without browning.
2 Add in the anise, candlenuts and pineapple. Continue to sauté for 2 minutes more.
3 Pour in the coconut milk. Season with salt and bring to the boil. Reduce the heat and simmer for approximately 10 minutes.
4 Remove the pan from the heat and discard the salam leaf.
5 Pour the sauce into a blender and process for 2 minutes until smooth. Yields 375 ml.

Saus Semur

SPICED SOYA SAUCE

> 30 ml peanut oil
> 20 g onions, peeled, finely diced
> 10 g garlic, peeled, finely diced
> 5 g ginger, peeled, finely diced
> 5 g black peppercorns, crushed
> 20 g brown sugar (gula Jawa)
> 6 dried cloves
> 2 g coriander seeds
> 1 g nutmeg powder
> 2 g cinnamon powder
> 200 ml dark sweet soya sauce
> 250 ml water
> salt

1 Heat the oil in a saucepan and sauté the onions, garlic and ginger for 2-3 minutes without browning. Stir frequently.
2 Add the peppercorns and brown sugar, and continue to sauté for 2 minutes more.
3 Mix in the cloves, coriander seeds, nutmeg and cinnamon powder. Pour in the sweet soya sauce and water. Season with salt. Bring the mixture to the boil, reduce the heat and simmer for 8-10 minutes. The sauce should have a syrupy consistency; if it does not, let it simmer some more until the desired consistency is achieved. Remove from the heat.
4 Pour the mixture through a sieve and discard all the solid ingredients. Yields 375 ml.

Saus Kacang Merah

RED KIDNEY BEAN SAUCE

> 30 ml peanut oil
> 20 g shallots (bawang merah), peeled, finely diced
> 10 g garlic, peeled, finely diced
> 5 g ginger, peeled, finely diced
> 10 g brown sugar (gula Jawa)
> 2 salam leaves
> 150 g red kidney beans, soaked overnight, boiled 45-60
>   minutes until soft
> 90 ml red chili juice (see page 23)
> 250 ml coconut milk (see page 22)
> salt

1 Heat the peanut oil in a saucepan and sauté the shallots, garlic and ginger in the oil until light brown, approximately 2-3 minutes.
2 Add the brown sugar, salam leaves and red kidney beans. Continue sautéing for 2 minutes more.
3 Pour in the chili juice and coconut milk, season with salt and bring to the boil. Reduce the heat and let the sauce simmer for 10 minutes, stirring frequently.
4 Remove the pan from the heat and discard the salam leaves.
5 Pour the sauce into a blender and purée for 2-3 minutes until smooth. Yields 500 ml.

Saus Acar Kuning

SOUR TURMERIC SAUCE

30 ml peanut oil
20 g ginger, peeled, finely chopped
20 g shallots (bawang merah), peeled, finely chopped
10 g garlic, peeled, finely chopped
1 bay leaf
1 lemon grass stalk, crushed
3 g turmeric powder
40 g candlenuts, ground
5 g white sugar
500 ml coconut milk (see page 22)
30 ml white vinegar
salt
pepper

1   Heat the oil in a pan and sauté the ginger, shallots, garlic, bay leaf and lemon grass for 2 minutes.
2   Add in the turmeric powder, candlenuts and sugar, and continue to sauté for 3-5 minutes.
3   Pour in the coconut milk and vinegar, and simmer for 10 minutes. Season with salt and pepper.
4   Remove from the heat and discard the bay leaf and lemon grass.
5   Pour the sauce into a blender and purée until smooth. Yields 500 ml.

Saus Pepaya

PAPAYA SAUCE

The fruitiness of the papaya makes this sauce a fine accompaniment to fowl and gamebirds. Only well-ripened, red-fleshed papayas should be used in order to acquire the right colour and flavour.

15 ml peanut oil
40 g shallots (bawang merah), peeled, finely diced
5 g garlic, peeled, finely diced
5 g ginger, peeled, finely diced
10 g lemon grass stalk, finely diced
200 g ripe papaya, peeled, diced
10 g white sugar
15 ml white vinegar
125 ml red chili juice (see page 23)
185 ml chicken stock (see page 24)
salt

1   Heat the peanut oil in a saucepan and sauté the shallots, garlic, ginger and lemon grass for 2 minutes in the hot oil until light brown.
2   Stir in the papaya, sugar and vinegar, and continue to sauté for 2 minutes more.
3   Pour in the chili juice and chicken stock, and season with salt. Reduce the heat and simmer for approximately 5-7 minutes, stirring from time to time. Remove the pan from the heat.
4   Pour the sauce into a blender and purée for 2 minutes until smooth. Remove from the blender and serve warm. Yields 500 ml.

Saus Bengkulu

BENGKULU SAUCE

Because of its relatively mild flavour, this sauce goes well with many dishes.

30 ml peanut oil
40 g shallots (bawang merah), peeled, finely diced
20 g garlic, peeled, finely diced
50 g red chilies, seeded, diced
10 g green chilies, seeded, diced
10 sweet basil leaves (kemangi)
100 g tomatoes, peeled, seeded, diced
150 ml lamb stock (see page 24)
2 g shrimp paste
salt

1   Heat the peanut oil in a saucepan and sauté the shallots, garlic and chilies for 2 minutes without browning.
2   Add in the basil leaves and tomatoes. Continue to sauté for 2 minutes more.
3   Add in the lamb stock and shrimp paste, bring to the boil and reduce the heat. Season the sauce lightly with salt and simmer at low heat for approximately 15 minutes.
4   Pour the sauce into a blender and process until smooth. Yields 400 ml.

Saus Tauco Sumatra

SUMATRAN BLACK BEAN SAUCE

45 ml peanut oil
40 g onions, peeled, finely diced
10 g garlic, peeled, finely diced
20 g red chilies, cut into strips
20 g green chilies, cut into strips
1 lemon grass stalk, finely diced
10 g greater galangal, peeled, finely diced
1 salam leaf
120 g sour finger carambolas, cut into strips
200 ml fermented black soya beans
125 ml water
60 ml dark sweet soya sauce
salt

1   Heat the oil in a pan and sauté the onions, garlic, chilies, lemon grass and greater galangal in the hot oil for 2-3 minutes, stirring constantly.
2   Add in the salam leaf, sour finger carambolas, fermented soya beans and water. Bring the mixture to the boil.
3   Add in the sweet soya sauce and simmer until the sauce starts to thicken, approximately 5-8 minutes.
4   Remove from the heat and discard the salam leaf.
5   Pour the sauce into a blender and process at high speed for 2-3 minutes. Remove from the blender and serve. Yields 375 ml.

SPICY COCONUT SAUCE

Saus Rendang
SPICY COCONUT SAUCE

30 ml peanut oil
50 g shallots (bawang merah), peeled, finely diced
10 g garlic, peeled, finely diced
10 g ginger, peeled, finely diced
10 g greater galangal, peeled, finely diced
20 g candlenuts, ground
1 lemon grass stalk, bruised
4 kaffir lime leaves
1 turmeric leaf
2 g coriander powder
375 ml red chili juice (see page 23)
250 ml coconut milk (see page 22)
salt

1   In a saucepan, heat the peanut oil and sauté the shallots, garlic, ginger and greater galangal for approximately 5 minutes until light brown.
2   Add the candlenuts, lemon grass, lime leaves, turmeric leaf and coriander powder. Continue to sauté for 2 minutes.
3   Pour in the chili juice and coconut milk, and season with the salt. Bring the mixture to the boil, reduce the heat and let it simmer until the sauce thickens, approximately 6-8 minutes. Stir the mixture from time to time.
4   Remove the pan from the heat and discard the lemon grass and lime leaves.
5   Pour the sauce into a blender and run machine at high speed for approximately 3-4 minutes until the sauce is smooth. Yields 625 ml.

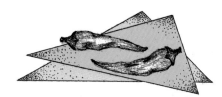

Saus Sambal Brambang
BRAMBANG SAUCE

260 g tomatoes, peeled, seeded, diced
20 g garlic, peeled, finely diced
120 g shallots (bawang merah), peeled, finely diced
20 g bird's eye chilies, seeded, diced
80 ml freshly squeezed lime juice
125 ml water
salt

1   Combine all the ingredients in a blender. Process for approximately 3-4 minutes until smooth.
2   Remove the pinkish sauce from the blender and refrigerate. Yields 500 ml.

NOTE: To make Sambal Brambang instead of Brambang Sauce, simply mix the above ingredients together without blending them. It should be left to marinate for an hour before use for the flavour to develop.

Saus Sambal Kecap
SWEET SPICY SOYA SAUCE

In this sauce, the bite of the chili cuts the heavy sweetness of the sweet soya sauce. It should always be served cold, and is a popular accompaniment to many dishes.

30 g shallots (bawang merah), peeled, finely diced
15 g garlic, peeled, finely diced
30 g red chilies, seeded, finely diced
10 g bird's eye chilies, seeded, finely diced
30 g tomatoes, peeled, seeded, diced
500 ml dark sweet soya sauce
45 ml freshly squeezed lime juice
salt

1   Combine all the ingredients and mix well.
2   Season with salt. Yields 500 ml.

SWEET SPICY SOYA SAUCE

Saus Gulai
INDONESIAN CURRY SAUCE

From Padang, the bustling port of west Sumatra, comes this hot curry sauce. Though several kinds of spices are used in the recipe, each spice carries its own distinct flavour which is easily detected in the sauce.

> 30 ml peanut oil
> 20 g shallots (bawang merah), peeled, finely diced
> 10 g garlic, peeled, finely diced
> 5 g ginger, peeled, finely diced
> 5 g greater galangal, peeled, finely diced
> 2 salam leaves
> 20 g candlenuts, ground
> 5 g turmeric root, finely diced
> 2 g anise powder
> 2 g cinnamon powder
> 2 g clove powder
> 1 g cardamom powder
> 30 ml tamarind water (see page 23)
> 90 ml red chili juice (see page 23)
> 500 ml coconut milk (see page 22)
> salt

1 Heat the oil in a saucepan and sauté the shallots, garlic, ginger and greater galangal in the oil over high heat for 3-4 minutes until light brown. Stir frequently.
2 Add in the salam leaves, candlenuts, turmeric and powdered spices. Continue to sauté for another 2 minutes over reduced heat.
3 Pour in the tamarind water and chili juice, and slowly add in the coconut milk. Season with salt.
4 Bring the mixture to the boil, then reduce the heat and simmer for approximately 10 minutes, stirring constantly.
5 Withdraw the pan from the heat and discard the salam leaves.
6 Pour the sauce into a blender and process until smooth, approximately 3-4 minutes. Serve hot. Yields 500 ml.

Saus Belimbing Wuluh
SOUR FINGER CARAMBOLA SAUCE

The sour *belimbing wuluh* is commonly used throughout Indonesia as a mild substitute for vinegar in fish and meat dishes. It is also eaten as a pickle or raw in salads. This sour sauce goes well with pork, lamb, poultry and fish.

> 30 ml peanut oil
> 40 g shallots (bawang merah), peeled, finely diced
> 5 g garlic, peeled, finely diced
> 5 g ginger, peeled, finely diced
> 5 g lemon grass stalk, finely diced
> 10 g shrimp paste
> 200 g sour finger carambolas, diced
> 20 g candlenuts, ground
> 5 g turmeric powder
> 60 ml red chili juice (see page 23)
> 375 ml coconut milk (see page 22)
> salt

1 Heat the peanut oil in a saucepan. Sauté the shallots, garlic, ginger and lemon grass in the hot oil for 2 minutes without browning.
2 Add the shrimp paste and sour carambolas. Continue to sauté for another 2 minutes.
3 Add in the candlenuts and turmeric powder and sauté for an additional 2 minutes.
4 Pour in the chili juice and coconut milk and season lightly with salt. Bring the mixture to the boil, reduce the heat and simmer for approximately 10 minutes.
5 Pour the sauce into a blender and process for 2 minutes until smooth. Yields 625 ml.

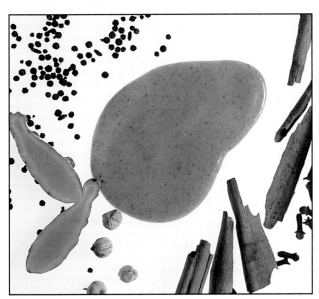

INDONESIAN CURRY SAUCE

Saus Dabu-dabu Manado

DABU-DABU SAUCE

This thin, fiery sauce is served uncooked and cold, even when accompanying hot dishes.

> 60 g red chilies, seeded, diced
> 10 g bird's eye chilies, seeded, diced
> 30 g shallots (bawang merah), peeled, finely diced
> 250 g tomatoes, peeled, seeded, diced
> 30 ml white vinegar
> 160 ml chicken stock, cold (see page 24)
> salt
> white pepper

1 Put the chilies, shallots, tomatoes and vinegar in a blender. Process until smooth.
2 Pour the mixture into a bowl, add in the chicken stock and season with salt and pepper. Mix well. Yields 500 ml.

NOTE: When chicken stock is mixed with the sauce, it can be served with meat or chicken dishes. If the sauce is to accompany fish dishes, use fish stock instead.

Saus Jeruk

ORANGE SAUCE

> 30 ml peanut oil
> 30 g shallots (bawang merah), peeled, finely diced
> 10 g garlic, peeled, finely diced
> 5 g greater galangal, peeled, finely diced
> 5 g ginger, peeled, finely diced
> 30 g candlenuts, ground
> 1 lemon grass stalk, crushed
> 15 g turmeric root, finely diced
> 2 g coriander powder
> 10 g brown sugar (gula Jawa)
> 125 ml coconut milk (see page 22)
> 250 ml unsweetened orange juice
> salt

1 Heat the oil in a saucepan and sauté the shallots, garlic, greater galangal and ginger for about 1-2 minutes, until the ingredients are light brown.
2 Add in the candlenuts, lemon grass, turmeric root, coriander powder and brown sugar. Sauté for a further 2 minutes.
3 Pour in the coconut milk and orange juice, and season with salt. Bring the mixture to the boil. Reduce the heat and let it simmer for about 20 minutes, stirring frequently.
4 Remove the pan from the heat and discard the lemon grass.
5 Pour the sauce into a blender and process for 2 minutes until smooth. Serve hot. Yields 375 ml.

Saus Asam Manis

SWEET SOUR SAUCE

This sauce is light red in colour. One should be able to taste the ginger in it. If not, increase the amount of ginger by 2-5 g at a time.

> 30 ml vegetable oil
> 40 g shallots (bawang merah), peeled, finely diced
> 5 g garlic, peeled, finely diced
> 20 g ginger, peeled, finely diced
> 250 g tomatoes, peeled, seeded, diced
> 40 g sugar
> 45 ml white vinegar
> 125 ml water
> salt

1 Heat the oil in a saucepan. Sauté the shallots, garlic and ginger in the hot oil for 2 minutes without browning.
2 Add in the tomatoes, sugar, white vinegar and water. Season with salt and bring to the boil. Reduce the heat and let the sauce simmer for 5 minutes.
3 Pour the sauce into a blender and process at high speed for 2 minutes until the sauce is smooth. Yields 500 ml.

Saus Kacang Madu

PEANUT HONEY SAUCE

Although lots of honey is produced in Indonesia, honey is rarely used in traditional cooking. Nonetheless, this sweet sauce makes a fine complement to chicken, duck or lamb. It is important that a strong-tasting honey be used, otherwise the peanut taste will predominate.

> 30 ml peanut oil
> 40 g shallots (bawang merah), peeled, finely diced
> 5 g garlic, peeled, finely diced
> 10 g ginger, peeled, finely diced
> 150 g peanuts, roasted, ground
> 10 g lemon grass stalk, finely diced
> 60 ml red chili juice (see page 23)
> 150 ml honey
> 375 ml water
> salt

1 Heat the oil in a saucepan and sauté the shallots, garlic and ginger in the hot oil for 2 minutes without browning.
2 Add in the peanuts and lemon grass and continue to sauté for 2 minutes.
3 Pour in the chili juice, honey and water. Season with salt and bring the mixture to the boil.
4 Reduce the heat and let the sauce simmer for approximately 8-10 minutes, stirring slowly.
5 Pour the sauce into a blender and process 2 minutes. The sauce should have a silky consistency. Yields 625 ml.

Saus Rica-rica
RICA-RICA SAUCE

This sauce hails from Manado in north Sulawesi, where it (or variations of it, but always featuring tomatoes) is used on practically everything. This particular Rica-rica Sauce is good, served hot or cold, with fish. It is also a fine accompaniment for poultry.

30 ml vegetable oil
30 g shallots (bawang merah), peeled, finely diced
10 g garlic, peeled, finely diced
5 g ginger, peeled, finely diced
60 g red chilies, seeded, finely diced
1 salam leaf
30 g candlenuts, ground
200 g tomatoes, peeled, seeded, diced
5 g turmeric powder
250 ml coconut milk (see page 22)
60 ml red chili juice (see page 23)
salt

1   Heat the oil in a saucepan. Add the shallots, garlic, ginger and chilies and sauté for 2-3 minutes without browning.
2   Add in the salam leaf and candlenuts, and continue to sauté for 2 minutes more.
3   Add in 150 g of the tomatoes and the turmeric powder, and sauté for another 2 minutes. Pour in the coconut milk and chili juice. Season with salt.
4   Bring the mixture to the boil, reduce the heat and simmer until the sauce thickens, approximately 8 minutes. Stir constantly.
5   Remove the pan from the heat and discard the salam leaf.
6   Pour the sauce into a blender and process until smooth, approximately 2-3 minutes.
7   Remove the sauce from the blender. Just before serving, add in the remaining diced tomatoes. Yields 625 ml.

NOTE: Should the sauce become too thick, add a small amount of chicken stock.

Saus Sambal Godok
WHITE BEANCURD SAUCE

30 ml peanut oil
30 g shallots (bawang merah), peeled, finely diced
10 g garlic, peeled, finely diced
10 g greater galangal, peeled, finely diced
4 salam leaves
15 g candlenuts, ground
100 g white beancurd, diced
40 g long beans, diced
90 ml red chili juice (see page 23)
250 ml coconut milk (see page 22)
salt

1   Heat the peanut oil in a saucepan. Add the shallots, garlic, greater galangal and salam leaves and sauté for 2 minutes without browning.
2   Add in the candlenuts and continue to sauté for 2 minutes.
3   Add in the beancurd and long beans, and sauté for 2 minutes more.
4   Pour in the chili juice and coconut milk, and season with salt. Bring to the boil, reduce the heat and simmer for approximately 10 minutes or until the sauce thickens.
5   Withdraw the pan from the heat and discard the salam leaves.
6   Pour the mixture into a blender and process at high speed until smooth. Serve hot. Yields 500 ml.

Saus Bumbu Rujak
SPICY RUJAK SAUCE

Use this *rujak* sauce with fish and beef dishes. It is yellow in colour and should be served hot.

30 ml peanut oil
10 g garlic, peeled, finely diced
30 g shallots (bawang merah), peeled, finely diced
10 g ginger, peeled, finely diced
10 g greater galangal, peeled, finely diced
5 g lemon grass stalk, finely diced
1 salam leaf
5 g white sugar
20 g candlenuts, ground
2 g turmeric powder
10 ml white vinegar
90 ml red chili juice (see page 23)
400 ml coconut milk (see page 22)
salt

1   Heat the peanut oil in a saucepan. Sauté the garlic and shallots until light brown, approximately 2-3 minutes.
2   Add in the ginger, greater galangal, lemon grass and salam leaf, continuing to sauté for a further 1-2 minutes without letting the new ingredients take colour.
3   Stir in the sugar, candlenuts and turmeric powder, and continue to sauté for another minute.
4   Pour in the vinegar, chili juice and coconut milk. Season with some salt. Then bring the mixture to the boil, reduce the heat and simmer for 8-10 minutes or until the sauce starts to thicken.
5   Remove the pan from the heat and discard the salam leaf.
6   Pour the sauce into a blender and purée at high speed for 2-3 minutes. Remove from the blender and serve. Yields 500 ml.

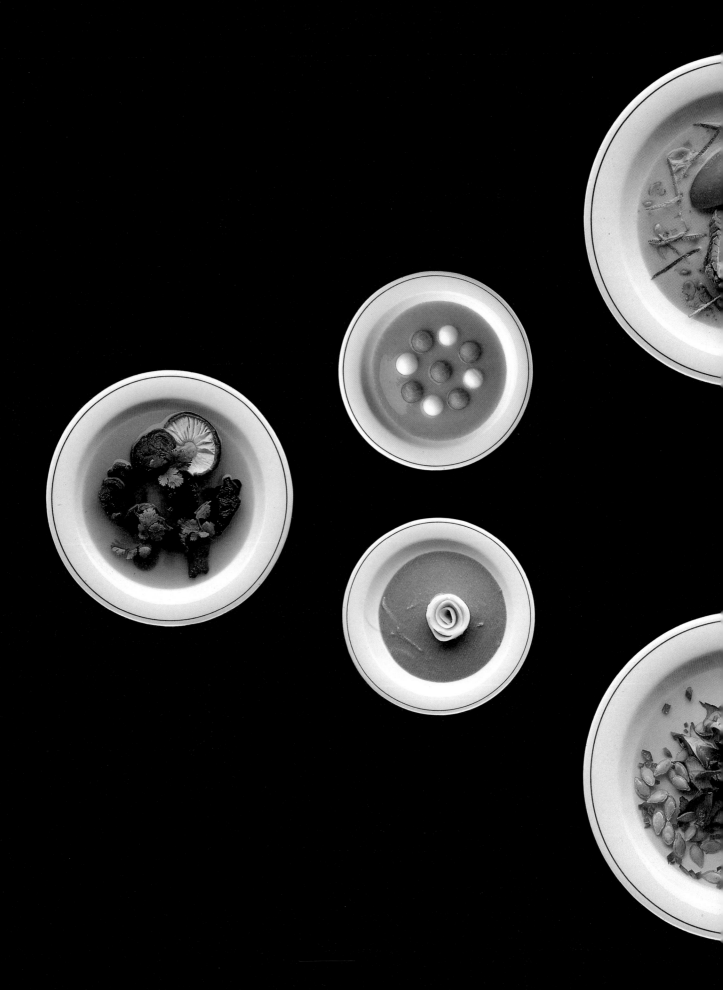

SOUPS AND APPETIZERS

SOUPS

Soto Jawa Timur
EAST JAVANESE CHICKEN SOUP

STEP 1: Chicken Soup
> 15 ml vegetable oil
> 10 g garlic, peeled, finely diced
> 5 g ginger, peeled, finely diced
> 5 g turmeric root, peeled, finely diced
> 2 g shrimp paste
> 320 ml chicken stock (see page 24)
> 375 ml coconut milk (see page 22)
> salt
> ground white pepper
> 120 g chicken meat, diced

1 Heat the vegetable oil in a shallow stockpot. Add in the garlic, ginger and turmeric root and sauté in the oil for 2 minutes without browning.
2 Stir in the shrimp paste and continue to sauté for approximately 2 minutes, until the paste has been thoroughly mixed in.
3 Pour in the chicken stock and gradually add in the coconut milk, stirring frequently. Season with salt and pepper, but use salt sparingly.
4 Bring the soup to the boil, then reduce the heat and let it simmer for 20 minutes, to absorb the flavours. Stir constantly to prevent the coconut milk from settling. Remove the pot from the heat.

STEP 2: Garnish and Presentation
> 40 g dried glass noodles, soaked in warm water for 20 minutes
> 40 g sour finger carambolas, sliced thinly
> 10 g shallots (bawang merah), peeled, sliced thinly, deep-fried

1 Arrange the glass noodles, sour finger carambola slices and fried shallots in individual soup plates.
2 Ladle in the soup made in Step 1 and serve immediately.

Sop Siwalan
PALM NUT SOUP

This beautifully mild soup features the fruit of the versatile Palmyra tree. If palm nuts are not available, use fresh water chestnuts instead.

> 30 ml vegetable oil
> 10 g shallots (bawang merah), peeled, finely diced
> 10 g garlic, peeled, finely diced
> 5 medium-sized red chilies, sliced
> 160 g chicken meat, skinned, diced
> 160 g palm nuts, boiled until crunchy — about 20 minutes
> 40 g carrot, peeled, finely diced
> 2 g nutmeg powder
> 1 litre chicken stock (see page 24)
> salt
> 1 nutmeg, grated

1 Heat the oil in a shallow stockpot and sauté the shallots, garlic and red chilies for 2 minutes, until they look glazy.
2 Stir in the chicken meat, palm nuts and carrots, and sauté for 2 minutes more.
3 Sprinkle the nutmeg powder over the mixture. Pour in the chicken stock and season with salt.
4 Bring the stock to the boil, reduce the heat and simmer for 10 minutes over low heat.
5 Remove from the heat and sprinkle the freshly grated nutmeg over the soup just before serving.

Sop Kacang Merah
RED KIDNEY BEAN SOUP WITH GINGER

STEP 1: Soup
> 10 ml peanut oil
> 40 g onions, peeled, finely diced
> 40 g shallots (bawang merah), peeled, finely diced
> 5 g garlic, peeled, finely diced
> 10 g ginger, peeled, finely diced
> 5 g greater galangal, peeled, finely diced
> 150 g red kidney beans, soaked overnight, boiled until soft — 45 minutes to 1 hour
> 500 ml clear chicken stock (see page 24)
> 125 ml coconut milk (see page 22)
> salt
> white pepper

1 Heat the peanut oil in a saucepan and sauté the onions, shallots, garlic, ginger and greater galangal until soft. Do not let them brown.
2 Add in the kidney beans, toss and continue to cook for another 2 minutes.
3 Pour the chicken stock over the mixture and bring to the boil. Reduce the heat and let the soup simmer, stirring often, until all the ingredients are soft.
4 Withdraw the pan from the heat; pour the soup into a blender and purée it until silky.
5 Return the soup to the pan and continue to cook, gradually adding in the coconut milk, for another 5 minutes. Season with salt and pepper.

STEP 2: Garnish and Presentation
> 20 g red kidney beans, soaked overnight, boiled until soft — 45 minutes to 1 hour
> 10 g ginger, cut into fine strips
> 10 g red chilies, cut into fine strips
> 4 sprigs coriander leaves

1 Divide the kidney beans into 4 equal parts and put a portion in each soup bowl. Arrange the ginger and red chili julienne in the bowls.
2 Ladle in the soup made in Step 1 and top each bowl with a sprig of coriander leaves.

Sop Cendawan Indonesia

INDONESIAN MUSHROOM SOUP

STEP 1: Broth
15 ml peanut oil
50 g shallots (bawang merah), peeled, finely chopped
10 g garlic, peeled, finely chopped
5 g lemon grass stalk, finely chopped
10 g fresh coriander leaves
50 g dried black Chinese mushrooms, soaked in warm water
for 1 hour, chopped
50 g dried wood fungus, soaked in warm water for 1 hour,
chopped
1 litre chicken stock (see page 24)
ground white pepper
ground nutmeg
5 g fresh ginger, chopped
salt

1 Heat the oil in a stockpot or saucepan and sauté the shallots in the hot oil until they look glazy.
2 Add in the garlic, lemon grass, coriander leaves, mushrooms and wood fungus and continue to sauté for 2-3 minutes.
3 Pour in the chicken stock and the remaining seasoning ingredients; add salt to taste. Bring the broth to the boil, then let it simmer for 1 hour, stirring occasionally.
4 Strain the liquid through a cheesecloth or fine wire sieve into another pot. Keep hot.

NOTE: In order to intensify the mushroom flavour of the soup, cook the chicken stock with 200 g of dried wood fungus for 30 minutes before using the stock for the soup.

STEP 2: Garnish and Presentation
40 g dried black Chinese mushrooms, soaked in warm water
for 1 hour
40 g dried wood fungus, soaked in warm water for 1 hour
4 lemon grass stalks, peeled, washed
8 sprigs coriander leaves

1 Put a portion of the mushrooms and wood fungus in each soup plate.
2 Ladle in the broth made in Step 1 and garnish with the lemon grass stalks and coriander leaves.

Soto Solo Kasuhnanan

BEEF BROTH SOLO KASUHNANAN

This clear beef broth with fermented bean cake is named after the palaces of the ancient capital of Solo.

STEP 1: Beef Broth
15 ml vegetable oil
30 g shallots (bawang merah), peeled, finely diced
5 g garlic, peeled, finely diced
5 g ginger, peeled, finely diced
1.5 litres beef stock (see page 24)
2 g coriander powder
2 salam leaves
5 g brown sugar (gula Jawa)
260 g boneless beef — topside, top round or inside round
salt
ground white pepper
10 g red chilies, stem removed, sliced into rings

1 Heat the vegetable oil in a shallow stockpot and sauté the shallots, garlic and ginger in the oil for 2 minutes, without colouring.
2 Pour in the beef stock and add in the coriander powder, salam leaves and brown sugar.
3 Bring the soup to boiling point and then add in the beef. Season with salt and pepper.
4 Reduce the heat and let it simmer over low heat for approximately 40-50 minutes. From time to time skim the scum off the surface so that the broth remains clear.
5 When the beef is cooked, remove it from the broth and let it cool before slicing and putting to one side.
6 Pour the clear broth through a sieve and discard the remains.
7 Pour the broth back into the stockpot. Add in the sliced chilies and let it simmer for 2 minutes.

STEP 2: Garnish and Presentation
40 g red chilies, seeded, sliced into rings
40 g stringbeans, cut into thin strips
40 g beansprouts, cleaned
40 g fermented bean cake, steamed for 5 minutes, cubed
4 salam leaves

1 Arrange a portion of the chilies, stringbeans, beansprouts, fermented bean cake and beef slices in each individual soup bowl.
2 Ladle in the broth made in Step 1, garnish with the salam leaves and serve immediately.

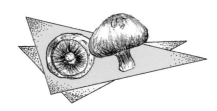

PUMPKIN LEAF SOUP WITH PRAWNS

Sop Daun Labu Udang Rebon

PUMPKIN LEAF SOUP WITH PRAWNS

This spicy, smooth soup has a strong taste of pumpkin leaves.

STEP 1: Soup
> 30 ml vegetable oil
> 20 g shallots (bawang merah), peeled, finely diced
> 15 g garlic, peeled, finely diced
> 10 g shrimp paste
> 40 g tomatoes, peeled, seeded, diced
> 60 g young pumpkin leaves, cut into strips, blanched
> 625 ml coconut milk (see page 22)
> 150 g grey baby prawns, shelled, deveined
> salt

1 Heat the oil in a shallow stockpot and sauté the shallots and garlic for 2 minutes, until glazy.
2 Stir in the shrimp paste and continue to sauté until the paste has been thoroughly mixed in.
3 Add in the diced tomatoes and young pumpkin leaves. Sauté for another 2 minutes.
4 Pour in the coconut milk and bring to the boil. Reduce the heat and simmer for 10 minutes. Stir from time to time to prevent the coconut milk from settling.
5 Season with salt. Then add in the baby prawns and continue to simmer for 2 minutes more.
6 Remove the soup from the stockpot and pour it into a blender. Purée the mixture at high speed for 2-3 minutes.

STEP 2: Garnish and Presentation
> 2 large prawns, cleaned, shell on, blanched for 1 minute
> 20 g red chilies, seeded, finely diced
> 5 g green chilies, seeded, finely diced

1 Slice the prawns in half lengthwise and clean out the heads. Fill the cavity with the diced chilies.
2 Ladle the hot soup made in Step 1 into individual soup plates. Place a prawn on top for garnish.

BIRD'S NEST SOUP WITH QUAIL EGGS

Sop Sarang Burung Karangbolong

BIRD'S NEST SOUP WITH QUAIL EGGS

STEP 1: Soup
> 560 ml chicken stock, cold (see page 24)
> 100 g chicken, minced or ground
> 2 egg whites
> 20 g shallots (bawang merah), peeled, chopped
> 10 g garlic, peeled, chopped
> 10 g celery stick, diced
> 10 g leeks, diced
> 3 lemon grass stalks, crushed
> 4 bird's nests, whole, cleaned, soaked in warm water for a short while
> salt
> pepper

1 Combine all the ingredients in a stockpot. Season with salt and pepper and bring to simmering point.
2 When all the ingredients have risen to the surface, after approximately 15 minutes, reduce the heat and simmer for another 30 minutes.
3 Strain the liquid carefully through a wet cheesecloth. The broth should be golden in colour. Reheat before serving.

STEP 2: Garnish and Presentation
> 1 bird's nest, soaked for 30 minutes in lukewarm water to remove impurities
> 1 green bell pepper, cut into diamonds, blanched
> 6 quail eggs, cooked in boiling salt water for 4 minutes, shelled, halved
> 20 g carrots, peeled, finely diced, blanched

1 Arrange the above garnish ingredients in individual soup bowls.
2 Remember to reheat the soup before ladling it into the bowls.

INDONESIAN MUSHROOM SOUP

BEEF BROTH SOLO KASUHNANAN

SPINACH COCONUT SOUP

Sop Bobor

SPINACH COCONUT SOUP

This is a rich, sweet-tasting soup. Water convolvulus leaves may be used instead of spinach for the soup.

STEP 1: Soup
    30 ml vegetable oil
    15 g onions, peeled, finely diced
    5 g garlic, peeled, finely diced
    10 g lesser galangal, peeled, finely diced
    1 salam leaf
    1 lemon grass stalk, crushed
    3 g coriander powder
    15 g brown sugar (gula Jawa)
    500 ml chicken stock (see page 24)
    250 ml coconut milk (see page 22)
    100 g spinach leaves, stems removed
    80 g young coconut meat, diced
    salt

1 Heat the vegetable oil in a shallow stockpot. Sauté the onions, garlic and lesser galangal for 2 minutes without browning.
2 Add in the salam leaf, lemon grass, coriander powder and brown sugar. Sauté for another 2-3 minutes until the sugar has dissolved.
3 Pour in the chicken stock and gradually add in the coconut milk, stirring frequently. Bring to the boil.
4 Add in the spinach leaves and diced coconut meat. Season with salt. Reduce the heat and let the soup simmer over low heat for 15 minutes.
5 Remove the pot from the heat. Discard the salam leaf and lemon grass.
6 Pour the mixture into a blender and purée for 2-3 minutes.

NOTE: If fresh coconut is not available, use shredded, dried coconut flakes instead, but be sure to soak them first in lukewarm water for at least 10 minutes.

STEP 2: Garnish and Presentation
    20 small young spinach leaves
    80 g young coconut meat

1 Serve a portion of the soup made in Step 1 in each soup bowl.
2 Use young and tender spinach leaves and the coconut to garnish each bowl.

Sop Pelangi Pagi

CLEAR PRAWN SOUP WITH LEMON GRASS

STEP 1: Clarification
    150 g red snapper fillet, skinned
    20 g garlic, peeled
    20 g carrot, peeled
    20 g leeks, use bottom part only
    2 egg whites
    1 lemon grass stalk, crushed
    1 bay leaf
    10 ml chili juice (see page 23)
    20 g tamarind pulp
    750 ml clear fish stock, cold (see page 24)

1 Mince or grind the red snapper finely together with the garlic, carrots and leeks. Put the mixture into a bowl.
2 Stir in the egg whites, then add in the lemon grass, bay leaf, chili juice and tamarind pulp. Mix well.
3 Put this mixture in a stockpot, add in the cold fish stock and bring slowly to the boil, stirring the soup occasionally.
4 Reduce the heat and let the soup simmer until the solid ingredients float to the top, approximately 15 minutes.
5 Withdraw from the heat and using a large soup ladle, push the solid ingredients aside. Strain the liquid through cheesecloth or a fine wire sieve into another pot. Keep the broth hot.

NOTE: When preparing the stock for this recipe, use half the amount of fish and bones given in the recipe on page 24 and mix with an equal amount of prawns.

STEP 2: Garnish and Presentation
    2 tomatoes, peeled, seeded, cut into diamonds
    4 baby corns, blanched, cut into 1-cm pieces
    1 lemon grass stalk, finely diced
    12 sweet basil leaves (kemangi)
    12 medium-sized prawns, shelled, cleaned, tail on, blanched
        for 2 minutes in the fish stock

1 Divide the garnish ingredients equally into 4 portions and arrange them in individual soup bowls.
2 Pour the warm soup made in Step 1 over the garnish and serve immediately.

Sop Kecipir dari Betawi

ASPARAGUS BEAN SOUP

This soup should be seasoned mildly to allow the aroma of the asparagus bean leaves to be fully appreciated. If asparagus beans are unavailable, use snowpeas instead; however, the snowpeas will take considerably less time than the asparagus beans to cook.

STEP 1: Asparagus Bean Broth
500 ml chicken stock (see page 24)
5 g salt
2 g sugar
150 g asparagus beans

1   Pour the stock into a stockpot, season with the salt and sugar, then bring it to the boil.
2   Drop the asparagus beans into the boiling water, reduce the heat and simmer for approximately 30-40 minutes.
3   Withdraw the pot from the heat and pour the mixture into a blender. Process for 2-3 minutes.
4   Strain the liquid through a fine sieve and discard the solid remains.

STEP 2: Soup
15 ml vegetable oil
10 g shallots (bawang merah), peeled, finely diced
60 g green asparagus beans, cut into 1-cm long pieces
10 g red chilies, seeded, finely diced
120 g asparagus beans, cut into triangles, blanched for 2-5 minutes
20 g pumpkin seeds, dried, roasted

1   In a shallow stockpot, heat the vegetable oil and sauté the shallots, green asparagus beans and chilies in the oil for 2 minutes. Stir constantly and do not let the ingredients take colour.
2   Pour in the asparagus bean broth made in Step 1 and simmer over low heat for 10 minutes.
3   Add the blanched asparagus beans and continue to simmer for 2 minutes more.
4   Sprinkle the roasted pumpkin seeds over the soup just before serving.

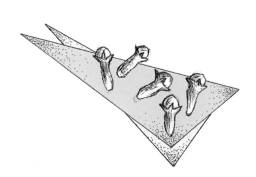

Soto Makassar

MAKASSAR SOUP

This is a traditional soup from Ujung Pandang in Sulawesi. Here is our own version of a fine-tasting beef soup with the interesting underlying sourness of kaffir lime juice.

STEP 1: Beef Broth
1.5 litres water
1 lemon grass stalk, crushed
2 garlic cloves, peeled
10 coriander leaves
5 g salt
160 g beef shoulder, boned

1   Pour the water into a shallow stockpot. Add in the lemon grass, garlic and coriander leaves. Season with the salt and bring to the boil.
2   Add in the beef and let it cook at reduced heat, approximately 45 minutes, until the meat is tender. (There should only be about 500 ml of liquid left after this step.)
3   Withdraw the pot from the heat and allow the meat to cool in the stock. Remove the beef and slice it.

STEP 2: Soup and Presentation
15 ml peanut oil
80 g raw peanuts, shelled, skinned
20 g shallots (bawang merah), peeled, finely diced
5 g garlic, peeled, finely diced
5 g ginger, peeled, finely diced
40 g candlenuts, chopped
45 ml salty soya sauce
2 g coriander powder
salt
30 ml freshly squeezed lime juice
20 g tomato, peeled, seeded, diced or cut into sections
2 g kaffir lime rind, finely sliced

1   In a separate pot, heat the peanut oil and cook the raw peanuts over low heat. Stir frequently until the peanuts become light brown in colour, approximately 3 minutes. Remove about half of the peanuts from the pot and keep aside.
2   Add in the shallots, garlic, ginger and candlenuts. Sauté for 2 minutes.
3   Stir in the soya sauce and add the coriander powder. Pour in the beef broth made in Step 1 and season lightly with salt. Taste and adjust.
4   Bring the soup to the boil, reduce the heat and simmer for 10 minutes only, to allow the flavour to be absorbed.
5   Stir in the lime juice, then remove the soup from the heat.
6   Pour the soup into a blender and run at high speed for 2-3 minutes.
7   Remove from the blender and ladle the soup into individual bowls. Garnish with the beef slices, the remaining peanuts, the tomatoes and lime rind.

PAPAYA SOUP

Sop Pepaya
PAPAYA SOUP

30 ml vegetable oil
20 g shallots (bawang merah), peeled, finely diced
5 g garlic, peeled, finely diced
10 g red chilies, seeded, finely diced
2 g bird's eye chilies, finely diced
2 g ginger, peeled, finely diced
2 g turmeric root, peeled, finely diced
10 g candlenuts, finely chopped
2 salam leaves
200 g young green papaya, peeled, seeded, cubed
l litre chicken stock (see page 24)
salt
16 unripe (white) papaya balls
20 ripe (yellow) papaya balls

1   Heat the vegetable oil in a shallow stockpot. Sauté the next 6 ingredients for 2-3 minutes without browning.
2   Add in the candlenuts and salam leaves and continue to sauté for another 2 minutes.
3   Add in the papaya and pour the chicken stock over the mixture. Season lightly with salt.
4   Bring the soup to the boil. Then reduce the heat and simmer for 10-15 minutes, stirring from time to time, until the papaya becomes soft.
5   Withdraw the pot from the heat. Discard the salam leaves.
6   Pour the soup into a blender and purée for 2-3 minutes at high speed.
7   Remove the soup from the blender, divide into 4 portions and garnish with the papaya balls.

CLEAR PRAWN SOUP WITH LEMON GRASS

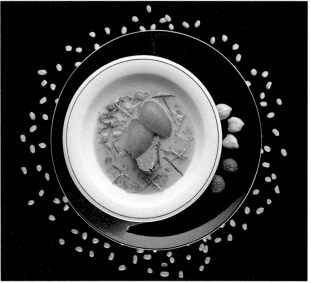

ASPARAGUS BEAN SOUP

MAKASSAR SOUP

APPETIZERS

Selada Bebek Danau Toba

DUCK BREAST TOBA

Lake Toba, a magnificent crater lake, lies in the highlands of Sumatra. Duck, a popular dish here, is frequently served with a fiery green chili sauce.

STEP 1: Fiery Green Chili Sauce
(Saus Bumbu Cabe Hijau)

30 ml peanut oil
40 g shallots (bawang merah), finely diced
10 g garlic, finely diced
100 g green chilies, seeded, finely diced
1 lemon grass stalk
10 g greater galangal, finely diced
3 kaffir lime leaves
40 g candlenuts, ground
15 g turmeric powder
60 ml tamarind water (see page 23)
500 ml water
salt

1 Heat the peanut oil in a frying pan. Sauté the shallots and garlic until they are light brown.
2 Add the chilies, lemon grass, greater galangal and kaffir lime leaves, and continue to sauté for 2 minutes.
3 Add in the ground candlenuts and turmeric powder. Continue to sauté for another 5 minutes.
4 Turn down the heat, stir in the tamarind water and simmer over a low flame for approximately 15-20 minutes, stirring frequently.
5 Pour in the water, increase the heat and cook until the sauce thickens, approximately 6-9 minutes.
6 Remove the lemon grass and lime leaves, and let the sauce cool. Yields 675 ml.

STEP 2: Cooking and Presentation

2 x 250 g duck breasts
salt
pepper
30 ml peanut oil
250 ml Fiery Green Chili Sauce, cold
80 g oyster or button mushrooms, sautéed in butter

1 Season the duck breasts with the salt and pepper.
2 Heat the peanut oil in a frying pan and place the duck breasts in the hot oil, skin side down.
3 Fry the duck over medium heat evenly on each side for approximately 5 minutes. Remove the meat from the pan and let it cool for 5 minutes.
4 Spread a layer of the sauce on each plate.
5 Slice the duck breasts and arrange the slices on the plates.
6 Garnish with the mushrooms.

Ikan Lidah Isi Tahu Sumedang

SOLE FILLETS ON RICA-RICA SAUCE

This dish is a combination of fish and sauce served hot with a cold garnish.

STEP 1: Poached Sole Fillets

160 g sole meat, boned, diced
80 g prawns, shelled, deveined
80 g lobster meat
5 g garlic, peeled, finely diced
10 g shallots (bawang merah), peeled, finely diced
1 egg
60 ml cream (33% fat)
salt
ground white pepper
20 g firm white beancurd, diced finely
8 x 60 g sole fillets
250 ml fish stock (see page 24)

1 Mince or grind the sole meat, prawns and lobster meat finely and put in a chilled bowl.
2 Work in the garlic, shallots, egg, cream, salt and pepper with a wooden spatula.
3 Fold in the beancurd and chill this mixture in a refrigerator for 2 hours.
4 Put the sole fillets, skin side down, on a board and spread with the seafood beancurd mixture. Fold the fillets into triangular shapes.
5 Place the fillets in a shallow pan just large enough to hold them.
6 Pour in the fish stock and cover with greased parchment or waxed paper.
7 Poach the fillets in the stock gently for 12-15 minutes. Remove from the heat and keep the fish warm in the stock.

STEP 2: Garnish and Presentation

20 g red chilies, seeded, finely diced
40 g yam bean, peeled, diced
60 g mango, peeled, diced
20 sweet basil leaves (kemangi)
125 ml Rica-rica Sauce, hot (see page 39)

1 Mix the red chilies, yam bean and mango together to make a salad.
2 Place 2 poached sole fillets on each plate.
3 Garnish with the chili, yam bean and mango salad, the basil leaves and hot sauce.

Pepes Jamur

MUSHROOM AND CHICKEN EN COCOTTE

Most mushrooms in Java grow near Mount Dieng, where the climate is wet and humid. The traditional type, *jamur merang*, grows on old rice stalks left in padi fields after harvest. This is a recipe for a warm appetizer served on a cold spicy sauce.

STEP 1: Mushroom and Chicken Cocotte

> 4 *white cabbage leaves*
> 100 *g chicken breast meat, cut into strips*
> 50 *g straw or button mushrooms, cut into strips*
> 10 *g shallots (bawang merah), peeled, cut into strips*
> 10 *g red chilies, seeded, cut into strips*
> 1 *egg, whisked*
> 5 *ml freshly squeezed lime juice*
> *salt*

1 Blanch the cabbage leaves in boiling water for 2 minutes. Remove and dip immediately into iced water.
2 Preheat the oven to 250°C. Then line 4 small soufflé moulds or coffee cups with 1 cabbage leaf each.
3 In a bowl, mix together the chicken strips, mushrooms, shallots and chilies.
4 Stir in the egg and lime juice. Season with the salt.
5 Pour the mixture into the moulds or cups and "cover" with the overhanging cabbage leaves.
6 Place the moulds in a roasting pan and pour in enough hot water to reach halfway up the moulds. Poach in the preheated oven for approximately 25 minutes.
7 Remove the moulds from the pan. Keep them warm.

STEP 2: Salad

> 20 *g red chilies, seeded, cut into strips*
> 20 *g turnip, peeled, cut into strips*
> 20 *g carrot, peeled, cut into strips*
> 20 *g cucumber, seeded, cut into strips*
> 20 *g white cabbage, shredded*
> 30 *ml peanut oil*
> 30 *ml freshly squeezed lime juice*
> *salt*

1 Blanch the red chilies, turnips and carrots in boiling water for 2 minutes. Cool in iced water and drain.
2 Combine all the vegetables in a bowl.
3 Add in the peanut oil and lime juice, mix well and season with the salt.

STEP 3: Sauce and Presentation

> 20 *g red chilies, seeded, diced finely*
> 120 *g mangoes, cubed*
> 125 *ml sugar syrup (see page 23)*
> 45 *ml freshly squeezed lime juice*
> 30 *ml water*
> *salt*

1 Combine all the ingredients together and blend for 3-4 minutes until smooth. Serve the sauce cold. Yields 250 ml.
2 Flip the cooked mushroom and chicken mixture out of the moulds and cut each in half. Pour some cold sauce on each plate and arrange 2 halves on the sauce.
3 Garnish with the salad made in Step 2.

Udang dengan Daun Pakis dan Saus Tauco

PRAWNS ON FERNTOP SALAD

Pakis are delicate fernlike plants which grow wild in the highlands of Bali, Java and particularly Sumatra. Here they are used in a recipe of our own invention. It is served cold.

STEP 1: Steamed Wrapped Prawns

> 100 *g white perch or bass meat*
> 100 *g prawn meat*
> 20 *g shallots (bawang merah), peeled, finely diced*
> 10 *g garlic, peeled, finely diced*
> 125 *ml cream (33% fat)*
> *salt*
> 1 *egg*
> 20 *g firm white beancurd, diced*
> 20 *g beansprouts, cleaned*
> 8 *x 100 g prawns, shelled, deveined*

1 Chop the fish and prawn meat into fine pieces and put into a blender with the shallots, garlic and cream. Season with salt and blend until smooth, approximately 2-3 minutes.
2 Add in the egg and continue to blend for 30 seconds more.
3 Put this mixture into a cold bowl. Add the diced beancurd and beansprouts. Mix well with a wooden spatula.
4 Press this mixture around each prawn.
5 Place the prawns on a tray and steam them for 15 minutes. Remove from the steamer.

STEP 2: Salad and Presentation

> 40 *g carrot, cut into strips, blanched*
> 40 *g beansprouts, blanched*
> 40 *g red chilies, cut into strips, blanched*
> 185 *ml Sumatran Black Bean Sauce, cold (see page 35)*
> 20 *ferntops*

1 Mix the blanched vegetables with 60 ml of the Sumatran Black Bean Sauce to make a salad.
2 Pour a layer of the remaining sauce on each plate.
3 Place a portion of the salad on the sauce.
4 Slice the prawns and arrange the slices on the plates.
5 Garnish with the ferntops.

CHICKEN BREAST WITH FERNTOPS

Selada Ayam Bali

BALI CHICKEN SALAD

500 ml chicken stock (see page 24)
2 x 150 g boneless chicken breasts, skinned
20 g sweet basil leaves (kemangi)
20 g kaffir lime leaves
20 g long bean leaves
160 ml Bali Sauce, cold (see page 27)
20 g red chilies, finely diced

1   Heat up the chicken stock in a pan.
2   Gently poach the chicken breasts in the hot stock for 20 minutes. Remove the pan from the heat and let the meat cool in the stock.
3   Remove the breasts from the stock when cooled. Pat dry with a paper towel and cut each breast into 6-8 slices.
4   Clean and wash all the leaves. Put them in a bowl with the chicken. Add in the Bali Sauce and toss.
5   Arrange the leaves and meat on each plate. Sprinkle with the diced chilies.

BALI CHICKEN SALAD

Ayam Isi Tauge Bumbu Bali

CHICKEN BREAST WITH FERNTOPS

STEP 1: Beansprout Stuffing

250 g chicken meat, diced
60 ml cream (33% fat)
1 egg
10 g red chilies, seeded, diced
20 g beansprouts, cleaned
salt

1   Mince or grind the chicken meat until fine.
2   Place the minced chicken meat in a blender with the cream, and process for 1-2 minutes. Gradually add in the egg and blend together for a short while until mixture becomes very fine and smooth.
3   Put the chicken mixture in a bowl, add in the chilies and beansprouts and stir well with a wooden spatula. Season with the salt and set aside.

STEP 2: Poached Chicken Breasts

4 x 100 g boneless chicken breasts, skinned
500 ml chicken stock (see page 24)

1   Place the chicken breasts skin side down on a flat surface and make an incision with a small pointed knife in the breast from the breast tip to the wing
2   Fill a piping bag with the stuffing made in Step 1 and pipe it into the breasts until they have plumped out. Secure the incision to prevent the stuffing from coming out.
3   Place the stuffed breasts in a pan and pour in the chicken stock. Poach the breasts gently for approximately 15 minutes.
4   Take the pan from the heat and let the chicken breasts cool in the stock.
5   When cool, remove the breasts and slice evenly.

STEP 3: Garnish and Presentation

4 leeks
8-12 fern stalks with leaves and stems
125 ml Bali Sauce, cold (see page 27)

1   Blanch the leeks and ferns in boiling water for 2 minutes. Cool immediately by plunging into iced water.
2   Spread a layer of the cold Bali Sauce on each plate.
3   Place a leek on the sauce.
4   Arrange slices of the chicken breast next to the leek and garnish with a rolled fern stalk.

CALAMARE WITH CUCUMBER SAUCE

MANADONESE LOBSTER SALAD

DUCK BREAST ON BITTER GOURD SALAD

Lalaban Dada Bebek dengan Pare

DUCK BREAST ON BITTER GOURD SALAD

STEP 1: Roast Duck Breast
30 ml peanut oil
20 g shallots (bawang merah), peeled, diced
10 g garlic, peeled, diced
10 g lemon grass stalk, diced
5 g greater galangal, peeled, diced
2 g freshly ground cloves
2 g turmeric powder
12 sweet basil leaves (kemangi), chopped
2 x 300 g boneless duck breasts
salt

1 Heat the peanut oil in a frying pan. Sauté the shallots, garlic, lemon grass and greater galangal in the hot oil for 2-4 minutes until light brown.
2 Add the ground cloves, turmeric powder and basil leaves and continue to sauté for 2 minutes. Remove the pan from the heat and let the marinade cool.
3 Brush the marinade evenly onto both sides of the duck breasts. Let the meat marinate in the refrigerator for 5 hours. Then preheat the oven to 280°C.
4 Roast the duck breasts in the preheated oven for 5 minutes on each side. Remove from the oven and keep warm.

NOTE: If 300 g boneless duck breasts are not available, increase the number of breasts to make up the amount.

STEP 2: Spicy Peanut Sauce (Saus Bumbu Kacang)
30 ml peanut oil
100 g raw peanuts, shelled
60 g red chilies, seeded, diced
15 g bird's eye chilies, seeded, diced
45 g candlenuts, ground
5 g lesser galangal, peeled, chopped
15 g garlic, peeled, finely chopped
15 g shallots (bawang merah), peeled, finely chopped
60 ml freshly squeezed lime juice

1 Heat half of the peanut oil in a flat pan.
2 Add the peanuts and fry them until they are light brown, approximately 5 minutes. Take them out and drain off the excess oil.
3 Heat up the remaining peanut oil in the pan. Add the chilies, candlenuts, lesser galangal, garlic and shallots. Sauté for 3-5 minutes until light brown. Remove from the pan.
4 Combine the peanuts with the sautéed mixture and mince or grind this until fine.
5 Put the ground mixture in a frying pan, stir in the lime juice and boil for 5 minutes. (Use only freshly squeezed lime juice — bottled juice is too strong.) Then remove the sauce from the heat and let it cool. Yields 325 ml.

STEP 3: Salad and Presentation
40 g bitter gourd
80 g young coconut meat, cut into strips
20 sweet basil leaves (kemangi)
30 ml freshly squeezed lime juice
salt
160 ml Spicy Peanut Sauce, cold

1 Slice the bitter gourd into rounds. Take out the seeds and keep them, then blanch the bitter gourd for 1-2 minutes.
2 Combine all the ingredients, except the sauce, in a salad bowl. Season with salt.
3 Arrange portions of the salad on individual plates. Sprinkle the bitter gourd seeds over the salad.
4 Slice the duck breasts and arrange the slices next to the salad. Serve the sauce on the side.

Cumi-cumi dan Saus Ketimun

CALAMARE WITH CUCUMBER SAUCE

STEP 1: Cucumber Sauce
90 ml palm wine
10 g shallots (bawang merah), peeled, finely diced
375 ml fish stock (see page 24)
200 g cucumbers, peeled, seeded, cut
salt
5 ml freshly squeezed lime juice

1 Mix the palm wine with the shallots and bring to the boil in a pan. Boil until the liquid has reduced to two-thirds.
2 Pour in the fish stock and reduce again to two-thirds.
3 Blanch the cucumber in boiling salt water for 2 minutes. Then place in a blender with the palm wine mixture.
4 Blend together until well mixed and fine. Season with salt and the lime juice. Serve the sauce hot. Yields 500 ml.

STEP 2: Cooking and Presentation
15 ml peanut oil
240 g squid, body tube only, cleaned with ink sac removed, cut into strips
2 g ginger, peeled, finely diced
5 g garlic, peeled, finely diced
10 g shallots (bawang merah), peeled, finely diced
5 g red chilies, seeded, finely diced
5 g green chilies, seeded, finely diced
salt
160 ml Cucumber Sauce, hot
4 small cucumbers, each carved or turned into 12 pieces

1 Heat the oil in a frying pan. Sauté the squid together with the ginger, garlic, shallots and chilies in the hot oil for 3-5 minutes. Season with salt and keep hot.
2 Pour some of the hot sauce onto each plate. If desired, sprinkle on some diced cucumber skin.
3 Arrange a portion of the squid on the plates and garnish with the turned cucumbers.

Selada Udang Karang Gohu

MANADONESE LOBSTER SALAD

STEP 1: Papaya Salad

> 180 g young green papaya, peeled — half, cut into strips;
>   half, carved or turned
> 5 g ginger, peeled, finely diced
> 20 g red chilies, seeded, finely diced
> 15 g sugar
> 30 ml white vinegar
> 30 ml water
> salt

1   Combine all the ingredients and season with the salt. Let the salad marinate in the refrigerator for 2 hours.
2   Use a sieve or colander to drain off the liquid from the salad before serving.

STEP 2: Lobster Simmered in Coconut

> 250 ml coconut milk (see page 22)
> 5 g turmeric powder
> 5 g coriander powder
> 20 g shallots (bawang merah), peeled, finely diced
> 20 g leeks, finely diced
> 320 g shelled lobster (about 2 tails or 1 cold-water lobster)

1   Bring the coconut milk to the boil in a saucepan.
2   Add the turmeric, coriander, shallots and leeks and boil for 2 minutes. Reduce the heat to simmering point.
3   Put the lobster in the coconut milk and let it simmer for 15 minutes. The lobster meat should turn a light yellow colour.
4   Remove the pan from the heat and allow the lobster to cool in the liquid.
5   Then remove the lobster from the liquid and slice the meat evenly.

STEP 3: Garnish and Presentation

> 125 ml Spicy Bajak Sauce, hot (see page 27)
> 20 kenikir leaves

1   Put 2-3 tablespoons of the hot sauce on each plate.
2   Arrange the papaya salad made in Step 1 on the sauce.
3   Place the slices of lobster next to the salad.
4   Garnish with the kenikir leaves.

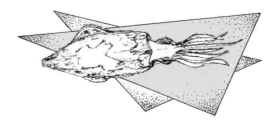

Selada Ikan Muara

SEAFOOD SALAD MUARA

STEP 1: Baked Seafood

> 15 ml vegetable oil
> 20 g shallots (bawang merah), peeled, finely diced
> 5 g garlic, peeled, finely diced
> 30 g candlenuts, ground
> 10 g brown sugar (gula Jawa)
> 15 g turmeric powder
> 30 ml water
> salt
> 160 g perch or white bass fillets
> 160 g pomfret fillets
> 4 x 50 g prawns, shelled, deveined
> 86 g squid, only the body tube, washed, cleaned, ink sac
>   removed, cut into rings

1   Heat the vegetable oil in a frying pan and sauté the shallots and garlic for 2-3 minutes.
2   Add in the candlenuts, brown sugar and turmeric powder. Continue to sauté for 2 minutes more.
3   Pour in the water, season with salt, then remove from the heat and let the marinade cool.
4   Preheat the oven to 350°C.
5   Cut 4 pieces of aluminium foil large enough to wrap up each type of fish or seafood. Brush the foil lightly with oil.
6   Place each type of seafood separately on the pieces of greased foil and brush the marinade evenly on all the seafood pieces.
7   Fold each piece of foil over its contents, forming a neat, tightly-sealed package.
8   Bake the wrapped seafood packages in the pre-heated oven as follows: perch or bass, approximately 8-10 minutes; pomfret, approximately 6 minutes; prawn, approximately 6 minutes; squid, approximately 10 minutes.
9   Open the packages and let the seafood cool. Slice the fish.

STEP 2: Salad and Presentation

> 80 g long beans, parboiled, cut into strips
> 80 g beansprouts, cleaned
> 20 g red chilies, seeded, cut into strips
> 90 ml Spicy Rujak Sauce (see page 39)
> 20 sweet basil leaves (kemangi)

1   Mix the long beans, beansprouts and chilies together to make a salad.
2   Place a portion of the salad on each plate.
3   Arrange the fish and seafood pieces on the salad.
4   Pour some of the sauce over half of the fish and seafood pieces and leave the other half without sauce.
5   Garnish with sweet basil leaves.

Burung Dara dengan Selada Kacang

PIGEON BREAST ON PEANUT SALAD

STEP 1: Roast Pigeon Breasts
30 ml peanut oil
4 x 50 g boneless pigeon breasts
salt
pepper
4 x 20 g chicken livers

1   Preheat the oven to 250°C.
2   Heat 20 ml of the peanut oil in a flat pan.
3   Season the pigeon breasts with salt and pepper and brown them on both sides in the hot oil.
4   Put the pan into the preheated oven and roast the pigeon breasts until they are done as liked. (It will take about 5 minutes for medium.) While roasting, baste the meat frequently to keep it moist.
5   Remove the breasts from the pan and keep warm.

6   Season the chicken livers with salt and pepper.
7   Heat the remaining peanut oil in a pan and sauté the chicken livers in the hot oil for 3 minutes. Remove and keep warm.

STEP 2: Salad and Presentation
120 g fern stems, blanched, chopped
20 g peanuts, roasted, chopped
180 ml Peanut Sauce, cold (see page 29)
10 g red chilies, diced

1   Combine the fern stems, peanuts and 60 ml of the Peanut Sauce in a bowl. Mix well.
2   Spoon some of the remaining sauce on each plate and place a portion of the ferns and peanuts on it.
3   Slice the warm pigeon breasts and chicken livers. Arrange sices of the meat on the cold salad.
4   Sprinkle with the diced chilies.

SQUID ON MANGO COCONUT SAUCE

RED SNAPPER FILLETS WITH MUSSELS

FRESHWATER PRAWN CIREBON

Kukus Cumi-Cumi dengan Saus Mangga
SQUID ON MANGO COCONUT SAUCE

This dish can be served as an appetizer, a salad, or even as a main course.

STEP 1: Poached Stuffed Squid
160 g snapper fillets, cubed
125 ml cream (33% fat)
10 g dried black wood fungus, soaked in warm water for 1 hour, cut into strips
1 red chili, seeded, diced finely
10 sweet basil leaves (kemangi), cut into strips
½ egg white
salt
4 squid, body tube only, washed, ink sac removed
500 ml fish stock (see page 24)

1 Put the cubed fish fillets in a blender with the cream. Blend until the mixture is silky.
2 Put the mixture in a cold bowl and stir in the black wood fungus, chili, sweet basil leaves and egg white. Mix well and season with salt.
3 Fill the squid with the fish and mushroom mixture. Secure the opening with a toothpick.
4 Preheat the oven to 180°C.
5 Warm the fish stock in a pan, add in the squid and cover with a buttered piece of parchment paper.
6 Poach the squid gently for 10 minutes in the preheated oven. The squid must be cooked over low heat and not for a very long time, otherwise the meat becomes rubbery.
7 Remove the pan from the oven and keep the squid warm in the stock.

STEP 2: Mango Coconut Sauce (Saus Mangga)
120 g mango flesh
60 g young coconut flesh
15 ml freshly squeezed lime juice
salt

1 Put the mango, coconut and lime juice in a blender and process until silky.
2 Remove from the blender and season with salt. Heat the sauce. Since mango spoils quickly, don't prepare this sauce too early. Yields 125 ml.

STEP 3: Garnish and Presentation
16 pieces ripe mango, turned or carved
4 wood fungus, soaked in warm water for 1 hour, sliced
120 g young coconut, scooped out with a spoon

1 Remove the squid from the fish stock and pat dry with paper towels. Slice each squid into 4-5 pieces.
2 Put 2 tablespoons of the Mango Coconut Sauce on each plate.
3 Arrange the squid slices on the sauce.
4 Garnish with the mango, wood fungus and young coconut.

Kakap Merah dengan Kerang Hijau
RED SNAPPER FILLETS WITH MUSSELS

STEP 1: Poached Snapper Fillets
120 g mussels
480 g red snapper fillets
10 sweet basil leaves (kemangi), cut into strips
salt
500 ml fish stock (see page 24)

1 Rinse the mussels, scrub off the beard and steam them until the shells open, approximately 3-5 minutes. Discard any which do not open. Rinse off any sand and extract the flesh from the shell. Clean and keep a few of the shells.
2 Place the snapper fillets side by side, skin side down, on a piece of cheesecloth.
3 Place a mussel in the middle of each fish fillet and sprinkle with the strips of basil leaves. Season with salt. Save the extra mussels for garnishing the dish.
4 Roll all the fillets in the cheesecloth into a sausage shape and tie the ends of the cloth with string.
5 Place the wrapped fillets in a pan just large enough to hold them. Pour in the fish stock.
6 Place the pan over low heat and simmer gently for 10 minutes.
7 Withdraw the pan from the heat and let the fillets cool in the stock.
8 Remove the roll from the stock. Discard the cheesecloth and slice the fillets.

STEP 2: Presentation
250 ml Pesmol Sauce, hot (see page 30)
20 sweet basil leaves (kemangi)

1 Pour some Pesmol Sauce on each plate.
2 Arrange the sliced fillets on the plate.
3 Garnish with the basil leaves and the remaining mussels and the cleaned shells.

Ikan Mas Bumbu Rujak
GOLDEN CARP WITH SPICY RUJAK SAUCE

500 ml fish stock (see page 24)
480 g golden carp fillets
12 cashewnut leaves, cut into fine strips
60 ml Spicy Rujak Sauce, cold (see page 39)
20 g young coconut meat, cut into strips
20 g ripe mango flesh, cut into strips
40 g water apples, cut into strips

1 Heat up the fish stock in a saucepan. Poach the golden carp fillets in the stock for 8-10 minutes
2 Remove the pan from the heat and let the fillets cool in the stock.
3 Arrange 3 cashewnut leaves on each plate.
4 Place a portion of the fillets on the plate and top with the cold sauce.
5 Garnish with the strips of fruit.

Udang Galah Sungging

FRESHWATER PRAWN CIREBON

Udang galah are popular all over Indonesia, and in Cirebon, in Java, the rivers are still filled with these prawns. In this recipe, the steamed prawns and Pesmol Sauce are served hot while the salad and Rujak Sauce are cold.

STEP 1: Steamed Prawns
   30 g prawns, cleaned, shelled, finely chopped
   30 g white bass or snapper meat, boned, diced
   1 egg
   125 ml cream (33% fat)
   20 g carrot, peeled, finely diced
   10 g red chilies, finely diced
   10 g stringbeans, finely diced
   20 g celery sticks, finely diced
   10 x 50 g freshwater or jumbo prawns, heads removed,
      deveined, shelled except for the tail

1   Put the chopped prawns and fish meat in a blender. Process until very fine.
2   Gradually add in the egg, cream, carrots, chilies, stringbeans and celery and process until smooth.
3   Press about 30-50 g of the blended mixture on each freshwater prawn, following the contours of the prawn. Wrap each prawn in greased plastic wrap (cling film).
4   Steam the prawns for 10 minutes. Remove from the steamer, take off the plastic wrap and keep warm.

STEP 2: Salad and Presentation
   30 g water chestnuts, diced
   30 g young green mango, diced
   20 g pineapple, diced
   20 g red chilies, diced
   20 ml Rujak Sauce, cold (see page 30)
   60 ml Pesmol Sauce, hot (see page 30)
   32 sweet basil leaves (kemangi)

1   Combine the water chestnuts, young mango, pineapple and chilies into a salad. Toss lightly with the Rujak Sauce.
2   Put 3 teaspoons of hot Pesmol Sauce on each plate.
3   Slice each prawn in half and arrange the halves on the sauce.
4   Garnish with the basil leaves and the cold salad.

Selada Kakap dan Belut

SNAPPER AND EEL SALAD

In the night, farmers in Java and Bali go to their rice fields in hope of catching eels. Although smaller than the eels raised in pens, these wild eels are just as delicious. This salad is fiery hot in taste.

   100 g white snapper fillets
   100 g red snapper fillets
   100 ml fish stock (see page 24)
   100 g smoked eel
   100 ml Dabu-dabu Sauce, cold (see page 38)
   80 g stringbeans, cut in strips
   50 g red chilies, cut in strips
   12 long bean leaves
   12 sweet basil leaves (kemangi)

1   Preheat the oven to 180°C.
2   Poach the snapper fillets in the fish stock in the preheated oven for approximately 15 minutes. Remove the fish from the stock and let it cool.
3   Cut the fish and smoked eel into strips.
4   Pour a little Dabu-dabu Sauce onto each plate.
5   Toss the stringbeans, red chilies and long bean leaves together to make a salad, and arrange on the plates.
6   Place the strips of fish and eel on the plates next to the salad and garnish with the basil leaves.

Udang Raja dengan Acar Kuning

LOBSTER WITH YELLOW PICKLES

STEP 1: Boiled Lobster
   1 litre water
   5 g salt
   150 g onions, peeled, cubed
   200 g carrots, peeled, cubed
   1 lemon grass stalk, bruised
   2 x 300 g spiny or rock lobster tails, or 1 x 600 g cold-water
      lobster

1   Put the water, salt, onions, carrots and lemon grass in a stockpot and bring to the boil.
2   Add the lobster and boil for 10 minutes.
3   Remove the lobster from the pot and discard the stock. Let the lobster cool, then break the lobster meat out of the shell and cut it into even slices Chill.

STEP 2: Garnish and Presentation
   4 portions Yellow Pickles, cold (see page 126)
   16-20 sweet basil leaves (kemangi)
   125 ml Spicy Bajak Sauce, cold (see page 27)

1   Place a portion of the pickles in the middle of each plate.
2   Arrange the cold lobster slices on the plate and garnish with the sweet basil leaves.
3   Spoon a little of the sauce onto the lobster slices.

STRINGBEAN SALAD WITH MUSSELS

Selada Buncis Karang Hijau

STRINGBEAN SALAD WITH MUSSELS

Mussels are found in the seabeds to the east and west of Jakarta. The flavour of these mussels is less strong than that of mussels found in colder waters.

45 ml peanut oil
20 ml palm wine
40 g shallots (bawang merah), peeled, finely diced
salt
2 g black peppercorns, crushed
10 ml fish stock (see page 24)
200 g mussels, cleaned, shelled
200 g stringbeans
100 g onions, peeled

1 Combine the first 5 ingredients in a bowl to make the vinaigrette. Mix well using a whisk. Chill.
2 Heat the fish stock in a small saucepan. Blanch the mussels in the hot stock for 2 minutes and leave them aside to cool.
3 Blanch the stringbeans and onions in boiling water for 1-2 minutes, then plunge them immediately into iced water, to retain crispness.
4 Cut the onions and some of the beans into strips and arrange them on individual plates with the whole beans, as illustrated. Pour the vinaigrette over the vegetables.
5 Garnish with the mussels.

NOTE: If red onions are available, they may be used to add colour to the dish.

Selada Udang Bungkus Tahu

WRAPPED PRAWNS

STEP 1: Steamed Wrapped Prawns

100 g white perch or grouper, boned, skinned, diced
40 g prawns, shelled, deveined, diced
10 g shallots (bawang merah), peeled, finely diced
salt
80 ml cream (33% fat)
1 egg
60 g firm white or yellow beancurd, diced
6 x 60 g prawns, shelled, deveined

1 Mince or grind the diced fish and prawns finely, then put in a blender with the shallots and season with salt. Run the blender for 1 minute.
2 Gradually add in the cream and blend for another 30 seconds. With the blender still running, slowly add in the egg. Stop when the mixture is smooth.

3 Spoon the mixture into a bowl and fold in the beancurd cubes with a wooden spatula.
4 Press some of the fish beancurd mixture all round each prawn, then place them in a steamer. Cover with a lid and steam for about 15 minutes. Remove the prawns and keep them warm.

STEP 2: Garnish and Presentation

125 ml Sour Turmeric Sauce, hot (see page 35)
40 g firm white or yellow beancurd, cut into leaf shapes
20 g red chilies, cut into diamonds
20 g yam bean or water chestnuts, cut into leaf shapes

1 Put a layer of the hot sauce on each plate.
2 Slice the prawns evenly and arrange a portion of the slices on the sauce.
3 Garnish with the beancurd, chili and yam bean pieces.

Ikan Kembang Saus Bumbu Bali

MACKEREL ON BALI SAUCE

STEP 1: Baked Mackerel Fillets

4 x 120 g mackerel fillets, halved
15 ml peanut oil
15 g shallots (bawang merah), peeled, finely diced
5 g garlic, peeled, finely diced
60 ml chili juice (see page 23)
60 ml tomato juice
2 kaffir lime leaves
5 ml tamarind water (see page 23)
salt

1 Place the fillets in a shallow dish, skin side down.
2 Mix the remaining ingredients together and sprinkle this over the fillets. Let them marinate overnight in the refrigerator.
3 Preheat the oven to 300°C.
4 Brush a baking tray with a little peanut oil and heat it in the oven.
5 Place the fillets, skin side down, on the hot tray. Bake them in the oven for approximately 10 minutes.
6 Remove the tray from the oven and lift the fillets from the tray. Keep them warm.

STEP 2: Garnish and Presentation

20 g potatoes, boiled, diced
20 g pumpkin, boiled, diced
10 g red chilies, diced
1 kaffir lime leaf, finely shredded
120 ml Bali Sauce, hot (see page 27)

1 Combine the potatoes, pumpkin, red chilies and kaffir lime leaf together. Mix well and chill in the refrigerator.
2 Place the mackerel fillets on individual plates.
3 Garnish with the salad and dab with the hot sauce.

Dada Ayam Isi Tahu dengan Daun Kol

BEANCURD-STUFFED CHICKEN BREAST

Westerners may not think of Indonesia as a source of cabbage, but in fact much of the cabbage used in Southeast Asia is exported from the north Sumatran city of Medan, where the vegetable grows in abundance on Brastagi Mountain.

STEP 1: Chicken Beancurd Stuffing

160 g chicken breast meat
125 ml cream (33% fat)
1 egg, whisked
50 g firm white beancurd, finely diced
10 g red chilies, finely diced
5 g garlic, finely diced
salt

1 Dice the chicken meat and grind or mince it finely. Then, put it in a blender and process until very fine.
2 In a cold bowl, combine the chicken, cream and egg. Mix well.
3 Add in the beancurd and red chilies, and season with the garlic and salt. Set the stuffing mixture aside.

STEP 2: Steamed Chicken Breasts

2 x 140 g boneless chicken breasts, skinned
10 g shallots (bawang merah), peeled, sliced, deep-fried
3 g kaffir lime leaves, cut into fine strips
4-5 white cabbage leaves, blanched

1 With a small pointed knife, cut a lengthwise opening along the thin edge of the chicken breasts.
2 Put half of the stuffing made in Step 1 into a piping bag and pipe through the incision in the chicken breasts until they become round and full.
3 Spread the remaining stuffing on top of the chicken breasts to a thickness of 1 cm.
4 Sprinkle the deep-fried shallots and lime leaf julienne on top of the chicken breasts.
5 Wrap each chicken breast in blanched cabbage leaves. Place them in a steamer.
6 Steam the chicken for approximately 10-15 minutes. Remove from the heat and keep warm.

STEP 3: Salad and Presentation

40 g water apples, diced
40 g young green mango, peeled, diced
40 g water chestnuts, peeled, diced
40 g young green papaya, peeled, diced
15 g red chilies, finely diced
20 g sweet potato, finely diced
60 ml Rujak Sauce, cold (see page 30)
8 fresh whole kaffir lime leaves
125 ml Rica-rica Sauce, cold (see page 39)
3 g kaffir lime leaves, cut into fine strips

1 Combine the water apple, mango, water chestnut, green papaya, red chili and sweet potato pieces with the Rujak Sauce into a salad. Set this aside.
2 Cut each chicken breast into 4 triangles.
3 Put 2 whole lime leaves on each plate.
4 Use the Rica-rica Sauce and the salad to garnish each plate.
5 Top the salad with the lime leaf julienne.

NOTE: If kaffir lime leaves are not available, substitute sweet basil leaves.

Pepes Ikan Emas Darawati

CARP WITH DARAWATI SAUCE

The Darawati area near Bandung in west Java is famous for its fish ponds. Virtually anyone who can afford it has one, even if it is half a hectare or less.

STEP 1: Baked Carp Fillets

20 g shallots (bawang merah), peeled, finely chopped
5 g garlic, peeled, finely chopped
20 g candlenuts, ground
5 g lemon grass stalk, finely diced
2 kaffir lime leaves, shredded
10 sweet basil leaves (kemangi), cut into strips
salt
400 g carp fillet, skinned, cut into 4 pieces

1   Blend the first 7 ingredients together and spread this mixture evenly on top of the fish fillets. Let the fish marinate overnight in the refrigerator.
2   Preheat the oven to 300°C.
3   Take the fish out of the marinade and put one fillet on top of a second with the marinated sides facing inwards.
4   Wrap each pair of fillets tightly in oiled aluminium foil and place the wrapped fillets on a baking tray.
5   Bake the fillets in the preheated oven for approximately 10 minutes. Then remove the fillets from the oven, unwrap the aluminium foil and let the fish cool completely.

STEP 2: Darawati Sauce (Saus Darawati)

15 ml peanut oil
15 g shallots (bawang merah), peeled, finely diced
5 g garlic, peeled, finely diced
1 lemon grass stalk, finely diced
5 g ginger, peeled, finely diced
30 g candlenuts, ground
5 g shrimp paste
125 ml chili juice (see page 23)
250 ml coconut milk (see page 22)
5 g tamarind pulp
6 sweet basil leaves (kemangi)
salt

1   Heat the oil in a frying pan and sauté the shallots, garlic, lemon grass and ginger for 3-4 minutes without browning.
2   Stir in the candlenuts and shrimp paste, and continue to sauté for a further 3 minutes until the shrimp paste has been absorbed in the mixture.
3   Add the chili juice, coconut milk, tamarind pulp and basil leaves, and season lightly with salt. Bring the mixture to the boil and let it cook slowly.
4   Remove from the heat as soon as the sauce begins to thicken. Leave it to cool. Yields 375 ml.

STEP 3: Garnish and Presentation

40 g shallots (bawang merah), peeled
125 ml Darawati Sauce, cold
80 g beansprouts, cleaned
10 g turmeric leaves, cut into very fine strips

1   Blanch the shallots in boiling water for 3 minutes. Remove and let them cool.
2   Pour a layer of Darawati Sauce on each plate.
3   Slice the fish fillets and place the slices on the sauce.
4   Garnish with the blanched shallots, the beansprouts and turmeric leaves.

Makanan Laut Pantai Selatan

SOUTH BEACH SEAFOOD MEDLEY

STEP 1: Sautéed Seafood

80 g white perch or snapper fillets, skinned
80 g pomfret, skinned, boned
80 g shelled spiny or rock lobster (approximately 1 tail)
80 g prawns, shelled, deveined
5 g turmeric powder
2 g coriander powder
5 g shallots (bawang merah), peeled, finely diced
5 g garlic, peeled, finely diced
125 ml coconut milk (see page 22)
30 ml peanut oil
salt

1   Cut the perch or snapper fillet, pomfret and lobster into medallions. Place these in a shallow dish with the prawns.
2   Sprinkle the seafood with the turmeric, coriander, shallots and garlic. Pour in the coconut milk, mix well and let the seafood marinate at room temperature for 30 minutes.
3   Drain off the coconut milk marinade.
4   Heat the peanut oil in a frying pan and sauté the seafood over high heat for 2-3 minutes until light brown. Remove from the pan.

STEP 2: Garnish and Presentation

160 g young green papaya, scooped out with a melon baller, blanched
160 g chayote, parboiled, sliced
4 sprigs kenikir leaves
125 ml Spicy Beansprout Sauce, hot (see page 30)

1   Arrange the blanched papaya and chayote in a circle on each plate.
2   Place the sautéed seafood in the centre.
3   Garnish with the kenikir leaves and the hot sauce.

NOTE: The kenikir leaves may be replaced with chervil or tarragon leaves.

FISH AND SEAFOOD

Ikan Lidah Pantai Florida

SOLE FLORIDA BEACH

STEP 1: Pan-fried Sole

> 4 x 320 g sole, head, skin and maw removed
> salt
> 40 g shallots (bawang merah), peeled, finely diced
> 40 g spring onions, peeled, finely diced
> 15 g turmeric powder
> 60 ml peanut oil

1 Season the sole with salt. Sprinkle the shallots, spring onions and turmeric powder on both sides of the fish.
2 Heat the peanut oil in a frying pan and fry the sole on each side for 3-4 minutes. Remove from the pan and keep warm.

STEP 2: Garnish and Presentation

> 15 ml peanut oil
> 20 g shallots (bawang merah), peeled, sliced into strips
> 10 g garlic, peeled, sliced into strips
> 20 g red chilies, seeded, sliced into strips
> 40 g Candied Mango, sliced into strips (see page 123)
> 2 cup leaves, sliced into strips
> 250 ml White Beancurd Sauce, hot (see page 39)

1 Heat the peanut oil in a frying pan. Add in the shallots, garlic and chilies and sauté for 2 minutes without browning.
2 Add the mango and cup leaves. Sauté for another minute and remove from the heat. Keep warm.
3 Spoon some of the White Beancurd Sauce on the plate.
4 Place a sole on the sauce and arrange the sautéed garnish next to the fish.

Lele Sembilang Tapos

CATFISH EEL TAPOS

STEP 1: Steamed Catfish Eel Fillets

> 8 x 80-100 g catfish eel fillets, skin on
> salt
> 30 ml Rica-Rica Sauce, cold (see page 39)
> 2 carrots, sliced thinly lengthwise into medium-sized pieces, blanched

1 Place the catfish eel fillets, skin side down, on a flat surface. Season lightly with salt and brush with the Rica-rica Sauce. Top each fillet with the blanched carrot strips.
2 Roll each fillet into a tight roll and fasten the ends with a toothpick or skewer.
3 Place the rolled fillets in a steamer and steam for approximately 10-14 minutes. Remove and keep warm.

STEP 2: Garnish and Presentation

> 20 g candied snakefruit sections
> 20 g tomatoes, peeled, seeded, quartered
> 15 ml mango juice
> 160 ml Rica-rica Sauce, hot (see page 39)
> 16 sweet basil leaves (kemangi)

1 In a bowl, combine the snakefruit and tomatoes. Mix in the mango juice. Set this salad aside.
2 Pour some of the hot Rica-rica Sauce onto the centre of each plate.
3 Cut the steamed fillets into approximately 2-cm rolls and arrange these on top of the sauce.
4 Garnish with the fruit and tomato salad and the sweet basil leaves.

NOTE: After catfish eel has been steamed, its black skin tends to stick to utensils or fingers and will come off easily; to avoid this peeling off of skin, be sure to wet utensils or fingers with water.

Gurame Tauco Sumatra

CARP IN BLACK BEAN SAUCE

Most traditional fish farming was carried out in west Java and it is relatively new to west Sumatra. This particular dish has a fairly strong flavour.

> 600-750 g carp fillets, cut into 12 pieces of 50-60 g
> 15 ml freshly squeezed lime juice
> salt
> 15 ml vegetable oil
> 60 ml fish stock (see page 24)
> 180 ml Sumatran Black Bean Sauce (see page 35)
> 80 g cucumbers, turned or cut into wedges, blanched
> 15-20 long beans, blanched
> 3 red chilies, seeded, cut into diamonds

1 Place the fillets in a shallow dish and sprinkle with the lime juice and salt. (Do not use bottled lime juice — it is too strong in taste). Marinate for 20 minutes.
2 Heat the oil in a shallow frying pan. Sauté the carp fillets over high heat on both sides quickly for 1-2 minutes, to give them colour.
3 Drain off all the oil. Pour in the fish stock and Black Bean Sauce. Simmer the carp in this liquid over low heat for 2-4 minutes. Remove from the heat.
4 Heat more oil in another pan and sauté the blanched cucumbers for 2 minutes, tossing constantly. Season with salt. Remove and keep warm.
5 Set 3-4 carp pieces on each plate and garnish with the remaining sauce in the pan, the cucumbers, long beans and chilies.

Buntil Ikan Emas dan Daun Talas
GOLDEN CARP IN TARO LEAVES

The light bitterness of the taro and kenikir leaves is a pleasant contrast to the sweet sour sauce.

STEP 1: Steamed Golden Carp Fillets
8 x 50 g golden carp fillets
8 taro leaves large enough to wrap the fish fillets, blanched
salt
turmeric powder
5 g red chilies, seeded, finely diced
5 g green chilies, seeded, finely diced
2 kenikir leaves, finely chopped

1 Place each carp fillet on a blanched taro leaf.
2 Season the fillets with salt and turmeric powder.
3 Sprinkle the chilies and chopped kenikir leaves over the fish.
4 Fold the taro leaf over and wrap into tight packets.
5 Steam the fish in a steamer for approximately 6-8 minutes. Turn off the heat but keep the fish hot.

STEP 2: Garnish and Presentation
180 ml Sweet Sour Sauce, hot (see page 38)
½ cup kenikir leaves

1 Pour some of the hot sauce on each plate.
2 Slice the steamed fillets diagonally into triangles, or squares.
3 Arrange the fillets on top of the sauce and garnish with the kenikir leaves.

Ikan Sembilang Labu Siam Pedas
CATFISH EEL WITH WHITE BEANCURD

From the front the *ikan sembilang*, or *lele* as it is sometimes called, looks like a catfish; from the rear, it looks like an eel. Despite its ugly look, it is a tasty fish which inhabits the estuaries of many of Indonesia's rivers, flitting between the sea and the river. If *ikan sembilang* is not available, catfish may be used.

STEP 1: Catfish Eel Stuffing
120 g catfish eel fillets, minced
40 g prawns, shelled, deveined, minced
20 g shallots (bawang merah), peeled, finely diced
1 g turmeric powder
40 g bitter gourd, diced
20 g young coconut meat, diced
1 egg, whisked
60 ml cream (33% fat)
salt
ground white pepper

1 Place the minced fish and prawn in a blender. Add the shallots and season with the turmeric powder. Process for 2-3 minutes until smooth. Remove and place in a cold bowl.
2 Add the bitter gourd and coconut meat to the mixture and mix in the egg. Stir well with a wooden spoon.
3 Add in the cream slowly, then season with salt and pepper. Blend well with a wooden spatula until the cream is well mixed in.
4 Chill for 1 hour in a refrigerator before using.

STEP 2: Steamed Catfish Eel Fillets
8 x 100 g catfish eel fillets, leave black skin on
salt
10 g red chilies, seeded, cut into fine strips

1 Place 4 of the catfish eel fillets, skin side down, on a flat surface and season with salt.
2 With a spatula, spread the stuffing made in Step 1 evenly over the fillets. Sprinkle the chili strips over the stuffing, then place the remaining fillets, skin side up, over this and wrap tightly with kitchen plastic wrap.
3 Place the wrapped fillets in a steamer and steam for approximately 15-20 minutes. Switch off the steamer but keep the fish hot.

STEP 3: Spicy Chayote Sauce (Saus Labu Siam Pedas)
15 ml peanut oil
20 g shallots (bawang merah), peeled, finely diced
5 g garlic, peeled, finely diced
5 g greater galangal, peeled, finely diced
60 g red chilies, seeded, finely diced
1 salam leaf
-375 ml coconut milk (see page 22)
100 g chayote, parboiled, diced
salt

1 Heat the peanut oil in a saucepan. Sauté the shallots, garlic, greater galangal and chilies in the oil for 3-4 minutes until the ingredients are light brown.
2 Add in the salam leaf and coconut milk. Bring to the boil.
3 Add in the parboiled chayote. Season with some salt and reduce the heat. Simmer for 10 minutes.
4 Remove the pan from the heat and discard the salam leaf before pouring the mixture into a blender.
5 Blend the sauce for 2-3 minutes until smooth. Serve hot. Yields 500 ml.

STEP 4: Garnish and Presentation
180 ml Spicy Chayote Sauce, hot
80 g firm white beancurd, cubed or cut into shapes

1 Pour some of the hot sauce on each plate.
2 Place the steamed fish on the sauce.
3 Garnish with the beancurd.

CATFISH EEL TAPOS

GOLDEN CARP IN TARO LEAVES

CARP IN BLACK BEAN SAUCE

CATFISH EEL WITH WHITE BEANCURD

RED SNAPPER FROM EAST JAVA

FRIED COCONUT PRAWNS

Udang Perkasa

FRIED COCONUT PRAWNS

The combination of fried spinach leaves, prawns and the light, sweet hot sauce is something new in Indonesian cuisine.

STEP 1: Vegetable Garnish

1 egg white
5 g cornflour
12 spinach leaves
250 ml vegetable oil
15 ml peanut oil
40 g shallots (bawang merah), peeled, finely chopped
20 g red chilies, seeded, cut into strips
120 g canned sweetcorn kernels, drained
salt

1   Using a whisk, beat the egg white together with the cornflour until thoroughly mixed, but not stiff, approximately 1 minute. Dip the spinach leaves into the batter mixture.
2   Heat the vegetable oil in a pan to 280°C. Fry the spinach leaves in the hot oil for 1 minute until crisp. Remove and keep warm. (Save the oil for frying the prawns later on.)
3   Heat the peanut oil in a frying pan. Sauté the shallots and chilies in this oil for 1 minute without browning.
4   Add in the sweetcorn kernels and sauté for another minute. Season with salt, remove from the heat and keep warm.

STEP 2: Sambal Sauce (Saus Sambal Goreng)

15 ml peanut oil
40 g shallots (bawang merah), peeled, finely diced
5 g garlic, peeled, finely diced
20 g candlenuts, ground
40 g tomatoes
1 lemon grass stalk, crushed
3 salam leaves
20 g brown sugar (gula Jawa)
120 ml chili juice (see page 23)
250 ml coconut milk (see page 22)
15 ml vinegar
salt

1   Heat the peanut oil in a saucepan. Add the shallots and garlic, and sauté for 3 minutes until light brown.
2   Add the candlenuts, tomatoes, lemon grass and salam leaves; then stir in the brown sugar. Sauté for a further 2 minutes.
3   Pour in the chili juice, coconut milk and vinegar. Bring the mixture to the boil, reduce the heat and simmer until the sauce thickens, approximately 5-7 minutes. Season with salt.
4   Remove the pan from the heat and discard the lemon grass and salam leaves.
5   Pour the sauce into a blender and process until smooth, approximately 3-4 minutes. Yields 500 ml.

STEP 3: Coconut Prawns and Presentation

8 x 40-60 g prawns, shelled, deveined, tail on
30 ml freshly squeezed lime juice
salt
50 g flour
1 egg, whisked
100 g grated coconut
vegetable oil left over from Step 1
160 ml Sambal Sauce, hot

1   Sprinkle the prawns with the lime juice and season with salt. Then dust the prawns with the flour and dip them into the beaten egg. Finally, roll the prawns in the grated coconut.
2   In a deep pan, heat the vegetable oil to 280°C. Deep-fry the prawns quickly for 3-4 minutes, then place them on kitchen paper to allow the oil to drip off. Serve hot.
3   Place 3 deep-fried spinach leaves on each plate.
4   Slice the prawns lengthwise and arrange them on the plates.
5   Sprinkle with the grated coconut and serve with the sautéed vegetables from Step 1 and hot Sambal Sauce.

Ikan Pedang Nelayan

SWORDFISH ON PUMPKIN SAUCE

In most parts of the world, swordfish is an expensive game fish. In Indonesia, they're often just hauled out with nets. If you can't get swordfish, use marlin.

4 x 180-200 g pieces of swordfish steaks, boned
5 g lemon grass stalk, finely diced
anise powder
salt
45 ml peanut oil
80 g pumpkin, cut into any shape desired, blanched
80 g chayote, cut into any shape desired, blanched
180 ml Pumpkin Sauce, hot (see page 29)
4 pumpkin leaves, blanched
12-16 star anise

1   Season the swordfish steaks with the lemon grass, anise powder and salt.
2   Heat half of the peanut oil in a frying pan to 200°C. Pan-fry the fish on each side for approximately 4-5 minutes. Withdraw the pan from the heat.
3   Using a different frying pan, heat the remaining oil and sauté the pumpkin and chayote over medium heat, tossing well, for 2-3 minutes. Season with salt. Remove from the heat and keep warm.
4   Pour some of the hot sauce on each plate. Top the sauce with the pumpkin leaves.
5   Arrange the sautéed vegetables on the pumpkin leaves and sprinkle a few star anise over them.
6   Slice the fish steaks open from the side, lengthwise, into 2 flat steaks.
7   Place them on the plate so that the pan-fried side shows as well as the inner section of the fish steak.

Kakap Merah Banyuwangi

RED SNAPPER FROM EAST JAVA

Probably the best known fish throughout Indonesia, *kakap merah* is excellent whether grilled, steamed, baked or pan-fried. Any other good-tasting member of the snapper family can be used as a substitute.

STEP 1: Pan-fried Red Snapper Fillets
> 20 g red chilies, seeded, finely diced
> 20 g green chilies, seeded, finely diced
> 10 g shallots (bawang merah), peeled, finely diced
> 5 g garlic, peeled, finely diced
> rind of 1 lime, finely diced
> 10 ml freshly squeezed lime juice
> 4 x 120 g red snapper fillets, skin on
> 30 ml vegetable oil

1 Combine the first 6 ingredients to make the marinade. Mix well.
2 Place the snapper fillets in a dish, skin side down, add the marinade and marinate for 2 hours.
3 Heat the vegetable oil in a frying pan. Place the marinated fillets skin side down in the pan and fry on each side for 2-3 minutes. Remove and keep warm.

STEP 2: Garnish and Presentation
> 15 ml vegetable oil
> 50 g beansprouts, cleaned
> 40 g red chilies, seeded, cut into strips
> 40 g green chilies, seeded, cut into strips
> salt
> 160 ml Banyuwangi Sauce, hot (see page 31)

1 Heat the vegetable oil in a frying pan. Stir-fry the beansprouts and chilies in the hot oil, tossing constantly, for 2-3 minutes. Season with salt. Remove and keep warm.
2 Pour a layer of the hot sauce on each plate.
3 Slice each fillet into 6 pieces and place these slices on the sauce.
4 Garnish with the sautéed vegetables.

Udang Windu Surabaya

TIGER PRAWNS SURABAYA

Several prawn species are popular in Indonesia: the *udang putih* — banana or white prawn, the freshwater *udang galah* — giant blue prawn — which is often raised in ponds, and the *udang windu*, featured in this recipe.

STEP 1: Chili Prawn Sauce (Saus Sambal Udang)
> 30 ml vegetable oil
> 30 g shallots (bawang merah), peeled, finely diced
> 10 g garlic, peeled, finely diced
> 10 g ginger, peeled, finely diced
> 10 g greater galangal, peeled, finely diced
> 5 g shrimp paste
> 100 g prawns, shelled, diced
> 1 lemon grass stalk, crushed
> 20 g candlenuts, ground
> 125 ml chili juice (see page 23)
> 125 ml coconut milk (see page 22)
> salt

1 Heat the oil in a saucepan. Sauté the shallots, garlic, ginger and greater galangal for 2 minutes in the oil, without letting the ingredients brown.
2 Add the shrimp paste, prawns, lemon grass and candlenuts. Continue to sauté for 2-3 minutes until light brown.
3 Pour in the chili juice and coconut milk, season lightly with salt, then bring to the boil. Reduce the heat and let the sauce simmer, stirring frequently, until it thickens, approximately 8-10 minutes.
4 Remove the pan from the heat and discard the lemon grass stalk.
5 Pour the sauce into a blender and purée until smooth, approximately 3 minutes. Serve hot. Yields 375 ml.

STEP 2: Cooking and Presentation
> 30 ml peanut oil
> 20 x approximately 40 g tiger prawns, cleaned, shelled, deveined, tail on, head removed
> 20 g shallots (bawang merah), peeled, cut into fine strips
> 10 g ginger, peeled, cut into fine strips
> 20 g red chilies, seeded, cut into fine strips
> 20 g young green mango, cut into fine strips
> salt
> 180 ml Chili Prawn Sauce, hot

1 Heat the peanut oil in a large frying pan, preferably a wok, to 220-240°C.
2 Sauté the prawns, shallots, ginger, chilies and green mango strips quickly over high heat for 2-3 minutes. Season with salt. Serve immediately otherwise the prawns will dry out.
3 Put some of the hot sauce on a deep plate or large soup plate.
4 Arrange the sautéed prawns and vegetables on the sauce.

FILLET OF HALIBUT MADURA

Kukus Ikan Sebelah Madura

FILLET OF HALIBUT MADURA

STEP 1: Poached Halibut Fillets

4 Indian halibuts, skinned
20 g red chilies, in julienne strips
20 g sweet basil leaves (kemangi), washed, stems removed
ground white pepper
125 ml fish stock (see page 24)

1   Cut each halibut into 4 fillets.
2   Place 8 of the fillets on a flat surface and sprinkle with the chili strips. Top with the basil leaves and season with the ground pepper. Put the remaining 8 fillets on top.
3   Place the fillets in a flat pan and poach gently in the fish stock for 5-8 minutes.
4   Remove from the stock and cut the fillets into diamonds. Keep them warm.

STEP 2: Garnish and Presentation

40 g shallots (bawang merah), peeled
40 g potatoes, peeled, cubed or in balls
40 g carrots, peeled, cubed or in balls
20 g long beans, diced
10 ml peanut oil
3 g garlic, peeled, finely diced
180 ml Banyuwangi Sauce, hot (see page 31)
60 ml Sour Turmeric Sauce, hot (see page 35)
2 long beans, blanched

1   Blanch the shallots, potatoes, carrots and long beans in salt water for ½-1 minute.
2   Heat the peanut oil in a pan. Sauté the blanched vegetables with the garlic for 2 minutes in the hot oil. Remove and keep warm.
3   Pour the Banyuwangi Sauce in a circular fashion in the centre of each plate and add 1 tablespoon of Sour Turmeric Sauce on top.
4   Arrange the cut fillets on the sauces.
5   Garnish with the sautéed vegetables and the blanched long beans tied in a knot.

Ikan Ekor Kuning Sungai Musi

FUSILIER WITH MINT NOODLES

The *ikan ekor kuning* is a particularly attractive fish with a bright yellow tail fin, and it is one of the prime products of Indonesia's burgeoning aquaculture. Any small perch can be used as a substitute.

STEP 1: Pineapple Sauce (Saus Nanas)

30 ml vegetable oil
40 g shallots (bawang merah), peeled, finely diced
5 g lemon grass stalk, finely diced
250 ml freshly blended pineapple juice
210 ml chili juice (see page 23)
60 ml tamarind water (see page 23)
salt

1   Heat the vegetable oil in a saucepan. Add the shallots and lemon grass and sauté for 2 minutes without browning.
2   Pour in the pineapple juice, chili juice and tamarind water. Season with salt.
3   Bring the mixture to the boil, reduce the heat and simmer for approximately 5-7 minutes, stirring occasionally.
4   Remove the pan from the heat and pour the mixture into a blender. Process until smooth. Yields 375 ml.

STEP 2: Cooking and Presentation

480 g fusilier fillets
10 g turmeric powder
10 g ginger, peeled, finely diced
15 g rice flour
30 ml peanut oil
10 g red chilies, cut into strips
160 g cooked broad egg noodles
250 ml Pineapple Sauce, hot
10 g mint leaves

1   Let the fusilier fillets marinate in the turmeric powder and ginger for 1 hour.
2   Dust the fillets lightly with the rice flour.
3   Heat half of the peanut oil until very hot in a frying pan. Sauté the fillets quickly, about 2-3 minutes on each side, in the oil. Remove and keep warm.
4   Sauté the chili strips in the remaining peanut oil for a minute. Add the cooked noodles and sauté for 1 minute. Remove from the pan.
5   Put a little of the hot Pineapple Sauce on each plate.
6   Arrange the noodles and sautéed fish fillets on the sauce. Garnish with the mint leaves.

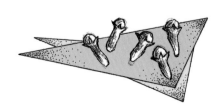

Frigate Mackerel Southwest Java

Grey Mullet with Sweetcorn

Fusilier with Mint Noodles

Ikan Tongkol Krakatau

FRIGATE MACKEREL SOUTHWEST JAVA

In general, mackerels are well known throughout Southeast Asia, and the frigate mackerel especially so in Indonesia. If this variety is not available, any other mackerel will do for this recipe.

STEP 1: Pan-fried Mackerel Steaks
4 x 150-160 g pieces of frigate mackerel steaks, skinned,
boned
80 ml tamarind water (see page 23)
15 ml freshly squeezed lime juice
salt
25 ml peanut oil

1   Place the mackerel steaks in a bowl and pour the tamarind water and lime juice over them. Let the mackerel marinate in the refrigerator for 1 hour.
2   Remove the mackerel steaks from the marinade and pat them dry with kitchen paper towels. Season with salt.
3   Heat the peanut oil in a frying pan to 220°C. Pan-fry the mackerel steaks quickly on each side for approximately 4-5 minutes. Remove and keep warm.

STEP 2: Vegetables and Presentation
20 ml peanut oil
20 g shallots (bawang merah), peeled, finely diced
5 g greater galangal, peeled, finely diced
5 g shrimp paste
5 g red chilies, seeded, finely diced
40 g young green mango, cut into fine strips
40 g white radish, cut into fine strips
salt
375 ml coconut milk (see page 22)
8 white radish leaves, blanched

1   In a saucepan, heat the peanut oil and sauté the shallots and greater galangal without colouring for about 1 minute.
2   Mix in the shrimp paste and chilies. Sauté over medium heat for 2 minutes.
3   Add in the mango and radish strips and continue to sauté for 2 minutes more. Season with salt.
4   Pour in the coconut milk and bring the mixture to the boil. Reduce the heat and simmer for approximately 4-5 minutes. Remove from the heat and keep the contents warm.
5   Ladle the vegetables into a large soup plate and put a small portion of it on individual plates.
6   Slice each of the mackerel steaks and arrange the pieces in a crescent on the plate.
7   Garnish with the radish leaves and serve immediately.

Ikan Belanak Isi Jagung Semarang

GREY MULLET WITH SWEETCORN

Ikan belanak is very similar to the grey mullet found in the West. Although, it is not widely used in Indonesia, it is a fine, sweet seasonal fish.

STEP 1: Grey Mullet Stuffing
100 g grey mullet fillet, minced
10 g shallots (bawang merah), peeled, finely diced
5 g garlic, peeled, finely diced
10 g grated coconut
1 egg white
90 ml cream (33% fat)
salt
20 g canned sweetcorn kernels, drained

1   Place the minced fish in a blender and purée until smooth, about 3-4 minutes. Transfer the fish to a cold bowl.
2   Add the shallots, garlic, coconut and egg white to the bowl. Mix well with a wooden spoon.
3   Add in the cream, season with salt and mix in the sweetcorn kernels. Blend the cream well into the mixture.
4   Place the stuffing in a refrigerator and let it rest for 1 hour before using.

STEP 2: Cooking and Presentation
4 x 200 g grey mullet fillets, skin on
salt
pepper
15 ml peanut oil
60 g canned sweetcorn kernels, drained
10 g red chilies, seeded, cut into fine strips
4-8 cup leaves, blanched
160 ml Pesmol Sauce, hot (see page 30)

1   Place two of the fillets, skin side down, on a flat surface and season with salt and pepper.
2   With a spatula, spread the stuffing made in Step 1 evenly on the fillets, then place the remaining fillets, skin side up, over the stuffing. Press the fish to make the fillets look even.
3   Wrap the stuffed fillets in kitchen plastic wrap and place the fish in a steamer. Steam for approximately 15 minutes. Turn off the heat but keep the fish hot.
4   Heat the peanut oil in a frying pan. Sauté 40 g of the sweetcorn kernels and the chilies for 2 minutes. Season with salt. Remove from the heat.
5   Spoon the vegetables into the cup leaves. Tie these into bundles using pieces of chives or lemon grass.
6   Pour some of the hot Pesmol Sauce on each plate.
7   Cut the steamed fillets small enough to have 3-4 pieces per serving.
8   Arrange the pieces on the plates.
9   Put the stuffed cup leaves on the sauce. Garnish with the remaining sweetcorn kernels.

Pindang Ekor Kuning

FUSILIER ON PINDANG SAUCE

This fish is served with a mild and light sweet sauce.

STEP 1: Poached Fusilier Fillets
250 ml fish stock (see page 24)
640 g fusilier fish fillets
salt
pepper

1 Preheat the oven to 180°C.
2 Heat the fish stock in a pan just large enough to hold the fillets.
3 Season the fillets with salt and pepper, and put them in the pan. Cover with a piece of buttered parchment paper and poach in the preheated oven for approximately 10-12 minutes. Remove and keep the fish warm in the stock.

STEP 2: Pindang Sauce (Saus Pindang)
15 ml peanut oil
25 g shallots (bawang merah), peeled, chopped finely
25 g red chilies, seeded, finely chopped
25 g green chilies, seeded, finely chopped
25 g candlenuts, ground
500 ml coconut milk (see page 22)
100 g starfruit, chopped
10 g ginger, peeled, finely chopped
5 g greater galangal, peeled, finely chopped
5 g turmeric powder
1 salam leaf
1 lemon grass stalk
salt

1 Heat the peanut oil in a frying pan and sauté the shallots and chilies for 2 minutes in the oil.
2 Add in the candlenuts and continue to sauté until the ingredients are light brown in colour.
3 Pour in the coconut milk and bring the mixture to the boil, stirring frequently.
4 Add in the starfruit, ginger, greater galangal, turmeric powder, salam leaf and lemon grass.
5 Let the sauce simmer for approximately 8-10 minutes, until it starts to thicken.
6 Remove from the heat and discard the lemon grass and salam leaf.
7 Pour the sauce into a blender and process until smooth, about 2-3 minutes. Remove from the blender and keep warm. Yields 500 ml.

STEP 3: Garnish and Presentation
160 ml Pindang Sauce, hot
24 mint leaves
120 g yam bean, peeled, cut into diamonds
80 g red chilies, seeded, cut into diamonds

1 Pour some of the Pindang Sauce on each plate.
2 Arrange a portion of the poached fusilier fillets on the sauce.
3 Garnish with the mint leaves, yam bean and chilies.

Ikan Kembung Lelaki dengan Saus Kunyit

MACKEREL WITH TURMERIC SAUCE

Ikan kembung, or mackerel, is a favourite fish throughout Indonesia and it is good grilled, steamed or baked. Here, it is accompanied with a spicy turmeric sauce and a slightly sour, hot shallot relish.

STEP 1: Turmeric Sauce (Saus Kunyit)
15 ml peanut oil
20 g shallots (bawang merah), peeled, finely diced
5 g garlic, peeled, finely diced
5 g greater galangal, finely diced
5 g ginger, peeled, finely diced
15 g turmeric powder
80 ml red chili juice (see page 23)
375 ml coconut milk (see page 22)
salt

1 In a saucepan, heat the peanut oil and sauté the shallots, garlic, greater galangal and ginger in the oil for 2-3 minutes, stirring constantly, without browning.
2 Add the turmeric powder and continue sautéing over low heat for another minute.
3 Pour in the chili juice and coconut milk. Season with salt. Bring the mixture to the boil, reduce the heat and simmer for approximately 10 minutes.
4 Remove from the heat. Do not blend or strain this sauce. Serve hot. Yields 375 ml.

STEP 2: Cooking and Presentation
8 x 100-120 g striped mackerel fillets, skin on
salt
30 ml freshly squeezed lime juice
30 ml peanut oil
180 ml Turmeric Sauce, hot
80 g Chili Tomato Pickles, cold (see page 127)
10 g turmeric leaves, cut into fine strips

1 Place the mackerel fillets in a shallow dish and season with salt and the lime juice. Marinate for ½ hour.
2 Remove the mackerel from the marinade and brush lightly with the oil.
3 Place the fillets on a hot grill or griddle, skin side down first, and cook on each side for approximately 3-4 minutes. Remove the fish from the heat and keep warm.
4 Cut the mackerel fillets into triangles or diamonds and arrange some pieces on each plate.
5 Pour the hot sauce between the fish pieces.
6 Set the pickles on the sauce and garnish with the turmeric leaf strips.

BARBECUED RED SNAPPER

Kakap Merah Bakar Belimbing Wuluh
BARBECUED RED SNAPPER

800 g-1 kg red snapper fillets, red skin on
salt
ground white pepper
30 ml peanut oil
120 g sour finger carambolas, sliced
40 g yam bean, peeled, cut into shapes
5 g red chilies, sliced
180 ml Sour Finger Carambola Sauce, hot (see page 37)

1 Cut the red snapper fillets into 8 even 100-125 g pieces or medallions.
2 Season the fish with salt and pepper. Brush lightly with half of the oil.
3 Place the fish on a rack over a hot barbecue and cook each side for approximately 2-3 minutes. Remove from the barbecue and keep hot.
4 Heat the remaining oil in a frying pan. Sauté the sour finger carambolas, yam bean and chilies over medium heat for 1 minute, tossing well. Season with salt. (The yam bean and carambola should be crunchy and crisp.) Remove from the heat.
5 Pour some of the sauce on each plate.
6 Arrange the sautéed vegetable garnish on the sauce and place a few pieces of the fish on the sauce.

LOBSTER MOUSSE ON PANCAKE NET

SPINY LOBSTER TELUK BAYUR

FUSILIER ON SHRIMP SAUCE

Udang Barong Teluk Bayur
SPINY LOBSTER TELUK BAYUR

Every morning fishermen bring in their catch of spiny lobster to the west Sumatran port of Teluk Bayur. If cooked properly, the meat is as firm and succulent as that of any cold-water lobster.

STEP 1: Steamed Lobster
4 x 150-200 g spiny or rock lobster tails, shelled
2 g coriander leaves, finely chopped
20 g shallots (bawang merah), peeled, finely diced
10 g leeks, finely diced
20 g candlenuts, ground
250 ml coconut milk (see page 22)

1   Place the lobster tails on a shallow dish.
2   In a bowl, combine the coriander, shallots, leeks and candlenuts. Pour in the coconut milk and mix well with a whisk.
3   Pour this mixture over the lobster and let it marinate for 4 hours in a refrigerator.
4   Remove the marinated lobster from the marinade and wrap each tail tightly with kitchen plastic wrap. Tie up the ends with twine or kitchen string.
5   Place the lobsters in a steamer, steam for approximately 15-18 minutes. Remove and keep hot.

NOTE: If Atlantic or cold-water lobsters are used, the meat in two claws is roughly equivalent in amount to that in a tail, so half the number of lobsters are required.

STEP 2: Teluk Bayur Sauce (Saus Santan Teluk Bayur)
15 ml peanut oil
20 g shallots (bawang merah), peeled, finely diced
2 g garlic, peeled, finely diced
5 g ginger, peeled, finely diced
5 g greater galangal, peeled, finely diced
5 g red chilies, seeded, finely diced
5 g shrimp paste
500 ml coconut milk (see page 22)
salt

1   Heat the peanut oil in a saucepan. Sauté the shallots, garlic, ginger and greater galangal in the oil over low heat for 2-3 minutes, without browning. Stir constantly.
2   Add the red chilies and shrimp paste and continue to saute for 2 minutes more.
3   Pour in the coconut milk, season lightly with salt and bring the mixture to the boil. Let it simmer for approximately 8 minutes until the sauce thickens.
4   Pour the sauce in a blender and process it for 2 minutes. Serve hot. Yields 250 ml.

STEP 3: Vegetables and Presentation
15 ml peanut oil
40 g young coconut meat, diced
80 g Candied Mango — 8 slices left whole; the remainder diced (see page 123)
salt
180 ml Teluk Bayur Sauce, hot

1   Heat the peanut oil in a frying pan and sauté the diced coconut and mango in it, tossing well, for 2-3 minutes. Season with salt. Remove from the heat and keep hot.
2   Pour some of the hot sauce across each plate.
3   Put a small mound of the sautéed fruit next to the sauce.
4   Unwrap the lobsters and slice them into scallop shapes.
5   Set the lobster scallops on the sauce and garnish with the mango slices.

Ikan Bakar Bakasem
FUSILIER ON SHRIMP SAUCE

STEP 1: Shrimp Sauce (Saus Udang)
60 g peeled shrimps
10 g brown sugar (gula Jawa)
15 ml white vinegar
salt
15 ml vegetable oil
20 g shallots (bawang merah), peeled, finely diced
5 g garlic, peeled, finely diced
10 g ginger, peeled, finely diced
½ lemon grass stalk, finely diced
1 kaffir lime leaf
20 g turmeric root, finely diced
50 g tomatoes, peeled, seeded, diced
250 ml coconut milk (see page 22)

1   Combine the raw shrimps with the brown sugar, white vinegar and salt. Marinate for 4 hours.
2   Heat the vegetable oil in a saucepan. Sauté the shallots, garlic, ginger, lemon grass, lime leaf and turmeric root in the hot oil for 3-4 minutes without browning.
3   Stir in the marinated shrimp mixture and continue to sauté for 2 minutes.
4   Add the tomatoes and coconut milk. Bring the mixture to the boil and simmer until the sauce thickens, approximately 8 minutes.
5   Remove from the heat and discard the lime leaf.
6   Pour the sauce into a blender and process until fine. Remove and keep warm. Yields 375 ml.

STEP 2: Cooking and Presentation
4 x 150 g fusilier fish fillets
salt
pepper
15 ml vegetable oil
160 ml Shrimp Sauce, hot
20 g red chilies, finely diced
4 sweet basil leaves (kemangi)

1   Season the fish fillets with salt and pepper.
2   Brush the fillets lightly with the oil, then place in a hot pan, skin side down, and cook evenly on both sides for 3 minutes each. Remove and keep warm.
3   Pour a little of the hot sauce on each plate.
4   Place the cooked fillets on top of the sauce.
5   Garnish with the chilies and basil leaves.

Roti Jala dengan Udang Raja

LOBSTER MOUSSE ON PANCAKE NET

In northern Sumatra, a favourite snack is *roti jala*, a type of pancake, topped with lamb curry. Here is a new version with lobster mousse.

STEP 1: Lobster Mousse

200 g lobster meat
10 g shallots (bawang merah), peeled, finely chopped
20 g ginger, peeled, finely chopped (set aside a little for seasoning the scallops)
5 g coriander powder (set aside a little for the scallops)
15 ml chili juice (see page 23)
salt
pepper
1-2 egg whites
125 ml cream (33% fat)
4-5 mustard green leaves, blanched
4 x 10-15 g scallops

1 Dice the raw lobster meat and put it into a blender. Add in the shallots, ginger and coriander powder and chili juice. Season with salt and pepper.
2 Blend for 3-4 minutes until smooth.
3 Remove the mixture from the blender and place it in a bowl. Refrigerate until the mixture is cold.
4 Work the egg whites and cream into the mixture with a wooden spatula. Set the mousse aside.
5 Line 4 soufflé moulds or small coffee cups with some of the blanched mustard green leaves.
6 Season the scallops with the remaining coriander powder and ginger.
7 Wrap the scallops one by one with the remaining pieces of mustard green leaves.
8 Half-fill the moulds or cups with the mousse mixture. Add 1 wrapped scallop and top with more of the mousse until the mould or cup is almost filled. Fold the leaves over to make a cover.
9 Poach the mousse gently in a waterbath in the oven at 180°C for approximately 15 minutes. Remove and keep warm.

STEP 2: Pancake Net (Roti Jala)

50 g white flour
1 egg
10 g ginger, peeled, finely grated
100 ml coconut milk (see page 22)

1 Combine the ingredients to form a pancake batter. Make sure the batter is thin. If it is too thick, add more coconut milk.
2 Take a small empty can and pierce 3 holes, about 1-2 mm in diameter, in the bottom in a triangle formation.
3 Heat a teflon pan (or a flat pan with very little oil). Pour the batter into the perforated can and spin the pancake batter into the pan in a net fashion.
4 Fry the pancake for 1 minute on either side.

NOTE: This recipe makes 10-12 roti jalas of approximately 15-20 g each.

STEP 3: Presentation

4 Pancake Nets
36 fresh white or green asparagus tips, blanched
4 small red chilies, stem on, slit from halfway down to the tip, seeded
160 ml Chili Basil Sauce, hot (see page 28)

1 Place a pancake net on each preheated plate.
2 Free the mousse from the moulds, cut each mousse in half and place the halves on top of the pancake.
3 Garnish with the asparagus tips and chilies.
4 Serve the sauce on the side.

NOTE: A thin crepe can be used in place of a roti jala.

Ikan Kembung Perempuan

MACKEREL WITH TOMATOES

8 x 30-40 g short-bodied mackerel fillets, skin on
80 ml green chili juice (see page 23)
80 ml coconut milk (see page 22)
salt
45 ml peanut oil
60 g green chilies, sliced
40 g tomatoes, peeled, seeded, diced
20 g dried Chinese black mushrooms, soaked, sliced
5 g ginger, peeled, finely diced
180 ml Green Chili Sauce, hot (see page 30)

1 Place the mackerel fillets in a shallow dish and pour over the chili juice and coconut milk. Let them marinate in the refrigerator for 1 hour.
2 Remove the fillets from the marinade and dry them with kitchen paper towels. Season lightly with salt.
3 Brush the fillets with a little oil and place the fish, skin side down first, on a rack over a barbecue. Cook each side for approximately 2 minutes. Remove from the barbecue and keep hot.
4 Heat the remaining oil in a frying pan and sauté the green chilies over medium heat, stirring constantly, for 2 minutes.
5 Add in the tomatoes and mushrooms and season with salt and the ginger. Continue to sauté for another minute. Remove from the heat.
6 Pour some of the hot Green Chili Sauce on each plate. Spoon the sautéed vegetables on the sauce.
7 Set the fish on the vegetables. Arrange 2 slices per plate, with one piece skin side up and the other skin side down.

NOTE: Bigger mackerel fillets may be used but be sure to increase the cooking time.

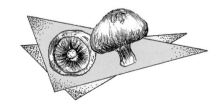

CATFISH EEL WITH PECEL SAUCE

Cobek Lele Saus Pecel

CATFISH EEL WITH PECEL SAUCE

STEP 1: Poached Catfish Fillets

25 g shallots (bawang merah), peeled, finely chopped
10 g garlic, peeled, finely chopped
10 g red chilies, seeded, finely chopped
16 sweet basil leaves (kemangi), cut into strips
5 g turmeric powder
5 ml tamarind water (see page 23)
salt
4 x 120 g catfish fillets, skin on, halved
250 ml fish stock (see page 24)

1   Combine the first 7 ingredients to make the marinade. Mix well.
2   Place the fillets skin side down in a shallow pan.
3   Sprinkle the marinade over the fillets and let them marinate in the refrigerator for 2 hours.

4   Preheat the oven to 180°C, then take the fillets out of the refrigerator.
5   Roll up each fillet and fasten with a skewer.
6   Place the fillets in a pan and pour in the fish stock.
7   Poach the fillets in the preheated oven for approximately 15 minutes.
8   Remove the fillets from the oven and keep them warm in the stock.

STEP 2: Garnish and Presentation

120 ml Sweet Spicy Pecel Sauce, hot (see page 31)
100 g mango flesh, scooped out with a melon baller
100 g young coconut meat, cut into strips
24 turmeric leaves, cut into fine strips

1   Spread some of the hot sauce on each plate.
2   Slice the catfish fillets and arrange 2-3 slices by the sauce.
3   Garnish with the mango and coconut flesh and turmeric leaf strips.

KING PRAWNS IN COCONUT SAUCE

Udang Saus Opor

KING PRAWNS IN COCONUT SAUCE

25 g shallots (bawang merah), peeled, finely chopped
10 g garlic, peeled, finely chopped
30 g red chilies, — 10 g finely chopped; 20 g cut into rounds
25 g candlenuts, ground
5 g ginger, peeled, finely chopped
1 lemon grass stalk, finely chopped
salt
24 x 40 g king prawns, cleaned, shelled, deveined
15 ml peanut oil
60 g ripe mango flesh, scooped out with a melon baller
30 g young green papaya flesh, scooped out with a melon baller
60 ml fish stock (see page 24)
180 ml coconut milk (see page 22)

1   Combine the shallots, garlic, finely chopped chilies, candlenuts, ginger, lemon grass and salt to make the marinade. Mix well.
2   Put the cleaned prawns in a shallow bowl and sprinkle with the marinade. Let them marinate in the refrigerator for 2 hours.
3   After 2 hours, drain off all the marinade from the prawns
4   Heat the peanut oil in a frying pan and sauté the prawns over high heat for 2 minutes.
5   Add in the mango and papaya balls, fish stock and coconut milk. Simmer for 2 minutes.
6   Remove from the heat. Take the prawns out of the sauce and arrange 5-6 of them on each plate.
7   Place a few mango and papaya balls next to the prawns.
8   Put a spoonful of sauce on the plate, sprinkle with the sliced chilies and serve immediately.

Sotong Kukus dengan Saus Kenikir

SQUID WITH GREEN SAUCE

The kenikir leaf gives a light green tint to the sauce in this dish.

STEP 1: Poached Stuffed Squid

16 mussels
100 g white perch, skinned, boned, cubed
60 ml cream (33% fat)
½ egg white
10 g dried black Chinese mushrooms, soaked in warm water
    for 1 hour, cut into strips
15 g red chilies, seeded, cut into strips
12 sweet basil leaves (kemangi), cut into strips
salt
ground white pepper
4 x 120 g squid, body tube only, washed, ink sac removed
250 ml fish stock (see page 24)

1 Clean and steam the mussels as described on page 58. Extract the mussels from their shells and set aside.
2 Mince or grind the perch until fine, then process in a blender for 2 minutes.
3 Keeping the blender running, gradually add in the cream and process for another minute. Then work in the egg white slowly, but blend only for another 5 seconds until the mixture becomes smooth.
4 Transfer the mixture to a cold bowl. Add the mussels, black mushrooms, chilies and basil leaves. Mix well with a wooden spatula, season and place in a refrigerator for 2 hours.
5 After 2 hours, remove the mixture from the fridge and use it to stuff the squid.
6 Roll each squid in a piece of cheesecloth and tie up the ends.
7 Heat the fish stock in a pan just big enough to hold the squid. Put in the squid and let them simmer in the stock for 15 minutes.
8 Withdraw the pan from the heat. Take the squid out of the stock (save the stock for making the sauce), untie the cheesecloth and slice the squid in half lengthwise.

STEP 2: Green Sauce (Saus Kenikir)

10 g kenikir leaves
20 g spinach leaves
185 ml fish stock left over from Step 1
20 g shallots (bawang merah), peeled, finely chopped
5 g garlic, peeled, finely chopped
15 g red chilies, seeded, finely chopped
40 g coconut meat
12 sweet basil leaves (kemangi)
90 ml red chili juice (see page 23)

1 Blanch the kenikir and spinach leaves in boiling water for 2 minutes.
2 Bring the fish stock to the boil in a saucepan, then add in the shallots, garlic, chilies, coconut meat, basil leaves and chili juice. Cook until all the ingredients are soft, around 10-12 minutes.

3 Pour the contents of the pan into a blender. Add in the blanched kenikir and spinach leaves and blend until smooth.
4 Remove the sauce from the blender. Taste and adjust the seasoning if necessary. Serve hot. Yields 375 ml.

STEP 3: Garnish and Presentation

20 g brown sugar (gula Jawa)
30 ml tamarind water (see page 23)
15 g red chilies, seeded, diced
5 g bird's eye chilies, sliced
80 g water apples, sliced
125 ml Green Sauce, hot

1 Dissolve the brown sugar in the tamarind water and add in the chilies.
2 Pour this mixture over the water apple slices. Toss well.
3 Place a portion of the water apple slices on each plate.
4 Arrange the squid slices next to the fruit and garnish with the hot sauce.

Ikan Bawal Putih Saus Sambal Godok

STEAMED WHITE POMFRET

One of the most highly prized fish, the white or silver pomfret has delicious flesh which comes off easily from its bones. It also requires very little cooking time. Plaice or any flat fish may be used as a substitute for pomfret, but the flavour is not the same.

4 x 300 g white pomfrets, cleaned
20 g lesser galangal, peeled, finely diced
20 g shallots (bawang merah), peeled, finely diced
salt
60 ml red chili juice (see page 23)
180 ml White Beancurd Sauce, hot (see page 39)
10 g sweet basil leaves (kemangi), finely chopped
120 g Chili Tomato Pickles (see page 127)

1 Place the pomfrets in a shallow dish and add the lesser galangal and shallots. Season with salt and pour on the chili juice.
2 Leave the fish to marinate in the refrigerator for 1 hour.
3 Drain off the marinade and place the marinated fish in a dish in a steamer and steam for approximately 15-18 minutes.
4 Turn off the heat but keep the fish hot.
5 Pour some of the hot sauce on individual serving plates.
6 Sprinkle the chopped basil leaves on the sauce.
7 Set a pomfret on the sauce and garnish with the pickles.

Ikan Bawal dari Bengkulu

BENGKULU BLACK POMFRET

Although black pomfret ranks second to its white variety, it is still a very good fish.

4 x 250-300 g black pomfrets, cleaned
5 g ginger, peeled, finely diced
30 ml freshly squeezed lime juice
salt
45 ml peanut oil
10 g shallots (bawang merah), peeled, finely diced
5 g lesser galangal, peeled, finely diced
20 g red chilies, seeded, cut into fine strips
5 g ginger, peeled, cut into fine strips
120 g water convolvulus, stems on
ground white pepper
180 ml Bengkulu Sauce, hot (see page 35)

1 Place the pomfrets in a shallow dish, sprinkle the ginger on top and pour in the lime juice.
2 Let the fish marinate in the refrigerator for 1 hour.
3 Remove the pomfrets from the marinade and dry them with kitchen paper towels. Season with salt.
4 Heat half of the peanut oil in a frying pan to 220°C. Pan-fry the pomfrets on each side for approximately 4 minutes. Remove and keep hot.
5 In a large frying pan, heat the remaining oil and sauté the shallots, lesser galangal, chilies and ginger quickly for 1 minute over high heat, until the shallots are light brown.
6 Add in the water convolvulus, season with some salt and pepper and continue to sauté over high heat for another minute. Remove immediately from the pan.
7 Place a portion of the sautéed vegetables on each plate and arrange a pomfret next to the vegetables.
8 Serve with the hot Bengkulu Sauce.

Ikan Garoupa Saus Tauge Pedas

GROUPER ON SPICY BEANSPROUT SAUCE

4 x 160 g grouper fillets
20 g shallots (bawang merah), peeled, finely diced
5 g garlic, peeled, finely diced
salt
30 ml peanut oil
250 ml Spicy Beansprout Sauce, hot (see page 30)
120 g fresh coconut meat, cut into strips
20 mint sprigs

1 Sprinkle the fillets with the shallots and garlic. Season with salt.
2 Heat the peanut oil in a frying pan. Fry the fillets quickly on each side for 2 minutes. Remove.
3 Place the grouper fillets on individual plates.
4 Pour some of the hot sauce next to the fillets.
5 Garnish with the coconut strips and mint sprigs.

Ikan Ekor Kuning Isi Udang Windu

FUSILIER AND TIGER PRAWN

STEP 1: Poached Fusilier Fillets
40 g candlenuts, ground
10 g shallots (bawang merah), peeled, finely diced
2 g garlic, peeled, finely diced
2 g turmeric powder
60 ml coconut milk (see page 22)
12 x 40-50 g fusilier fish fillets, skin on
salt
12 x 30 g tiger prawns, shelled, deveined
500 ml fish stock (see page 24)

1 In a bowl, combine the candlenuts, shallots, garlic, turmeric powder and coconut milk. Mix well with a wooden spoon. The marinade should be a slightly thick paste.
2 Place the fusilier fillets, skin side down, on a flat surface. Season lightly with salt, then brush the marinade on the fish.
3 Place 1 prawn on each fillet and fold the fillet over so that it forms a tight triangular parcel. Secure the ends with a toothpick.
4 Place the fillets in a pan and pour in the fish stock.
5 Poach the fillets for approximately 5-7 minutes. Turn off the heat but keep the fillets hot in the stock.

STEP 2: Garnish and Presentation
30 ml peanut oil
80 g asparagus beans, blanched, sliced
40 g coconut meat, cut into strips
salt
180 ml Sweet Sour Sauce, hot (see page 38)
10 g kenikir leaves, finely chopped

1 In a frying pan, heat the peanut oil and sauté the asparagus beans and coconut meat quickly for 2 minutes without browning. Season with salt, then remove from the heat and keep hot.
2 Pour some of the hot sauce on one side of each plate and place 2-3 poached fusilier fillets on the sauce.
3 Arrange the sautéed asparagus beans and coconut in the centre of the plate. Sprinkle on the chopped kenikir leaves.

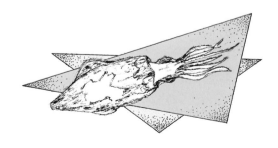

MEAT AND
POULTRY

MEAT

Gulai Korma Kambing
MELAYU LAMB STEW

STEP 1: Lamb Stew
30 ml peanut oil
90 g shallots (bawang merah), peeled, finely diced
20 g garlic, peeled, finely diced
1 lemon grass stalk, finely diced
10 g ginger, peeled, finely diced
600 g boneless leg of lamb, cubed
5 g white pepper powder
2 g coriander powder
2 g nutmeg powder
2 g fennel seeds, crushed
100 g tomatoes, peeled, seeded, diced
1 litre coconut milk (see page 22)
salt
500 ml lamb stock (see page 24)

1   Preheat the oven to 180°C.
2   Heat the peanut oil in a braising pan. Add in the shallots, garlic, lemon grass and ginger. Sauté, stirring constantly, for 2-3 minutes. Do not let the ingredients colour.
3   Add the lamb cubes and continue to sauté over high heat until the meat is browned.
4   Season with the pepper, coriander, nutmeg and fennel. Sauté for 2 minutes more.
5   Add in the tomatoes and pour in the coconut milk. Season with salt. Put on the lid of the braising pan and place it in the preheated oven.
6   Braise the meat for approximately 60-90 minutes, stirring occasionally with a wooden spoon. Use the lamb stock to thin the sauce when it gets too thick or starts to stick to the bottom of the pan.
7   Remove from the oven and keep the stew warm.

NOTE: Instead of lamb leg, a cheaper cut such as lamb shoulder may be used, but a longer braising time is needed.

STEP 2: Garnish and Presentation
15 ml peanut oil
4 young green mangoes, sliced, blanched
nutmeg powder
salt
9-12 sprigs coriander leaves
12 dried black Chinese mushrooms, soaked in warm water for 1 hour, sliced, sautéed in oil
3 tomatoes, peeled, seeded, quartered

1   Heat the peanut oil in a frying pan, add in the green mangoes and season with nutmeg powder and salt. Sauté the mangoes for 1-2 minutes.
2   Ladle the lamb stew into serving plates.
3   Garnish with the sautéed green mango, coriander sprigs, sautéed·mushrooms and tomato quarters.

Daging Sapi Muda Saus Ebi
VEAL WITH DRIED SHRIMP SAUCE

STEP 1: Dried Shrimp Sauce (Saus Ebi)
30 ml peanut oil
50 g dried shrimps, ground
40 g shallots (bawang merah), peeled, finely chopped
20 g garlic, peeled, finely chopped
10 g ginger, peeled, finely chopped
10 g greater galangal, peeled, finely chopped
1 lemon grass stalk, finely chopped
5 g turmeric root, finely diced
15 g candlenuts, ground
30 g brown sugar (gula Jawa)
30 ml chili juice (see page 23)
30 ml tamarind water (see page 23)
500 ml coconut milk (see page 22)
salt

1   Heat the peanut oil in a saucepan. Sauté the dried shrimps, shallots and garlic until light brown.
2   Add the ginger, greater galangal and lemon grass. Continue to sauté for 2 minutes more.
3   Add the turmeric, candlenuts and brown sugar, and sauté for another 2 minutes.
4   Pour in the chili juice, tamarind water and coconut milk, and season with salt. Bring the mixture to the boil. Then reduce the heat and simmer for approximately 10 minutes, stirring frequently.
5   Pour the sauce into a blender and process for 2-3 minutes until smooth. Serve hot. Yields 500 ml.

STEP 2: Cooking and Presentation
500 g veal fillet, fat and sinew removed
4 tablespoons direndam marinade (see page 23)
salt
45 ml peanut oil
120 g bitter gourd, sliced, blanched
250 ml Dried Shrimp Sauce, hot
20 g red chilies, seeded, cut into diamonds, blanched
20 g green chilies, seeded, cut into diamonds, blanched

1   Preheat the oven to 180°C.
2   Brush the veal fillet with the marinade and season with salt.
3   Heat 30 ml of the peanut oil in a roasting pan. Put the veal fillet into the pan and roast in the oven for approximately 18-20 minutes, basting occasionally in order to prevent the meat from drying out. Remove and keep warm.
4   Heat the remaining oil in a frying pan and sauté the bitter gourd for 1 minute.
5   Spread a thin layer of the hot sauce on each plate.
6   Slice the fillet into 4 portions. Place the slices on the sauce.
7   Garnish with the sautéed bitter gourd, and sprinkle with the chilies.

Daging Sapi Muda dan Pete Cina

VEAL FILLET WITH JAVANESE PARKIA

Veal loin or pork fillets can also be used in this recipe.

STEP 1: Roast Veal Fillets

4 x 160 g pieces veal fillet, fat and sinew removed
10 g lemon grass stalk, finely diced
5 g garlic, peeled, finely diced
1 g turmeric powder
salt
15 ml peanut oil

1 Place the veal fillets on a plate and rub with the lemon grass, garlic and turmeric powder.
2 Put the veal in a refrigerator and let it marinate for 2 hours.
3 Season the veal with salt just before cooking.
4 Preheat the oven to 200°C.
5 Heat the peanut oil in a small roasting pan or tray and put the fillets into the pan. Sear each side for 1 minute.
6 Put the pan into the preheated oven and roast the meat for approximately 15-18 minutes. Baste occasionally to keep the meat moist.
7 Remove the fillets from the roasting pan and keep them warm.

STEP 2: Garnish and Presentation

25 ml peanut oil
160 g sweet potatoes, cut into diamonds, blanched
10 g brown sugar (gula Jawa)
salt
80 g Javanese parkia pods, blanched
5 g shallots (bawang merah), peeled, finely diced
250 ml Honey Chili Sauce, hot (see page 31)
20 g Javanese parkia seeds

1 Heat 15 ml of the peanut oil in a shallow frying pan. Sauté the sweet potatoes and brown sugar in the oil for 3-4 minutes, tossing frequently, until the sugar has dissolved completely and coated the potatoes. Season with a little salt and remove the pan from the heat.
2 In another pan, heat the remainder of the oil and sauté the parkia and shallots for 2 minutes, tossing from time to time. Season with a dash of salt and remove from the heat.
3 Pour some of the hot Honey Chili Sauce onto each plate.
4 Cut each veal fillet into 1-cm thick slices and place the slices in a line next to the sauce.
5 Garnish the plate with the sautéed sweet potatoes and parkia.
6 Sprinkle the green parkia seeds on the sauce.

Daging Bistik Jawa

ROAST JAVANESE BEEF FILLET

STEP 1: Roast Beef Fillet

720 g beef fillet, fat and sinew removed
2 g coriander powder
2 g nutmeg powder
5 g lemon grass stalk, finely diced
salt
30 ml peanut oil

1 Preheat the oven to 160°C.
2 Season the beef fillet with the coriander powder, nutmeg powder, lemon grass and salt.
3 Pour the oil into a roasting pan and heat it to a high temperature on the stove top. Sear the meat quickly on all sides in the pan.
4 Transfer the pan to the preheated oven and roast the fillet, basting frequently until it is cooked as liked (about 25 minutes, for medium).
5 Remove the pan from the oven and let the meat rest in the pan for 10 minutes before cutting.

STEP 2: Sweet Beef Sauce (Saus Bistik Jawa)

30 ml peanut oil
30 g shallots (bawang merah), peeled, finely diced
10 g garlic, peeled, finely diced
10 g candlenuts, ground
15 g coriander seeds, ground
5 g nutmeg powder
375 ml dark sweet soya sauce
125 ml beef stock (see page 24)

1 Heat the peanut oil in a saucepan and sauté the shallots and garlic for 2 minutes without browning.
2 Add in the candlenuts, coriander and nutmeg. Continue to sauté for another minute.
3 Pour in the sweet soya sauce and beef stock. Bring the mixture to the boil, then reduce the heat. Simmer slowly for 10 minutes, stirring from time to time. The sauce should be syrupy in consistency and served hot. Yields 500 ml.

STEP 3: Garnish and Presentation

8 small round aubergines (terung engkol), halved, or 400 g
  aubergine, sliced
50 g shallots (bawang merah), peeled
50 g carrot, peeled, carved
50 g young green papaya, peeled, carved
15 ml peanut oil
250 ml Sweet Beef Sauce, hot
4 sprigs coriander leaves

1 Blanch the aubergines, shallots, carrot and papaya in turn in boiling water for 2 minutes. Drain.
2 Heat the peanut oil in a frying pan. Add in the vegetables and sauté briefly for 1 minute without colouring. The vegetables should remain crunchy.
3 Spread some of the sauce on each plate.
4 Slice the roast beef into 8-12 pieces and place 2-3 slices on the sauce on each plate.
5 Garnish with the vegetables and coriander.

MELAYU LAMB STEW

VEAL WITH DRIED SHRIMP SAUCE

VEAL FILLET WITH JAVANESE PARKIA

Roast Javanese Beef Fillet

Beef with Marinated Beansprouts

Hot and Sour Lamb Medallions

Kambing Gaya Asam Pedas

HOT AND SOUR LAMB MEDALLIONS

STEP 1: Baked Wrapped Lamb Medallions

> 30 ml peanut oil
> 5 g garlic, peeled, finely diced
> 20 g shallots (bawang merah), peeled, finely diced
> 20 g straw or button mushrooms, sliced
> 30 g leeks, cut into fine strips
> 10 g chilies, cut into fine strips
> salt
> 6 x 60 g lamb medallions
> turmeric powder
> 2 g ginger, peeled, finely diced
> 8 white cabbage leaves approximately 10 x 10 cm in size, blanched

1 In a frying pan, heat half the peanut oil and sauté the garlic and shallots for 2 minutes, until glazy.
2 Add in the mushrooms, leeks and chilies and season with salt. Continue to sauté for 2 minutes more. Remove from the heat and let the mushroom-leek mixture cool at room temperature. Set aside.
3 Season the lamb with a little turmeric powder, salt and the ginger.
4 Preheat the oven to 200°C.
5 Heat the remaining oil in a pan over heat. Put the meat in the pan and sear quickly on each side for 30 seconds. Remove immediately from the pan.
6 Place each lamb medallion on a cabbage leaf. Top each piece with a portion of the mushroom-leek mixture. Fold the leaf over and wrap the lamb tightly into a small parcel.
7 Place the wrapped lamb medallions on a greased baking tray and put the tray in the preheated oven. Bake the lamb for approximately 8-10 minutes. Remove and keep warm.

STEP 2: Hot Sour Sauce (Saus Kunyit Asam Pedas)

> 30 ml peanut oil
> 20 g shallots (bawang merah), peeled, finely diced
> 5 g garlic, peeled, finely diced
> 5 g ginger, peeled, finely diced
> 2 g greater galangal, peeled, finely diced
> 30 g candlenuts, ground
> 2 g turmeric powder
> 2 kaffir lime leaves
> 30 ml red chili juice (see page 23)
> 60 ml tamarind water (see page 23)
> 250 ml coconut milk (see page 22)
> salt

1 Heat the peanut oil in a saucepan and sauté the next 4 ingredients for 2-3 minutes, stirring frequently to prevent browning.
2 Add in the candlenuts, turmeric powder and lime leaves. Continue sautéing for 2 minutes more.
3 Pour in the chili juice, tamarind water and coconut milk. Season with salt. Bring the mixture to the boil, reduce the heat and simmer for 6-8 minutes.

4 Remove the pan from the heat and discard the lime leaves.
5 Pour the sauce into a blender and purée for 2-3 minutes. Remove and serve hot. Yields 375 ml.

STEP 3: Presentation

> 250 ml Hot Sour Sauce, hot.
> 25 g long bean leaves, cut into fine strips but 4 left whole
> 4 cabbage leaves, blanched
> 6 red chilies, seeded, cut into fine strips

1 Pour some of the hot sauce on each plate.
2 Slice the lamb medallions in half. Arrange on the sauce.
3 Garnish with a long bean leaf, a cabbage leaf and the shredded chilies and bean leaves.

Empal Basah dengan Urap Tauge Kedele

BEEF WITH MARINATED BEANSPROUTS

This dish offers an interesting taste combination of hot spiced beef with a cold spicy sour sauce which is contrasted with the bitterness of the papaya leaves. The double procedure of simmering (or boiling) beef and then pan-frying in order to seal in the meat juices is widely practised in many places in Indonesia.

> 600 g beef fillet, fat and sinew removed
> 2 g coriander powder
> 2 g cumin powder
> salt
> 750 ml beef stock (see page 24)
> 20 ml peanut oil
> 250 ml Sambal Brambang (see page 36)
> 160 g Coconut-marinated Beansprouts (see page 122)
> 8 papaya leaves, blanched

1 Season the beef fillet with the coriander, cumin and salt. Rub the spices well into the meat.
2 Heat the beef stock in a stockpot and bring to the boil. Reduce the heat to simmering point.
3 Put the fillet in the stock and let it simmer for 25-30 minutes. Remove and let the meat rest for 5-7 minutes before slicing it thinly.
4 In a frying pan, heat the peanut oil and sear the meat slices over high heat on both sides for 15-20 seconds. Serve immediately.
5 Pour some of the sambal onto each plate.
6 Arrange the marinated beansprouts to one side of the sauce.
7 Place the beef slices on the sauce.
8 Garnish with the papaya leaves.

Panggang Kambing Isi
LAMB WITH SPICY VEAL STUFFING

STEP 1: Spicy Veal Stuffing
100 g boneless veal shoulder or leg, finely minced
20 g shallots (bawang merah), peeled, finely diced
2 g garlic, peeled, finely diced
1 egg
125 ml cream (33% fat)
5 g salt
1 g white pepper powder
5 g red chilies, seeded, finely diced
5 g carrot, finely diced

1   Combine the minced veal, shallots and garlic in a blender. Blend until smooth, approximately 2-3 minutes.
2   Remove the mixture from the blender and put it in a cold bowl. Use a wooden spatula to mix in the egg thoroughly.
3   Slowly add in the cream, then season with the salt and pepper. Add the chilies and carrot and mix until the cream is blended well into the mixture.
4   Place this stuffing in a refrigerator and let it rest for 1 hour before using.

STEP 2: Lamb Marinade
45 ml peanut oil
40 g shallots (bawang merah), peeled, finely diced
10 g garlic, peeled, finely diced
1 lemon grass stalk, finely diced
10 g ginger, peeled, finely diced
10 g greater galangal, peeled, finely diced
40 g candlenuts, ground
10 g turmeric powder
5 g black peppercorns, crushed
salt

1   Heat the peanut oil in a frying pan and sauté the shallots and garlic for 2-3 minutes, stirring constantly.
2   Add the lemon grass, ginger and greater galangal. Continue to sauté for another 2-3 minutes.
3   Stir in the candlenuts, turmeric powder and black peppercorns, and season with salt. Continue sautéing for another 3 minutes.
4   Remove from the heat and let the mixture cool at room temperature before using. .

STEP 3: Roast Stuffed Lamb Racks
4 x 400 g lamb racks, with about 6-7 rib bones
4 mustard green leaves, blanched .
30 ml peanut oil

1   Bone the lamb racks but leave the rib bones attached to the meat. Use a sharp knife to make an incision between the rib bones and the roll of meat, but do not separate the two.
2   Flap down the roll of meat so that it is at right angles to the rib bones. Flatten the meat part with a cleaver or chopper to approximately 1.5 cm in thickness. Top the meat part with a blanched mustard green leaf.

3   Use a wooden spatula to spread the stuffing made in Step 1 on the mustard green leaf.
4   Fold the lamb meat over the stuffing towards the rib bones into a tight sausage shape. Tie the roll with twine or string.
5   Place the rolled lamb in a pan and pour the marinade made in Step 2 over it. Let the lamb marinate in a refrigerator for 2 hours.
6   Preheat the oven to 180°C, then remove the lamb from the fridge and drain off the excess marinade.
7   Heat the peanut oil in a roasting pan and place the lamb rolls in the pan. Sear them quickly on all sides until golden brown.
8   Place the roasting pan in the preheated oven and roast for 10 minutes, basting frequently to keep the meat moist.
9   Remove the lamb from the pan and keep it warm for 5 minutes in order to retain the meat juices.

STEP 4: Presentation
250 ml Peanut Honey Sauce, hot (see page 38)
10 g black peppercorns
2 red chilies, sliced
2 green chilies, sliced

1   Pour a thin layer of the sauce on each plate.
2   Cut each lamb roll into 3-4 slices and place these pieces on the sauce.
3   Sprinkle the peppercorns over the sauce and garnish with the chilies.

Daging Saus Ubi Jalar
BEEF ON SWEET POTATO SAUCE

4 x 150 g pieces beef fillet, fat and sinew removed
salt
pepper
75 ml peanut oil
120 g ferntops
80 g sweet potatoes, blanched, cut into balls with a melon baller
250 ml Sweet Potato Sauce, hot (see page 28)
10 bird's eye chilies, diced

1   Season the beef fillet with salt and pepper.
2   Use 60 ml of the oil to brush on the meat.
3   Cook the meat under a medium-hot grill or on a griddle for 3 minutes each side. Remove and keep warm.
4   Heat the remaining oil in a frying pan. Sauté the ferntops and sweet potatoes over medium heat for 1-2 minutes. Season with salt, remove from the heat and keep warm.
5   Pour some of the hot sauce in the centre of each plate. Sprinkle the diced chilies on the sauce.
6   Arrange the vegetables around the sauce.
7   Slice each piece of beef in half and arrange the slices on the sauce.

NOTE: The meat may be fried instead of grilled.

LAMB FILLET BENGKULU

GRILLED PORK CHOPS NORTH SULAWESI

Bakar Iga Kambing Bengkulu

LAMB FILLET BENGKULU

STEP 1: Pan-fried Lamb Fillets
10 g coriander powder
10 g kaffir lime leaves, finely chopped
5 g nutmeg powder
4 x 150 g pieces lamb fillet
salt
15 ml peanut oil

1 Combine the first 3 ingredients to make the marinade.
2 Put the lamb fillets in the marinade and let them sit overnight in the refrigerator.
3 Drain off the excess marinade and season the fillets with salt.
4 Heat the peanut oil in a pan to 200°C and sauté the fillets on each side for approximately 4 minutes.

STEP 2: Garnish and Presentation
15 ml peanut oil
160 g young green papaya, peeled, sliced into thin strips
10 g red chilies, seeded, diced
salt
250 ml Bengkulu Sauce, hot (see page 35)
4 young papaya leaves, blanched
20 carved potatoes, boiled in turmeric water (see page 123)
20 kaffir lime leaves

1 Heat the peanut oil in a pan and sauté the papaya julienne and red chilies for 2 minutes. Season with salt.
2 Spread a layer of the hot sauce on each plate.
3 Spoon a portion of the sautéed papaya into each papaya leaf and arrange this on the sauce.
4 Slice the lamb fillets and arrange the slices around the papaya julienne.
5 Garnish the dish with the potatoes and lime leaves.

Iga Babi Saus Dabu-dabu Manado

GRILLED PORK CHOPS NORTH SULAWESI

STEP 1: Grilled Pork Chops
30 ml dark sweet soya sauce
30 ml tomato juice
20 g shallots (bawang merah), peeled, finely diced
5 g garlic, peeled, finely diced
2 g ginger, peeled, finely diced
pinch of nutmeg powder
4 x 140-160 g boneless pork chops
salt
15 ml peanut oil

1 In a bowl, combine the first 6 ingredients and blend well with a whisk.
2 Brush this marinade on the pork chops and let them marinate in a refrigerator for 2 hours.
3 Drain off the excess liquid and season the meat with salt. Brush the meat lightly with the peanut oil.
4 Place the pork chops on a hot griddle or under a hot grill and cook on each side for 5-6 minutes. Keep warm.

STEP 2: Garnish and Presentation
120 ml Dabu-dabu Sauce, cold (see page 38)
100 g Sambal Brambang (see page 36)
8 kaffir lime leaves

1 Spoon a little of the Dabu-dabu Sauce on each plate.
2 Place a portion of the sambal next to the sauce.
3 Slice the grilled chops and arrange the meat on the sambal.
4 Garnish with the lime leaves.

BEEF ON SWEET POTATO SAUCE

LAMB MEDALLIONS IN FIERY SPICES

LAMB WITH SPICY VEAL STUFFING

Kambing Bumbu Bajak

LAMB MEDALLIONS IN FIERY SPICES

STEP 1: Grilled Lamb Medallions
30 ml peanut oil
20 g shallots (bawang merah), peeled, finely diced
2 g garlic, peeled, finely diced
5 g red chilies, seeded, finely diced
20 g peanuts, ground, deep-fried
30 ml dark sweet soya sauce
5 ml freshly squeezed lime juice
15 ml tamarind water (see page 23)
30 ml water
12 x 50 g lamb medallions, fat and sinew removed
salt

1 Heat half of the peanut oil in a saucepan and sauté the shallots, garlic and red chilies until slightly browned.
2 Add in the peanuts and continue to sauté for another minute.
3 Pour in the sweet soya sauce, lime juice, tamarind water and water. Simmer this marinade mixture for 5-7 minutes.
4 Withdraw the pan from the heat and let the marinade cool completely before using.
5 Season the lamb medallions with salt and brush the marinade on both sides of the meat.
6 Brush the remaining oil on the medallions and cook them under a grill or on a hot griddle for 2-3 minutes on each side. Remove and keep warm.

STEP 2: Garnish and Presentation
15 ml peanut oil
80 g potato balls, scooped with a melon baller, boiled in
*   turmeric water (see page 123)*
salt
250 ml Spicy Bajak Sauce, hot (see page 27)
4 Stuffed Mustard Green Leaves, hot (see page 119)
4 mustard green leaves, blanched

1 Heat the oil in a frying pan and add in the turmeric potato balls. Sauté for 2 minutes without browning, then season with salt. Remove the pan from the heat.
2 Pour some of the hot sauce onto each plate and place 2 or 3 medallions on the sauce.
3 Garnish with the sautéed potato balls, stuffed mustard greens and a blanched mustard green leaf.

NOTE: The meat may be fried instead of grilled.

Daging Masak Tauco

MEDALLIONS OF BEEF TAUCO

STEP 1: Tomato Tauco Sauce (Saus Tomat Tauco)
30 ml peanut oil
40 g shallots (bawang merah), peeled, finely diced
10 g garlic, peeled, finely diced
20 g red chilies, seeded, finely diced
20 g green chilies, seeded, finely diced
200 g tomatoes, peeled, seeded, diced
160 ml fermented yellow soya beans
250 ml water

1 In a saucepan, heat the peanut oil and sauté the shallots, garlic and chilies in the oil for 2-3 minutes, without browning, stirring constantly.
2 Stir in the tomatoes, fermented soya beans and water. Bring the mixture to the boil and then reduce the heat and simmer for 5-6 minutes.
3 Taste the sauce and adjust if necessary. The fermented soya beans will make the sauce salty and this may be adjusted by adding a small amount of water if it is too salty. Remove from the heat.
4 Pour the sauce into a blender and process for 2-3 minutes until smooth. Remove from blender and keep hot. Yields 375 ml.

STEP 2: Tauco Beef Medallions
8-12 x 60 g beef medallions
salt
20 black peppercorns, crushed
30 ml peanut oil
200 ml Tomato Tauco Sauce, hot

1 Season the beef medallions with the salt and peppercorns.
2 Heat the peanut oil in a frying pan.
3 Place the beef in the pan and sear quickly over high heat for 30 seconds on either side.
4 Pour the Tomato Tauco Sauce into the pan, reduce the heat and let the meat simmer for 4-5 minutes, so that the beef absorbs the flavour of the sauce.

STEP 3: Garnish and Presentation
40 g tomatoes, peeled, seeded, diced
5 g green chilies, seeded, finely diced
black peppercorns
12 kaffir lime leaves

1 Take the beef medallions out of the sauce and arrange the meat in the centre of individual plates.
2 Pour the sauce over the meat.
3 Mix the diced tomatoes with the chilies. Put a mound of this to one side of the meat. Sprinkle on some black peppercorns and garnish with the lime leaves.

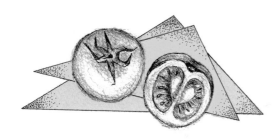

Lidah Sapi Bumbu Kuning

OX TONGUE IN COCONUT MILK

STEP 1: Boiled Ox Tongue
2 litres water
10 g garlic cloves, peeled, crushed
20 g shallots (bawang merah), peeled, crushed
10 g ginger, peeled, crushed
1 leek, use the bottom half only
1 x 800 g piece ox tongue

1 Pour the water into a stockpot and bring to the boil. Drop the garlic, shallots, ginger and leek into the boiling water.
2 Add in the ox tongue. Reduce the heat and simmer for approximately 1½-2 hours, until the tongue is cooked. To check whether the ox tongue is ready, remove it from the hot stock and pinch the tip with your thumb and forefinger. If your fingers go through the meat easily, then it is done.
3 Remove the ox tongue from the stock and cool it in cold water.
4 Quickly peel off and discard the thick outer skin.
5 Slice the tongue into 1-cm thick slices. Keep hot.

STEP 2: Sauce and Presentation
30 ml peanut oil
20 g shallots (bawang merah), peeled, finely diced
2 g garlic, peeled, finely diced
5 g ginger, peeled, finely diced
10 g turmeric root, finely diced
20 g candlenuts, ground
1 g coriander powder
500 ml coconut milk (see page 22)
120 g leeks, sliced into rounds
20 g red chilies, seeded, sliced into rounds
1 g cumin powder
salt
2 spring onion stalks, cut into 4-cm lengths

1 In a deep frying pan, heat half of the peanut oil and sauté the shallots, garlic, ginger and turmeric root for 2 minutes, stirring constantly to prevent browning the ingredients.
2 Mix in the candlenuts and coriander powder and continue to sauté for 2 minutes more.
3 Pour in the coconut milk and bring the mixture to the boil. Put the ox tongue slices in the coconut mixture and simmer for 5-8 minutes. Remove from the heat and keep the meat warm in the sauce.
4 Meanwhile, heat the remaining peanut oil in a separate frying pan. Add the leeks and red chilies, and season with the cumin powder and salt. Sauté, tossing well, for 2 minutes. Remove the pan from the heat and keep the vegetables warm.
5 Pour some of the strained coconut sauce onto each plate.
6 Arrange the tongue slices on the sauce.
7 Garnish with the sautéed leeks, red chilies and spring onions.

NOTE: If fresh turmeric root is not available, substitute with 2 g turmeric powder.

Paha Kambing Panggang Sambal Kecap

ROAST MARINATED LEG OF LAMB

This is an interesting dish, served hot, with a cold sauce.

STEP 1: Roast Rolled Leg of Lamb
45 ml peanut oil
20 g shallots (bawang merah), peeled, finely diced
35 g garlic, peeled, finely diced
10 g ginger, peeled, finely diced
5 g clove powder
5 g coriander powder
5 g turmeric powder
2 lemon grass stalks, crushed
2 kaffir lime leaves
2 g black peppercorns, ground
salt
600 g boneless leg of lamb

1 Pour 30 ml of the peanut oil into a bowl. Add the shallots, garlic, ginger, clove, coriander and turmeric powder. Stir briskly with a whisk until the ingredients are well mixed.
2 Add in the lemon grass, lime leaves and peppercorns. Season this marinade with some salt.
3 Place the lamb in a large bowl. Pour the marinade over the lamb, turning the meat over a few times so that the marinade is distributed evenly on the meat. Place in the refrigerator for 12 hours.
4 Preheat the oven to 180°C. Then remove the marinated lamb from the fridge, season with a little salt and roll up the meat. Secure the roll with kitchen string.
5 Heat 15 ml of the peanut oil in a roasting pan and roast the meat in the oven for approximately 30-40 minutes, turning the roll from time to time. Baste constantly to keep the meat moist. When done, remove the roast from the oven and keep hot.

STEP 2: Garnish and Presentation
15 ml peanut oil
120 g chayote, blanched, cubed
salt
120 ml Sweet Spicy Soya Sauce, cold (see page 36)
4 kaffir lime leaves
1 tomato, peeled, seeded, quartered
black peppercorns
4 lemon grass stalks, finely peeled

1 Heat the peanut oil in a frying pan and sauté the chayote for 2 minutes. Season with salt. Remove the vegetable from the pan and keep hot.
2 Untie the string from the lamb roll and slice the meat into 8 even slices.
3 Pour a little of the cold sauce onto each plate.
4 Arrange 2 slices of lamb on the sauce and garnish with the sautéed chayote, the lime leaf, a tomato quarter, black peppercorns and lemon grass.

PORK FILLET WITH CARAMBOLA

LAMB LEG WITH PECEL SAUCE

Daging Babi Belimbing Wuluh
PORK FILLET WITH CARAMBOLA

Two types of carambola are featured in this recipe: the small and sour-tasting *belimbing wuluh*, which serves as the base for the sauce, is counteracted by the sweetness of the relatively larger starfruit (*belimbing manis*), which is more commonly eaten raw, as a dessert, but is used here as a garnish.

> *4 x 140 g pieces pork fillet, fat and sinew removed*
> *coriander powder*
> *turmeric powder*
> *salt*
> *pepper*
> *30 ml peanut oil*
> *2 medium-sized starfruit*
> *3 sour finger carambolas, sliced*
> *250 ml Sour Finger Carambola Sauce, hot (see page 37)*
> *60 g black glutinous rice or wild rice, cooked*
> *2 red chilies, halved*

1. Season the pork fillets with a little coriander, turmeric, salt and pepper.
2. Heat half of the peanut oil in a frying pan and fry the fillets in the hot oil on each side for 6-7 minutes, basting occasionally with the oil.
3. Remove the meat from the pan and keep warm.
4. Slice the starfruit to get the star cross-section. Heat the remaining peanut oil in a flat frying pan and quickly sauté the starfruit and sour finger carambola slices for 1 minute on each side. Season with salt. Remove the pan from the heat.
5. Pour some of the hot sauce onto each plate.
6. Slice the pork fillets into finger-thick slices and arrange them in a line on top of the sauce. Garnish with the sautéed fruit, cooked black glutinous rice and chili half.

NOTE: Soak the glutinous rice grains for 2-3 hours before cooking, or the cooked rice will be very hard.

Paha Kambing Jawa Timur Saus Pecel
LAMB LEG WITH PECEL SAUCE

STEP 1: Roast Lamb Leg

> *60 ml peanut oil*
> *30 g shallots (bawang merah), peeled, finely diced*
> *30 g onion, peeled, finely diced*
> *20 g garlic, peeled, finely diced*
> *20 g candlenuts, ground*
> *600 g boneless lamb leg, rubbed with salt inside, tied firmly*

1. Heat half of the oil in a frying pan. Add in the shallots, onions, garlic and candlenuts and sauté for 3-4 minutes until golden brown. Leave to cool.
2. Rub the lamb leg with the mixture. Let it marinate for 4 hours in a refrigerator.
3. Preheat the oven to 200°C.
4. Heat the remaining oil in a roasting pan.
5. Place the lamb leg in the pan and roast it in the oven for 30-40 minutes, basting frequently.
6. Remove the lamb leg from the oven and the roasting pan, and let it rest for 10 minutes.

STEP 2: Garnish and Presentation

> *500 ml water*
> *50 g carrot, peeled, cut into fine strips*
> *50 g long beans, cut into thin lengths*
> *50 g cucumber, peeled, seeded, cut into fine strips*
> *50 g water convolvulus*
> *20 g beansprouts, cleaned*
> *250 ml Sweet Spicy Pecel Sauce, hot (see page 31)*
> *120 g fermented bean cake, fried, cut into shapes*
> *10 g sweet basil leaves (kemangi)*

1. Bring the water to the boil. Boil the carrot, long beans and cucumber for 1 minute in the water.
2. Add in the water convolvulus and beansprouts. Continue to boil for another minute. Drain.
3. Pour some of the hot sauce on each plate. Place portions of the vegetables on the sauce.
4. Slice the lamb leg and place on the vegetables. Garnish with bean cake, basil and remaining sauce.

OX TONGUE IN COCONUT SAUCE

BEEF BRAINS WITH BITTER GOURD

ROAST MARINATED LEG OF LAMB

Otak Godok dengan Pare

BEEF BRAINS WITH BITTER GOURD

Indonesians by and large love to eat brains and other offal. In this recipe, the natural sweetness of the brains is contrasted with the bitterness of the bitter gourd.

STEP 1: Beef Brains in Sauce
4 x 120 g beef brains
1 litre water
salt
2 salam leaves
500 ml White Beancurd Sauce (see page 39)

1. Soak the beef brains in very cold water for 6 hours to clean off all the blood and impurities. The water should be changed hourly and the brains will become very white as a result.
2. Pour the litre of water into a pot. Sprinkle in some salt and drop the salam leaves into the water. Bring the water to simmering point.
3. Add in the washed beef brains and continue to simmer for 5 minutes.
4. Remove the brains from the water and cool them off in iced water. When cool, peel off the fine transparent outer skin.
5. Pour the White Beancurd Sauce into a separate pot and bring it to a simmer. Put the brains in the sauce and cover the pot with a lid. Simmer for approximately 5-7 minutes. Stir occasionally, so that the brains absorb the flavour of the sauce.
6. Remove the pot from the heat and keep the brains warm in the sauce.

STEP 2: Vegetables and Presentation
30 ml vegetable oil
20 g bitter gourd, sliced, blanched
40 g tomatoes, peeled, seeded, sliced
20 g red chilies, seeded, diced
salt
white pepper
8 salam leaves
12 spring onions

1. In a frying pan, heat the vegetable oil and sauté the bitter gourd, tomatoes and chilies for 2 minutes, stirring frequently. Season with salt and pepper.
2. Spoon some of the sauce from the pot onto each plate.
3. Take the beef brains out of the pot and place them whole on the sauce.
4. Garnish the plate with the sautéed tomatoes, chilies, bitter gourd, the salam leaves and spring onions.

NOTE: Even after blanching, bitter gourd remains extremely bitter, hence, only a small amount is needed for this dish.

Daging Malbi

BRAISED BEEF MALBI

STEP 1: Braised Beef
60 ml peanut oil
30 g shallots (bawang merah), peeled, finely diced
10 g garlic, peeled, finely diced
600 g beef (top or bottom round or topside), cubed
5 g ginger, peeled, finely diced
5 g greater galangal, peeled, finely diced
30 g brown sugar (gula Jawa)
1 salam leaf
salt
125 ml tomato juice
500 ml coconut milk (see page 22)
60 ml dark sweet soya sauce
500 ml beef stock (see page 24)

1. Preheat the oven to 180°C.
2. Heat the peanut oil in a deep braising pan on top of the stove. Add the shallots and garlic and sauté until they are light brown, about 2-3 minutes.
3. Add in the beef and continue to sauté over high heat until all the meat has been seared a light brown.
4. Reduce the heat and add in the ginger, greater galangal, brown sugar and salam leaf. Continue to sauté an additional 2-3 minutes, then season with salt.
5. Stir in the tomato juice, coconut milk and sweet soya sauce.
6. Cover the braising pan with a lid and place it in the preheated oven. Cook for 1½-2 hours, gradually adding as much of the stock as necessary to prevent the sauce from becoming too thick and sticking.
7. Remove the pan from the oven and keep warm.

STEP 2: Vegetables and Presentation
15 ml peanut oil
6 small round aubergines (terung engkol), quartered,
    blanched for 2 minutes in salt water
60 g yam bean, blanched, cubed
60 g long beans, blanched, cut into thin lengths
40 g tomatoes, peeled, seeded, diced

1. In a separate pan, heat the oil and sauté all the vegetables in the hot oil for 2-3 minutes. Season with salt.
2. Serve the braised beef on individual plates and garnish with the sautéed vegetables.

NOTE: If small aubergines are not available, use 300-350 g aubergine cut in 1-cm cubes and blanched.

Gulai Kambing Pangandaran
BONELESS LAMB RACK PANGANDARAN

This recipe features a fiery, spicy accompanying sauce which is served cold with the hot lamb dish.

STEP 1: Roast Rolled Lamb Racks
- 4 x 150 g boneless lamb racks
- 10 g shallots (bawang merah), peeled, finely diced
- 5 g garlic, peeled, finely diced
- 20 g candlenuts, ground
- 5 g ginger, finely diced
- 1 lemon grass stalk, finely diced
- 2 g turmeric powder
- salt
- pepper
- 20 ml vegetable oil

1. Using a cleaver or chopper, slightly flatten the lamb racks.
2. In a bowl, combine the next 5 ingredients. Mix well. Rub this mixture on both sides of the lamb.
3. Sprinkle on the turmeric powder, salt and pepper. Let the lamb marinate overnight in a refrigerator.
4. Preheat the oven to 180°C. Then remove the marinated lamb from the refrigerator.
5. Roll each piece into a sausage shape and tie with string.
6. Put the oil in a roasting pan and heat it in the oven. Place the lamb rolls in the pan and roast for approximately 8-10 minutes. Occasionally baste the lamb with the dripping to keep the meat moist.
7. Withdraw the pan from the oven and let the lamb rest in the pan for 3-4 minutes before cutting.

STEP 2: Garnish and Presentation
- 15 ml vegetable oil
- 8 long beans, blanched
- 4 perkedels (see pages 118, 119)
- 250 g Brambang Sauce (see page 36)

1. Heat the oil in a pan and sauté the beans for 2 minutes, then fry the perkedels for 4 minutes.
2. Slice the lamb rolls and arrange them on individual plates.
3. Garnish with the long beans and perkedel, and serve with the cold sauce.

Otak Sapi Muda Bukit Tinggi
BRAISED CALF BRAINS BUKIT TINGGI

- 4 x 120-140 g calf brains
- 500 ml beef stock (see page 24)
- 60 ml white vinegar
- salt
- 4 mustard green leaves, blanched
- 250 ml Indonesian Curry Sauce, hot (see page 37)
- 10-15 g turmeric leaves, cut into very fine strips
- 80 g vegetable pickles, cold (see pages 126-7)

1. Clean the brains as described in Beef Brains with Bitter Gourd (see page 98).
2. Pour the beef stock into a stockpot and add in the vinegar. Season with salt. Bring the stock to the boil, reduce the heat to simmering point.
3. Add the calf brains to the stock and simmer for 6-8 minutes.
4. Remove the brains from the stock and cool them in iced water.
5. Peel off the transparent outer skin and discard this, then wrap each brain in a mustard green leaf and place the wrapped pieces in a small saucepan.
6. In a separate pan, heat up the Indonesian Curry Sauce until it simmers. Pour this sauce over the wrapped calf brains and simmer them gently for approximately 2-4 minutes.
7. Remove the brains from the sauce and cut each parcel in half.
8. Place 2 pieces on each plate and pour the sauce over the meat.
9. Garnish the plates with the strips of turmeric leaves and vegetable pickles.

Kambing Kecap Saus Gulai
LAMB CHOPS GULAI

- 45 ml dark sweet soya sauce
- 10 g shallots (bawang merah), peeled, finely diced
- 2 g garlic, peeled, finely diced
- 5 ml freshly squeezed lime juice
- salt
- 12 x 50-60 g lamb chops
- 30 ml peanut oil
- 8 spring onions, use lower half only
- 4 cabbage leaves, cut into squares
- 1 g anise powder
- 250 ml Indonesian Curry Sauce, hot (see page 37)

1. Mix the sweet soya sauce with the shallots, garlic, lime juice and salt.
2. Brush this mixture on both sides of the lamb chops and let them marinate in the refrigerator for 2 hours.
3. Dip the marinated lamb chops in some peanut oil, place them on a hot griddle or under a hot grill and cook on both sides for approximately 3-4 minutes, until medium-done. Remove and keep warm.
4. In a flat frying pan, heat the remaining peanut oil and sauté the spring onions and cabbage for 1-2 minutes. Season with the anise, toss well and continue to sauté for another 2 minutes. Withdraw the pan from the heat.
5. Pour the hot sauce onto the plates.
6. Set 3 lamb chops on the sauce on each plate and garnish with the sautéed vegetables.

Daging Bakar Kecap Saus Rendang
BEEF ON SPICY COCONUT SAUCE

STEP 1: Grilled Beef Fillet
20 g shallots (bawang merah), peeled, finely diced
5 g garlic, peeled, finely diced
10 g red chilies, seeded, finely diced
5 ml freshly squeezed lime juice
30 ml dark sweet soya sauce
salt
4 x 160 g pieces beef fillet, fat and sinew removed
30 ml vegetable oil

1   Combine all the ingredients, except for the fillet and oil, in a bowl. Mix well.
2   Brush this marinade on both sides of the fillets and marinate in the fridge for 1 hour.
3   Drain off the marinade and season the beef with a little salt.
4   Dip the meat into the vegetable oil and then cook it under a hot grill or over a hot griddle for 4 minutes on each side. Remove the meat from the heat and keep it warm.

STEP 2: Garnish and Presentation
30 ml vegetable oil
120 g beansprouts, cleaned
10 g red chilies, seeded, cut into strips
salt
coriander powder
250 ml Spicy Coconut Sauce, hot (see page 36)
4 mustard greens, blanched, cut into half

1   Heat the oil in a frying pan and add the beansprouts and chilies. Sauté the vegetables in the oil briskly for 2 minutes. Season with salt and a dash of coriander powder. Remove from the heat.
2   Pour a portion of the hot sauce onto each plate.
3   Arrange the meat on the sauce. Garnish with the sautéed vegetables and the mustard greens.

Daging Sapi Muda Saus Cabe Hijau
VEAL WITH GREEN CHILI SAUCE

8 x 60 g veal medallions, fat and sinew removed
3 g ginger, peeled, finely diced
3 g greater galangal, peeled, finely diced
salt
30 ml peanut oil
12 dried black Chinese mushrooms, soaked in warm water for 1 hour
8 Red Chilies with Veal Stuffing (see page 118)
250 ml chicken stock (see page 24), or water
250 ml Green Chili Sauce, hot (see page 30)
2 green chilies, seeded, diced

1   Season the veal medallions with the ginger and greater galangal. Leave the meat to marinate in a refrigerator for 1 hour before using.
2   Take the meat out of the refrigerator and season with salt.
3   Use half the amount of peanut oil to brush on the meat. Grill the veal medallions on each side for approximately 3-4 minutes under a hot grill or on a hot griddle. Remove and keep warm.
4   Heat the remaining oil in a separate frying pan and add in the black mushrooms. Season with salt. Sauté, tossing well, for 2 minutes. Remove from the heat but keep the mushrooms warm.
5   Poach the stuffed chilies in chicken stock for approximately 4-5 minutes. Remove from the stock and cut in half.
6   Spoon 3 tablespoons of the hot sauce onto each plate. Slice the medallions in half and place on the sauce.
7   Place the stuffed chilies in the centre of each plate. Garnish with the sautéed mushrooms and sprinkle with the diced chilies.

LAMB LOIN AND PUMPKIN

Kambing Labu Merah

LAMB LOIN AND PUMPKIN

4 x 150 g pieces lamb loin, cut off a rack, boned, fat and
sinew removed
2 g anise powder
salt
pepper
30 ml peanut oil
60 g shallots (bawang merah), peeled, finely diced
120 g pumpkin, diced, blanched
250 ml Pumpkin Sauce, hot (see page 29)
20 g roasted pumpkin seeds
10 g green chilies, seeded, diced
12 star anise
4 kaffir lime leaves

1 Season the lamb with the anise, salt and pepper.
2 Heat half of the peanut oil in a frying pan. Sauté the lamb at 180°C for approximately 10 minutes, turning the meat occasionally. Remove and keep warm.
3 In a flat frying pan, heat the remaining oil and sauté the shallots and diced pumpkin for 2-3 minutes. Stir constantly. Season with some anise and salt. Remove from the pan and keep warm.
4 Pour some of the hot Pumpkin Sauce onto each plate.
5 Slice each lamb loin into 8-10 pieces and arrange the slices in a circle on the sauce.
6 Place the sautéed shallots and pumpkin in the centre of the plate, ringed by the lamb slices. Sprinkle with the pumpkin seeds and diced chilies.
7 Garnish with the star anise and lime leaf.

Iga Kambing Saus Ubi Jalar
LAMB RACK ON SWEET POTATO SAUCE

Good quality New Zealand lamb is highly recommended due to its fine taste, but if you prefer a stronger-tasting lamb, use the British or French.

STEP 1: Roast Lamb Racks

4 x 250-300 g lamb racks, on the bone, fat cover removed, fat and meat tissue between the rib bones should be cut out from the tips of the bones approximately 2 cm down
5 g greater galangal, peeled, finely diced
1 lemon grass stalk, diced
2 g turmeric powder
1 garlic clove, peeled, finely diced
salt
15 ml peanut oil

1 Preheat the oven to 200°C.
2 Season the lamb racks with the greater galangal, lemon grass, turmeric powder, garlic and salt.
3 Pour 15 ml of the peanut oil into a roasting pan and heat it very hot on the stove top.
4 Place the lamb racks in the roasting pan and sear quickly, approximately 1 minute, on each side.
5 Then roast the meat in the preheated oven for about 10-12 minutes, basting frequently, until the lamb is medium-done.
6 Remove the racks from the oven and keep them warm.

STEP 2: Vegetables and Presentation

30 ml peanut oil
40 g sweet potato, diced, blanched
40 g bamboo shoots, diced, blanched
salt
pepper
250 ml Sweet Potato Sauce, hot (see page 28)

1 Heat the peanut oil in a frying pan. Sauté the sweet potatoes and bamboo shoots together for about 2-3 minutes. Season with salt and pepper.
2 Carve one chop off each lamb rack and leave the rest whole.
3 Form a pattern on the individual plates with the hot sauce.
4 Set the whole lamb rack on the sauce.
5 Place the sautéed vegetables next to the lamb rack and arrange the remaining lamb chop on the vegetables.

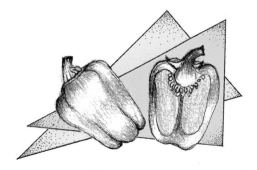

Daging Panggang Banda Aceh
BEEF FILLET BANDA ACEH

STEP 1: Fiery Acehnese Sauce (Saus Bumbu Aceh)

100 g dry shredded coconut flakes
15 ml peanut oil
20 g shallots (bawang merah), peeled, finely diced
10 g garlic, peeled, finely diced
30 g red chilies, seeded, finely diced
30 g green chilies, seeded, finely diced
3 g bird's eye chilies, seeded, finely diced
1 lemon grass stalk, bruised
10 g tamarind pulp
5 g clove powder
5 g coriander powder
5 g white pepper powder
pinch of turmeric powder
500 ml water
salt

1 Sauté the dry shredded coconut flakes in a hot pan without any fat or oil until they are light brown. Remove from the pan.
2 Heat the oil in the pan and sauté the shallots, garlic, chilies and lemon grass for 2 minutes.
3 Stir in the tamarind paste and clove, coriander, pepper and turmeric powder, together with the roasted coconut flakes. Continue to sauté for 2 minutes more.
4 Add in the water and bring to the boil. Season with salt, then reduce the heat. Let the mixture simmer for approximately 20 minutes.
5 Withdraw the pan from the heat and discard the lemon grass.
6 Pour the sauce into a blender and purée at high speed for 2-3 minutes. Remove from the blender and serve. Yields 750 ml.

STEP 2: Grilled Beef Fillet

4 x 150 g pieces beef fillet, fat and sinew removed
salt
4 tablespoons direndam marinade (see page 23)
160 g pumpkin, skinned, seeded, blanched, cubed
15 ml vegetable oil

1 Season the fillet with the salt and brush on the marinade.
2 Grill the beef on each side for approximately 4 minutes. Remove from the grill and keep the meat warm.
3 Sauté the pumpkin in the oil and season with salt.

STEP 3: Presentation

250 ml Fiery Acehnese Sauce, hot
12 Stuffed Mustard Green Leaves, hot (see page 119)
10 g red chilies, seeded, finely diced

1 Spoon a little of the hot sauce onto each plate.
2 Place the fillet on top of the sauce and garnish with the Stuffed Mustard Green Leaves and sautéed pumpkin.
3 Sprinkle the diced red chilies over the dish.

Rendang Kambing Kota Baru

LAMB IN SPICY COCONUT SAUCE

STEP 1: Braised Lamb Loins

30 ml peanut oil
20 g shallots (bawang merah), peeled, finely diced
2 g garlic, peeled, finely diced
40 g candlenuts, ground
2 g turmeric powder
2 g coriander powder
1 lemon grass stalk, finely diced
salt
4 x 150 g lamb loin chops, fat and sinew removed
4 large white cabbage leaves, blanched
500 ml Spicy Coconut Sauce, hot (see page 36)

1   Pour the peanut oil into a bowl. Add the shallots, garlic and candlenuts. Sprinkle the turmeric and coriander powder over the mixture. Add the lemon grass and season with salt. Mix well, using a whisk, until the mixture becomes a thick paste. (To adjust the consistency of the marinade, add more candlenuts to make the paste thicker; if it is too thick, add more peanut oil.)
2   Brush this marinade evenly on the lamb and let it marinate in a refrigerator for 2 hours.
3   Preheat the oven to 180°C. Then remove the lamb from the refrigerator.
4   Sear the lamb at high heat in a frying pan for 1 minute on each side.
5   Remove the meat from the pan and wrap each piece tightly in a blanched cabbage leaf.
6   Place the wrapped lamb in a small braising pan and pour the hot Spicy Coconut Sauce over the meat. Cover with the lid and braise in the preheated oven for 10 minutes, stirring occasionally. Withdraw the pan from the heat, but leave the meat in the pan.

NOTE: During the braising process, the thickness of the sauce may cause the meat to stick to the bottom of the pan and consequently burn. Add a little lamb stock to free the meat.

STEP 2: Garnish and Presentation

15 ml peanut oil
100 g straw mushrooms, quartered
60 g long beans, blanched
1 g turmeric powder
salt
15 ml lamb stock (see page 24)

1   In a shallow frying pan, heat the peanut oil and add the mushrooms and long beans. Season with the turmeric powder and salt. Sauté quickly, tossing well, for 2 minutes.
2   Pour in the lamb stock and continue sautéing until the liquid has evaporated.
3   Remove the lamb loins from the braising pan and slice each into 2 pieces. Arrange the pieces in the middle of the plate. Pour the remaining sauce over the meat and garnish with the sautéed vegetables.

Daging Sapi Muda Bungkus Daun Talas

VEAL FILLET IN TARO LEAVES

The large, dark green taro leaves impart a slightly bitter flavour to the veal; no other leaf will do the same.

STEP 1: Veal Fillets

20 g shallots (bawang merah), peeled, finely diced
30 g candlenuts, ground
15 g turmeric powder
2 g coriander powder
250 ml coconut milk (see page 22)
5 g salt
4 x 120 g pieces veal fillet, fat and sinew removed
15 ml peanut oil
4 taro leaves, blanched in boiling salt water for 1-2 minutes

1   Combine the shallots, candlenuts, turmeric powder, coriander powder, coconut milk and salt in a bowl to make the marinade. Mix well.
2   Place the veal fillets in an earthenware dish and pour the marinade mixture on top.
3   Leave the meat to marinate for 1 hour.
4   Preheat the oven to 180°C.
5   Heat the peanut oil in a frying pan.
6   Remove the pieces of veal from the marinade and sear quickly over high heat in the hot oil for 1 minute on each side. Then wrap the meat in the taro leaves.
7   Place the wrapped meat on a slightly oiled baking sheet and bake for approximately 8-10 minutes in the preheated oven.
8   Remove the meat from the oven and keep warm.

STEP 2: Garnish and Presentation

15 ml peanut oil
80 g snowpeas, blanched
80 g carrots, peeled, carved, blanched
40 g water apples, cut into strips
salt
250 ml Spicy Coconut Sauce, hot (see page 36)
8 cashewnut leaves

1   Heat the peanut oil in a frying pan. Sauté the snowpeas, carrots and water apples in the oil for 1 minute. Season with salt and keep warm.
2   Spread a layer of the hot sauce on each plate.
3   Cut each veal fillet into 4 slices and place the pieces on the sauce.
4   Garnish with the sautéed vegetables and cashewnut leaves.

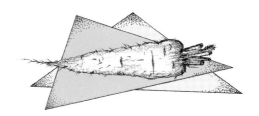

POULTRY

Dada Bebek Saus Jeruk

DUCK BREAST ON ORANGE SAUCE

STEP 1: Roast Duck Breasts

4 x 200 g boneless duck breasts
5 g ginger, peeled, finely diced
5 g lemon grass stalk, finely diced
salt
ground white pepper
15 ml peanut oil

1 Season the duck breasts with the ginger, lemon grass, salt and pepper. Let them marinate for 2 hours, then preheat the oven to 200°C.
2 Heat the oil in a frying pan and sear the duck breasts for 1-2 minutes on each side until brown.
3 Place the pan in the oven for 8-10 minutes. Turn the breasts over frequently and baste. Remove from the oven and keep warm.

STEP 2: Garnish and Presentation

250 ml Orange Sauce, hot (see page 38)
10 g green peppercorns
10 ml peanut oil
160 g oyster mushrooms
40 g dried black Chinese mushrooms, soaked in warm water
for 1 hour, sliced
salt

1 Cover the plate with the hot Orange Sauce and sprinkle the peppercorns on the sauce.
2 Slice each breast very thinly and arrange the slices on the sauce.
3 Heat the peanut oil in a flat, wide frying pan. Sauté the oyster and black mushrooms for 2 minutes, stirring constantly. (Oyster mushrooms are very fine and delicate and require very little cooking time.) Season with salt, remove from the heat and serve immediately with the duck.

CHICKEN BREAST ON SPICED PEANUTS

CHICKEN ON HONEY CHILI SAUCE

DUCK IN PEANUT PINEAPPLE SAUCE

105

Ayam Sumbawa

CHICKEN ON HONEY CHILI SAUCE

Much of the best Indonesian honey comes from the volcanic island of Sumbawa, where bees gather nectar from the flower-festooned forests.

STEP 1: Grilled Chicken Breasts

60 ml honey
20 g shallots (bawang merah), peeled, finely diced
5 g garlic, peeled, finely diced
15 ml tamarind water (see page 23)
4 x 150-160 chicken breasts, boned except for the wing
25 ml peanut oil

1 Combine the honey, shallots, garlic and tamarind water in a bowl. Stir well with a whisk.
2 Brush this marinade on either side of the chicken breasts and let them marinate for 2 hours in a refrigerator.
3 After the chicken breasts have marinated, quickly dip them into the peanut oil.
4 Using a hot griddle or a charcoal or gas grill, cook the chicken at a high temperature on each side for approximately 4 minutes. Remove the meat from the grill and keep warm.

STEP 2: Garnish and Presentation

20 ml peanut oil
80 g asparagus beans, sliced
40 g candied nutmeg
10 g red chilies, seeded, cut into strips
salt
250 ml Honey Chili Sauce, hot (see page 31)

1 Heat the oil in a frying pan and sauté the asparagus beans, candied nutmeg and chilies quickly, tossing well, for 2 minutes. Season with salt. Remove the pan from the heat.
2 Spread the hot Honey Chili Sauce on the plates.
3 Arrange the sautéed vegetable mixture on the sauce.
4 Cut each chicken breast lengthwise into 2 and place the slices on the sauce and vegetables.

Itik Danau Laut Tawar

DUCK IN PEANUT PINEAPPLE SAUCE

STEP 1: Braised Duck

1 x 1.5-2 kg duck
20 g garlic, peeled, finely diced
20 g ginger, peeled, finely diced
110 ml freshly squeezed lime juice
salt
30 ml peanut oil
80 ml freshly squeezed pineapple juice
500 ml Peanut Sauce, hot (see page 29)
80 g fresh pineapple, diced

1 Take the duck, split it down the middle lengthwise and remove the backbone completely with a sharp knife. Then joint the duck and put all the pieces in a bowl.
2 Sprinkle the garlic and ginger over the duck. Pour 80 ml of lime juice over the meat and let it marinate in the refrigerator for 4-5 hours.
3 Preheat the oven to 180°C. Then take the duck out of the marinade and dry it with kitchen paper towels. Season with salt and set aside.
4 Heat the peanut oil in a small roasting pan over high heat and add in the duck pieces. Sear the meat quickly on each side for approximately 1-2 minutes, or until the meat is light brown.
5 Put the pan in the preheated oven and roast for approximately 10 minutes. Turn the pieces over from time to time and baste frequently.
6 Remove the pan from the oven, turn the oven down to 160°C, and drain off the fat and oil from the pan. Leave the duck pieces in the pan.
7 Pour the remaining lime juice, the pineapple juice, Peanut Sauce and diced pineapple into the pan with the duck. Return the pan to the oven and braise for 45 minutes.
8 After braising, remove the duck pieces, leaving the sauce in the pan.
9 Remove all bones from the duck breasts, except the wing bone. Then cut each duck breast into thin slices lengthwise, and split the legs into 3-4 pieces. Set aside and keep warm.
10 Take the sauce out of the pan, process in a blender for 2-3 minutes until it becomes a fine purée. Keep the sauce hot.

STEP 2: Garnish and Presentation

15 ml peanut oil
40 g raw peanuts, shelled
1 g cinnamon powder
salt
20 g green chilies, seeded, diced
40 g yam bean, turned or carved

1 Heat the oil in a frying pan and sauté the peanuts until golden brown. Season with the cinnamon and salt.
2 Pour a layer of the warm sauce from Step 1 on each plate. Sprinkle on the sautéed peanuts and diced chilies.
3 Arrange 2 pieces of the duck leg with some slices of the duck breast on the sauce.
4 Garnish with the yam bean.

Semur Ayam Bumbu Kacang

CHICKEN BREAST ON SPICED PEANUTS

STEP 1: Semur Marinade
15 ml peanut oil
10 g shallots (bawang merah), peeled, finely diced
2 g garlic, peeled, finely diced
2 g ginger, peeled, finely diced
1 g nutmeg powder
60 ml tomato juice
30 ml dark sweet soya sauce

1   In a pan, heat the peanut oil and sauté the shallots, garlic and ginger without letting them brown.
2   Add in the nutmeg powder, tomato juice and sweet soya sauce. Bring the mixture to the boil, reduce the heat and simmer until the marinade thickens.
3   Remove the pan from the heat, pour the marinade into a bowl and set it aside to cool.

STEP 2: Roast Chicken Breasts
4 x 150 g chicken breasts, boned except for the wing
salt
20 ml peanut oil

1   Place the chicken breasts in a bowl or dish and pour the marinade made in Step 1 over the meat. Place in a refrigerator to marinate for 2 hours.
2   Preheat the oven to 180°C. Then take out the marinated chicken breasts, drain off the excess liquid and season them with salt.
3   Heat the peanut oil in a shallow roasting pan or tray inside the preheated oven. Place the chicken breasts in the pan and roast for approximately 5-8 minutes, turning occasionally and basting frequently. (The chicken breasts may stick to the bottom of the roasting pan, so loosen the meat carefully when turning the breasts or removing them from the pan.)
4   Remove the pan from the oven and keep warm.

STEP 3: Garnish and Presentation
20 ml peanut oil
4 small round aubergines (terung engkol), quartered, or
*   300 g sliced aubergines, blanched in salt water*
salt
120 g Candied Mango, cut into slivers (see page 123)
250 ml Peanut Sauce, hot (see page 29)
20 g peanuts, shelled, peeled, deep-fried, finely chopped

1   Heat the peanut oil in a shallow frying pan and sauté the blanched aubergines for 2 minutes, stirring constantly. Season with salt.
2   Stir in the candied mango and continue to sauté for another minute. Remove and keep warm.
3   Pour some of the hot Peanut Sauce onto each plate. Sprinkle the chopped peanuts on the plate.
4   Cut each roast chicken breast, from the tip to the round end, into 3-5 long slices. Place the slices on the plate and garnish with the sautéed aubergines and mango.

Ayam Paniki

CHICKEN PANIKI

The original recipe for this hails from Manado in north Sulawesi.

STEP 1: Spring Chickens
60 ml peanut oil
25 g shallots (bawang merah), peeled, finely diced
10 g garlic, peeled, finely diced
50 g red chilies, seeded, finely diced
10 g lemon grass stalk, finely diced
5 g ginger, peeled, finely diced
15 g turmeric powder
2 kaffir lime leaves
500 ml coconut milk (see page 22)
salt
4 x 180-220 g boned spring chickens, each cut into 6-8
*   pieces*

1   Heat 30 ml of the peanut oil in a large saucepan. Add in the shallots, garlic, chilies, lemon grass and ginger. Sauté for 2 minutes without browning.
2   Add the turmeric powder and kaffir lime leaves, and continue to sauté for 2 minutes more.
3   Pour in the coconut milk and bring to the boil, stirring frequently. Season with salt.
4   Preheat the oven to 280°C and heat the remaining peanut oil in a roasting pan in the oven.
5   Place the chicken pieces in the saucepan. Cover with a lid and simmer for approximately 5 minutes.
6   Remove the half-cooked chicken from the sauce and keep the sauce warm over low heat.
7   Place the chicken pieces in the oil heated in the roasting pan and roast the chicken in the preheated oven for approximately 8-10 minutes, basting from time to time. Then remove the roasting pan from the oven and take out the chicken pieces. Keep warm.
8   Remove the saucepan from the heat and discard the kaffir lime leaves.
9   Pour the sauce into a blender and process until smooth. Remove and keep warm.

STEP 2: Garnish and Presentation
15 ml peanut oil
3 starfruit, cut into sections
2 red chilies, cut into rings
12 melinjo leaves — 4 cut into fine strips; 8 blanched
salt

1   Heat the peanut oil in a frying pan and sauté the starfruit, chilies and melinjo leaf strips for 1 minute. Season with salt, then remove from the heat.
2   Spread some of the warm sauce on each plate.
3   Arrange the chicken pieces in the middle of the plate, on the sauce.
4   Garnish with the sautéed starfruit slices, chili rings and strips of melinjo leaves. Top with the blanched melinjo leaves.

QUAILS ON CURRIED VEGETABLES

Burung Puyuh Ujung Kulon

QUAILS ON CURRIED VEGETABLES

20 ml dark sweet soya sauce
20 ml palm wine
10 ml vegetable oil
15 g garlic, peeled, finely chopped
salt
4 quails
120 g glass noodles, soaked 5 minutes, cut into short lengths
4 dried black Chinese mushrooms, soaked for 1 hour, sliced
20 g peanuts, chopped
40 g chicken liver, boiled for 2-3 minutes, chopped
20 g shallots (bawang merah), peeled, finely diced
200 g chicken breast meat, diced
10 g ginger, peeled, finely diced
10 coriander leaves
20 ml peanut oil
4 portions Curried Vegetables (see page 123)

1 Mix the sweet soya sauce, palm wine, vegetable oil and 5 g garlic together to make the marinade. Season with salt.
2 Brush this marinade onto the quails and leave them to marinate for 1 hour.
3 Combine the noodles with the black mushrooms, peanuts, chicken liver, shallots and chicken breast. Mix well and add in the rest of the garlic, the ginger, coriander and salt to make the stuffing.
4 Preheat the oven to 200°C. Then stuff the marinated quails with the noodle filling. Secure the opening with a toothpick.
5 Place the quails in a roasting pan and brush them with some peanut oil. Roast them in the preheated oven for approximately 20 minutes.
6 Remove the quails from the oven and cut each in half. Arrange these on the Curried Vegetables. The vegetables used on page 123 can be varied according to taste.

PIGEON BREAST ON NUTMEG SAUCE

CHICKEN BREAST BANTEN

PEANUT HONEY CHICKEN

Ayam Kintuk Banten

CHICKEN BREAST BANTEN

STEP 1: Fried Chicken Breasts
4 x 120 g boneless chicken breasts, skinned
15 g turmeric powder
20 g candlenuts, ground
20 g shallots (bawang merah), peeled, finely diced
10 g garlic, peeled, finely diced
10 g lemon grass stalk, finely diced
10 g greater galangal, peeled, cut into fine strips
10 g sweet basil leaves (kemangi)
salt
30 ml peanut oil

1   Use a small, pointed knife to slice each chicken breast open lengthwise. Spread them out on a flat surface.
2   Mix together the next 6 ingredients.
3   Sprinkle the mixture on the open chicken breasts. Top with the basil leaves and season with salt.
4   Fold the chicken breasts back into their original shape. Secure the opening with a toothpick.
5   Heat the oil in a frying pan and fry the chicken breasts on each side for approximately 4-5 minutes. Remove from the pan and keep warm.

STEP 2: Banten Coconut Sauce (Saus Kintuk Banten)
30 ml peanut oil
20 g shallots (bawang merah), peeled, finely diced
5 g garlic, peeled, finely diced
30 g torch ginger, diced
50 g sour finger carambolas, diced
2 g nutmeg powder
5 g sugar
30 ml tamarind water (see page 23)
60 ml chili juice (see page 23)
250 ml coconut milk (see page 22)
salt

1   Heat the peanut oil in a saucepan. Sauté the shallots and garlic in the hot oil for 2 minutes.
2   Add in the torch ginger and sour finger carambola, and continue to sauté for another 2 minutes.
3   Add the nutmeg powder and sugar, and sauté for a further 2 minutes.
4   Pour in the tamarind water, chili juice and coconut milk. Season with salt and bring the mixture to the boil. Reduce the heat and simmer for approximately 10 minutes, stirring frequently.
5   Remove from the heat and pour the mixture into a blender. Process at high speed for 2-3 minutes until the sauce becomes smooth. Remove from the blender and keep warm. Yields 375 ml.

STEP 3: Garnish and Presentation
250 ml peanut oil
50 g dried glass noodles
250 ml Banten Coconut Sauce, hot
80 g leeks, sliced, blanched
20 g red chilies, seeded, diced
basil leaves

1   Heat the peanut oil in a pan to 350°C. Fry the dried glass noodles in the hot oil, stirring frequently, until they are light brown and crispy. This should happen very quickly.
2   Remove the noodles from the hot oil and drain them on kitchen paper. Keep warm.
3   Pour some of the hot sauce onto each plate.
4   Set the deep-fried noodles on the sauce.
5   Slice the chicken breasts vertically into 4 and place the slices by the deep-fried noodles.
6   Garnish with the leeks, diced chilies and basil leaves.

Ayam Saus Kacang Madu

PEANUT HONEY CHICKEN

This is a very tasty dish on a sweet spicy sauce which is well complemented by the fruit salad.

STEP 1: Sautéed Chicken Breasts
4 x 150-160 g chicken breasts, boned except for the wing
30 ml red chili juice (see page 23)
20 g shallots (bawang merah), peeled, finely diced
5 g ginger, peeled, finely diced
salt
30 ml peanut oil
250 ml Peanut Honey Sauce (see page 38)

1   Place the chicken breasts in a shallow dish.
2   In a bowl, combine the chili juice, shallots and ginger. Stir well with a whisk.
3   Pour this marinade over the chicken breasts and put them in a refrigerator to marinate for 4 hours.
4   Remove the marinated chicken breasts from the marinade and drain off the excess liquid. Season them with salt.
5   Heat the oil in a frying pan and sauté the chicken on each side for approximately 3-4 minutes, turning occasionally and basting with the oil. Remove from the pan and keep hot.
6   Pour out all the excess fat from the pan. Then, using the same pan, deglaze with the Peanut Honey Sauce and keep this boiling for 2 minutes. Withdraw the pan from the heat and keep the sauce hot.

STEP 2: Garnish and Presentation
15 ml peanut oil
40 g mangosteen segments
20 g water apples, sliced
10 g young green mango, finely sliced
salt

1   Heat the peanut oil in a frying pan and add in all the fruits. Sauté quickly for 1 minute and season lightly with salt. Remove from the heat.
2   Spread some of the hot Peanut Honey Sauce on each plate.
3   Cut the chicken breasts open, butterfly style, and arrange on top of the sauce.
4   Garnish with the sautéed fruits.

Dada Burong Dara dan Saus Pala

PIGEON BREAST ON NUTMEG SAUCE

Pigeon is a favourite dish on the island of Timor, where people go hunting for them in the rugged rock formations and wide expanses of bush.

STEP 1: Sautéed Pigeon Breasts
60 ml dark sweet soya sauce
20 g shallots (bawang merah), peeled, finely diced
5 g red chilies, seeded, finely diced
30 ml freshly squeezed lemon juice
16-20 x 30-40 g boneless pigeon breasts
salt
30 ml peanut oil
250 ml Nutmeg Sauce (see page 31)

1 Pour the sweet soya sauce into a bowl and add in the shallots, chilies and lemon juice. Stir the marinade well with a whisk.
2 Place the pigeon breasts in another bowl.
3 Pour the marinade over the pigeon breasts and let them marinate in the refrigerator for 4 hours to allow the meat to absorb the flavour.
4 Remove the marinated meat from the refrigerator and season with salt.
5 Heat the peanut oil in a frying pan. Sauté the pigeon breasts quickly on each side for approximately 2 minutes. Remove the meat from the pan and keep warm.
6 Drain off the oil from the pan and pour in the Nutmeg Sauce. Boil quickly for 2-3 minutes; withdraw the pan from the heat but keep the sauce hot.

STEP 2: Garnish and Presentation
15 ml peanut oil
40 g beansprouts, cleaned
5 g carrot, peeled, cut into strips
10-15 g kenikir leaves

1 Heat the peanut oil in a pan. Add in the beansprouts and carrots. Sauté, tossing quickly, for 2 minutes. Season with salt. Remove the vegetables from the heat and keep warm.
2 Spread some of the hot sauce in the centre of each plate.
3 Place the sautéed vegetables on the sauce.
4 Place 4-5 pigeon breasts on and around the vegetables.
5 Garnish with the kenikir leaves.

Burung Dara Isi Saus Semur

PIGEONS ON SPICED SOYA SAUCE

STEP 1: Roast Stuffed Pigeons
4 x 100 g pigeons, boned except for the legs
salt
300 g chicken meat, minced
10 g red chilies, seeded, finely diced
10 g green chilies, seeded, finely diced
2 g coriander powder
2 g cumin powder
80 ml cream (33% fat)
30 ml peanut oil

1 Spread the pigeons, skin side down, on a flat surface and rub lightly with salt. Set aside.
2 Process the chicken meat in a blender for 2-3 minutes until smooth. Remove from the blender and put in a cold bowl.
3 Add in the chilies, coriander and cumin powder. Slowly stir in the cream and season with salt. Combine this stuffing mixture well with a wooden spatula.
4 Preheat the oven to 180°C. Heat the oil in a roasting pan in the oven.
5 Spoon an even amount of the stuffing onto each pigeon.
6 Fold up the pigeons and shape them to their original form. Secure the opening with a toothpick.
7 Place the stuffed pigeons, breast side up, in the roasting pan and roast the pigeons in the oven for 35 minutes. Baste frequently to keep the meat moist. Remove the pigeons from the oven and keep them warm.

STEP 2: Garnish and Presentation
peanut oil for deep-frying
80 g sweet potatoes, cut into strips, blanched
salt
cinnamon powder
250 ml Spiced Soya Sauce, hot (see page 34)
10 g green chilies, sliced

1 Heat the peanut oil in a deep pan and deep-fry the sweet potato strips until golden. Drain off the oil, then sprinkle the salt and cinnamon powder over the sweet potato strips and keep them hot.
2 Spread some of the hot sauce on each plate.
3 Cut each pigeon in half, starting at the leg. Place the 2 halves on the sauce, one piece skin side down and the other, skin up.
4 Garnish with the fried sweet potato and chili slices.

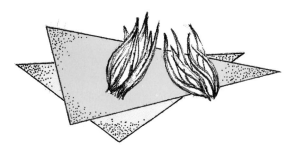

Ayam Saus Kacang Merah
CHICKEN WITH RED KIDNEY BEANS

STEP 1: Sautéed Chicken Breasts
4 x 150-160 g boneless chicken breasts
60 ml red chili juice (see page 23)
30 g brown sugar (gula Jawa)
10 g shallots (bawang merah), peeled, finely diced
5 g ginger, peeled, finely diced
salt
25 ml peanut oil

1 Place the chicken breasts in a small dish.
2 Pour the chili juice into a saucepan and bring to the boil. Mix in the brown sugar and simmer until the sugar has dissolved. Remove from the heat and let the liquid cool at room temperature.
3 When the sugared chili juice has cooled, make the marinade by adding the shallots, ginger and garlic to it.
4 Pour the marinade over the chicken breasts and refrigerate for 4 hours to allow the meat to absorb the flavour.
5 Remove the marinated chicken from the refrigerator and season with salt.
6 Heat the oil in a frying pan. Sauté the chicken on each side for approximately 3-4 minutes. Remove and keep warm.

STEP 2: Garnish and Presentation
20 ml peanut oil
80 g red kidney beans, soaked overnight, boiled until soft
8 long beans, blanched, tied in loops or braided
250 ml Red Kidney Bean Sauce, hot (see page 34)
2 red chilies, diced

1 Heat the oil in a pan and sauté the kidney beans and long beans for 1-2 minutes. Season with salt and withdraw the pan from the heat but keep the beans warm.
2 Cut each chicken breast lengthwise into 3-4 slices.
3 Pour the hot sauce onto individual plates. Arrange the chicken slices on the sauce.
4 Set the long beans on the plates and fill the loops with the sautéed kidney beans and the diced chilies.

Ayam Gulung Urap-urapan Saus Kemangi
CHICKEN WITH SPICY COCONUT STUFFING

Urap-urapan is a traditional boiled vegetable dish which is marinated with shredded coconut. Here it is used as a stuffing, thus resulting in a spicy dish on a mild, delicate sauce.

STEP 1: Spicy Coconut Stuffing
120 g grated coconut
80 g beansprouts, cleaned, blanched
60 ml red chili juice (see page 23)
20 g shallots (bawang merah), peeled, finely diced
10 g garlic, peeled, finely diced
10 g lesser galangal, peeled, finely diced
10 g lemon grass stalk, finely diced
½ egg, whisked
salt

1 Combine all the ingredients in a bowl and mix well with a wooden spatula.

NOTE: If fresh coconut is not available, use dried grated coconut soaked in warm water, then drained.

STEP 2: Steamed Chicken Breasts
4 x 100-140 g boneless chicken breasts, skinned
salt

1 Flatten each chicken breast with the flat side of a cleaver or chopper until the meat is 5 mm thick. Spread it out on a flat surface.
2 Season the chicken lightly with salt.
3 Spoon the stuffing made in Step 1 on the chicken breasts and spread it evenly with a spatula.
4 Roll each breast into a tight sausage shape and wrap each roll in kitchen plastic wrap. Tie the ends with twine or string.
5 Place the wrapped chicken rolls in a steamer and steam for 18-20 minutes.
6 Remove the rolls from the steamer and let them rest for 5 minutes before removing the plastic wrap. Set them aside and keep warm.

STEP 3: Garnish and Presentation
10 g yam bean, cut into wedges, blanched
250 ml Chili Basil Sauce, hot (see page 28)
4 sweet basil leaves (kemangi)

1 Pour a layer of the hot sauce onto each plate.
2 Slice each chicken roll into 4-6 and arrange the slices on the sauce.
3 Garnish with the sweet basil leaves and yam bean.

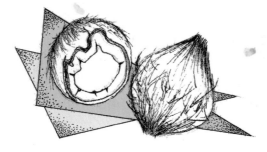

CHICKEN WITH SPICY COCONUT STUFFING

BABY CHICKEN BURA-HAY

CHICKEN WITH RED KIDNEY BEANS

Ayam Saus Kuning Bura-hay
BABY CHICKEN BURA-HAY

This chicken dish, stewed in coconut milk with spices, is deliciously sweet.

STEP 1: Stewed Baby Chickens
> 4 baby chickens or Cornish game hens, backbone removed
> 2 g anise powder
> 2 g coriander powder
> 2 g turmeric powder
> salt
> 30 ml tamarind water (see page 23)
> 30 ml peanut oil
> 250 ml coconut milk (see page 22)

1 Flatten the baby chickens and lay them out like butterflies.
2 Season the baby chickens with the anise, coriander, turmeric and salt. Sprinkle the tamarind water over them and let them marinate in the refrigerator for approximately 8 hours.
3 Preheat the oven to 160°C, then take the chickens out of the fridge.
4 Heat the peanut oil in a stewing pan over high heat to approximately 200°C. Place the chickens in the hot pan and sear on each side for 2 minutes.
5 Pour in the coconut milk and cover the pan.
6 Place the stewing pan in the preheated oven and stew for approximately 15-18 minutes, stirring. Remove the chickens from the oven and keep warm.

STEP 2: Bura-hay Sauce (Saus Kuning Bura-hay)
> 15 ml peanut oil
> 30 g shallots (bawang merah), peeled, finely diced
> 15 g garlic, peeled, finely diced
> 5 g ginger, peeled, finely diced
> 5 g greater galangal, peeled, finely diced
> 1 lemon grass stalk, crushed
> 1 salam leaf
> 20 g candlenuts, ground
> 5 g turmeric root, finely diced
> 5 g anise powder
> 2 g coriander powder
> 30 ml tamarind water (see page 23)
> 375 ml coconut milk (see page 22)
> salt

1 Heat the oil in a saucepan and sauté the shallots and garlic in the oil until light brown.
2 Add in the ginger, greater galangal and lemon grass, and continue to sauté for 2 minutes more.
3 Add the salam leaf and candlenuts, sprinkle in the turmeric root, anise and coriander, and sauté for an additional 2 minutes.
4 Pour in the tamarind water and coconut milk, and season with salt. Bring the mixture to the boil, reduce the heat and simmer for about 10 minutes.
5 Remove the pan from the heat and discard the lemon grass and salam leaf.
6 Pour the sauce into a blender and process until smooth. Serve hot. Yields 500 ml.

STEP 3: Garnish and Presentation
> 15 ml peanut oil
> 20 g red chilies, seeded, finely diced
> 160 g rice noodles, boiled for 4-6 minutes
> 40 g Javanese parkia
> 250 ml Bura-hay Sauce, hot

1 Heat the peanut oil in a frying pan. Sauté the chilies for 2-3 minutes, stirring constantly.
2 Stir in the noodles, season with salt and place a portion of this mixture on each plate.
3 Sauté the Javanese parkia for a minute, season with salt and put this aside.
4 Pour the hot Bura-hay Sauce on one side of the noodles.
5 Cut each chicken into pieces and place the pieces on the sauce. Garnish with the sautéed parkia.

Bebek Panggang Saus Bumbu Bajak
DUCK BREAST ON BAJAK SAUCE

> 2 x 300 g boneless duck breasts
> 1 g turmeric powder
> 1 tablespoon black peppercorns, crushed
> salt
> 30 ml peanut oil
> 24 x 10 g pieces pumpkin, turned or carved, blanched
> 8 long beans, blanched, twisted into loops or cut into lengths
> 250 ml Spicy Bajak Sauce, hot (see page 27)
> 5 g red chilies, seeded, finely diced

1 Season the duck breasts with the turmeric, crushed black peppercorns and salt.
2 Preheat the oven to 220°C.
3 Pour half of the peanut oil into a roasting pan and place over very high heat until the oil reaches approximately 240°C.
4 Place the duck breasts in the pan and sear each side for 1 minute only.
5 Place the roasting pan in the preheated oven and roast for 10-12 minutes, basting constantly and turning the breasts over every 2 minutes. Remove from the oven and set aside.
6 Heat the remaining peanut oil in a frying pan. Add the blanched pumpkin pieces and long beans. Sauté for 2-3 minutes, stirring frequently, then season with salt. Remove the pan from the heat.
7 Pour some of the hot Spicy Bajak Sauce onto each plate.
8 Cut the duck breasts horizontally into thin slices and place the slices on the sauce. Sprinkle with the diced red chilies.
9 Arrange the sautéed vegetables next to the duck.

NOTE: If the duck breasts are smaller than suggested in this recipe, make sure to adjust the oven temperature and cooking time to get the same result — browned on the outside and medium inside.

Burung Dara Isi dan Nanas

CORIANDER PINEAPPLE PIGEON

STEP 1: Sautéed Stuffed Pigeon Breasts

30 ml vegetable oil
20 g shallots (bawang merah), peeled, finely diced
40 g leeks, finely diced
40 g carrot, peeled, finely diced
60 g pineapple, finely diced
salt
12 x 40-50 g pigeon breasts, boned except for the wing
pepper

1 Heat half the vegetable oil in a frying pan and sauté the shallots and leeks in the oil without browning.
2 Add the carrots and sauté for 2 minutes. Remove from the heat and let the mixture cool.
3 Stir the pineapple into the sautéed mixture and set this stuffing mixture aside.
4 Use a pointed knife to make a lengthwise incision in the thin side of each pigeon breast.
5 Fill the incision with the pineapple mixture.
6 Heat the remaining oil in a frying pan. Fry the pigeon breasts on each side for approximately 3 minutes. Remove from the heat and keep warm.

STEP 2: Coriander Pineapple Sauce
(Saus Ketumbar Nanas)

30 ml vegetable oil
40 g shallots (bawang merah), peeled, finely diced
5 g garlic, peeled, finely diced
15 g coriander leaves
60 g brown sugar (gula Jawa)
200 g pineapple, peeled, diced
60 ml chili juice (see page 23)
30 ml freshly squeezed lime juice
salt

1 Heat the peanut oil in a saucepan and sauté the shallots, garlic and coriander leaves for 3 minutes without browning.
2 Stir in the brown sugar and continue to sauté for another 2 minutes.
3 Add in the pineapple and sauté for 2 minutes more.
4 Pour in the chili and lime juices, season with salt and bring the mixture to the boil. Reduce the heat and simmer for approximately 5-8 minutes, stirring from time to time.
5 Remove the pan from the heat and pour the sauce into a blender. Process until fine and smooth. Remove and keep warm. Yields 250 ml.

STEP 3: Garnish and Presentation

160 ml Coriander Pineapple Sauce, hot
80 g pineapple, peeled, diced
60 g water apples, diced
16 coriander leaves

1 Spread a layer of the sauce on each plate.
2 Slice the pigeon breasts and place the pieces on the sauce.
3 Garnish with the fruits and coriander leaves.

Ayam Kaliurang

KALIURANG CHICKEN

This is a light, slightly sour dish.

STEP 1: Braised Spring Chickens

2 x 800 g spring chickens, backbone removed
30 ml peanut oil
salt
60 g shallots (bawang merah), peeled, finely diced
10 g greater galangal, peeled, finely diced
100 g sour finger carambolas, peeled, diced
1 lemon grass stalk, finely diced
2 kaffir lime leaves
10 g red chilies, seeded, finely diced
500 ml coconut milk (see page 22)
160 ml chicken stock, hot (see page 24), or water

1 Flatten the chickens and lay them out like butterflies on a flat surface.
2 Heat the peanut oil in a deep frying pan which is large enough to hold both chickens next to each other.
3 Season the chickens with salt and put them in the pan, skin side down. Brown quickly over high heat for 2-3 minutes on each side.
4 Reduce the heat, then add the next 6 ingredients to the pan. Sauté for another 2-3 minutes.
5 Pour in the coconut milk and let the chickens simmer for approximately 15-20 minutes. Add the chicken stock or water a little at a time to thin the coconut milk sauce when it gets too thick during the simmering process.
6 Remove the chickens from the sauce and keep them warm in a separate pan.
7 Discard the lime leaves, then pour the sauce into a blender and purée for 2-3 minutes until smooth.
8 Pour the sauce back over the chickens and keep both hot.

STEP 2: Garnish and Presentation

60 g ripe papaya, peeled, seeded, diced
2 kaffir lime leaves, finely cut into strips
5 ml freshly squeezed lime juice
4 x 30-40 g sour finger carambolas, finely sliced

1 Combine the papaya, lime leaves and lime juice in a bowl. Mix well and set aside.
2 Remove the chickens from the sauce, cut them into 8 pieces and arrange on individual plates.
3 Arrange the sour finger carambola slices next to the chicken pieces. Place the papaya garnish next to them.
4 Garnish with the sauce.

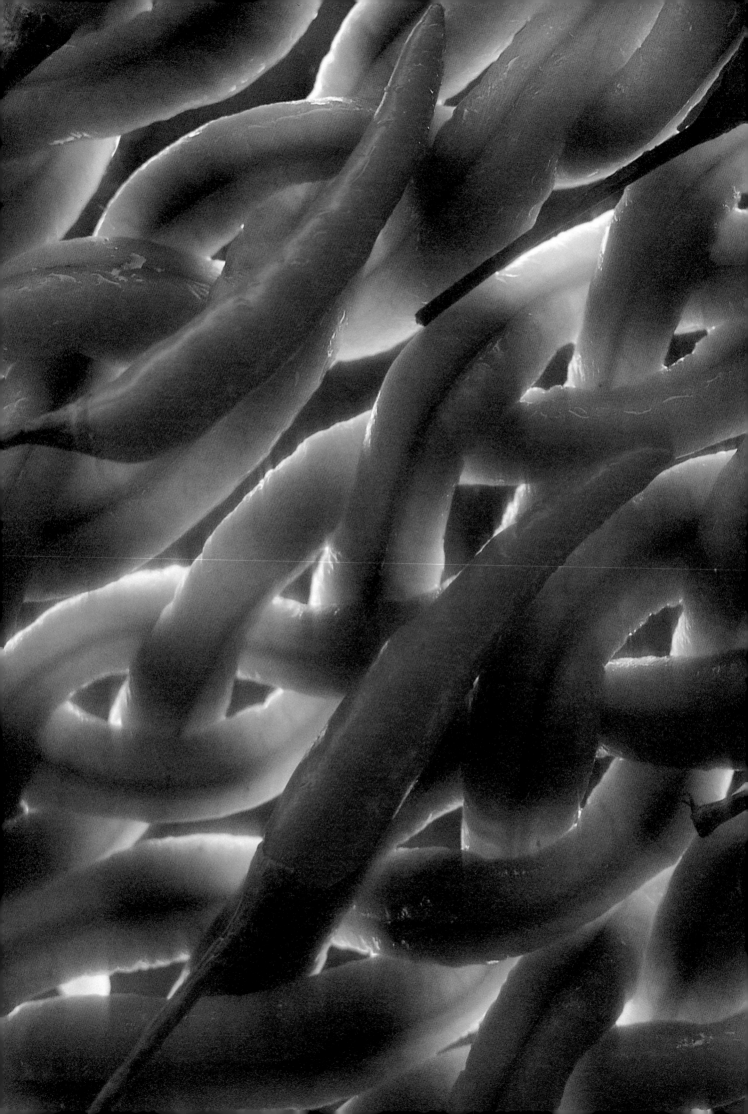

VEGETABLES
AND PICKLES

VEGETABLES AND PICKLES

VEGETABLES

Botok Kroket

RED BEAN CROQUETTES

80 g potatoes, boiled, peeled
5 ml peanut oil
5 g garlic, peeled, finely diced
2 g lesser galangal, peeled, finely diced
20 g shallots (bawang merah), peeled, finely diced
80 g red kidney beans, soaked overnight, boiled for 1 hour
    until soft, diced
salt
2 eggs

1 Mash the boiled potatoes until fine. Do not use any milk or butter when doing this.
2 In a frying pan, heat the peanut oil and add in the garlic, lesser galangal and shallots. Sauté for 2 minutes without browning. Remove from the pan and allow to cool.
3 Add the mashed potatoes and kidney beans to the sautéed ingredients. Season with salt. Add 1 egg to the mixture. Mix well with a wooden spatula.
4 Form the mixture into balls, squares, half-moons or any other shape you like.
5 Break the other egg and separate the white from the yolk. Use the yolk to brush the top of the croquettes.
6 Cook the croquettes on a griddle over high heat until slightly brown.

Ubi Jalar Masak Santan Gula Merah

SWEET POTATO GRATIN

vegetable oil
320 g sweet potatoes, peeled, sliced
250 ml coconut milk (see page 22)
1 egg yolk
60 g brown sugar (gula Jawa)
6 dried cloves
1 g nutmeg powder
salt

1 Preheat the oven to 200°C.
2 Grease a large earthenware or ovenproof dish with vegetable oil and place the sliced potatoes, one layer deep, in the greased dish.
3 Mix the coconut milk, egg yolk, brown sugar, cloves, nutmeg powder and salt with a whisk. Pour the mixture over the potatoes.
4 Place the dish in the preheated oven and bake for approximately 15-20 minutes.

Cabe Merah Isi dengan Sapi Muda

RED CHILIES WITH VEAL STUFFING

100 g veal, minced or ground
20 g shallots (bawang merah), peeled, finely diced
2 g garlic, peeled, finely diced
5 g red chilies, finely diced
½ egg yolk
salt
ground white pepper
8 medium-sized red chilies, seeded, stems removed
250 ml chicken stock, hot (see page 24)

1 Place the minced veal in a bowl. Add in the shallots, garlic, diced chilies and egg yolk. Season with salt and pepper.
2 Mix well with a wooden spatula until smooth.
3 Put the veal mixture into a piping bag with a small-holed nozzle.
4 Pipe the stuffing into the chilies, but only until they are three-quarters-full so that there is room for the stuffing to expand during the poaching process.
5 Place the stuffed chilies in a shallow pan. Add in the hot chicken stock and poach gently at 80°C for approximately 5-7 minutes.
6 Remove the chilies from the hot stock. Use them as a garnish or as a vegetable to accompany veal dishes.

Perkedel Jagung

SWEETCORN PERKEDEL

120 g potatoes, boiled, peeled
100 g canned sweetcorn kernels, drained
20 g lemon grass stalk, finely diced
10 g red chilies, seeded, finely diced
1 egg
salt
ground white pepper
oil for shallow frying

1 Mash the potatoes until fine. Do not use any butter or milk when doing this. Then use a wooden spoon to mix in the other ingredients, seasoning with salt and pepper.
2 Shape the mixture into 8 round or square patties (perkedel).
3 Sauté these perkedel quickly in hot vegetable oil on each side for 2 minutes. Serve with hot meat dishes.

Perkedel Ayam
CHICKEN PERKEDEL

200 g potatoes, boiled, peeled
15 ml vegetable oil
5 g garlic, peeled, finely diced
20 g shallots (bawang merah), peeled, finely diced
20 g leeks, finely diced
100 g chicken meat, minced or diced finely
salt
ground white pepper
nutmeg powder
2 eggs
oil for shallow frying

1 Mash the potatoes until fine. Do not use any butter or milk when doing this.
2 Heat the vegetable oil in a frying pan and sauté the garlic, shallots and leeks over medium heat for 2 minutes without browning. Stir constantly.
3 Add in the chicken and continue to sauté for 5 minutes more. Withdraw the pan from the heat.
4 In a bowl, combine the sautéed mixture with the hot mashed potatoes. Season with salt, pepper and nutmeg.
5 Break 1 egg and drop it in the mixture. Mix well with a wooden spoon.
6 Shape the mixture into patties (perkedel) of 40 g.
7 Beat the other egg with a whisk in another bowl. Dip each patty in the beaten egg before frying it for 2 minutes on each side in hot oil.

NOTE: Minced lamb or beef may be used instead of chicken.

Tauco Minang
GREEN BEANS MINANG

15 ml peanut oil
20 g shallots (bawang merah), peeled, finely diced
10 g garlic, peeled, finely diced
10 g greater galangal, peeled, finely diced
5 g shrimp paste
50 g green chilies, seeded, sliced
100 g long beans or stringbeans, cut in lengths
180 ml fermented black soya beans
375 ml coconut milk (see page 22)

1 Heat the peanut oil in a saucepan. Add in the shallots, garlic and greater galangal and sauté over high heat until light brown.
2 Reduce the heat and add in the shrimp paste, chilies and beans; continue to sauté over medium heat for 3 minutes more. Stir constantly.
3 Add in the fermented soya beans and coconut milk. Let the mixture simmer for approximately 3-5 minutes. Serve hot.

Kol Isi Rebung
BAMBOO SHOOTS IN CABBAGE LEAVES

15 ml peanut oil
20 g shallots (bawang merah), peeled, finely diced
1 red chili, seeded, finely diced
5 g garlic, peeled, finely diced
20 g leeks, finely diced
150 g bamboo shoots, diced
1 egg white, whisked
salt
white pepper
8 white cabbage leaves about 10-12 cm in size, blanched

1 Heat the peanut oil in a frying pan. Add in the shallots, chili and garlic and sauté over medium heat for 2 minutes, stirring constantly.
2 Add in the leeks and bamboo shoots and continue to sauté for 2 minutes more.
3 Withdraw the pan from the heat and let the mixture cool before mixing in the egg white with a wooden spoon. Season with salt and pepper.
4 Preheat the oven to 240°C.
5 Spoon a little of the bamboo shoot mixture onto each cabbage leaf. Fold the leaf over into a ball or a roll.
6 Place the folded cabbage leaves on an oiled baking sheet and cook in the preheated oven for approximately 10-15 minutes. Serve hot.

Sawi Hijau Isi Tauge
STUFFED MUSTARD GREEN LEAVES

15 ml peanut oil
20 g shallots (bawang merah), peeled, finely diced
5 g garlic, peeled, finely diced
1 red chili, seeded, finely diced
120 g beansprouts
salt
4 mustard green leaves, blanched

1 Heat the peanut oil in a frying pan. Sauté the shallots, garlic and chili for 1-2 minutes until light brown.
2 Add in the beansprouts and continue to sauté for 1 minute, until the beansprouts begin to turn slightly soft. Season with salt. Then remove the pan from the heat.
3 Flatten the mustard green leaves with the flat side of a cleaver or chopper and spread them out on the table top.
4 Divide the beansprout mixture into 4 batches. Place a portion of the mixture in the middle of each leaf.
5 Fold the leaf over the mixture and wrap it into a small tight ball. Tie with a piece of lemon grass or twine into a small bundle.
6 Steam for 1-2 minutes before serving.

Bamboo Shoots in Cabbage Leaves

Green Beans Minang

Stuffed Mustard Green Leaves

Urap Sayuran

COCONUT VEGETABLES

The Indonesian word *urap* means a vegetable dish with fresh or dried grated coconut.

80 g grated coconut
5 g shrimp paste
10 g lesser galangal, finely diced
10 g white sugar
80 g long beans, cut into thin lengths, blanched
80 g white cabbage, sliced finely, blanched
80 g spinach leaves, sliced, blanched
80 g beansprouts, cleaned, blanched
salt
sliced cucumber (optional)

1 Dry-fry the grated coconut in a pan, without oil, until the coconut becomes light brown, approximately 4-5 minutes. Stir constantly. During this process, the coconut oil is extracted, thus there is no need for oil.
2 Add in the shrimp paste and lesser galangal. Then mix in the sugar and continue sautéing over medium heat for 5 minutes more.
3 Withdraw the pan from the heat. Put the mixture in a bowl and let it cool at room temperature.
4 When cooled, add in the vegetables and season with salt. Toss well. Serve with sliced cucumbers if desired.

NOTE: If this is served as a main dish, it is enough for 4-6 persons; if served as an accompaniment, it is sufficient for 8-10 persons.

Urap Tauge Kedele
COCONUT-MARINATED BEANSPROUTS

80 g beansprouts, cleaned
5 g lesser galangal, peeled, finely diced
15 g brown sugar (gula Jawa)
3 g shrimp paste
salt
80 g coconut meat, cut into strips
10 g red chilies, seeded, cut into strips
5 g lemon grass stalk, finely diced
20 g grated coconut

1 Blanch the beansprouts in boiling water for 1 minute and plunge immediately in iced water to cool.
2 Pound together the lesser galangal, brown sugar, shrimp paste and a little salt with a pestle in a stone mortar until the mixture becomes a fine paste.
3 Combine the beansprouts, coconut meat, red chilies and lemon grass in a bowl. Add in the pounded paste and grated coconut. Mix well.
4 Let the mixture sit in a refrigerator for 2 hours to allow the flavours to be absorbed before serving.

Kukus Pare Sindang Laya
STUFFED BITTER GOURD

4 x 250 g bitter gourds
15 ml peanut oil
20 g shallots (bawang merah), peeled, finely diced
5 g garlic, peeled, finely diced
10 g red chilies, seeded, finely diced
220 g grated coconut
15 g brown sugar (gula Jawa)
10 g tamarind pulp
salt
2 eggs, whisked

1 Cut each bitter gourd lengthwise and scrape out the seeds and soft flesh. Discard the seeds, but retain the flesh.
2 Heat the peanut oil in a saucepan. Add in the shallots, garlic and red chilies. Sauté for 2 minutes without browning.
3 Stir in the young coconut, bitter gourd flesh, brown sugar and tamarind pulp. Season with salt. Sauté for 3 minutes more. Then remove the pan from the heat and let the mixture cool.
4 When cool, stir in the eggs and stuff the hollowed bitter gourd halves with the mixture.
5 Put the halves together and tie with kitchen string.
6 Steam the stuffed bitter gourds for 20 minutes.
7 Remove from the steamer and untie the string. Serve warm.

Tumis Bayam
STIR-FRIED SPINACH

The local variety of spinach has roundish leaves and comes in 2 colours, green or dark reddish-purple.

30 ml peanut oil
20 g onions, peeled, finely diced
10 g garlic, peeled, finely diced
20 g red chilies, seeded, cut into strips
250 g red spinach leaves
250 g green spinach leaves
salt
pepper

1 Heat the peanut oil in a frying pan. Sauté the onions, garlic and chilies in the oil for 1 minute over medium heat without browning the ingredients.
2 Add in the spinach and continue to sauté for 2-3 minutes. Season with salt and pepper. Serve.

Sayur Bumbu Jawa
VEGETABLES IN SPICED COCONUT MILK

30 ml peanut oil
10 g garlic, peeled, finely diced
30 g shallots (bawang merah), peeled, finely diced
10 g ginger, peeled, finely diced
5 g greater galangal, peeled, finely diced
5 g turmeric root, peeled, finely diced
50 g candlenuts, ground
500 ml coconut milk (see page 22)
180 g long beans, cut into short lengths, blanched for 2 minutes
20 g red chilies, seeded, cut into strips, blanched for 2 minutes
20 g green chilies, seeded, cut into strips, blanched for 2 minutes
30 ml white vinegar
10 g white sugar
salt
pepper

1 Heat the peanut oil in a shallow saucepan and sauté the garlic, shallots, ginger, greater galangal and turmeric root over medium heat for 2 minutes without colouring.
2 Add the candlenuts and continue to sauté for 2 minutes more.
3 Pour in the coconut milk and bring to the boil. Reduce the heat to simmering point.
4 Add the blanched beans and chilies, and simmer for 5-7 minutes.
5 Finally add in the vinegar and sugar, and season with salt and pepper. Simmer for 1 minute more, then serve immediately.

NOTE: If the sauce becomes too thick during the simmering process, add some water to thin it down.

Sayur Asam
SOUR VEGETABLES

15 ml peanut oil
30 g shallots (bawang merah), peeled, finely diced
5 g shrimp paste
15 g brown sugar (gula Jawa)
20 g tamarind paste
1 litre chicken stock (see page 24), or water
60 g young jackfruit sections
60 g young chayote, peeled, sliced
60 g baby corns, sliced
60 g long beans, sliced into lengths
60 g peanuts, shelled
10 g melinjo leaves
40 g melinjo nuts
salt
pepper

1   Heat the peanut oil in a shallow wide saucepan. Add the shallots and shrimp paste, and sauté over low heat for 2-3 minutes.
2   Add the brown sugar and tamarind paste, and continue to sauté for 1-2 minutes.
3   Pour in the chicken stock or water and bring to the boil. Let it boil for 5 minutes.
4   Turn down the heat and add in the remaining ingredients. Simmer for 5-8 minutes.
5   Remove from the heat and serve the vegetables in the stock.

NOTE: If either melinjo nuts or melinjo leaves are not available, drop them from the recipe as there is no substitute.

Kentang dan Kunyit
TURMERIC POTATOES

This is a basic recipe and the amounts can be increased or decreased proportionately. It can be used for all kinds of potatoes, either carved, cubed, whole, etc. The idea is to use the turmeric to give a bright yellow colour to the potatoes.

500 ml water
5 g turmeric powder
2 g turmeric root, sliced
salt
1 kg potatoes

1   Combine the first 4 ingredients in a pot and bring the liquid to the boil.
2   Add in the potatoes and cook as long as you would when using plain water to boil potatoes.

Sayur Masak Kari
CURRIED VEGETABLES

15 ml vegetable oil
10 g garlic, peeled, finely diced
45 g onions, peeled, finely diced
5 g fresh turmeric root, peeled, finely diced
30 g candlenuts, ground
250 ml coconut milk (see page 22)
60 g carrot, peeled, cubed
60 g cauliflower, cleaned, cubed
60 g stringbeans, sliced
20 g red chilies, seeded, sliced
water
15 ml vinegar
salt

1   Heat the vegetable oil in a frying pan and sauté the garlic, onions and turmeric in the hot oil for 1 minute without browning.
2   Add in the candlenuts and continue to sauté for 1 minute more without letting the ingredients colour.
3   Pour in the coconut milk and bring the mixture to the boil.
4   Add in the carrots and cauliflower, turn down the heat and let the mixture simmer until the vegetables are still crunchy, approximately 6-8 minutes.
5   Add the stringbeans and chilies and simmer for another 4 minutes. Use the water to thin the coconut milk mixture when it gets too thick during the simmering process.
6   Finally add the vinegar and season with salt. Serve hot.

Manisan Mangga
CANDIED MANGO

This *manisan* (candied fruit or sweetmeat) can be served cold as a relish or side dish, or hot, sautéed and added to main course dishes as a garnish.

120 g green young mango flesh, cut into fine strips
50 g white sugar
375 ml water
10 g red chilies, seeded, cut into fine strips
salt

1   Mix the mango strips together with the sugar in a bowl.
2   Boil the water and pour the hot water over the sugared mangoes.
3   Let the mangoes cool at room temperature before placing the bowl in a refrigerator to marinate overnight.
4   Drain off the liquid, add the strips of chili and season with salt. Mix well.

PICKLED GREEN MANGOES

PULASARI PICKLES

PICKLED PALM HEARTS

YELLOW PICKLES

MIXED PICKLES

CABBAGE AND BEANSPROUT PICKLES

PICKLES

The word *acar* literally means "pickle" or "pickled". Essential to the pickling process are ingredients such as vinegar, sugar, salt and water. There are many kinds of *acars*, and they are usually served as side dishes to accompany the meal.

Acar Rujak Poh
PICKLED GREEN MANGOES

> *240 g young green mango flesh, cut into strips*
> *20 g red chilies, seeded, cut into strips*
> *20 g green chilies, seeded, cut into strips*
> *375 ml water*
> *2 pandanus leaves*
> *60 ml white vinegar*
> *40 g white sugar*
> *10 g salt*
> *1 cinnamon stick*

1   Put the mangoes and chilies in a bowl.
2   In a saucepan, combine the water, pandanus leaves, vinegar, sugar and salt. Boil for 5 minutes.
3   Remove from the heat and discard the pandanus leaves. Add in the cinnamon stick.
4   Pour the liquid over the mangoes and chilies and let them soak for a minimum of 2 hours. Drain off the liquid prior to serving this as a garnish.

Acar Pulasari
PULASARI PICKLES

> *50 g carrot, carved into balls*
> *80 g yam bean, peeled, scooped out with a melon baller*
> *80 g kedongdong flesh, scooped out with a melon baller*
> *30 g shallots (bawang merah), peeled*
> *20 g red chilies, seeded, sliced into rounds*
> *20 g green chilies, seeded, sliced into rounds*
> *60 ml white vinegar*
> *60 g white sugar*
> *5 g salt*

1   Combine all the ingredients in a bowl and mix well with a wooden spoon.
2   Let the vegetables soak for a minimum of 2 hours and drain off the liquid if using as a garnish.

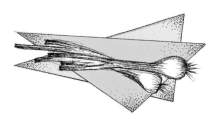

Acar Pondoh
PICKLED PALM HEARTS

> *200 g palm hearts, cut into diamonds*
> *30 g red chilies, seeded, finely diced*
> *30 g green chilies, seeded, sliced into fine strips*
> *30 g small shallots (bawang merah), peeled, diced*
> *300 ml water*
> *2 lemon grass stalks, crushed*
> *30 ml white vinegar*
> *30 g white sugar*
> *10 g salt*

1   Place the palm hearts, chilies and shallots in a bowl.
2   Combine the rest of the ingredients in a saucepan and boil the mixture for 10 minutes.
3   Remove the lemon grass and pour the hot liquid over the vegetable mixture.
4   Let the vegetables soak for a minimum of 2 hours, and drain off the liquid if using as a garnish.

Acar Kuning
YELLOW PICKLES

> *30 ml peanut oil*
> *20 g shallots (bawang merah), peeled, finely diced*
> *5 g garlic, peeled, finely diced*
> *10 g greater galangal, peeled, finely diced*
> *15 g red chilies, seeded, sliced into strips*
> *20 g candlenuts, ground*
> *5 g turmeric powder*
> *5 g brown sugar (gula Jawa)*
> *1 lemon grass stalk, bruised*
> *2 salam leaves*
> *5 ml white vinegar*
> *250 ml coconut milk (see page 22)*
> *40 g carrots, peeled, cut into strips, blanched for 4 minutes*
> *40 g cauliflower florets, blanched for 2 minutes*
> *40 g stringbeans, cut into strips, blanched for 2 minutes*
> *40 g cucumber, seeded, cut into strips*
> *salt*

1   Heat the oil in a flat frying pan and sauté the shallots, garlic, greater galangal and chilies for 2 minutes without browning.
2   Stir in the candlenuts, turmeric powder and brown sugar, and continue to sauté for another 2 minutes without burning.
3   Add the lemon grass, salam leaves, vinegar and coconut milk. Bring to the boil.
4   Then mix in the carrots, cauliflower florets and stringbeans. Cook in the mixture until the vegetables are semi-soft, approximately 2 minutes.
5   Finally add in the cucumber, season with salt and cook for 1 minute more. Remove from the heat, let the pickles cool, then store in the refrigerator.

Acar Campur-campur
MIXED PICKLES

250 ml water
30 ml white vinegar
30 g white sugar
5 g salt
20 g bird's eye chilies, stems removed
20 g red chilies, seeded, sliced into fine strips
20 g green chilies, seeded
180 g cucumber, skin on, seeded, cut into shapes
40 g carrot, peeled, cut into shapes
20 g onion, peeled, sliced into strips

1   Pour the water into a saucepan, add the vinegar, sugar and salt, and bring to a rapid boil.
2   Add in the remaining ingredients and boil for 1-2 minutes. Then remove from the heat and let the vegetables cool in the liquid.
3   When cool, refrigerate the pickles. The liquid could be drained off if the pickles are to be used as a garnish.

Acar Kol dengan Tauge
CABBAGE AND BEANSPROUT PICKLES

500 ml water
30 g white sugar
5 g salt
30 ml white vinegar
1 lemon grass stalk, crushed
2 pandanus leaves, or ¼ teaspoon pandan essence
120 g white cabbage, shredded
120 g beansprouts, cleaned
60 g carrot, peeled, cut into fine strips
20 g red chilies, seeded, finely diced

1   Pour the water into a saucepan. Add the sugar, salt, vinegar, lemon grass and pandanus leaves and bring to the boil. Let it boil until the liquid is reduced by half.
2   Remove from the heat and strain the liquid into another saucepan. Discard the lemon grass and pandanus leaf.
3   Bring the strained liquid back to the boil and add in the remaining ingredients. Let them boil for 1-2 minutes.
4   Remove the pan from the heat and let the vegetables cool in the liquid.
5   When cool, refrigerate the pickles. The liquid could be drained off if the pickles are to be used as a garnish.

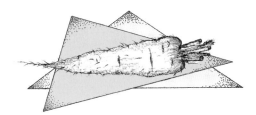

Dabu-dabu Lilang
CHILI TOMATO PICKLES

This is a very fiery garnish for meat dishes.

100 g ripe tomatoes, peeled, seeded, diced
40 g red chilies, sliced
20 g bird's eye chilies, sliced
40 g shallots, peeled, sliced
5 ml white vinegar
10 ml freshly squeezed lime juice

1   Combine all the ingredients in a bowl and mix well.
2   Let the vegetables marinate for at least 20 minutes before using.

NOTE: This garnish is particularly fierce as it uses unseeded chilies. If you want it to be milder, remove the seeds before slicing the chilies.

Acar Bawang Merah
PICKLED SHALLOTS

300 g shallots (bawang merah), peeled
375 ml water
60 ml white vinegar
15 g salt

1   Place the whole shallots in a bowl.
2   In a saucepan, combine the water, vinegar and salt. Boil for 5 minutes, then pour the boiling liquid over the shallots.
3   Let the mixture cool before putting it in a refrigerator. The shallots should be allowed to soak in the liquid for a minimum of 2 hours. Drain off the liquid if using as a garnish.

Acar Belimbing Wuluh
PICKLED SOUR FINGER CARAMBOLAS

140 g sour finger carambolas, sliced
30 g red chilies, seeded, cut into strips
30 g shallots (bawang merah), peeled, cut into strips
10 g dill
375 ml water
45 ml white vinegar
15 g salt
30 g white sugar

1   Put the sour finger carambolas, chilies, shallots and dill in a bowl.
2   In a saucepan, combine the water, vinegar, salt and sugar. Bring the mixture to the boil and let it boil for 5 minutes, then pour over the vegetables.
3   Let the vegetables soak in the liquid for at least 2 hours. Then drain off the liquid and serve the vegetables as a garnish.

DESSERTS, SHERBETS AND SYRUPS

DESSERTS

Martabak Manis dan Kacang Merah
PANCAKE WITH RED KIDNEY BEANS

This is a very popular dessert throughout Indonesia.

300 g flour
300 ml water
75 g white sugar
10 g baking soda
10 g yeast powder
salt
3 egg whites, whisked until stiff
30 ml peanut oil
50 g unsalted peanuts, fried, ground
20 g chocolate vermicelli or finely chopped dark chocolate
60 ml condensed milk
250 ml Avocado Syrup (see page 143)
100 g red kidney beans, soaked overnight, boiled until soft — about 1 hour
2 avocados, cut into sections

1   Combine the flour, water, 25 g of the sugar, baking soda, yeast and salt in a bowl. Stir vigorously with a whisk until a smooth batter results.
2   Strain this pancake batter through a fine sieve into another bowl.
3   Use a whisk to mix in the stiffly beaten egg whites, then let the mixture rest for 25 minutes.
4   Grease a cast-iron pan or heavy omelette pan, preferably teflon, about 30 cm in diameter and 3-4 cm in depth with the peanut oil, and heat it.
5   Pour half of the batter into the hot pan, cover with a lid and cook for approximately 15 minutes over low heat.
6   Take off the lid and sprinkle half the ground peanuts, chocolate vermicelli, condensed milk and half the remaining sugar on top of the pancake. Then loosen the edges with a spatula and fold the pancake in half.
7   Remove this 'D' shaped pancake from the pan, put it on a cutting board and cut it into triangles.
8   Arrange 2 triangles on each plate. Serve hot with the Avocado Syrup and sprinkle with the kidney beans, avocado sections and chopped peanuts.
9   Repeat this process with the other half of the batter.

NOTE: If you do not have a pan of the recommended size, just make more pancakes, but be sure to pour the batter 1 cm thick into the pan since it has to be baked very slowly. Also, if your pan is made of aluminium or a very thin material, decrease the temperature more.

Es Kopi dengan Jambu Biji
COFFEE PARFAIT WITH GUAVA COMPOTE

STEP 1: Coffee Parfait
4 egg yolks
100 g white sugar
15 g Java coffee powder
125 ml boiling water
90 ml liquid whipping cream
250 ml whipping cream, whipped until stiff

1   Cream the egg yolks with the sugar in a mixing bowl.
2   In a smaller bowl, dissolve the coffee powder in the boiling water. Pour this into the bowl with the creamed egg yolks, and stir in the liquid whipping cream. Mix well.
3   Pour this mixture into a saucepan and slowly bring to the boil over low heat for 2-3 minutes, stirring constantly with a whisk.
4   Dip a wooden spoon into the hot mixture and pull it out. If the mixture coats the wooden spoon lightly, it is cooked enough. Remove immediately from the heat.
5   Strain the mixture through a fine sieve into a bowl. Let it cool completely.
6   Carefully fold in the stiffly whipped cream with a whisk or wooden spoon. Then pour this mixture into a 750-1000 ml mould or 4 individual moulds. Freeze until solid.

NOTE: If Java coffee is not available, use any other strong coffee.

STEP 2: Guava Compote
500 ml water
250 g white sugar
30 ml freshly squeezed lime juice
1 x 5 g stick cinnamon
250 g ripe guavas, peeled, seeded, cut into 8-10 sections

1   Pour the water into a stockpot and bring it to the boil. Add in the sugar, lime juice and cinnamon. Boil for 5 minutes.
2   Add the guava pieces and reduce the heat. Simmer for 5-8 minutes.
3   Remove the pot from the heat and let the guavas cool in the syrup.
4   Pour the mixture into a bowl and refrigerate.

STEP 3: Presentation
roasted coffee beans
mint sprigs
mango pieces
1 guava, quartered

1   Remove the parfait from the mould.
2   Garnish with the coffee beans, mint sprigs, mango and guava, and serve with the guava compote made in Step 2.

Srikaya Palembang

PALEMBANG COCONUT MOUSSE

6 eggs
50 g white sugar
100 g coconut cream
400 ml warm water
50 g brown sugar (gula Jawa)
180 ml Coconut Syrup (see page 142)
watermelon
4 pandanus leaves

1 Break the eggs into a bowl, add in the white sugar and stir vigorously with a whisk until the mixture becomes creamy but not foamy. Set this aside.
2 Prepare the coconut milk by whisking the coconut cream with the warm water in a bowl.
3 Pour the coconut milk into a saucepan and add in the brown sugar. Heat this for approximately 2-3 minutes, but do not let it boil or bubble.
4 Remove the pan from the heat and strain the coconut milk through a fine sieve into a bowl. Blend in the egg and sugar mixture with a whisk. Stir well.
5 Preheat the oven to 150°C.
6 Pour the mixture into small coffee cups or individual soufflé moulds. Set the cups in a shallow pan, pour hot water into the pan to reach half-way up the cups.
7 Place the pan in the preheated oven and poach gently for 40-50 minutes. Check occasionally that the water in the pan does not boil. If the water starts boiling, reduce the heat immediately and add some cold water to stop the bubbling.
8 Remove the cups or moulds from the pan and let them cool before removing the mousse.
9 Decorate with the Coconut Syrup, watermelon and pandanus leaves.

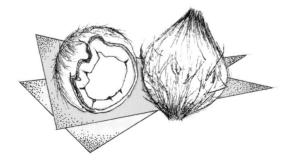

Lapis Pepe Buah Segar

RICE FLOUR LAYERS WITH FRUITS

Steamed rice flour cakes or rice cakes are popular in many parts of Indonesia. This particular layer cake will go well with any of the tropical fruit syrups given in this chapter.

125 g coconut cream
450 ml warm water
150 g rice flour
150 g white sugar
60 g brown sugar (gula Jawa)
½ teaspoon pandanus leaf juice or pandan essence
250 ml Soursop Syrup (see page 143)
120 g ripe papaya flesh, cubed or sliced
120 g ripe mango flesh, cubed or sliced
120 g mangosteen sections
8 pandanus leaves

1 Prepare the coconut milk by whisking together the coconut cream with the warm water.
2 In another bowl, combine the rice flour, coconut milk and white sugar. Stir vigorously with a whisk until it becomes a smooth mixture.
3 Divide this mixture into 3 even parts and place each portion in a bowl of its own.
4 Use a wooden spoon to mix the brown sugar into 1 portion of the mixture. Colour the second portion green with the pandanus juice. Leave the third portion uncoloured.
5 Pour the plain (uncoloured) mixture into a 800-ml rectangular or round cake mould.
6 Set the mould in a steamer or rice cooker and steam the mixture for approximately 5 minutes. Remove the mould from the steamer and let it cool for 2-3 minutes.
7 Pour the green-coloured mixture on top of the uncoloured one and return the mould to the steamer. Steam this for about 5 minutes, then let it cool.
8 Now pour the brown mixture on top and steam the cake for 25-30 minutes. Remove the mould from the steamer.
9 Let the cake cool completely, then put it in the refrigerator for at least 2 hours.
10 Remove the cake from the mould and cut it into portions.
11 Pour the Soursop Syrup next to the cake and decorate with the fruits and pandanus leaves.

NOTE: If pandanus leaf juice is not available, use any other green colouring agent. To make cakes with 6 thinner layers, cook the first 5 layers for 5 minutes each, then the last layer need only be cooked for 15 minutes.

PANCAKE WITH RED KIDNEY BEANS

COFFEE PARFAIT WITH GUAVA COMPOTE

PALEMBANG COCONUT MOUSSE

PAPAYA COCONUT PUDDING

RICE FLOUR LAYERS WITH FRUITS

BLACK AND WHITE CAKE

Kue Hitam Manis

BLACK AND WHITE CAKE

Grapes are grown in Indonesia in the northern part of Bali, around the city of Singaraja. This recipe combines a coconut pudding with a grape topping.

STEP 1: Coconut Pudding
150 g coconut cream
500 ml warm water
25 g cornflour
100 g white sugar
60 g grated coconut

1 Prepare the coconut milk by whisking together the coconut cream with the warm water. Put this in the fridge to cool.
2 Mix 60 ml of the cold coconut milk with the cornflour. Set this aside.
3 Pour the remaining coconut milk into a saucepan and add the sugar. Bring this to the boil.
4 Add in the grated coconut, reduce the heat and let the mixture simmer for approximately 5 minutes. Stir constantly with a whisk.
5 Gradually stir in the coconut-cornflour mixture, and continue simmering until the mixture starts to bind and get thick. Then remove the pan from the heat.
6 Line a tray with a piece of waxed or parchment paper and set a cake ring of about 14 cm in diameter and 4 cm in depth on top.
7 Pour the coconut mixture into the ring and let it cool at room temperature while making the topping for the cake.

STEP 2: Cake Topping and Presentation
100 ml water
15 g white sugar
150 g black grapes, peeled, seeded
15 g gelatine powder
180 ml Coconut Syrup or Kolak Sauce (see page 142, 143)
120 g grapes, peeled, quartered

1 Pour the water into a saucepan and bring to the boil. Add in the sugar and black grapes and boil for 2-3 minutes. Then pour this mixture into a blender and purée for 1-2 minutes.
2 Remove the grape purée from the blender and strain through a fine sieve or cheesecloth into a bowl.
3 Stir the gelatine powder into the strained liquid with a whisk and leave it to cool.
4 As soon as the liquid starts to thicken, pour it on top of the cake and spread it evenly over the cake's surface. Place the cake in the fridge for approximately 2 hours.
5 When set, remove the cake from the fridge and take off the cake ring.
6 Slice up the cake evenly and arrange the slices on serving plates.
7 Decorate with the Coconut Syrup or Kolak Sauce and grape quarters.

Poding Kelapa Lapis Pepaya

PAPAYA COCONUT PUDDING

STEP 1: Papaya Coconut Pudding
150 g coconut cream
500 ml warm water
200 g ripe papaya, peeled, seeded, sliced paper thin
30 g cornflour
60 g white sugar
50 g grated coconut

1 In a bowl, prepare the coconut milk by whisking the coconut cream with the warm water. Cool it in the refrigerator.
2 Line a rectangular 500-ml mould with the papaya slices so that the ends of the slices hang over the rim of the mould by 2-3 cm on each side.
3 Mix the cornflour with 100 ml of the cold coconut milk and set aside.
4 Pour the remaining coconut milk into a saucepan and bring it to the boil. Add in the sugar and grated coconut. Reduce the heat and let the mixture simmer for approximately 5 minutes, stirring constantly with a wooden spoon.
5 Add the coconut-cornflour mixture to the saucepan and continue to simmer for another 2 minutes.
6 Remove the pan from the heat and let the mixture cool for 2-3 minutes before pouring it into the papaya-lined mould.
7 Fold the overhanging papaya slices over the mixture and let it cool completely before placing the mould in a refrigerator for approximately 4 hours.
8 When set, remove the pudding from the mould and slice evenly.

STEP 2: Presentation
180 ml Pineapple Syrup (see page 142)
100 g ripe papaya flesh, scooped out with a melon baller
100 g young coconut meat, cut into strips

1 Pour some of the syrup on each plate.
2 Set 2-4 slices of the pudding on the syrup.
3 Garnish with the papaya and the fresh coconut strips rolled into balls.

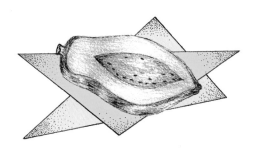

Cendole dengan Es Krim Nangka

JACKFRUIT CENDOLE

Avocado, Banana, Coconut Syrup or Kolak Sauce can be used to accompany this dessert as alternatives to the Jackfruit Syrup suggested, and the jackfruit in the batter can be replaced by young coconut or pineapple.

80 g coconut cream
250 ml warm water
100 g flour
90 ml milk
120 g brown sugar (gula Jawa)
1 egg
120 g jackfruit flesh, diced
peanut oil for frying
500 ml Jackfruit Sherbet (see page 138)
180 ml Jackfruit Syrup (see page 142)

1   Prepare the coconut milk by whisking together the coconut cream and warm water.
2   Combine this coconut milk with the flour, milk and brown sugar in a bowl. Blend in the egg and stir the mixture vigorously to form a smooth batter.
3   Strain the batter through a fine sieve.
4   Use a wooden spoon to mix in the diced jackfruit.
5   Grease a small teflon or omelette pan (approximately 10-12 cm in diameter) with a little peanut oil. Heat it.
6   Fry pancakes, using 60 ml of the batter at one time, for approximately 1-2 minutes on each side. The mixture will make around 8-9 pancakes.
7   Remove the pancakes from the pan and let them cool.
8   Place 2-3 pancakes on each plate. Spoon on some Jackfruit Sherbet and decorate with the syrup and pieces of fruit.

Sri Rasa Ketan

RICE CAKE

250 g glutinous white rice
80 g coconut cream
250 ml warm water
50 g white sugar
250 ml water
50 ml pandanus leaf juice or 15 ml pandan essence
180 ml Banana Syrup (see page 143)
4 small sweet bananas, peeled
8 pandanus leaves
watermelon pieces

1   Soak the glutinous white rice for 4 hours in plenty of cold water. Drain off the water and wash the rice with fresh cold water 2-3 times, until the water becomes clear. Drain off all excess water.
2   Prepare the coconut milk by whisking together the coconut cream and warm water.

3   Combine the washed rice, sugar, coconut milk, water and pandanus leaf juice in a saucepan. Bring this mixture to the boil, constantly stirring with a wooden spoon; then reduce the heat and simmer for approximately 30 minutes.
4   Place a cake ring approximately 14 cm in diameter in a rice steamer. Pour half of the rice mixture into the ring, cover the steamer with a lid and steam for 25-30 minutes.
5   Remove the rice cake from the ring, set it aside on a plate and repeat the steaming procedure for the remaining half of the mixture.
6   After the steamed rice cakes have cooled, cut them into wedges. Place pieces on each plate and decorate with the Banana Syrup, bananas, pandanus leaves and watermelon.

Apel Malang

POACHED APPLE ON SAPODILLA SYRUP

1.5 litres water
250 g sugar
2 x 5 g sticks cinnamon
10 cloves
45 ml freshly squeezed lime juice
4 medium-sized apples, washed
250 ml Sapodilla Syrup (see page 142)
lime leaves
4 sapodillas, peeled, seeded, cut into sections

1   Pour the water into a stockpot. Add in the sugar, cinnamon sticks, cloves and lime juice. Bring to the boil.
2   Add apples and reduce the heat. Let the apples simmer in the mixture for 8-10 minutes.
3   Remove the pot from the heat and pour the contents into a bowl. Let the apples cool completely in the syrup.
4   When cool, remove the apples from the syrup and, using a sharp, pointed knife, make 12 downward incisions from the top in the skin of each apple. Peel alternate sections of the skin from top to bottom, but leave a part of the skin on when you reach the bottom. (See picture.)
5   Spread a layer of the Sapodilla Syrup on each plate.
6   Place the poached apple in the middle of the sauce and garnish with the lime leaves and sapodilla.

NOTE: If time permits, leave the apples in the syrup overnight in a refrigerator. This will allow the apples to absorb fully the syrup.

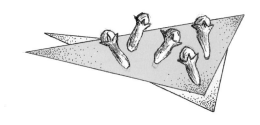

POACHED APPLE ON SAPODILLA SYRUP

JACKFRUIT CENDOLE

RICE CAKE

STARFRUIT SHERBET WITH CINNAMON

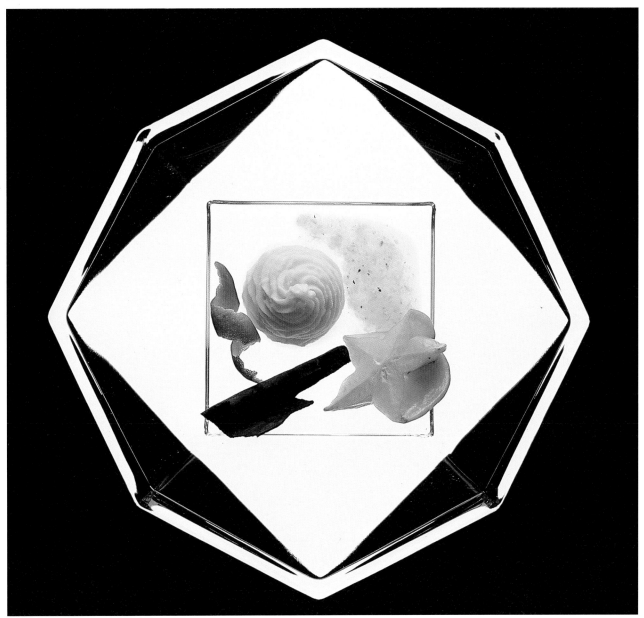

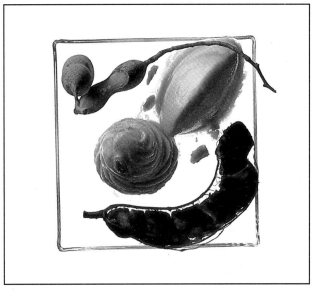

JACKFRUIT SHERBET

TAMARIND SHERBET

SHERBETS

If you do not have an electric ice cream machine to freeze your sherbets, follow the procedure below:

1. Place the mixture in a large bowl and put it in a freezer.
2. After 30-40 minutes, a layer of ice will form. Using a balloon whisk or an electric hand-mixer, whisk the mixture vigorously. Return the mixture to the freezer.
3. Repeat this process until the sherbet is frozen into a smooth mass. (The more you whisk, the smoother your sherbet will become.)

Obviously this process will take a longer time than if you have an electric ice cream machine handy. The results will also depend on how low (degrees below 0°C) the temperature of your freezer is set.

It should be noted that the freezing time given in these recipes are in accordance with our own electric ice cream machine. Depending on the make of the machine, the freezing time can range from 10-50 minutes, using the same quantity stated in the recipe. Therefore, you will have to make adjustments according to your own machine.

Es Krim Belimbing Manis
STARFRUIT SHERBET WITH CINNAMON

350 ml water
300 g starfruits, diced
75 g white sugar
1 x 5 g stick cinnamon
200 ml sugar syrup (see page 23)
30 ml freshly squeezed lime juice
½ egg white, lightly whisked

1. Bring the water to the boil in a saucepan.
2. Add in the next 3 ingredients and boil for 8-10 minutes.
3. Drain off all the liquid and discard the cinnamon stick.
4. Purée the starfruit in a blender for 2-3 minutes. Remove from the blender and strain this through a fine sieve into a bowl. Leave it to cool. This gives 300 g of starfruit purée.
5. Combine the starfruit purée, sugar syrup and lime juice in a bowl. Stir in the egg white with a whisk.
6. Put the mixture in an electric ice cream machine and freeze for approximately 20-25 minutes.

Es Krim Nangka
JACKFRUIT SHERBET

250 ml water
250 g jackfruit flesh, diced
150 g white sugar
15 ml freshly squeezed lime juice
1 pandanus leaf
½ egg white, lightly whisked

1. Bring the water to the boil in a saucepan.
2. Add in the jackfruit, sugar, lime juice and pandanus leaf. Reduce the heat and let the mixture simmer for 8-10 minutes.
3. Remove the pan from the heat and discard the pandanus leaf.
4. Pour the mixture into a blender and purée for 3-4 minutes. Then pour the mixture into a bowl to cool.
5. Mix in the egg white with a whisk.
6. Put the mixture in an electric ice cream machine and freeze for 15-20 minutes.

Es Krim Asam Jawa
TAMARIND SHERBET

This sherbet may be served between courses as a palate refresher, but decrease the amount of white sugar by half and serve only 30-40 ml per person.

550 ml water
300 g tamarind pulp
160 g white sugar
80 g brown sugar (gula Jawa)
½ egg white, lightly whisked

1. Prepare the tamarind juice by boiling 300 ml of the water with the tamarind pulp for about 10 minutes. Strain this through a fine sieve.
2. Combine the resulting tamarind juice with the remaining water in a saucepan. Add the sugar and boil for 5 minutes.
3. Remove from the heat and let the mixture cool.
4. When cool use a whisk to mix in the egg white.
5. Put this mixture in an electric ice cream machine and freeze for approximately 20 minutes.

Es Krim Kelapa Muda
YOUNG COCONUT SHERBET

300 g young coconut meat, diced
200 ml coconut milk (see page 22)
150 g white sugar
½ egg white, lightly whisked

1. Combine the coconut meat, coconut milk and sugar in a blender. Purée for 2-3 minutes, then pour the mixture into a bowl.
2. Mix in the egg white with a whisk.
3. Put the mixture in an electric ice cream machine and freeze for 20-25 minutes.

Es Krim Ketan Hitam

BLACK RICE SHERBET

A Coconut Syrup or Kolak Sauce will go well with this sherbet.

70 g black glutinous rice
475 ml water
60 ml rice wine
50 g white sugar
1 egg white, lightly whisked

1 Wash the black rice several times in plenty of cold water until the water becomes clear. Then soak the rice in fresh cold water for 12 hours.
2 Drain off all liquid from the rice, then bring 325 ml of water to the boil in a saucepan.
3 Add in the drained, washed rice and cook for approximately 20-25 minutes. Remove from the heat and let the rice cool in its liquid.
4 In another saucepan, bring the remaining 150 ml of water to the boil.
5 Add the rice wine and sugar, and let this syrup boil for approximately 5 minutes. Remove the pan from the heat and let it cool.
6 Pour the cooled syrup into a blender and add in the cooked black rice together with its liquid. Purée this for 2-3 minutes.
7 Remove the mixture from the blender and strain through a sieve into a bowl.
8 Mix in the egg white with a whisk.
9 Put the mixture in an electric ice cream machine and freeze for 15-20 minutes.

NOTE: Any rice wine may be used in making this sherbet but, if possible, choose a brown-coloured one.

Es Krim Brem Bali dengan Cengkeh

BALINESE RICE WINE SHERBET

125 ml water
150 g white sugar
325 ml rice wine
15 ml freshly squeezed lime juice
5 g whole cloves
½ egg white, lightly whisked

1 Bring the water to the boil in a saucepan.
2 Add in the sugar, rice wine, lime juice and cloves. Reduce the heat and simmer for approximately 8-10 minutes.
3 Remove the pan from the heat, discard the cloves and let the mixture cool.
4 When cool mix in the egg white with a whisk
5 Put the mixture in an electric ice cream machine and freeze for 15-20 minutes.

Es Krim Lada Hijau

GREEN PEPPERCORN SHERBET

This sherbet may also be served as a palate refresher between courses, but the quantity of sugar used in making the syrup must be decreased — only 250 g sugar to 500 ml water.

250 ml water
45 ml freshly squeezed lime juice
50 g whole green peppercorns
salt
600 ml sugar syrup (see page 23)
½ egg white, lightly whisked

1 Bring the water to the boil in a saucepan.
2 Add in 15 ml of the lime juice, all the peppercorns and the salt. Reduce the heat and simmer the mixture for 5 minutes.
3 Drain off all the liquid from the saucepan and set aside 15 g of the boiled green peppercorns.
4 In a blender, combine the remaining peppercorns, sugar syrup and the rest of the lime juice. Purée for 2-3 minutes.
5 Pour the mixture into a bowl and mix in the egg white with a whisk. Stir in the whole peppercorns.
6 Put the mixture in an electric ice cream machine and freeze for approximately 15-20 minutes.

Es Krim Durian

DURIAN SHERBET

375 ml water
200 g white sugar
280 ml coconut cream
1 pandanus leaf
400 g durian flesh
1 egg white, lightly whisked

1 Bring the water to the boil in a saucepan.
2 Add in the sugar, coconut cream, pandanus leaf and durian flesh. Reduce the heat and let this mixture simmer for approximately 10 minutes.
3 Remove the pan from the heat and discard the pandanus leaf.
4 Pour the mixture into a blender and purée at high speed for 2-3 minutes.
5 Remove from the blender and pour the mixture into a bowl to cool.
6 When cool, mix in the egg white with a whisk.
7 Put the mixture in an electric ice cream machine and freeze for approximately 15-20 minutes.

GUAVA SHERBET

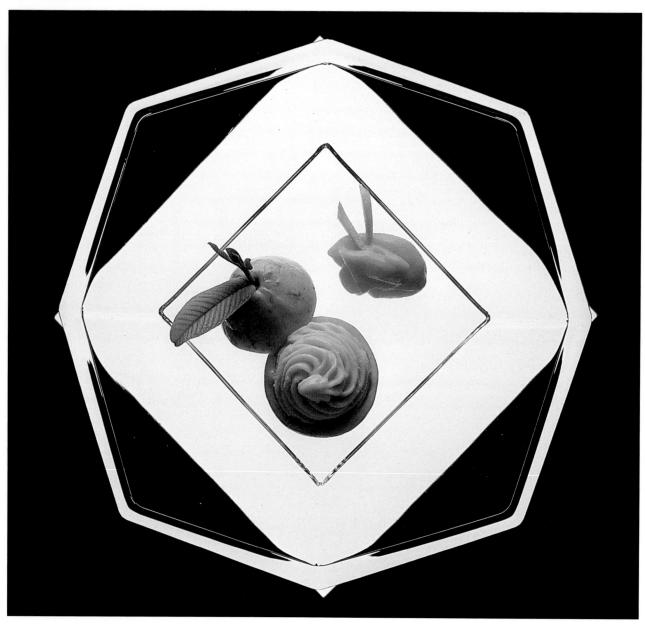

Es Krim Jambu Biji

GUAVA SHERBET

150 ml water
150 g white sugar
15 ml freshly squeezed lime juice
250 g guava, peeled, seeded, diced
½ egg white, lightly whisked

1 Bring the water to the boil in a saucepan.
2 Add in the sugar, lime juice and guava, and boil for 12-15 minutes.
3 Pour the mixture into a blender and purée for 3-4 minutes. Then remove from the blender and pour into a bowl to cool.
4 When cool mix in the egg white with a whisk.
5 Put the mixture in an electric ice cream machine and freeze for approximately 20-25 minutes.

DURIAN SHERBET

SOURSOP SHERBET

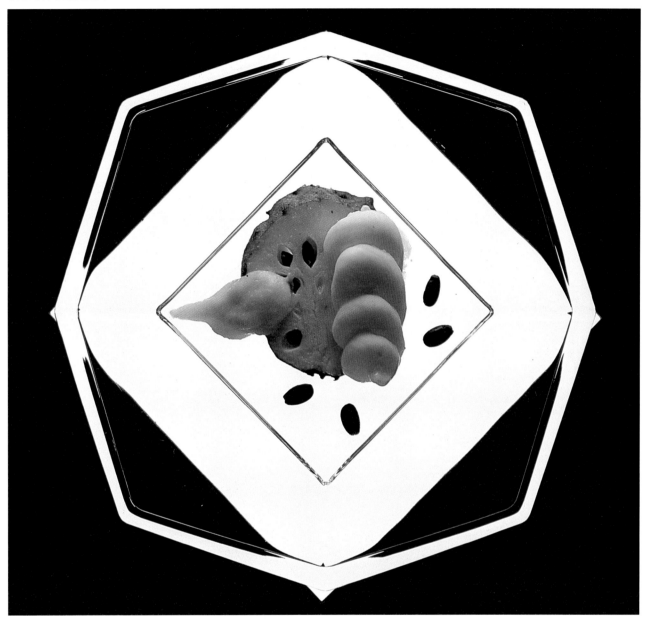

Es Krim Sirsak

SOURSOP SHERBET

400 g soursop, peeled, seeded
250 ml sugar syrup (see page 23)
15 ml freshly squeezed lime juice
½ egg white, lightly whisked

1 Combine the soursop, sugar syrup and lime juice in a blender, and purée for 2-3 minutes. Then pour the mixture into a bowl.
2 Mix in the egg white with a whisk.
3 Put the mixture in an electric ice cream machine and freeze for approximately 20 minutes.

SAPODILLA SHERBET

Es Krim Sawo

SAPODILLA SHERBET

400 g sapodilla, peeled, seeded, diced
300 ml sugar syrup (see page 23)
30 ml freshly squeezed lime juice
½ egg white, lightly whisked

1   Combine the sapodilla, sugar syrup and lime juice in a blender, and purée for 2-3 minutes. Then pour the mixture into a bowl.
2   Mix in the egg white with a whisk.
3   Put the mixture in an electric ice cream machine and freeze for approximately 20-25 minutes.

Es Krim Teh Parahiyangan

BLACK TEA SHERBET

This sherbet is also good when served between courses as a palate refresher. However, decrease the quantity of sugar to 80 g only and serve a small amount of sherbet per person.

500 ml water
10 g black Java tea leaves
150 g brown sugar (gula Jawa)
½ egg white, lightly whisked

1   Bring the water to the boil in a saucepan.
2   Add in the tea leaves and brown sugar. Boil rapidly for 3-5 minutes.
3   Remove from the heat, then strain the liquid through a fine sieve into a bowl and discard the tea leaves. Let the liquid cool.
4   Mix the egg white into the cooled liquid with a whisk.
5   Put the mixture in an electric ice cream machine and freeze for 20-25 minutes.

Es Krim Klengkeng

LYCHEE SHERBET

500 ml water
150 g white sugar
300 g lychees, peeled, seeded, diced
½ egg white, lightly whisked

1   Combine the water and sugar in a saucepan and boil for 5 minutes. Remove the pan from the heat and let the syrup cool.
2   Combine the syrup and lychees in a blender. Purée for 2-3 minutes, then pour this into a bowl.
3   Mix in the egg white with a whisk.
4   Put the mixture in an electric ice cream machine and freeze for 10-15 minutes.

Sirop Nanas

PINEAPPLE SYRUP

250 ml water
100 g white sugar
200 g ripe pineapple, peeled, diced
1 x 5 g stick cinnamon
10 medium-sized cloves
15 ml freshly squeezed lime juice

1   Bring the water to the boil in a saucepan.
2   Add in the other ingredients, then reduce the heat and let the mixture simmer for 10-12 minutes.
3   Remove from the heat and discard the cinnamon stick and cloves.
4   Pour the mixture into a blender and purée at high speed for 2-3 minutes. Let the syrup cool completely before using. Yields 375 ml.

Sirop Sawo

SAPODILLA SYRUP

250 g sapodilla, peeled, seeded, diced
60 ml sugar syrup (see page 23)
30 ml freshly squeezed lime juice
120 ml water

1   Combine all the ingredients in a blender.
2   Purée at high speed for 2-3 minutes. Remove from the blender and serve. Yields 400 ml.

Sirop Kelapa

COCONUT SYRUP

200 g fresh young coconut meat
100 ml sugar syrup (see page 23)

1   Combine the ingredients in a blender.
2   Purée at high speed for 2-3 minutes until velvety. Remove fom the blender and serve. Yields 250 ml.

Sirop Nangka

JACKFRUIT SYRUP

375 ml water
150 g jackfruit flesh, peeled, segments diced
1 x 5 g stick cinnamon
50 g white sugar

1   Bring the water to the boil in a saucepan.
2   Stir in the other ingredients, then reduce the heat and let the mixture simmer for 8-10 minutes.
3   Remove from the heat and discard the cinnamon.
4   Pour the mixture into a blender and purée at high speed for 2-3 minutes. Remove from the blender and serve. Yields 500 ml.

Saus Kayu Manis

CINNAMON SABAYON

This should be used either as a topping or a glaze.

5 egg yolks
140 g white sugar
3 g cinnamon powder
3 g ginger, finely diced
30 ml rice wine

1   Combine all the ingredients in a heat-resistant bowl.
2   Place the bowl in a hot water bath, making sure the water does not boil. Then beat the mixture in the bowl vigorously with a balloon whisk until it becomes creamy, approximately 2-3 minutes.
3   Remove from the hot water bath and continue stirring with the whisk until the mixture is cool, another 2-3 minutes. Use immediately. Yields 375 ml.

Sirop Pisang

BANANA SYRUP

It is best to prepare this syrup just before using it as bananas discolour very easily.

250 g ripe bananas, peeled, diced
60 ml sugar syrup (see page 23)
15 ml freshly squeezed lime juice

1   Combine all the ingredients in a blender.
2   Purée at high speed for 2-3 minutes. Remove from the blender and serve. Yields 250 ml.

Saus Kolak

KOLAK SAUCE

This is a very versatile sauce that can be served with many different hot or cold desserts, particularly those which contain bananas.

375 ml water
150 g brown sugar (gula Jawa)
15 g ginger, finely diced
5 g cornflour, dissolved in 15 ml cold water

1   Pour the water into a saucepan and bring it to the boil.
2   Add in all the other ingredients, reduce the heat and let the mixture simmer for approximately 8-10 minutes.
3   Remove the pan from the heat and strain the sauce through a fine sieve. Use hot or cold as desired. Yields 375 ml.

Sirop Sirsak

SOURSOP SYRUP

250 g soursop, peeled, seeded, diced
150 ml sugar syrup (see page 23)
15 ml freshly squeezed lime juice
60 ml water

1   Combine all the ingredients in a blender.
2   Purée the mixture at high speed for 2-3 minutes. Remove and serve. Yields 375 ml.

Sirop Apokat

AVOCADO SYRUP

This syrup should only be prepared shortly before serving since the avocado flesh turns brown very fast.

250 g avocado flesh, peeled, seeded, diced
90 ml sugar syrup (see page 23)
60 ml condensed milk
15 ml freshly squeezed lime juice
185 ml water

1   Combine all the ingredients in a blender and purée, at high speed, for 2-3 minutes.
2   Remove from the blender and serve. Yields 400 ml.

Sirop Melon

GREEN MELON SYRUP

250 g green melon flesh, peeled, seeded, diced
100 g icing sugar

1   Combine the ingredients in a blender. Purée for 2-3 minutes.
2   Remove from the blender and serve. Yields 250 ml.

Sirop Jambu Biji

GUAVA SYRUP

90 ml water
200 g ripe guavas, peeled, seeded, diced
100 g white sugar
120 ml canned guava juice
15 ml freshly squeezed lime juice

1   Bring the water to the boil in a saucepan.
2   Add the remaining ingredients, reduce the heat and allow to simmer for 10-12 minutes.
3   Remove the pan from the heat and pour the mixture into a blender. Purée at high speed for 2-3 minutes.
4   Remove the mixture from the blender and strain through a very fine sieve into a bowl. Let the syrup cool completely before using. Yields 400 ml.

GLOSSARY

GLOSSARY

In this section we have provided information on any ingredients used in the book which we feel might be unfamiliar to some readers. They are entered under their English name, followed by the Indonesian in brackets. In a few instances where there is no English translation, the entries are headed by the Indonesian word. The scientific name, where applicable, is given at the end of the entry.

ANISE (*jintan manis*). This aromatic seed may be used to flavour liquors and sweets. It is said that anise was known in Java before A.D. 1200 although it is not certain whether it was indigenous or had come from India. (*Pimpinella anisum*)

ASPARAGUS BEAN (*kecipir*). A winged bean with a very mild asparagus flavour, it is eaten raw when marinated or cooked as a vegetable. (*Psophocarpus tetragonolobus*)

AUBERGINE (*terung*). Also known as eggplant, this fruit vegetable is native to Southeast Asia. The larger variety has a shiny purple or white skin. The small, round variety, known as *terung engkol* in Indonesia, has a slightly bitter taste and is eaten either cooked or raw before it is ripe. When cooking aubergines, make sure that they are always firm and dry. (*Solanum melongena*)

BAMBOO SHOOT (*rebung*). The tender young ivory-white shoot of the bamboo. Crisp in texture and sweet in taste, it is mainly used in vegetable dishes and soups. Canned bamboo shoots are widely available. They should be boiled before use — 10 minutes if canned, 30 minutes if fresh. (*Bambusa*)

BASIL (*kemangi*) The local variety, *kemangi*, is milder in flavour than the basil found in Western countries. Another variety, *selasih*, grows wild in Indonesia and is more common elsewhere. Though it is used in salads, its flavour is inferior to that of *kemangi*, but whichever variety is available can be used. (*Ocimum americanum*; *O. basilicum*)

BEANCURD (*tahu*). Also known as *tofu*, this is made from soya bean milk and comes in soft, white blocks. It also can be compressed to make firmer white or yellow (coloured with turmeric) flat squares.

BEANSPROUT (*tauge*). The young sprouts of the green mung bean, these are used raw or cooked as a vegetable, in salads, in soups and in stuffings. They are easily available. (*Phaseolus aureus*)

BITTER GOURD (*peria* or *pare*). A dark green, bitter, cucumber-like vegetable with a wrinkled skin, it is usually pickled or cooked in curries when not quite ripe. Used as a vegetable, it can be cooked in the same ways as courgettes. (*Momordica charantia*)

BROWN SUGAR (*gula Jawa*). This very sweet, thick brown sugar is made from the sap of the flower of the coconut or Palmyra palm. A real home industry — every *kampung* (or village) makes *gula Jawa* — there is no large-scale commercial production, although it is sold at the markets in hard cakes. Any unrefined brown sugar may be used as a substitute.

CANDLENUT (*kemiri*). The hard nut of the candleberry tree. It has diverse uses — to this day, in remote villages, the nut is pounded with materials like cotton and copra to make candles, hence the common name "candlenut". *Kemiri* is roasted before it is used in cooking, then it is usually pounded and added as a binding agent to hot and cold sauces. When mixed with other spices and condiments, it may be eaten as a relish or used in curries. It is available in cans or sealed plastic packs in Asian food stores. The *kemiri* flavour is distinctive, but macadamia nuts or Brazil nuts may be used as substitutes if necessary. (*Aleurites moluccana*)

CARDAMOM (*kepulaga*). This grows wild in the lower hills of Java but is now widely cultivated throughout Indonesia. The oils obtained from the stems and leaves are used as flavourings, but it is the dried fruit which serves as a warm, aromatic spice. It can be purchased green, white or black — the colour depending on the drying method. Cardamom should always be used ground in order to release its oils. (*Amomum cardamomum*)

CASHEWNUT (*kacang mete* or *kacang monyet*). Native to the American tropics, the cashewnut plant was probably introduced to Southeast Asia by the Portuguese. The large, reddish cashew apple virtually hides the nut growing underneath. The ripe fruit and very young leaves are eaten raw and are much liked by the Javanese, who use the leaves as flavouring for rice. In the recipes in this book, we use the leaves cooked in vegetable dishes. (*Anacardium occidentale*)

CASSAVA (*ubi kayu*). A hardy, drought-resistant root plant seen along roadsides throughout Indonesia. The long brown tuber can be used as a vegetable, although several varieties are very bitter and are used only to make a type of flour. The young leaves resemble papaya leaves and are cooked as green vegetables. Tapioca is prepared from the starch. (*Manihot utilissima*)

CHAYOTE (*labu Siam*). A medium-sized, light green vegetable, slightly oval in shape and bearing a close resemblance to the cucumber in flavour. A soft squash may be used as a substitute. The young shoots of the plant are also eaten. (*Sechium edule*)

CHILI (*cabe*). Originally from Central America, this is now so basic to Indonesian cooking that virtually every household has several chili plants growing in the garden. Three types are commonly used: the long green chili, *cabe hijau*, which is the least hot; the long red chili, *cabe merah*, which is a bit hotter; and the bird's eye chili, or *cabe rawit*, a tiny dark green chili which is the hottest and most pungent of all. In all varieties, the seeds are the fieriest part of the chili. (*Capsicum*)

CINNAMON (*kayu manis*). The cinnamon tree is found in abundance in the mountains of Sumatra. The innermost layer of the bark is sold as thin, fragile quills used for flavouring meat, poultry and desserts. The spice is also available powdered, although the flavour and aroma disappears relatively quickly in this form. (*Cinnamomum cassia*; *C. zeylanicum*)

CLOVE (*cengkeh*). The clove tree is a native of the Maluku Islands, formerly the Moluccas or the Spice Islands. Cloves are actually the flower buds which are harvested and dried under the sun for days. The dried clove resembles a nail with a round tip and an elongated stem. Even in its powdered form, the clove retains its strong, aromatic flavour and is often used in soups and sauces. (*Eugenia aromatica*)

COCONUT (*kelapa*). One of the basics of Indonesian cooking. Coconuts at three stages of maturity are sold in Indonesian markets: *kelapa muda*, young coconut about 10 months old, has plenty of coconut water and transparent white flesh that can be scraped out with a spoon; *kelapa setengah tua* (literally middle-aged coconut) is about a year old and has firm flesh that is good for grating; and *kelapa tua*, the old nut in which most of the water has dried up and the flesh has become fibrous (this, unfortunately, is the age of most of the coconuts that reach cities in Western countries). Coconut milk, or *santan*, is made from grated coconut flesh (see page 22). When a recipe calls for grated coconut, dried grated coconut, soaked in water and then drained, may be a substitute. (*Cocos nucifera*)

CORIANDER (*ketumbar*). The seeds of this spice are used fresh, dried or powdered and one form should not be substituted for another. It is a strong spice and should be used sparingly. In Indonesia, fresh young coriander leaves are also used. (*Coriandrum sativum*)

CUMIN (*jintan putih*). The seeds are used as a spice, especially for seasoning curries, and are available both whole and in powdered form. They have a powerful aromatic flavour. Since different varieties range in strength and colour, it is wise to experiment to see which is most pleasing. (*Cuminum cuminum*)

CUP LEAF (*daun mangkok*). These leaves are traditionally used in Indonesia as platters in the same way as banana leaves. The leaves may also be boiled in vegetable dishes. (*Polyscias scutellerium*)

DILL (*adas manis*). The leaves of this herb are often used in flavouring pickles. The leaves (fresh or dried) as well as the seeds are also used in soups, fish and egg dishes and sauces. (*Anethum graveolens*)

DRIED SHRIMPS (*ebi*). Shelled, cleaned small prawns or shrimps that are subsequently steamed and sun-dried, they are widely used in soups, sauces, seafood and vegetable dishes and for making side dishes like *sambals* to accompany curries.

DURIAN. This nutritious, seasonal fruit is infamous for its strong smell. Fruits vary in size (from 20-35 cm), in texture and in flavour. All have a hard, dull greeny-yellow shell covered with sharp, pointed spines. This shell can be split open into 4-5 sections with 2-5 seeds encased in a soft, creamy pulp. The pulp is eaten raw, or used to make sherbets, ice creams, desserts, dessert sauces and candies. There are two durian seasons a year but the fruits are seldom seen in the West as they spoil easily. (*Durio zibethinus*)

FENNEL (*jintan*). This grows wild throughout the world and the leaves (fresh or dried), seeds and dried root are often used with fish. The seeds are sweet and have a licorice flavour. If not available, anise seeds make an acceptable substitute. (*Foeniculum vulgare*)

FERMENTED BEAN CAKE (*tempe*). This rather crunchy cake is made from boiled soya beans which have been pressed dry, then allowed to ferment. In Indonesian markets, *tempe* is usually available in rectangular slabs and may be fried as a snack. It is used in this book in salads and as a stuffing ingredient, as well as a garnish for soups. If *tempe* is not available, firm white beancurd is a possible substitute.

FERMENTED SOYA BEANS (*tauco*). A thick, strong, aromatic paste which is produced by fermenting either black or yellow whole soya beans. It is readily available, bottled or canned, in Asian food stores and may be labelled "Yellow Bean Sauce".

FERNTOP (*daun pakis* or *sayur paku*). The curled tip is cooked as a vegetable like fiddlehead or bracken fern, which makes a good substitute. (*Athyrium esculentum*)

GINGER (*halia*). This rhizome is native to Southeast Asia and it is available in root, powdered or pickled forms. The fresh root is used in most of the recipes in this book. (*Zingiber officinale*)

GREATER GALANGAL (*laos*). Less aromatic and pungent than lesser galangal (q.v.), it is always used fresh in Indonesia. The flowers can be used in salads. It also comes in powdered form. If not available, use ginger but double the amount. (*Languas galanga*)

GUAVA (*jambu biji*). This yellow-green fruit has a firm inner flesh filled with tiny seeds. There are many different types of guavas, but most common are the large fruits with rosy-pink or creamy-white flesh. Guavas are excellent for sherbets, ice creams and compotes. The juice has a delicate, sweet-sour taste and fragrant aroma. (*Psidium guajava*)

JACKFRUIT (*nangka*). Green in colour with thick, sharp spines, the young fruit is used mainly as a vegetable, but is eaten as a dessert when fully ripe. When ripe the pulp is yellow, with a waxy texture and very sweet taste. Its strong fragrance can overpower the scent of other ingredients. (*Artocarpus heterophyllus*)

JAVANESE PARKIA (*pete cina*). These flat pods are best eaten young as a vegetable either raw or cooked. Snowpeas may be served as a substitute. (*Leucaena glauca*)

KEDONGDONG. A small, oval-shaped green fruit with a slightly tart flavour and a fibrous round seed. The very young leaves can be eaten or cooked as a flavouring. (*Spondias cytherea*)

KENIKIR LEAF. This small leaf resembles a young carrot leaf. Kenikir has a sharp, bitter taste and is used in salads and sauces, or sometimes cooked as a vegetable. If necessary, chervil may be used as a substitute. (*Cosmos caudatus*)

ASPARAGUS BEAN

CASSAVA

AUBERGINE (TERUNG ENGKOL)

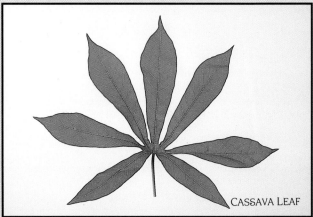

CASSAVA LEAF

BITTER GOURD

CUP LEAF

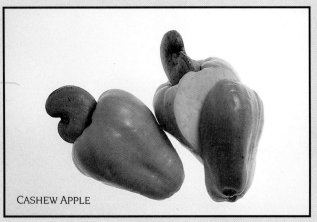

CASHEW APPLE

DURIAN

GINGER

MANGOSTEEN

GREATER GALANGAL

MACE

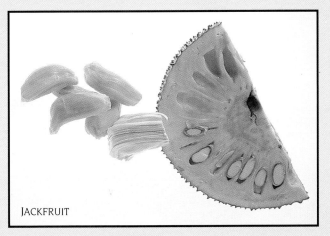

JACKFRUIT

MELINJO FRUIT

KEDONGDONG

MUSTARD GREEN

LEMON GRASS (*sereh*). This long, delightfully aromatic grass is a very popular flavouring for soups, fish, meats, sauces and curries. Fresh lemon grass stalks are now available in the United States and some countries in Europe. Although the powdered form is available, it should only be used as a substitute in the sauce recipes and the quantity should be reduced by two-thirds. (*Cymbopogon nardus*)

LESSER GALANGAL (*kencur*). This rhizome which originally came from India is used like greater galangal (q.v.), but more sparingly since it has a stronger, hotter flavour. Fresh *kencur* can be found in Asian food stores but, if it is not available fresh, the powdered form may be used instead. (*Kaempferia galanga*)

LIME. The two types of lime most commonly used in Indonesian cooking are the small, juicy lime (*jeruk nipis*) and the kaffir lime (*jeruk purut*). The latter has a dark green, wrinkled outer skin. The kaffir lime peel, which has a sharp bitter-sweet taste, is sometimes used in flavouring, and the highly acidic fruit, which does not have much juice, is used in *sambals*. The leaves are most commonly used in cooking. If no kaffir lime leaves are available, curry leaves may be used as a substitute.

LONG BEAN (*kacang panjang*). Sometimes called "the yard-long bean" because the thin pods can literally grow up to l metre in length. It is used extensively in these recipes either whole or cut in pieces. Stringbeans may be used as a substitute if necessary. (*Vigna sinensis* var. *sesquipedalis*)

MANGO (*mangga*). A pear-shaped tropical fruit with a smooth yellow or green skin. A ripe mango is sweet, its flesh creamy in texture. It is a popular dessert fruit and is also used in making sherbets, ice creams, compotes and sauces. The unripe mango is used in chutney, as well as salads; sliced and eaten raw with special sauces; or blended as a tart fruit juice. Unhappily, there is no substitute for fresh mango but it is widely available internationally nowadays. (*Mangifera indica*)

MANGOSTEEN (*manggis*). This round fruit has a smooth purple skin. It is extremely sweet with a delicate sweet-sour aftertaste when ripe. The snowy white flesh is segmented and has oval pits. Be careful when squeezing the fruit open because its thick rind contains mangostin, which stains. (*Garcinia mangostana*)

MELINJO. The small yellow or red-coloured fruit may be eaten raw, but it is not very tasty. The melinjo kernel is used to make *emping*, a flattened, thin cracker which is fried to a crisp and used as garnish for salads and soups. The leaves and young flowers are cooked and eaten like a vegetable. (*Gnetum gnemon*)

MUSHROOM. Although mushrooms grow wild on a number of the islands of Indonesia, they were not used in traditional cooking. Now there are three varieties being raised commercially in Java and Bali. They are the small, button-like straw mushroom, (*jamur*); the black Chinese mushroom (*jamur hitam*); and the oyster mushroom (*jamur tiram*).

MUSTARD GREEN (*sawi*). Popularly known by its Chinese name *caixin*, this pale green leafy plant is cooked as a vegetable. (*Brassica juncea*)

NOODLES. There are many types of Chinese noodles and they may be available either fresh or dried. Packaged dried noodles should be soaked in warm water before use to soften them. In the recipes in this book, noodles are used mainly for garnish.

Egg noodles are yellow as they are made from wheat flour and egg. Some varieties are available fresh, while others are only available dried.

Glass noodles are thin, brittle and semi-transparent. Sold dried in packets, they need not be soaked if they are to be deep-fried. When soaked they become almost transparent.

Rice noodles are thicker and whiter than glass noodles and they are the only type of noodle that is packaged wet.

NUTMEG (*pala*). The ripe fruit is oval, light yellow in colour and yields two aromatic spices: nutmeg, which is the seed inside the kernel and has a spicy sweet flavour; and mace, the red net which surrounds the kernel and has a stronger, more pungent flavour. Both are available dried or in powdered form. In Indonesia, the flesh of the fruit is traditionally candied, used in jams, cakes and tarts and as the syrup base for fruit drinks. The candied flesh may be available in packets in Asian food stores. (*Myristica fragrans*)

PALM HEART (*pondoh*). The centre of the palm tree obtained by cutting down the tree and splitting it near the base of the leaves. This is white, crunchy in texture and has a light, buttery-sweet flavour. It can be eaten raw or cooked and is used in salads and soups, as a vegetable, for garnish and as a filling for spring rolls. Available precooked in cans.

PALM NUT (*siwalan*). The sweetish, transparent, gelatinous substance extracted from the fruit of the Palmyra palm (*Borrassus flabellifer*). It is used mainly for desserts and sometimes in soups. Palm nuts can be bought in tins or jars.

PALM WINE. This is a fermented wine produced from the sap of the bruised young flower spikes of the Palmyra palm. It can be quite a potent brew and has a sweet, acid taste. A young white wine with a sweet, acid taste can be used as a substitute.

PANDANUS LEAF (*daun pandan*). This plant with long narrow leaves is commonly grown in Indonesian gardens. The leaves are used for fragrance, while the juice may be used for colouring. In Java, the leaves are sometimes used in preparing beancurd. A drop of vanilla can be used as a substitute in desserts if pandan essence is not available; in hot dishes, there is no substitute for the leaf. (*Pandanus amaryllifolius*)

PAPAYA (*pepaya*). A large, orange-fleshed fruit commonly eaten as a dessert. The green young papaya is cooked as a vegetable or pickled. (*Carica papaya*)

PEANUTS (*kacang tanah*). A highly nutritious underground legume. Vendors selling the roasted nuts are found in almost every Indonesian city and town. Peanuts are used extensively in Indonesian cooking, especially in sauces. *Oncom*, a fermented paste, is prepared from the ground nuts, and is usually eaten fried. (*Arachis hypogaea*)

PUMPKIN (*labu merah*). The local variety of the pumpkin has red flesh and a slightly rougher skin than the one found in the West. The leaves are also eaten in Indonesia. (*Cucurbita moschata*)

RAMBUTAN. A round, reddish fruit covered with soft spiny growth quite like hair (*rambut* in Indonesian), this is a seasonal dessert fruit. Its sweet, translucent white flesh bears a slight resemblance to the lychee in texture. (*Nephelium lappaceum*)

RED KIDNEY BEAN (*kacang merah*). This may vary from pink to maroon in colour. It is usually associated with another spicy cuisine as the basic ingredient of the Mexican dish, chili con carne. It has a floury texture and is fairly sweet in flavour. (*Phaseolus vulgaris*)

RICE WINE (*brem Bali*). Made from fermented boiled glutinous rice. A not-too-sweet Japanese *saki* or Chinese rice wine is an acceptable substitute.

SALAM LEAF. This tough, aromatic leaf, similar in shape and size to the bay leaf, is used to flavour soups, meat and fish dishes, as well as sauces. Bay leaf can be used as a substitute, but halve the quantity and expect a slightly different flavour. (*Eugenia polyantha*)

SAMBAL. This is usually a fragrant thick sauce or paste made with pounded chilies and other ingredients like shrimp paste, shallots and lime juice. It may be cooked or uncooked. (See page 26 for some recipes.)

SAPODILLA (*sawo* or *chiku*). A sweet, plum-sized fruit with smooth brown skin and a firm brown inner flesh. It is also known as chicle, and the sap is used as the base for making chewing gum. (*Manilkara achras*)

SHALLOT (*bawang merah*). An essential ingredient of Indonesian cooking. The local form is milder than the varieties generally found in the West. Although *bawang merah* is the ideal type to use, it can be replaced by any variety available.

SHRIMP PASTE (*terasi*). This strongly pungent paste is made from pounding shrimp heads to a pulp and then drying it in the sun. The dark, brownish-red paste is sold in round cakes or thick flat slabs in markets. It is used as a flavouring for soups, sauces, fish dishes, vegetables and *sambals*. It should be used sparingly and can last for a very long time if sealed and kept in the refrigerator or a cool dry place. *Terasi* or *belacan*, its Malay equivalent, can be bought from Asian food stores in small 20-50 g blocks.

SNAKEFRUIT (*salak*). This smallish, pear-shaped fruit of a squat, thorny palm has a brown, rough outer skin which is similar to snakeskin. The flesh is firm, starchy and rather crunchy with a sharp taste. Usually there are several segments with large brown pits. The sweetest and best *salak* are said to grow in Bali. (*Zalacca edulis*)

SOUR FINGER CARAMBOLA (*belimbing wuluh*). This light green, finger-like fruit is very sour and acid. It is used primarily in cooking soups, making sauces, as a pickle or garnish and may also be used as a vegetable. If not available, peeled and seeded gooseberries may be used as a substitute. (*Averrhoa belimbi*)

SOURSOP (*sirsak* or *durian belanda*). The long, heart-shaped fruit of a small tree. The skin is dark green with soft short spines. It usually weighs about 1 kg or more and its fragrant, white flesh is soft and juicy with tear-shaped black seeds in it. The flesh is eaten raw or can be used to make delicious drinks, sherbets, ice creams and fruit sauces. (*Annona muricata*)

SOYA BEAN (*kacang kedele*). This small yellow or black bean is an essential ingredient in several items basic to Indonesian cooking. The black bean is the basis for *kecap manis* (dark sweet soya sauce) and *kecap asin* (salty soya sauce). Soya bean milk is used to make *tahu* (beancurd). *Tauco* (fermented soya beans) is a paste made either from yellow or black soya beans, while *tempe* (fermented bean cake) is a cake made from fermented soya beans. (*Glycine soja*)

SOYA SAUCE (*kecap*). The Indonesian soya bean-based *kecap* comes in two varieties: the dark sweet *kecap manis* and the saltier *kecap asin*. The sweet *kecap manis* is used more often in this book, but both types may be found in Asian food stores. *Kecap manis* may be replaced by a sweet, dark Japanese or Chinese soya sauce, though the taste is not exactly the same. If no sweet variety is available, add a little brown sugar to the saltier soya sauce. *Kecap manis* keeps well without refrigeration.

SPINACH (*bayam*). *Bayam* is the tropical version of spinach and is widely cultivated. It has roundish, medium-sized green leaves which are cooked and eaten just like spinach. Another less common variety with reddish purple leaves is known as *bayam merah* or red spinach. Any spinach may be used as a substitute. (*Celosia argentea*)

STARFRUIT (*belimbing manis*). A sweet, yellow fruit which in cross-section looks like a five-pointed star, it is often eaten raw as a dessert and may be candied. (*Averrhoa carambola*)

SWEET POTATO (*ubi jalar* or *ubi manis*). A tuber with red, white or purple skin and white, red, orange or yellow flesh. It is eaten as a vegetable and sometimes cooked in sauces. The young leaves are also used in salads. (*Ipomoea batatas*)

TAMARIND (*asam*). The sour fruit of a large tree originally brought to Indonesia from India, it looks like the broad bean in shape but the skin is brown and very brittle. The flesh, which has tough fibres running through it, is green and very sour when immature. When ripe, the fruit turns brown and soft, but maintains its tart flavour. In Java, the pulp of the fruit is extracted and mixed with salt or sugar. The salted pulp is formed into blocks or balls and is called *asam kawak*. (*Tamarindus indica*)

TARO (*talas*). A staple food of Asia — the starchy tubers are boiled or fried, like potatoes. The huge, heart-shaped leaves must be boiled before eating. (*Colocasia esculentum*)

TORCH GINGER (*kecombrang* or *honje*). An exceptionally tall, aromatic native ginger widely cultivated for its reddish young flower shoots, which are either used raw in salads or cooked as a vegetable. (*Nicolaia elatior*)

TURMERIC (*kunyit*). A knobbly rhizome which looks rather like ginger but is bright orange beneath the rind. It is used fresh, dried or in powdered form to give a yellow colour to food. Always try to use the fresh root as the powdered form produces a slightly grainy texture. If only the powdered form is available, use half the quantity called for in the recipe. The broad, shiny leaves are also used for flavouring. (*Curcuma domestica*)

WATER APPLE (*jambu air*). This pretty, bell-shaped rosy-white fruit is very juicy and only slightly scented. It is normally eaten raw and used in salads and desserts. The similar rose apple is a slightly larger, oblong-shaped fruit with red-and-white striped skin. It is tastier than the water apple but more delicate. (*Eugenia aquea*; *E. malaccensis*)

WATER CHESTNUT. The dark-skinned corm of a wild sage, it should be peeled before being eaten, either raw or in soups. The flesh is crisp, white and slightly sweet. Available ready-peeled in cans. (*Eleocharis dulcis*)

WATER CONVOLVULUS (*kangkung*). A leafy vegetable with dark green, heart-shaped leaves and hollow stems, it grows wild or in cultivation in swampy areas of Asia. It is more delicate in flavour than the spinach of the West and is sometimes called swamp spinach. Extremely cheap, it is usually stir-fried or used raw in salads. (*Ipomoea aquatica*)

WHITE RADISH (*lobak*). There are two varieties: the white radish is preferable to the red for its milder taste. The radish and its green leaves may be used raw in salads or cooked as a vegetable, (*Raphanus sativus*)

WOOD FUNGUS (*jamur kuping*). This type of mushroom is sometimes called cloud ear fungus because it swells to a curled shape when soaked in water. Wood fungus is now extensively used in Indonesian cooking, especially in soups and vegetable dishes. It is sold in dried form and is normally greyish black in colour, but becomes brown and translucent when soaked in water. (*Auricularia polytricha*)

YAM BEAN (*bengkuang*). A sweet, starchy tuber which can be served raw in salads, but is more often cooked as a vegetable in this book. The brown outer skin should be peeled off before use; it keeps well if stored in a cool dry place. (*Pachyrrhizus bulbosus*)

PALM NUT

PANDANUS LEAF

RED SPINACH (BAYAM MERAH)

SALAM LEAF

SNAKEFRUIT

TORCH GINGER

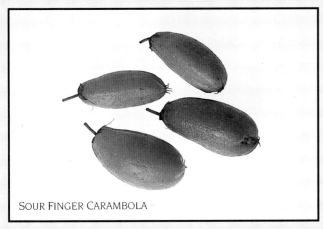

SOUR FINGER CARAMBOLA

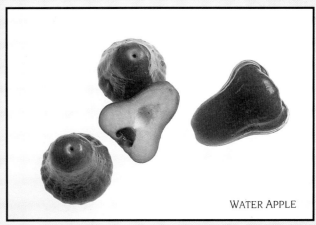

WATER APPLE

STARFRUIT

WATER CONVOLVULUS

TARO ROOT

YAM BEAN

Cooks in Indonesia do not normally weigh or measure ingredients because the practised cook goes very much by taste, sight and feeling when cooking. But for the benefit of those unfamiliar with Indonesian food and cuisine, all recipes in this book have been tested and their ingredients carefully weighed and measured. However, this does not mean that they cannot be changed; in fact, it is always a good idea to experiment, either increasing or decreasing the quantities in order to reach the desired flavour or spiciness. Tasting the food constantly during the cooking process is also most important. This book uses the metric system of measurement because it is the most accurate, but conversion charts are provided below for your reference.

GRAMS TO OUNCES	
g	*oz*
1	0353
10	.353
28	1
100	3.5
200	7
500	17.5
1000 or 1 kg	35.3 or 2.205 lb

To convert, multiply the number of grams by .0353 to get the number of ounces. Alternatively divide the gram figure by 31. The second method is easier but it will not be as accurate as the first method.

CENTIMETRES TO INCHES	
cm	*inch*
1	½
2.5	1
5	2
7.5	3
10	4
13	5
15	6
18	7
20	8
23	9
25	10
28	11
30	12

OUNCES TO GRAMS		
oz/lb	*Approx. g to nearest whole figure*	*Conversion to most convenient unit of 25 g*
1 oz	28 g	25 g
2 oz	57 g	50 g
3 oz	85 g	75 g
4 oz	113 g	125 g
5 oz	142 g	150 g
6 oz	170 g	175 g
7 oz	199 g	200 g
8 oz	226 g	250 g
9 oz	254 g	275 g
10 oz	283 g	300 g
11 oz	311 g	325 g
12 oz	340 g	350 g
13 oz	368 g	375 g
14 oz	396 g	400 g
15 oz	425 g	425 g
1 lb	453 g	500 g
1½ lb	679 g	750 g
2 lb	905 g	1 kg

LIQUID AND VOLUME MEASURES		
Metric	*Imperial*	*American*
2.5 ml	½ teaspoon	½ teaspoon
5 ml	1 teaspoon	1 teaspoon
15 ml	1 tablespoon	1 tablespoon
30 ml	2 tablespoons	2 tablespoons
45 ml	3 tablespoons	3 tablespoons
60 ml	4 tablespoons	¼ cup
75 ml	5 tablespoons	⅓ cup
90 ml	6 tablespoons	6 tablespoons
105 ml	7 tablespoons	7 tablespoons
125 ml	4 fl oz	½ cup
150 ml	¼ pint	⅔ cup
175 ml	6 fl oz	¾ cup
200 ml	⅓ pint	⅞ cup
250 ml	8 fl oz	1 cup
300 ml	½ pint	1¼ cups
350 ml	12 fl oz	1½ cups
400 ml	14 fl oz	1¾ cups
450 ml	¾ pint	2 cups
500 ml	18 fl oz	2¼ cups
600 ml	1 pint	2½ cups
750 ml	1¼ pints	3 cups
900 ml	1½ pints	3¾ cups
1 litre	1¾ pints	4¼ cups

DRY VOLUME MEASURES

In many American kitchens ingredients are measured in cups rather than by weight. The following chart is a useful reference for converting the metric measurement of dry ingredients into cups. It is based on all-purpose flour but, in fact, every dry ingredient has its own weight which is not necessarily the same as an equal volume of flour. This chart, therefore, shows only an approximation for any other dry ingredient.

All-purpose Flour

1 teaspoon	3 g
1 tablespoon	9 g
¼ cup	36 g
⅓ cup	46 g
½ cup	72 g
¾ cup	108 g
1 cup	144 g

Examples of volume (cup) conversions for other commonly used ingredients are as follows:-

Basil leaves, loosely packed, no stems	5 g	½ cup
Candlenut, ground	20 g	2 tablespoons
Chili, julienne	10 g	⅓ cup
Chili, diced	5 g	1 tablespoon
Coriander powder	2 g	½ tablespoon
	3 g	1 tablespoon
	5 g	1½ tablespoons
Coriander leaves, loosely packed	4 g	½ cup
Ginger, diced	5 g	1 tablespoon
Lemon grass, diced	5 g	1 tablespoon
Lime or lemon leaves	10 g	½ cup
Mace, dried	2 g	1 flake
Onions, diced	5 g	½ tablespoon
Peppercorns	30 g	1 tablespoon
Salam leaves, loosely packed	10 g	1 cup
Shallots, chopped	5 g	½ tablespoon
Tomato purée	10 g	1 tablespoon
Turmeric powder	2 g	½ tablespoon
	5 g	1 tablespoon

AMERICAN TERMINOLOGY

Listed below are the American equivalents for certain words used in this book.

UK/*American*
fillet/ tenderloin
prawn/ shrimp
courgette/ zucchini
spring onion/ scallion
aubergine/ eggplant
peanut/ groundnut
grill/ broil
tomato purée/ tomato paste

OVEN TEMPERATURE GUIDE

	Electricity		Gas Mark
	°C	°F	
Very cool	110	225	¼
	120	250	½
Cool	140	275	1
	150	300	2
Moderate	160	325	3
	180	350	4
Moderately hot	190	375	5
	200	400	6
Hot	220	425	7
	230	450	8
Very hot	240	475	9

TEMPERATURE CONVERSION

°C	°F	°C	°F	°C	°F
-40	-40	60	140	160	320
-34	-30	66	150	166	330
-29	-20	71	160	171	340
-23	-10	77	170	177	350
-18	0	82	180	182	360
-12	10	88	190	188	370
-6	20	93	200	193	380
-1	30	99	210	199	390
0	32	100	212	204	400
4	40	104	220	210	410
10	50	110	230	216	420
16	60	116	240	221	430
21	70	121	250	227	440
27	80	127	260	232	450
32	90	132	270	238	460
38	100	137	280	243	470
43	110	143	290	249	480
49	120	149	300	254	490
54	130	154	310	260	500

SPOON MEASURES: All spoon measures given in this book are level.

PINTS: The British and Australian pint is 20 fluid ounces as opposed to the American pint which is 16 fluid ounces.

NOTES FOR AUSTRALIAN USERS: In Australia the American 8-oz measuring cup is used in conjunction with the imperial pint of 20 fluid ounces. It is important to remember that the Australian tablespoon differs from both the British and American tablespoons. The British standard tablespoon holds 17.7 millilitres, the American 14.2 millilitres, and the Australian 20 millilitres. A teaspoon holds approximately 5 millilitres in all three countries.

SERVINGS: All these recipes serve 4 unless otherwise stated.

INDEX

NOTE: All entries with asterisks are sub-recipes.

ACKNOWLEDGEMENTS

The authors and editor would like to thank the *keluarga besar* of the Jakarta Hilton International Hotel, especially Michael Schuetzendorf, general manager, for backing the project and making this book possible; Clive Scott, food and beverage manager, for his encouragement and support; and Jane Kandou, secretary to the executive chef, for coping admirably with the additional workload this project imposed. Many thanks also to all the cooks of the kitchen brigade, and in particular to the following chefs whose knowledge, creativity and hard work helped the authors immeasurably: S. Johan Darussalam; Arief Susanto; Anton Panji; Bob Leonard; Endin Junaedi; Iwan Setiawan; Rudi Syafruddin; Toto Sunarto; Budiono; Boyke Permadi; Roychan Thaif; Ibnu Santoso; Harito Gentur Respati; Garry Salmons; Gerard Zysset.

Special thanks to: Yayasan Nusantara Jaya, its board members and staff, for promoting this new Indonesian cuisine, particularly Dr. Mochtar Kusuma-Atmadja, Judi Achjadi and also Anne Saxon, who first introduced the authors; the Directorate General of Tourism, under the direction of Joop Ave and Cri Murthi Adi, especially Luther Barrung in Jakarta, who ensured that we were warmly welcomed throughout the archipelago, and the offices in Ambon, Lampung, Manado and Ujung Pandang; Garuda Indonesia and Merpati Airlines; Iwan Tirta, for the use of his collection of *ikat* and *batik*; A.S. Wolfel of Hutschenreuther A.G. for the use of porcelain dinnerware; Mrs. Djuadi of Gracia in Jakarta for several dishes; and Clive Williams for his assistance at the cattle ranch.

Our thanks also to the many other people who gave their time and expertise, including: Des Alwi; Amiruddin Saharuna; Nuzwar Anwar; Dinas Perkebunan; Gina and Caesar Atienza; Rudy Badil; Nahrong Chivangkur; Gregory Churchill; Cokorda Isteri Manik; Dr. Darmawan Masud; Janet and Paul Drok; Arifin and Djohan Effendi; Elzhivago T.; I.G.N. Exawirya, Office of the Agricultural Counsellor, U.S. Embassy, Jakarta; Ramze Hasiboan, Association of Indonesian Pepper Exporters; Hanafi T. and Lie Doe Sen; H.M. Hasan; Locky Herlambang; Baktiawan Honandar; Doc Jarden; Jeffrey Kirana; John McGlynn; Kristina J. Melcher; Timothy Moley; Ny. Mariana; Bob Sadino; H. Sanuar; Mohd Samadikun Hardjodarsono; Dewi Soeprapto Onzko; Sumeleh; Charles Sutjiawan, Asosiasi Pala Indonesia; I. Gusti Made Sumung; Johny Sundah; Edwin Thebez; Andy Toth; C.H. Tulong; Timothy Watts; Jantje A. Worotitjan.

To Tina Miraflores Skrobanek, our deepest gratitude not only for all her excellent research and the seemingly endless typing of recipes, but also for her unfailing good humour and encouragement throughout the project, as well as a cheerful willingness to go anywhere — or just about anywhere — for a story. Finally, our appreciation to Angelina Phillips, the assistant editor, and to Woon Mee Lan, the designer, for their long hours of hard work pouring over recipes and layouts to put this book together.

Most of the photographs in this book are by Gerald Gay,
but pages 12, 15 (bottom) and 16 (top) are by
Suzanne Charlé, and pages 2-3, 8, 9, 10, 13, 14, 15 (top) and 17
are by Lawrence Lim.